THE

CONQUERORS, WARRIORS, & STATESMEN

OF

INDIA:

THE

CONQUERORS, WARRIORS, & STATESMEN

OF

INDIA:

AN HISTORICAL NARRATIVE OF THE PRINCIPAL EVENTS FROM THE INVASION OF MAHMOUD OF GHIZNI TO THAT OF NADER SHAH.

By SIR EDWARD SULLIVAN. Bart.

GYAN

Published by

Gyan Publishing House
5, Ansari Road
Daryaganj, New Delhi-110002
Phone: 011-47034999, 9811692060
E-mail: books@gyanbooks.com

Distribution Network
gyanbooks.com
India, USA, Canada, UK, Australia

ISBN: 978-93-6208-155-1 (PB)
First Published, 1866

2nd Impression 2024

Printed at: Gyan Press, Delhi.

THE CONQUERORS, WARRIORS, & STATESMEN OF INDIA
Author: EDWARD SULLIVAN

THE

CONQUERORS, WARRIORS, AND STATESMEN

OF

INDIA.

THE
CONQUERORS, WARRIORS, & STATESMEN
OF
INDIA:

AN HISTORICAL NARRATIVE OF THE PRINCIPAL EVENTS
FROM THE INVASION OF MAHMOUD OF GHIZNI TO THAT OF NADER SHAH.

BY SIR EDWARD SULLIVAN, BART.
AUTHOR OF
"LETTERS ON INDIA," "A TRIP TO THE TRENCHES," AND
"RAMBLES IN NORTH AND SOUTH AMERICA."

WITH A SKETCH MAP OF INDIA.

LONDON:
JOHN MURRAY, ALBEMARLE STREET.
1866.

PREFACE.

Lord Macaulay's unrivalled essays on Clive and Warren Hastings contain the following passages:

"The people of India, when we subdued them, were ten times as numerous as the Americans whom the Spaniards vanquished, and were at the same time quite as highly civilised as the victorious Spaniards. They had raised cities larger and fairer than Saragossa or Toledo, and buildings more beautiful and costly than Seville. They could show bankers richer than the richest firms of Barcelona or Cadiz, Viceroys whose splendour far surpassed that of Ferdinand the Catholic, myriads of cavalry, and long trains of artillery, which would have astonished the Great Captain.

"The empire which Baber and his Moguls reared in the sixteenth century, was long one of the most extensive and splendid in the world. In no European kingdom was so large a population subject to a single prince, or so large a revenue poured into the treasury. The beauty and magnificence of the buildings erected by the sovereigns of Hindostan, amazed even travellers who had seen St. Peter's. The innumerable retinues and gorgeous decorations which surrounded the throne of Delhi, dazzled even eyes which were accustomed to the pomp of Versailles. Some of the great Viceroys, who held their posts by virtue of commission from the Mogul, ruled as many subjects as the King of France or the Emperor of Germany. Even the deputies of these deputies might well rank, as to extent of territory and amount of revenue, with the Grand Duke of Tuscany, or the Elector of Saxony!"

And yet what do nineteen out of every twenty

men know of the civilisation, the cities, the merchants, warriors, and monarchs he refers to?

True, Elphinstone, Orme, and others, have written histories of India with a minuteness and a care that commands our admiration; but these works, learned and laborious, are too diffuse to become popular with the general readers.

It is a misfortune to our generation that Lord Macaulay did not write a history of India: to him it would have been a real labour of love, and he would have produced a series of word paintings that would have lasted as long as the English language.

The following pages were commenced after a journey through India and Ceylon some years ago: they do not lay claim to the rank of history; neither will they satisfy the "immortal longings" of the real student; but they may perhaps induce some who might not otherwise do so, to undertake the grateful task of writing a popular history of a country unequalled in the world for the magnificence of its natural aspects, and that has produced some of the noblest sovereigns, warriors, and statesmen that adorn the annals of any age, people or country.

The author has inserted nothing without authority, and he believes he has consulted every work or article that has been written on India, in the English or French languages.

RAVENHEAD, ST. HELEN'S,
LANCASHIRE.

CONTENTS.

CHAPTER I.

INTRODUCTORY.

CHAP. V.

A.D. 1026—1030.

CHAP. VI.

A.D. 1030—1040.

CHAP. VII.

A.D. 1044—1186.

CHAP. VIII.

A.D. 1191—1193.

CHAP. IX.

A.D. 1194—1235.

CHAP. X.

A.D. 1236—1286.

CHAP. XI.

A.D. 1287—1316.

CHAP. XII.

A.D. 1321—1387.

CHAP. XIII.

CHAP. XIV.

A.D. 1347—1422.

CHAP. XV.

A.D. 1422—1518.

CHAP. XXII.

CHAP. XXIII.

CHAP. XXIV.

CHAP. XXV.

CHAP. XXVI.

CHAP. XXVII.

To Binder.

Place Sketch Map of India at the end of the book.

Errata.

Page 4, line 14, *for* erudite learning *read* erudition
„ 26 „ 11, *for* Cossein *read* Cosseir
„ 26 „ 39, *for* et *read* e
„ 27 „ 16, *for* succombs *read* succumbs
„ 29 „ 19, *for* Gazi *read* Ghazi
„ 113 „ 3 from bottom, *for* these *read* those
„ 158 „ 3 from bottom, *for* missals *read* missives
„ 182 „ 3, *for* bears *read* bore
„ 212 „ 17, *for* slaughters *read* slaughter
„ 239 „ 1, *for* Hakim *read* Hatim
„ 256 „ 9, *for* interfere *read* intervene
„ 308 „ 15, *for* circumvent *read* compass
„ 349 „ 10, *for* or *read* nor
„ 370 „ 3 from bottom, *for* chuprattie *read* chupattie
„ 382 „ 4, *for* mohar *read* mohur

THE

CONQUERORS, WARRIORS, AND STATESMEN

OF

INDIA.

CHAPTER I.

INTRODUCTORY.

REMARKS ON THE EARLY HISTORY OF INDIA.—THE LEARNING AND PHILOSOPHY OF THE BRAHMINS. — CASTE AND THE OBSERVANCE OF "IMMEMORIAL CUSTOM."—DIVINITIES OF THE HINDOOS.—THE DOCTRINES OF BUDDHA AND BRAHMA.—THE VEDAS AND INSTITUTES OF MENU.

CHAP. I.

DURING the first quarter of the seventh century the Eastern world was lying fallow for the sword of the conqueror or the zeal of the enthusiast.

The fierce contests and alternate triumphs of Chosroe, the great Shah of Persia, and Heraclius, the chivalrous Emperor of the East, during a period of nearly twenty years, had shattered the monarchies and institutions of Asia,[1] and suffered the hostile creeds of Sabians, Magians, and Jews, the devilish doctrines of Manes[2] and Mazdak[3], and the gross idolatry of even the Christians themselves, to spread abroad antagonistic and uncertain notions of a future state incompatible with the peaceful existence of mankind.

It is not without design that Providence sanctions such marked convulsions of society.

This period is marked by two events that more than any others since the commencement of the Christian era have affected the destinies of the succeeding races of men.

In the year 602, the papal supremacy was authorised by Phocas, Emperor of the East; and twenty years later, Mahomed, an Arabian, of the tribe of Korëish, announced to his countrymen a divine revelation he was commanded to promulgate by the sword.

The former laid the foundation of the centralisation that has imparted such vitality to the faith of Christ; whilst the latter marks the date of the mighty revolution that transformed a race of wandering shepherds into the founders of mighty empires, and gave new aspirations of a future state to more than a fourth of the inhabitants of the globe.

It is not my intention to trace the wondrous career of conquest that, in little more than a hundred years, divided the civilised world amongst the three Caliphs of the Prophet, and diffused learning and the arts from the borders of China to Cordova and Fez: it is a marvellous narration, that has already engaged the pen of the learned and the eloquent, and will, through all time, afford fresh matter of interest and wonder to those who care to study the strange page of human destiny.

The splendour of the Fatimite Caliphs at Cairo, or of the Ommiades at Cordova, does not enter into our subject: we have rather to deal with the decline of the family of the Abbassides, who, for more than four hundred years, held their gorgeous court on the banks of the Tigris.

About A.D. 750, Almansor, of the family of Abbas, conquered Persia, and made Bagdad the seat of government; forty years later the caliphate attained its highest pitch of pride, under Haroun the Magnificent, who encouraged science, and extended his dominion from the Mediterranean to the frontiers of India; but these splendid possessions were too extended to remain long under one head: the several provinces of the empire soon became hereditary in the families of the governors. The viceroys were kings but in name, and in less than a hundred years the representative of the Abbassides merely retained the imperial dignity by the sufferance of independent subjects.

The most powerful of these viceroys was Ismael Samani, governor of Transoxiana and Khorassan, two magnificent provinces, that together comprised 1000 square miles of the most fertile and populous regions of Asia.

He assumed the title of king 885 A.D., and was the first of the dynasty of the Samanians, who for more than ninety years reigned vigorously in Bokhara, Transoxiana, Khorassan, Candahar, and Zabulistan, a great part of Persia, and Cabul[4], the land of the Affghans.

In the year 972 A.D., Munsur, of this dynasty, quarrelled with his lieutenant, Abistagi, who immediately seized and kept Khorassan and Affghanistan, and established his government at Ghizni, even then a considerable city. He was succeeded by Ismael Subuctugi, a Tartar soldier, who married his daughter, and rose by his energy to the chief command of his armies.

Ismael's territory included all the provinces held by his father-in-law, and during several fierce campaigns in India he annexed the Peshawur Valley, the Punjaub, and Moultan, together with many countries on the Indus.

His son, Mahmoud, succeeded to an empire that extended from the Caspian to the Indus; and it is with this "son of the slave of the slave, of the slave of the Caliph,"[5] that the ordinary era of the Mahomedan conquest of India commences. Before, however, following the daring campaigns that brought a new world under the Moslem yoke, and announced the creed of the Great Prophet of Mecca to millions, who, as yet, had known only the worship of Brahma and Boodh, we will take a cursory view of that country itself.

The fate of the Greek empire has been compared to the Rhine, that loses itself on land ere it finally mingles

BOOK I.

with the ocean: the stream of its history is lost in numberless insignificant channels before it has altogether ceased to exist.

The early history of India, on the other hand, resembles a river rising in a sandy soil and converging by a thousand trickling rills to the main channel: it is impossible to indicate the exact spot whence all proceed, and no one particular rill can be pronounced more important or well defined than the rest.

Time would fail to trace to their source the several races of men that, during the last forty centuries, have appeared and vanished, breaking like bubbles on the stream of Indian history and tradition.

Notwithstanding the vast labour and erudite learning visible in the earliest theological and philosophical works of the Hindoos, the science of history appears to have been but slightly cultivated; no reliable record of very ancient date has as yet been discovered, and the numerous compositions that supply its place have as much claim to the character of truthful narrative as the poems of Ossian or the voyages of the Odyssey.

Even where truth is apparently the text, their narrations are always incomplete and often impossible. The accounts of even very recent transactions are so clouded by allusions to their gods, that without the old Sanscrit grants of land, and Mahomedan annals, it would be impossible to discriminate between mythology and history. The entire omission of so world-renowned an event as Alexander's famous descent of the Indus, and the incessant introduction of the incarnate deities in their narratives of ordinary events, prove the imperfection of their traditions and the fanciful nature of their fables.[6]

Fortunately, the omissions of the Hindoos themselves are supplied by the very distinct and graphic narrations of some of the early Greek writers; and we are as much indebted to the elegant scholars who accompanied the expedition of Alexander for our knowledge of the wonders of the great peninsula two thousand years ago, as we are to the savants of Napoleon's army who unveiled the mysteries of the Delta of Egypt in the last century. Arrian, especially, whose history is entirely compiled from the evidence of eye-witnesses, gives us a very graphic account of the habits and customs of the natives of India twenty-one centuries ago; and it is rather startling to find that, upwards of 300 years before our era, when the whole of western Europe was peopled by skin-clad savages, who contested with wild animals the roots and nuts of their primeval forests, the companions of Alexander should have found on the banks of the Indus the strange social distinctions, the tinsel civilisation, the elaborate excellence in the arts and sciences, the laborious practice of metallurgy and pneumatics, the barbaric style of ornament, the division into castes, the daubing of the face with colours, and the slender make of the women, that even now, after a lapse of sixty generations, rivet the wonder and curiosity of the traveller.[7]

From these sources we learn that from the earliest ages of history, and history's elder sister, fable, up to the period of the first Mussulman invasion, Sanscrit was the current language of India, and the creed of Brahma its dominant faith; and there is ample evidence to prove that the priestly caste of the Brahmins had established a reputation for learning and philosophy hundreds of years before reading and writing were understood in the West. But the rare and meagre relations of conquerors and travellers scarcely lifted the veil of mystery that had through all time enshrouded the great peninsula of the East. It is not till the era of the first great Mussulman invasion, under Mahmoud, that the thousand and one bewildering streams of fable and tradition, along whose baffling course all who seek the truth must incontinently wander, emerge from the sands of time into the fair navigable stream of history.

There is every reason to credit the assertions of those

BOOK I.

learned few who have succeeded in mastering the Sanscrit records, that the Brahmins of ancient days were a highly polished and learned race, whose jurisprudence and literature bear evident testimony of a refined and philosophic people, to whom law and ethics had been a study and a profession.

It is said, there is scarcely a tenet of philosophy, from the code of Pythagoras to that of Plato, or a discovery in science, from the introduction of numerals[8] to the calculations of astronomy, whose rise cannot, in some degree, be traced to the Brahmins or Gymnosophists of India. The minor sciences and accomplishments seem to have played their part equally with the severer mental exercises in stimulating the civilisation of this strange people. From time immemorial the game of the four angas[9], or chess, appears to have solaced the leisure hours of the princes and sages of Hindostan; and hundreds of years before the fierce chaunts of the worshippers of Odin propitiated the virgins of the Valhalla; before Deborah and Barak sang the triumph of Israel; or Pythagoras discovered the divisions of the musical ratio, and Euclid reduced them to mathematical demonstration, the vina, or lute of the Hindoos, was heard amongst the palm groves of the East, tuned to scientific numbers[10], and sharing with the nightingale the admiration of mankind.[11]

"Immemorial custom," said the lawgiver of the Hindoos, "is transcendent law, approved in the sacred law, and in the code of divine legislation; let every man, therefore, of the three principal classes, who has due reverence for the supreme spirit that dwells in him, diligently and constantly observe immemorial custom."[12] So carefully has this injunction been observed by those to whom it was addressed, that, with the exception of a modification of language, and the introduction of some unimportant Mahomedan customs, it is doubtful whether any great difference exists between the Hindoos of to-day and those of whom we have the earliest notice; and it is probable that those Gymnosophists with whom Alexander conversed, under the high-arched shade of the banian tree, differed but slightly from the Brahmins and devotees, who now, after a lapse of 2000 years, daily assemble under the same noble tree for similar religious and philosophical purposes.

It is the opinion of those who have made it their especial study, that most of the habits and customs of the Hindoos are entirely unaffected by time; that caste — the inexplicable impediment to all permanent progress and enterprise, ancient as tradition, and beside which all other conditions of society are new — exists still in its pristine exclusiveness, ranking amongst the earliest and most remarkable institutions of mankind.[18]

There is no doubt whatever that the religion of Brahma is the most ancient in the world, and that in those far-distant days, in which facts are indistinct and dates uncertain, when Venus and Mercury were worshipped by the Greeks and Trojans, when the god Apis was courted with the wanton dances of the women of Memphis, and when the votaries of Zoroaster paid their vows to the rising and the setting sun, when Saul was King of Israel, and the religion of Christ dimly foreshadowed in the mystic words of Samuel and Job, the worship of the Hindoo Trinity was celebrated with the same rites and ceremonies, the same garlands of flowers, monotonous chaunts, and beating of drums, the same jewelled dancing girls and shaven priests that to this day distinguish the worship of Brahma throughout the whole peninsula of Hindostan; and at a time when the Phœnician priests drenched the altars of their Moloch with the blood of Canaanitish victims, and pitiless Druids quartered human sacrifices in the sacred groves of the early Britons, the fury of the great Hindoo idol at Juggernaut was propitiated with the same spirit of fanaticism that still kindles the devotion of thousands, who prostrate themselves under his car or mutilate themselves on his shrines.

BOOK I.

The Hindoo scripture and philosophy are contained in the four Vedas or Hymns, a very ancient Sanscrit compilation, asserted by the Brahmins to have been penned by the Divinity in person, and delivered by Brahma at the creation of the world for the benefit of mankind. Eastern scholars allow three of them an antiquity of upwards of 3000 years; but detect in the fourth the language and composition of a far more recent age. At present their purer precepts are somewhat supplanted by the Puranas, eighteen in number, which are supposed to be the work of the compilers of the Vedas, 900 B.C.

The holy caste of the Brahmins alone are permitted to read the Vedas; and the most fearful denunciations and punishments effectually prevent the perusal of them by any other class. The supreme doctrine of the Vedas is monotheism: they teach the existence of one God, the incarnation of truth and happiness, the two impalpable elements, who, under the form of Brahma, created the universe at his will. This is an article of faith that admits of no variation whatever.[14]

The Godhead is divided into three persons: Brahma, Vishnu, and Siva, representing respectively the creating, the preserving, and the destroying principles, the three mighty agencies by which nature works her miracles. The three persons of the triad have corresponding female divinities, regarded as their wives, and who represent the active principle possessed by each of them. Seresvati, the wife of Brahma, Lakshmi of Vishnu, and Parvati of Siva, share with their husbands the homage paid to the three great forces of nature, and are worshipped with various rites throughout the peninsula of Hindostan.

Brahma, the chief person of the Trinity, is not an object of worship, but of devout contemplation; and throughout India there is but one temple raised in his name.[15] It is to the other persons of the triad and their wives that the millions of Hindostan bow the knee of idolatry, and whose innumerable incarnations, or avatars, supply the

Hindoo Pantheon with the three hundred millions of deities that confound and bewilder all study and investigation. Vishnu, the preserver, the god of mercy, who, incarnate as Chrisna, deigned to shelter the lapwing's nest in the midst of the battle[16], and gave beatitude to the courtesan who, as the wall crushed her, pronounced his name, has ten principal incarnations, and together with his wife, the goddess of Fortune and Abundance, is the favourite deity of the Hindoos.

The most popular incarnations at the present day are those of Chrisna and Rama. Chrisna is worshipped by all the wealthy Hindoos, and by nearly all the women, who maintain that he is not merely an incarnation, but Vishnu himself; whilst the use of the latter name throughout India, as the ordinary friendly greeting, and the deafening shouts of Ram, Ram, that attend all religious processions, prove how intimately connected this deity is with their present conception of the Divine power.

Siva, the Destroyer, "the Prince of Death and God of War,"[17] adorned with a necklace of skulls, and represented as dancing over mangled corpses, and drinking blood from the skulls of the slain, is propitiated as the enemy of mankind, and frequently, in the place of Brahma, as the symbol of creative power. His worship is chiefly confined to the Brahmins[18], and to him are paid all the filthy and degrading rites that disgrace the religion of the Hindoos. He is the god of the Lingam, and is worshipped with bloody rites and sacrifices,—with mutilations and self-inflicted tortures. His wife is worthy of him; and under the name of Calee is represented as a black Medusa, with snakes for hair, and with every characteristic that can strike horror into the soul. In olden days, the favour of the fierce goddess was propitiated with human victims; and the most minute directions still exist for their proper execution[19]: an oblation of blood which has been rendered pure by holy test is declared equal to ambrosia; and the "learned" are instructed,

BOOK I.

when paying adoration to the goddess, to offer "blood and the head." Fortunately, the days are now passed when a cruel priesthood can add the terrors of human sacrifices to the other foul jugglery of their idolatrous worship. Innumerable Dii Minores contest with the supreme deities the worship of the multitude. Cama, the Indian cupid[20]; Indra, the god of the elements, "who guides the whirlwind and directs the storm;" Ganesea, or Gunputti, the god of wisdom, the favourite deity of Deccan; the sun, the moon, time, death, &c., all in turn receive the prayers and oblations of the credulous race.[21]

The Brahmins entirely deny the authenticity of all Jewish relation and mythology. They maintain that both Jewish and Christian religions are antagonistic to their Vedas; and they give a distinct account of an apostate from their faith, who established the Jewish heresy 5000 years ago.

The Hindoo religion is the only one in the world that seeks no proselytes or converts, and allows an equal chance of salvation to all creeds and denominations of the human race.

It is supposed that between 600 B.C. and 600 A.D. the heresy of Boodh or Buddha was very general in India; and there are many reasons for believing that during that lengthened period her millions swelled the ranks of that faith still the most numerous in the world.[22]

The Cingalese date the preaching of Buddha between 638 B.C. and 542 B.C.; and this chronology is generally credited. The new religion seems to have extended with marvellous celerity, and within a century of its rise to have become almost universal in the East.[23] Be that as it may, there is no doubt that the Buddhists were a powerful sect when Alexander invaded India; and that no violent persecution rose against them till the sixth or seventh century of our era, when they were nearly exterminated, and those who remained were forced to compromise their faith by allowing Gautama, or the ninth avatar of their supreme deity, Buddha, to be merely an incarnation of the second person of the Hindoo Trinity.[24]

It appears that they afterwards recovered a portion of their former numbers; for we read of them as being still a dominant sect in Benares in the eleventh century; since that period their sun has finally set in the peninsula, and the ancient faith of Brahma has regained its exclusive influence: but Buddhism, banished to the Celestial Empire, and the kingdoms of Ceylon and Siam, is still the creed of 300,000,000 of human beings—one-third of the whole race of man.

Buddhism was a reaction against Brahminism; and although much of the philosophy of each is drawn from the same source, and many of their peculiar rites and ceremonies are similar, their theology is as antagonistic as it is possible to imagine.

Brahminism is Pantheism, Buddhism is Nihilism: the former teaches that all things are God; the latter, that there is no God at all. The Brahminical theory resolves all things into spirit, exclusive of matter, the existence of which is denied. The Buddhist theory resolves all things into matter, to the exclusion of spirit, whose being it ignores. The followers of Brahma worship the Supreme Being under three hundred millions of forms; those of Buddha ignore the Deity altogether, and worship matter which is eternal.

Buddha was the apostle of a new faith; he broke with the traditional formalities of the past, and proclaimed, for the first time, in spite of castes and creeds, the equality of rich and poor, the foolish and the wise, the twice-born and the outcast: he abolished all caste, and elevated the character of saints and prophets above that of the priestly tribe, and substituted for an hereditary priesthood an organised hierarchy and monastic institutions.

Sworn to a life of continual suffering and self-denial, and enjoined to hide their good works and show only

BOOK I. their sins, his disciples penetrated to the uttermost regions of Asia, and even made proselytes in the centre of Europe.[25]

The strange doctrine of metempsychosis, that teaches the indiscriminate transmigration of the souls of men, into the forms of animals, insects, and even plants, till they have become sufficiently purified to be absorbed into the Divine essence, was first preached by Buddha, and is still held in all its primitive absurdity by the greater number of Hindoos[26] as well as Buddhists. They believe that immediately after death the spirit of man, that goeth upward[27], is wafted into the presence of its eternal judge, who passes sentence upon it, consigning it to happiness or misery, according to its deserts. So long as any impurity remains, the spirit is sent back again and again to tenant some earthly form; but when, by successive emanations, it has obtained perfect purity, it is received into paradise, and absorbed into the Deity. They believe that between each successive development they will pass a thousand years of happiness or misery in some of the numerous heavens or hells.[28] Nothing, they believe, can equal the happiness of those who die in the faith, and nothing can exceed the agony and torture of those who neglect it.

Whatever may have been the origin of this doctrine, its effect has undoubtedly been to instil into the hearts of its votaries the spirit of mercy towards the lower orders of creation. "From the meanest insect up to man thou shalt not kill," is the first commandment of Buddha, given to all, Hindoo and Buddhist, Brahmin as well as Sudra. "As many hairs as grow on the beard," says their lawgiver, "so many similar deaths shall the slayer of the beast, for his own satisfaction in this world, endure in the next, from birth to birth;" and though both Brahmins and Sudras do kill, there are still numerous castes who will not, under any consideration, willingly destroy life.

Where, but amongst the credulous votaries of this childish faith, will you meet with the tenderness that endows hospitals and places of refuge for worn-out animals[29]; that obliges the oil-mills[30] and the potter's wheel to suspend their revolutions for the four months in the year when insects most abound; and that enjoins its votaries to sit in the dark, rather than by luring a moth to the flame of the candle, to incur the crime of insect murder?

The civil polity of the Hindoos is based on the Institutes of Menu, the most minute and contradictory code of laws ever compiled by man.

According to the Brahmins, the Institutes share the antiquity of the Vedas, and were orally delivered by Menu about 1300 B.C., a period prior to the voyage of the Argonauts, or the expedition of the Greeks against Troy. They are twelve[31] in number, written in Sanscrit[32], the most refined and polished language in the world, and contain instruction and commands on everything connected with civil and religious exercises. They commence with the creation of the world, and convey distinct instructions for every act of a man's life, from his birth and his marriage[33] to his transmigration and final beatitude.

These Institutes are by turns perfectly just and fearfully cruel; whilst some of them breathe a spirit of forgiveness and mercy that might adorn the Christian faith[34], others are marked by a merciless ferocity unequalled in the laws of Draco.[35]

It is almost impossible to conceive that a code of morality that forbids a man to be querulous, even though in pain; to injure another even in thought; or to utter a word by which his fellow-creature can suffer uneasiness; that commands him to bless his enemy, and, like the sandal wood, to shed perfume on the axe that fells him,—can be the work of the same age that condemns a low-caste man to have his mouth burned for speaking lightly of a Brahmin, and sentences him who listens to the Vedas to have boiling oil poured into his ears!

BOOK I.

The code of Menu recognises the four great castes or divisions of the Hindoos, and the first chapter gives a minute account of their production from the body of Brahma[36], and of their distinct duties here on earth. The most particular relations are given respecting the destiny and position of these several castes; and whilst the Brahmins are enjoined to counsel and to pray, the Tchatryas or warriors to fight and to rule, the Bice to trade and to cultivate, the Sudra is warned that his is a condition of never-ending servitude, which it is death for him to violate. One entire chapter treats of the Chandalahs or outcasts; and it is impossible to conceive any institution of man more fierce and unrelenting than that which expels from the ordinary rights of existence one-fifth of all the races of Hindostan.[37]

The shastres[38] or commentaries tacked on to the Institutes of Menu, to foster the privileges or enlarge the influence of the Brahmins, are even yet more brutal; and the only marvel is, that during so many centuries the spirit of desperation has not roused this race of eastern helots to fierce and bloody revenge.

NOTES TO CHAPTER I.

[1] See Gibbon.

[2] Manes was a physician, and having mistaken the nature of the disease afflicting Prince Varanos, son of the King of Persia, was flayed alive, and his skin stuffed with chaff.

[3] Sale's Koran, vol. i. p. 49. D'Herbelot's Dictionary.

[4] Province of Ghizni called Zabulistan to distinguish it from Kabul.

[5] Ismael was the son of Subuctugi, the slave of Abistagi, the slave of Munsur, the slave of the Caliph.

[6] The Mahabharat, or "Great War," is merely a fanciful poem. The most authentic historical composition, in Sanscrit, appears to be the chronicles of the kings of Cashmere, entitled Radja Teringini, translated by Mr. Colebrooke in 1805. It is supposed to have been written B.C. 1148. The Ramayana and Mahabharat are the Iliad and Odyssey of Indian literature: they both relate the deeds of Vishnu; the first as incarnate in the person of Rama; the second in that of Chrisna. They are, however, far more diffuse than the works of Homer. The Ramayana has 100,000 lines; the Mahabharat, 400,000; the Iliad, 24,000; and the Æneid, 12,000. Mill, whose estimate of everything connected with the literature, civilisation, and even the wealth of the early Hindoos, is of the lowest, thus characterises these voluminous works: "Inflation, metaphor perpetual, and those the most violent and strained, often the most unnatural and ridiculous; obscurity, tautology, repetition, verbosity, confusion, incoherence distinguish the Mahabharat and Ramayana in a degree to which no parallel has yet been discovered."

[7] The following peculiarities enumerated by Arrian may be remarked to this day:—

1. Slender make of the women.
2. Living on vegetable food.
3. Divisions into castes; and perpetuation of trades in families.
4. Marriages at seven years of age, and prohibition of between different castes.
5. Men wearing earrings.
6. Daubing their faces with colours.
7. Only principal people use umbrellas.

Several other points of similarity are mentioned by Major Rennell.

[8] The Arabians, who introduced numerals into Europe, professed to have received them from the Indians.

[9] It was known by the name of Cheturanga, or the four angas, or members of an army, which are elephants, horses, chariots and foot soldiers. In the sixth century the King of India sent a chess-board to Nushïrwan, surnamed the Just, King of Persia. The game was entirely unknown in Persia; but such was the talent of Buzurg Chimere, sur-

named the Wise, Nushirwan's vizier, that after one explanation from the Indian ambassador, he sat down to play with him; the first game he obliged him to draw, the second he gave him stalemate, and the third checkmated him. The ambassador was so disgusted at being whipped at his own game that he refused to play any more. Buzurg then invented the game of backgammon, and sent it back to the King of India. The chess-board was intended to indicate, that in the great game of state, attention and capacity were better friends than fortune, the backgammon that attention and capacity cannot alone succeed, and that we must play the game of life according to the cards of fortune.

[10] "The Hindoo notes are seven, and transcend like ours by a sharp third." See musical modes of Hindoos in "Asiatic Researches," vol. iii.

[11] They have fallen off in their music; it is the crow and not the nightingale that now divides the traveller's irritation with the timboor and the oode, the present instruments in fashion. The timboor is a kind of lute, the oode a sort of guitar.

[12] Institutes of Menu, chap. i. sect. 108.

[13] The Egyptians probably recognised caste, "For a shepherd was an abomination to an Egyptian."

[14] "The prevailing character of the ritual of the Vedas is the worship of the personified elements: fire, the firmament, air, and water; of the sun, moon, and other elementary and planetary personages. It is also true that the worship of the Vedas is, for the most part, domestic worship, consisting of prayers and oblations offered in their own houses, not in temples, by individuals for individual good, and addressed to unreal presences, nor to real types. In a word the religion of the Vedas was not idolatry."—Professor Wilson.

[15] Pilgrimages are made in his name to the Brahma-Verta Ghaut, near Bithore (the stronghold of Nana Sahib), where, after he had performed a solemn sacrifice to celebrate the creation of the world, he left one of the pins of his slippers sticking in the steps. His solitary temple is at Pokher in Ajmere.

[16] The lapwing makes a peculiarly plaintive sound when disturbed from its nest. Chrisna hearing it as he was advancing to attack the Giants, stopped his elephant, and commanded the nest to be covered with a war bell.

[17] Har is the god of war, and his sacred bird is the goose! unde derivatur "goose-step."

[18] The priests of Vishnu marry, those of Siva do not. A strict worshipper of Vishnu will disapprove of suttee—Siva enjoins it.

[19] Read the Rudhiradhyaya or Sanguinary chapter. "Asiatic Researches," vol. v.

[20] Cama is now out of favour, which is an anomalous position for the god of love.

[21] The natives of India believe that the Sahibs worship Un-deva, the God of Food, or the Belly-god; for they assert that whatever we undertake or complete is celebrated by a dinner.

[22] Brahminical Hindooism may now be called the faith of Hindostan; but so late as the Mahomedan conquest of Mahmoud of Ghizni, the general system of faith in the provinces of Guzerat, Khandeesh, Aurunga-

bad, Bijapore and Koukan appears to have been the heterodox one of Hindooism or the Jaina religion.

[23] Buddhism extended to Russia, Sweden, north of Asia, Mongolia, Tartary, China, Thibet, Siam, Burmah and Ceylon. It was finally recognised in China, A.D. 65. For account of Buddhism in 7th century, A.D., see Voyages des Pèlerins Bouddhistes, vol. i.; Histoire de la Vie de Hionen-thuang et de ses Voyages dans l' Inde depuis l'an 629 jusqu'au 645, par Hoeili et Yeu-thsong, traduit du Chinois par Stanislaus Julien. Paris 1853.

[24] The Brahmins maintain that Vishnu, in his ninth avatar, assumed the form of Buddha, for the purpose of deluding the enemies of the gods.

[25] See review of "Les Pèlerins Bouddhistes" in *Times*, 1857. The instructions of Buddha to his disciples were not, "Go, ye saints, and show your miracles before all men," but "Live, ye saints, hiding your good works, and showing your sins."

[26] According to the tenets of metempsychosis nothing ever dies; the vital principle is merely transformed from one form to another, or a number of others. It is aptly illustrated by a lamp: one lamp is used to light another lamp; the element is not new but transmitted. Pythagoras was the first philosopher who professed the tenets of metempsychosis in Europe; he went so far as to say he remembered distinctly all the animals he had ever animated.

[27] Ecclesiasticus, chap. iii. v. 20.

[28] Their heaven is a perfect cessation of all pain; their hell one of gnawing serpents.

[29] There is one at Bombay at present, where they hire beggars for a feed of rice to sleep a night amongst the fleas and other agreeable companions.

[30] Mahrana Jey Sing, in reign of Jehangire, to inhabitants of Bakrole, printers, potters, and oilmen, commanding:—From the 11th Asar (June) to the full moon of Asog (Sept.), none shall drain the waters of the lake; no oil mills shall work, or earthen vessel be made during the four rainy months in the year.

Buddha was the son of Suddhodana, King of Kapilarastú, seeing a tigress starved and unable to feed her cubs, he made a charitable oblation of his body to be devoured by them!

[31] Institutes of Menu, chap. i.—Account of creation of the world.—2. Duties of sacerdotal castes: education of young Brahmins.—3. Time and duties of marriage. — 4. On economics and private morals.— 5. On diet and purification. — 6. Entirely on devotion. — 7. Right administration of Government. — 8. Important duties of kingly office.—9. Continuation of the same. — 10. On the mixed classes. — 11. Penance and expiation.—12. Transmigration and final beatitude.—Translated by Sir W. Jones.

[32] Sanscrit is compounded of "san" completion, "scrita" finished, hence it implies excessive polish. It is very voluminous, as may be imagined from its alphabet, compared with those of other languages:—

Greek	alphabet	24	letters.
Egyptian	"	25	"
Hebrew	"	22	"
English	"	26	"
Sanscrit	"	50	"

BOOK I.

The opinions of the following distinguished Eastern scholars will illustrate the beauty of the Sanscrit:—

Sir William Jones describes it as "a language of wonderful structure; more perfect than the Greek, more copious than the Latin, and more exquisitely refined than either."

Professor Wilson says that "the music of Sanscrit composition must ever be inadequately represented by any other tongue."

Halked describes it as "a language very copious and nervous, and far exceeding the Greek and Asiatic in the regularity of its etymology."

A German philologist declares Sanscrit as a written language to be raised to the highest pinnacle of perfection; whilst an enthusiastic Frenchman maintains that "it is the celebrated dialect perhaps spoken by the gods of Homer, and if not, worthy to be so!"

All reliable information regarding Sanscrit is wanting; it contains some identity with Greek and Latin. It is probable it was once the vernacular of Hindostan, but differed much in purity. The northern languages of India, Punjaubee, Bengalee, Guzeratee contain much Sanscrit; whereas the southern dialects, Tamul, Teloogoo and Canarese are independent. The Tamul is most pure; Mahratta contains a little Sanscrit.

There is such a flexibility in the language that it is hard to get at the exact meaning; the same composition variously analysed by grammatical rules may have sometimes three different meanings. There is a history that may be read either as a history of Rama or of Yuddhistira; two distinct stories are told in the same words! Tamul is equally comprehensive. On one occasion Mr. Percival heard a political eulogium read at a public meeting that had three meanings, one was an inscription of praise to Siva; another to a deceased benefactor, whose charities were particularly alluded to; the third was an encomium on the gentleman who presided at the meeting.—*The Land of the Veda.*

If every word has three meanings no wonder Europeans occasionally misunderstand their servants, and call them niggers and liars in consequence.

[33] The instructions regarding matrimony are judicious: a man is recommended not to marry any woman with red hair, deformed in her limbs, or an immoderate talker, or into a family that is subject to phthisis, epilepsy, or other hereditary diseases. "Let him," says this wise institute, "choose for his wife a girl whose form has no defect, who has an agreeable name, who walks gracefully, like a Phenicopteros, or like a young elephant (a doubtful compliment when we remember Momus's criticism on goddess of love), whose hair and teeth are equally beautiful, and whose body has exquisite softness!"—Chap. III.

[34] "Let not a man be querulous even though he be in pain; let him not injure another in deed or in thought; let him not even utter a word by which his fellow-creatures can suffer uneasiness, since that will obstruct his own progress to future beatitude."—Chap. II. on Education. Another pronounces "the duty of man, even in the moment of destruction, to consist not only in forgiving, but even in a desire to benefit his destroyer; as the sandal tree in the instant of its overthrow sheds perfume on the axe that fells it."

[35] If a low-caste man spoke with contempt of a Brahmin his mouth was to be burned. If he insulted him, his tongue was to be split. If he

assaulted him, he was to be put to death. If he listened to the reading of the Vedas, boiling oil was to be poured into his ears, &c., &c.

[36] Brahma produced the Brahmins from his mouth to signify wisdom. The Tchatrya from his arm to signify might. The Veisya or Bice from his thigh to signify labour. The Sudra from his feet to signify subjection.

[37] It is ordained that they exist remote from their fellow-creatures, amidst the filth and dirt of the suburbs; their sole wealth to consist in dogs and asses; their clothes must be the polluted mantles of the deceased; their dishes for food, broken pots; their ornaments, rusty iron; their food must be given them in potsherds at a distance, that the giver may not be defiled by the shade of their outcast bodies, &c. Their proper name is directed to be expressive of contempt, and the religious penance for killing them is the same as for killing a cat, a frog, a dog, a lizard, or such like animals. See Institutes of Menu, chaps. viii. and x. and indeed passim.

[38] See code of Gentoo laws, compiled at Benares by a number of learned Brahmins assembled for the purpose by Warren Hastings. Translated by Mr. Halked.

CHAP. II.

THE COMMERCE OF INDIA. — THE TRADE OF ARABIA WITH INDIA. — THE GOVERNMENT OF THE RAJAS AND THE POWER OF THE BRAHMINS. — PERSIAN INFLUENCE IN INDIA.—THE GREAT DIVISIONS OF THE COUNTRY.

BOOK I.

IN all ages of history the commerce of India has "enriched the nations and the kings of the earth:"[1] and from the days of Moses to our own, the shawls of Cashmere, the silks of Delhi, and the gold and ivory of Malabar, have adorned the palaces and decked the favourites of kings, and filled the coffers of princely traders.

To western nations, India has always been a region of gold and gems: redolent with "myrrh, aloes, and cassia;" the storehouse of the varied treasures of the East.[2] And, indeed, when we consider the length and breadth of the unceasing stream of wealth that has flown from Hindostan, beautifying, and civilising, and raising in its course some of the fairest cities that fill up the far distance in the background of history, we can scarcely wonder at its having, from the earliest ages, been considered the fountain-head of wealth, the El Dorado of conquerors and merchants, the theme of exaggeration and wonder to historians and romancers.

The trade of Arabia with India was probably the earliest commercial organisation in the world. At the regular seasons, permitted by the monsoons, the ports of Surat, the Concan, and Malabar, were visited by the hardy mariners of the Red Sea and the Persian Gulf[3]; whilst continuously during the hot season, long caravans, laden with the precious products of the far country, and piloted by the armed merchants of Persia and Samarcand, diverged from the frontier cities of Hindostan, and wound their weary way to the farthest frontiers of Asia.

The value of this overland trade, even in the days of fable, induced Cyrus to fix his seat of empire at Balkh[4], "the mother of cities;" and eventually made this "Mecca of the Magians"[5] the key to Central Asia, the connecting link between east and west. And whilst the maritime trade of India through the Red Sea enriched the fruitful land of Egypt under the Pharoahs[6]; beautified the temples of David and Solomon; raised proud Tyre, that city of perfect beauty[7], and made her merchants princes and her traffickers the honourable men of the earth: that by the Persian Gulf founded in the deserts of Arabia the queen city of Palmyra, and poured into her coffers the stream of wealth which raised, as if by magic, the gorgeous palaces and temples, whose shattered walls and crumbling columns, even now, after a lapse of fifteen centuries, tempt the curious and learned of the West to brave the scorching sun of Arabia and the hereditary hostility of the sons of Esau; and assembled within her walls the gallant band of citizen warriors who, for two centuries, held their own against the fierce hordes of Parthia, and the disciplined legions of Rome.

Some years later the Indian trade through Armenia enriched Erzeroom and Trebizond; and whilst the costly products of the far East ministered to the whims and fancies of the luxurious court of the great Theodosius, they enabled the panic-stricken inhabitants of Rome to purchase the clemency of the fierce destroyer, Alaric.[8] Later still, it was the wealth-bearing commerce of India that gilded the golden city of the Caliphs on the banks of the Tigris, and founded, on the shores of the Mediterranean, the maritime powers of Italy, whose rivalry enriched Europe, and terminated in the splendid triumph of the toga'd councillors of Venice.[9]

BOOK I.

But great as has always been the Indian trade, her merchants have never been an enterprising people, trading their own products in foreign ports or accompanying their caravans to distant lands. Hampered by the tyranny of caste, which necessitates the strictest rules of diet, and the observance of a multitude of sacred rites and ceremonious ablutions, and stigmatises as pollution all contact with an inferior, the high-caste native could never cross the ocean, but under great privation; and commanded by his lawgiver not to pass the Attock, or Forbidden, the most western of the rivers of the Punjaub, it is probable the merchant of India was unknown in cities more distant than Peshawur or Lahore.

The great maritime nations of the world, the Phœnicians, the Arabians, the Malays, the Portuguese, and Chinese, have each in turn possessed the maritime trade of India; whilst, on the southern banks of the Indus, the patient traders of Hindostan met the warrior merchants of Persia and Tartary, and exchanged their myrrh and their frankincense for western gold.

The natives of Hindostan have never sent forth fleets of commerce, nor have they as yet incurred the reproach of attempting foreign conquest or annexation. Their country has been overrun by Affghans, Moguls, Persians, and English, and partially occupied by French and Portuguese; they have been constantly invaded by their neighbours, and more than once have driven them back from their soil; but they have never in their turn become the aggressors; and it is probable that before the adventurous wars of Akbar and Aurungzebe no high-caste Hindoo, in arms, ever crossed the Indus, or ploughed the sea in search of foreign conquest.

It is only this unexampled isolation of the entire country, through countless ages of transition, that explains the fact, of two hundred millions of human beings, overrun by numerous conquering nations, deprived of their language, and, at times, sorely persecuted for their faith, remaining unaltered in a world of change, and preserving unimpaired the childish credulity in obscure tradition, that still imbues their every act and occupation, and renders venerable some of the most ordinary affairs and incidents of life.

From the earliest period of which we have any record, India has always been divided into large provinces or kingdoms, ruled over by rajas or kings.

The form of government of the rajas was monarchical, and, with the exception of the power of the priesthood, absolute. The kingly duties were all clearly defined, and entirely directed by, the laws of Menu. Never to recede from combat, to protect the people, and to honour the priests, was the highest duty of kings, and ensured their felicity.[10] Administration of justice in person, was the leading principle of their jurisprudence, and the revolutions of ages have in no degree lessened this primæval practice.[11]

Their councils consisted of a company of the most noble Brahmins, or priests, who sat on the right of the throne, and an equal number of noble Tchatryas, or warriors, who sat on the left, supposed respectively to represent the interests of peace and war.

The council of Brahmins might, and indeed did, condemn a bad king; but no amount of treason or crime could excuse the sovereign in taking the life of one of those holy men.

Apparently the power possessed by the Brahmins was irresistible. The king was instructed always to have a Brahmin as his first minister. His decisions, if contrary to the opinions of the Brahmins, would be null and void: even his family would refuse to obey him; and in all judicial matters he was really the executor of Brahminical decisions. But, on the other hand, he was exclusive master of the army and the revenue, which enabled him to counteract and dispense with the greater part of

BOOK I.

the judicature and legislative power of this ambitious hierarchy.

The Institutes of Menu strictly confined the kingly office to the Tchatrya, or raja tribe; but there is no doubt that ambitious members of the priestly caste constantly usurped supreme power, and that even individuals of the despised castes did occasionally break through the obstacle of their birth, and attain the regal dignity.[12]

In all Hindoo codes of law the king is declared lord paramount of the soil: he is the sole proprietor, and all land is held of him, on payment of a fixed sum. The exact proportion of this rent or land-tax appears to have varied from one-sixth to one-third of the entire produce of the soil; but it is probable it was considerably lighter under the native princes of the country than under their Moslem conquerors.[13] But whatever limit law or immemorial custom may have placed on the exactions of the sovereign, the same consideration did not extend to the Brahmins: they were absolute lords of all, and could, at will, help themselves to the best of everything they desired; and the boundless wealth that everywhere marked their domination, establishes their right to share the character of insatiable avarice, already enjoyed by the monks and priesthood of the West.[14]

We know little of the native sovereigns of India prior to the time of Mahmoud of Ghizni; and with one bright exception, their names have scarcely descended to posterity. Bicker-Magit, King of Malwa, who reigned in the first century of our era, occupies much the same position in the history, or rather tradition, of the Hindoos, that King Arthur does in our own. He was famed throughout India for his valour and success in war, and his careful cultivation of the arts of peace. Under his wise and benevolent reign the country attained unequalled prosperity. So firm was his justice, and so omnipotent his rule, that, according to the chroniclers of his day, "the magnet durst not exert its power on iron, or amber on the chaff of the field," without his permission. He died A.D. 89; and so great was the respect for his name, that even in the days of Akbar the greater number of Hindoos reckoned their time from his death.

It is probable that from very early ages the provinces west of the Indus were more or less tributary to the kings of Persia. Alexander the Great grounded his claim to the empire of India on the right of the ancient sovereigns of Persia, whose dynasty he had subverted; and 800 years later, Nushirvan[15], who was Shah of Persia when Mahomed was born, styled himself King of Persia and India. And although there is no record of their having ever passed the Indus, it is possible their power was acknowledged and respected by the monarchs of Hindostan; for we read that, A.D. 330, when Byram-Gore King of Persia, who had come to India, in disguise, to study the wise laws and regulations of that country, was discovered by the extraordinary feat of shooting an elephant dead with one arrow in the head, he was received with great homage by Basdeo King of Canouje.

At the period of Mahmoud's invasion, the Rajpoot was the dominant race in India. Hindostan[16] was divided into the four great kingdoms of Delhi, Canouje, Mewar, and Anhulwarra, and to the chief of one or another of these states the numerous petty princes of India paid homage and feudal service.

There was no supreme sovereign of India, but in any great emergency, the rajas, who united for defence, elected a head chief, with the title of Pal, or Protector, to whom they paid temporary allegiance. He who held this high office, at the date of the Mahomedan conquest, was the Rahtore sovereign of Canouje.

BOOK I.

NOTES TO CHAPTER II.

[1] Ezekiel xxvii.

[2] According to travellers, in India grew the fabled tree of pure gold, laden with fruit composed of the finest jewels, that originated the story of the cave of Aladdin.

[3] In the Institutes of Menu provision is made for losses incurred by adventurers at sea, which proves the antiquity of this commerce; probably it was principally confined to Guzerat.

[4] Balkh, called Um-ul-Belad, mother of cities. A block of white marble is still pointed out as the throne of Cyrus.

[5] Zoroaster was born at Balkh.

[6] The trade of India reached the Nile by Berenice, or Thebes by Cossein. The trade of Tyre was carried on by Arionzebe, at the head of the Gulf of Akaba, across part of Arabia Petræa to Rhinococura, or El Aryeh, not far from Gaza, thence to Tyre by sea.

[7] Ezekiel xxvii. xxviii.

[8] Amongst the articles of ransom that induced Alaric to raise the siege of Rome is mentioned 300lb. of pepper from Malabar.

[9] At one time Doria took Dandolo in triumph to Genoa.

[10] Menu.

[11] Mill.

[12] See Curtius's account of Xambranes, Supreme Raja of Canouje, and conversation of Sandrocottus with ambassadors of Seleucus.—Maurice, vol. ii. 35.

[13] The Sacontala, or Magic Ring, written by Calidas, B.C. 100, Act v. p. 53, and referring to a date supposed to be 1000 B.C., puts it at one-sixth; in the time of Shere the Affghan it was one-fourth; whilst the Ayeen Akbery, or Institutes of Akbar, states it at one-third; it is now two-thirds in parts of India. Act v. pp. 53—56: Chamberlain, *loquitur*:—"The sun yokes his bright steeds for the labour of many hours; the gale breathes by night and by day; the Prince of Serpents continually sustains the weight of this earth, and equally incessant is the toil of that man whose revenue arises from a *sixth* of his people's income."

[14] Their influence is thus summed up by Mill:—"By a system of priestcraft, built upon the most enormous, irrational, and tormenting superstitions that ever harassed and degraded any portion of mankind, their minds were enchained more intolerably than their bodies; in short, by despotism and priestcraft taken together, the Hindoos, in mind and body, were the most enslaved portion of the human race."

Fretri, pretri, monachi et pulli,
Mai non son satulli.

[15] A.D. 530. Nushirvan sent to the banks of the Ganges for a copy of Pilpay's Fables, described by Sir W. Jones as "the most beautiful, if not the most ancient, collection of apologues in the world." They were written about 1100 years ago by a Brahmin, and have been translated into twenty different languages, but are so mutilated as to be scarcely recognisable.

[16] Hindostan means, in general terms, the land of the Hindoos; but strictly speaking it is the land north of the Nerbudda.

CHAP. III.

A.D. 1000—1023.

ACCESSION OF MAHMOUD TO THE EMPIRE OF GHIZNI. — HIS SUCCESSFUL EXPEDITIONS AGAINST THE IDOLATERS OF INDIA. — THE ANNEXATION OF MOULTAN, PESHAWUR, AND THE GREATER PART OF SCINDE. — DESTRUCTION OF TANNASSAR, AND OF THE GREAT IDOL JUG-SOOM. — CASHMERE A PREY TO THE MUSSULMAN ARMY. — THE PLUNDER OF CANOUJE.—THE FALL OF MUTTRA. — THE AVARICE OF MAHMOUD.

CHAP. III. 1000.

ENGLAND and India cast aside the thick veil of fable and tradition, and take their places in the authentic page of history in the same century. It is at the Norman conquest, A.D. 1066, that the former emerges from the dim legends of Picts and Scots, and that the rude Saxon, the dialect of peasants, yields to the polished Norman, the language of courts ; and it is at the Moslem invasion of Mahmoud, A.D. 1000, that India breaks from the shadowy realms of bardic chroniclers, and that Sanscrit, the language of philosophy and science, gradually succombs to the rougher Urdu[1], "the language of camps."

After a successful reign of twenty years, Subuctugi died, and left the splendid empire of Ghizni to his son. He was a gallant and enlightened sovereign, who ruled with equity and justice, and his humanity and tenderness to animals has been perpetuated in one of the most charming tales of eastern romance.[2]

He made several fierce inroads into the Punjaub[3] ; and it was during these warlike parades that Mahmoud, his eldest son, acquired the knowledge of the wealth and idolatry of India, that kindled at once his avarice and his

BOOK I. zeal, and gave the earliest token[4] of his capacity for war and conquest.

1000. Mahmoud was absent in Khorassan, at the death of his father in Ghizni, and Ismael, his brother, had sufficient influence with the dying monarch to induce him to nominate him his successor. No sooner was Subuctugi dead, than Ismael seized the empire, and opening the royal treasuries, sought, by lavish gratuities, to secure the fidelity of the nobles and the troops; but Mahmoud was not a prince to be easily defrauded of his birthright. After trying in vain to induce his brother to resign his unjust usurpation, he marched against him, and regained at the sword point his capital and his crown. Comparative clemency marked the first victory of Mahmoud. Sending for his brother, he asked him what treatment he should have received if fortune had been reversed, and he had fallen into his power? Ismael replied, "that he should have imprisoned him for life in some castle, and indulged him with every pleasure but his liberty."[5] Mahmoud made no reply at the time, but shortly after acted on the suggestion, and confined him in the fortress of Georghan, where after many years of idleness and luxury, he subsequently died.

The character of Mahmoud had been early moulded by that of his father, Subuctugi; and from him he appears to have acquired that admiration of the arts and sciences, and that keen delight in battles, that made him at once the most magnificent monarch and the greatest warrior of the age. Even when young he displayed equally the spirit of the soldier and the liberal tastes of the scholar. During the lifetime of his father he enriched the capital with elegant buildings and costly gardens[6]; and the earnestness with which he opposed the acceptance of a magnificent ransom, that was to purchase Subuctugi's retreat from the territory of Jeipal King of Lahore, shows that even at that early age opportunity was alone wanting to initiate that career of conquest which has made his name famous through the world.

CHAP. III. 1000.

At the age of twenty-eight Mahmoud was the sole master of the dominion of his father.[7] Ghizni, his capital, was one of the finest cities in the East, and his supremacy was acknowledged from the frontiers of Persia to the banks of the Indus, and from Balkh to the Arabian Sea. He was, even at his accession, the most powerful sovereign of Asia; and when, shortly after, the last of the dynasty of the Samanians who reigned in Bokhara, and to whom he still paid a nominal allegiance, was ferociously put to death by Elek the Uzbek King of Cashgar, he remained without a rival throughout the East. The expeditions of his father had opened to Mahmoud the knowledge of the wealth of India and the idolatry of its inhabitants; and no sooner had he quieted his domestic foes and established his throne, than he swore on the Holy Koran[8] to seize the one and efface the other.

The Koran teaches that the highest dignity the faithful can attain is that of making war in person against the enemies of his religion; and in every page the gazi, or holy war against infidels, is elevated as the first and most imperative duty of the true believer.[9]

"The sword," says Mahomed, "is the key of paradise and hell. A drop of blood shed in the cause of God, a night spent in arms, is of more avail than two months of fasting and prayer. Whoever falls in battle, his sins are forgiven; at the day of judgment his wounds shall be resplendent as vermilion, and odoriferous as musk; and the loss of his limbs shall be replaced with the wings of angels and cherubims." During a period of three hundred years his warlike apostles, with fire, sword, and desolation, did not fail to execute these fierce mandates through the eastern world.

Those who perished in the holy crusade were supposed to go straight to Heaven; and all the eloquence and imagination of the prurient Prophet were employed to paint, in glowing terms, the liberal and intoxicating joys there awaiting them. Seventy-two wives of the girls of Para-

BOOK I. 1000. dise, formed entirely of musk, with eyes large as eggs and charms in proportion, waited impatient to greet the first approach of him whose thread of life was severed in battle with a Giaour[10]; whilst 80,000 servants, bearing 300 new dishes and 300 fresh kinds of wine, daily ministered to the immortal appetites of those gallant martyrs, to whom indigestion was unknown, and who were liable to no inconvenience from excess! When to such liberal promises of future bliss we add the immediate prospect of present wealth, we need not be surprised that the ruthless injunctions of the Prophet, to convert or slay, never lagged for want of willing hands to execute them.

From the earliest days of history the sword of proselytism has always been the keenest and most pitiless wielded by the hand of man; and ruthless as were the Mussulmans, they are not the only apostles who have sought to gratify their God with the lives, and themselves with the wealth, of rival worshippers. But it is a remarkable fact, that all who have made religion of any kind a cloak for conquest, have always been careful to turn their efforts to wealthy regions; and the identity of purpose that directed the Mussulman fanatics to India, and urged equally merciless Christians to Mexico and Peru, is so evident, that we are induced to suppose that[11]

> "Where there is no store of wealth
> Souls are not worth the charge of health;"

and that both must have been impelled by some imaginary command to save the wealthy communities first; no religion forbids the accumulation of this world's riches, or associates with their possession any diminution of future bliss.

India was, at this period, the richest country in the world; and it is possible the golden charms of Luckmee, the Hindoo goddess of wealth, influenced Mahmoud's choice in the selection of Hindostan as the field of his labours, quite as much as the vision of "a dark heaven of houris' eyes" in the Alderman's Paradise of the Prophet himself.

An additional inducement for invasion was presented by the nature of the inhabitants themselves. Both by creed and habit the Hindoos were pacific; and although the nations west of the Indus, constantly exposed to the inroads of the Persians, would necessarily learn the art of war, it is probable that, to the timid races of Hindostan and the southern Peninsula, the march of armies and the heralding of troops were almost as strange as to the natives of Peru in the days of Pizarro. The timid votaries of a God of Peace promised an easy victory to an army of fanatics, who served a God of Battles swift to shed blood!

During a period of twenty-four years Mahmoud made twelve distinct expeditions against the temples and cities of India, and on each occasion thousands of harmless Hindoos were consigned to Jehanum for every true believer who, in triumph, winged his upward flight to the eternal bowers of Paradise. Every object of the worship or veneration of the Hindoos was brutally destroyed; and the description of the amount of jewels and gold, and of the wealth of all kinds, that he brought back with him to Ghizni, resembles more a tale of the Arabian Nights than an authentic narration of history.[12]

It is not my intention to give a distinct account of these numerous invasions: the authorities are limited and very imperfect, and may excuse us an elaboration of succeeding tales of blood and slaughter, that, after all, may be incorrect. We will confine ourselves to the narration of those expeditions that are esteemed authentic, and that more immediately tended, to the establishment of Mussulman rule in Hindostan.

In A.D. 1001, after a few insignificant expeditions to the countries west of the Indus, Mahmoud, with 10,000 men, advanced to Peshawur, where he was met by Jeipal the Brahmin Raja of Lahore, with an army of 12,000 horse, 30,000 foot, and 300 chain elephants; the fortune of Mahmoud was in the ascendant. The Hindoo army

BOOK I. 1001. was defeated with great slaughter, and Jeipal himself taken prisoner; around the neck of this prince of ancient lineage, hung ten necklaces of jewels, one of which alone was valued at 82,000*l.* Jeipal was liberated on the payment of a great ranson; but having been twice defeated in battle, once by Subuctugi, and again by Mahmoud, he was, according to Hindoo law, declared unfit to reign; and having raised his son Anindpal to the throne, he mounted a funeral pile, and sacrificed himself to his gods.

After this victory Mahmoud returned to Ghizni, having established a Mahomedan governor in the Punjaub. During the next three years, Mahmoud, with fierce bands of Arabians, Turks, Affghans, and Chilligies, made three expeditions into the devoted provinces of the north-west. He annexed Moultan, the whole of the Peshawur Valley, and the greater part of Scinde; and exacted tribute from every sovereign from Cashmere to the mouths of the Indus. The most important of these expeditions was directed against the fortress and temple of Bimé, on the Rauvee, in the territory of Nagracot, a part of the Sewalic chain of mountains, north of the Punjaub.

Placed in a commanding situation, hallowed by the springs of the Jwálá-Mukhi, "the effulgent countenance," the holy burning fountain, surrounded by sacred groves, adorned with a celebrated college of Hindoo learning, Bimé was without doubt the strongest fortress and the most superb temple in the north of Hindostan. Nothing could exceed the lavish splendour of a structure roofed and paved with the precious metal; and 28,000 pounds of gold and silver plate; 1600 pounds of pure gold, in ingots; 80,000 pounds of silver bullion, and 800 pounds of different kinds of jewels, rewarded the sacrilege of its conquerors.[18]

Hitherto the expeditions of Mahmoud had been confined to the north and west of the Indus, and although he annually received immense subsidies from the rajas of Hindostan, he had never yet invaded their country; he now, however, determined to visit the land whence came so much gold, and in the 1011 A.D., he marched for Lahore, with the avowed intention of penetrating to the centre of Hindostan, and destroying the temple of Tannassar, esteemed most sacred in the country.

In vain was it urged by the ambassadors sent by Anindpal, King of Lahore, that Tannassar was the most cherished object of the worship of the Hindoos; that if the destruction of temples and idols was enjoined by the religion of Mahomed, he had already fulfilled his duty by the overthrow of Bimé; or that they offered the whole revenues of their masters to induce him to spare it; Mahmoud answered, that "it was an established tenet of the creed of Mahomed, that the more his followers destroyed idolatry, the greater would be their reward; that he was determined, with the assistance of God, to root out idolatry and therefore Tannassar must fall."

Situated on the banks of the sacred Sirsutty, about sixty miles from Delhi, Tannassar had, from the earliest ages, been a spot esteemed most holy by the Hindoos. It had been the imperial residence of the first supreme monarchs of Hindostan; and was connected with the exploits of their gods, and the justice of their most ancient kings; it was the Mecca of the Hindoos; its presiding deity, Jug-Soom, belonged to a former race of immortals; and was believed to have existed before the creation of the world; but the prayers of idolaters, and the claims of immemorial tradition, could not arrest for one instant the fierce will of Mahmoud. Every temple was destroyed, every shrine pillaged, and Jug-Soom himself, torn from the spot he had occupied for a thousand years, was broken up into innumerable fragments, and sent to pave the streets of Ghizni, Mecca, and Bagdad.

From Tannassar, the destroyer marched to the ancient city of Delhi. Canouje was now the capital of Hindostan; but Delhi, standing on the site of Indraput, the

BOOK I. 1011. capital of the country in the days of fable, was still famed for its ancient splendour, its beautiful gardens, and aromatic groves, and for being the mart of the commerce and handiwork of Hindostan. The kings of Delhi numbered amongst their vassals one hundred and eight subordinate princes, and claimed supremacy over all the countries westward, to the Indus, embracing the lands watered by its arms, from the foot of the Himalayas to the Aravulli chain. In this fertile region, producing in some places three crops a year, watered by the Ganges and the Jumna, decked with an infinite variety of exquisite flowers, and producing in profusion most of the fruits of Persia, Turkey, and Hindostan, Mahmoud wished to remain and establish his seat of empire. He was only deterred by the great distance that lay between it and his own capital, and the warlike character of the intervening nations. After plundering the city, he restored the sceptre to the native sovereign, and returned to Ghizni, laden with immense treasure, and forty thousand male and female captives.

But Mahmoud was not content with sacking temples and destroying the works of man; he must needs lay his ruthless hand on the fairest work of nature, and loose his fierce soldiers on the land of perpetual spring, the envy of paradise, the world-renowned valley of Cashmere.

This happy valley was eighty miles long, and thirty broad, and watered throughout its length by the holy stream of the Ghelum, called from its purity the River of Paradise. Surrounded by the grandest mountains in the world, adorned with magnificent cataracts, and splendid trees; tempered during the whole year with genial showers; studded with violets, roses, narcissus, peaches, apricots, and all the fruits and flowers of a temperate clime, Cashmere did indeed present the aspect of Eden, and was unequalled for loveliness throughout the world.

The inhabitants were, from their beauty, supposed to be of Divine origin, to whom their charming country furnished the life of gods. "I happened once to visit Cashmere," says the Persian poet, Rafied'din. "If you will attend I'll give a description of that country. I have seen Irak and India, Khorassan and Persia, but no place equal to Cashmere in beauty and excellence of climate. During the whole year, from Cashmere to the borders of Cathay, the air, tempered by gentle showers, has all the mildness of spring; there are flowers and green herbage, plains and running streams; palaces, cupolas, and public buildings beautiful to view. On every side are rising grounds, crystal springs and lofty trees, amid mountains covered with nut trees, apple trees, and fig trees. Festivity and pleasure peculiarly abound there. In mirth and revelry the Cashmerians pass away their time on silken cushions. They all wear shawls, whether of illustrious birth or of the lowest class. How shall I describe the lovely damsels of that country? for, in my opinion, the young moon is not equal to them in beauty; with lips sweet as sugar, in stature like the graceful pine, fragrant as jessamine, whatever side you look at those nymphs appear like the sun or moon. A thousand secret snares, like the links of a chain, are laid in the waving ringlets of those fair plunderers of hearts. When these lovely nymphs loose their flowing tresses, a thousand captive hearts issue from the points of every hair. There are innumerable youths handsome as Joseph; a thousand damsels, with pouting lips, fair as Zuleekha [14], and charming as the houris; all fresh, young, and blooming,—all in sweetness like sugar candy, sugar and milk."

CHAP. III. 1013.

Such was the fair land of Cashmere to which Mahmoud, in the year 1013, bent his destructive steps. He met with little opposition; and after plundering the valley of its great wealth, converting its peaceful idolaters at the sword's point, and bearing away some of the fairest of its houris, he returned to Ghizni; but, as might be supposed, one glimpse of a region that so nearly answered the description of the paradise promised by their prophet,

BOOK I. 1018. could not satisfy the immortal longings of such true believers as Mahmoud and his army. Two years later he returned, and again was this happy valley a prey to a fierce and avaricious soldiery.

The lust of conquest increases with its gratification. Every expedition of Mahmoud was the prelude of another, and every succeeding conquest laid the foundation of more. The wealth he had seen at Delhi and Tannassar had taught him that it was in those central regions of Hindostan he must expect his most ample spoil, and thither he determined to return.

After settling some difficulties[15] with his northern neighbours, the kings of Charism and Bokhara, he wintered his army at Balkh, and in the year 1018, "as soon as the sun began to awaken the children of spring," he marched at the head of 100,000 horse and 30,000 foot, raised in the countries of Turkestan and Khorassan, for Canouje, the renowned capital of Hindostan.[16]

A weary march of three long months through an unexplored country, and the passage of vast mountains and rapid rivers, separated him from his much-coveted prize. His route lay through Peshawur and the southern extremity of Cashmere; and, keeping close to the mountains, he entered Hindostan from the direction of Thibet; but it was not till the heats of summer began to parch the plains of Hindostan that he reached Canouje.[17] "Canouje, on the Ganges," says the Persian historian, "was a city that raised its head to the skies, and that in strength and structure might safely be said to have no equal." Built B.C. 800, and the capital of India, in the time of Alexander, it had, for fifteen centuries, been the residence of the supreme Raja of the Hindoos. Its walls were said to be 100 miles in circumference, and its population may be estimated from the fact, that 30,000 vendors of betel, and 60,000 singers and musicians supplied the masticating propensities, and ministered to the pleasures of the countless multitudes of this the most

1018.

populous city in India. 80,000 men in armour, 300,000 horse, covered with "pakhur," or quilted mail, 300,000 infantry, and of bowmen and battle-axes 200,000, besides a cloud of elephants bearing warriors, known from its size as the "Lame Host," because in a march the van had reached its camping-ground e'er the rear was in motion, composed the army of the king of Canouje.

So rapid was the march of Mahmoud, and so unexpected the direction of his onslaught, that his fierce horsemen were already pillaging the suburbs of the capital before the fact of his invasion was actually realised by the terrified inhabitants. The fierce manners and warlike aspect of the hardy Affghan and Tartar bands struck terror into the hearts of the enervated inhabitants of the capital, who fled in all directions from their destroying sabres.

The Maharaja of Canouje was Korra[18], a prince of the Rajpoot or warrior caste, who, affecting the height of regal pomp and splendour, was wanting in the dauntless chivalry and unflinching devotion that distinguished the poorest of his noble race. No sooner was an enormous ransom demanded, with the alternative of instant and general plunder, than it was immediately paid; and Korra completed his humiliation by embracing the Mahomedan faith. But such conduct met with no sympathy from the princes of Hindostan. Since the days of Brahma no prince of Rajpoot descent had ever compromised his faith for life or possessions. Three years later an alliance was formed amongst the neighbouring princes, and the craven Korra put to death, with his whole family.

Three days only did Mahmoud remain in Canouje, extorting the hoarded wealth and converting the pagan souls of terrified Hindoos, when he turned his steps to Meerut, distant about sixty miles, and after a sharp siege added its wealth to the plunder of the capital. He then marched towards Muttra, and *en route* attacked Mavin,

BOOK I. 1018.

a strong fort on the banks of the Jumna. Very different was the conduct of its prince, Calchander, to that of Korra. Finding, after a gallant defence, that his cause was hopeless, he slew his wife and children sooner than allow them to fall into the hands of the enemy of his gods, and then killed himself.

Muttra or Mathura, the next object of Mahmoud's avarice, was situated on the Jumna, about eighteen miles from Agra, on the road to Delhi: it was the very centre of that holy district, within which was the seat of whatever was refined in Hindooism, and whose language was the purest dialect of India.[19] It was the birthplace of Chrisna, the eighth and most holy avatar of Vishnu, and was at that time esteemed the most sacred city of India; its very name was always repeated with reverential awe; and throughout a circuit of one hundred miles the country was esteemed holy.

The god Chrisna was supposed to spend his leisure and take his diversion at Gokul, a small town and island in the Jumna below Muttra, and to select Muttra as the scene of his sterner acts. This was the scene of his childish frolics and of the pastoral avatar that made him the darling god of the Hindoo women. Here were the sacred forests of Vindra, where he disported with Radha, his favourite mistress, and her eight beautiful handmaids; and here was first instituted the sacred dance of the Gopi, or nine mistresses of Chrisna, that assembled the "girls of the idol," selected for their beauty from among all the dancing girls of Hindostan.

"Here," says Mahmoud in a letter to his ministers, "there are a thousand edifices as firm as the faith of the faithful, most of them of marble, besides innumerable temples; nor is it likely that this city has attained its present condition, but at the expense of millions of dinars. The treasures of a kingdom expended yearly during two centuries would not suffice to raise the thousand marble palaces and the innumerable temples that here raise their turrets to the skies." It may be that Mahmoud exaggerated the magnificence of his conquest, in order that he might claim greater merit for its complete destruction. Be that as it may, it is probable that, at this period, Muttra was the most elaborately adorned city in the East. Composed chiefly of shrines and temples, thronged with pilgrims and dancing girls, and defended by priests, this holy city fell an easy prey to the conquerors. Neither Chrisna[20] nor his worshippers found any mercy at the hands of these ruthless fanatics; the most sacred shrines and most holy temples were wantonly pillaged and destroyed. All, priests, pilgrims and Bayaderes, were barbarously slaughtered, and for twenty days this city of temples was given over to the lust and cruelty of northern butchers.

But fierce and ruthless as was the conquest of Mahmoud, there was much that even he could not destroy. Many of the structures, cemented and hardened by a thousand years, resisted even his attempts at destruction. Much remained after he was gone; and no sooner had the last Moslem soldier departed, than the worship of Chrisna was recommenced with all its lavish splendour. New and more elaborate temples rose on the ruins of the old; fresh troops of shaven Brahmins ministered at the shrines of new and more costly idols; devotees from the utmost limits of India crowded to regild with their wealth the mutilated shrines of their darling god; and the girls of the idol once more established their claim to the palm of beauty and grace.

The wealth acquired by Mahmoud on this occasion was immense; and the five great idols of pure gold, with eyes of rubies and ornaments of priceless gems, with another of massive gold, weighing more than half a ton, adorned with a sapphire weighing six pounds[21], long served as the inspiriting theme of past triumph and the incitement to future conquest. Laden with spoils and crowned with victory, the return of Mahmoud was naturally slow

BOOK I. 1018.

and tedious; but when at length he did reach his mountain home, he paraded before his astonished subjects the wealth of India, borne by 350 elephants and followed by 50,000 captives. And some days later, holding high festival on the plains that spread below his rocky capital, he seated himself on a throne of massive gold, and surrounded by his courtiers on others of silver, he exhibited, on tables of gold and silver, jewels and precious work and embroidery, such as it had never entered into their hearts to conceive, and distributed to the meanest present some portion of the glittering spoil of Ind,—no wonder that eager champions of Islam started up on all sides, and begged to be led again, and at once, into the golden land of the accursed idolaters!

The private spoil quite equalled that of the Sultan himself. Slaves were selling at 4*s.* a head; and as if by the stroke of a magician's wand, the needy population of Ghizni became one of the most wealthy and luxurious in the East. Few cities have ever exceeded the wealth and splendour of Ghizni at this period of her history. The accumulated plunder of eight expeditions, and the treasure of the richest shrines and cities in the world were devoted to embellishing this Alpine capital: built on a rock nearly 300 feet above the surrounding plains, bounded by distant mountains, and crowned with a profusion of buildings, whose delicate tracery exhibited the perfection of Saracenic design, little imagination is required to realise in Ghizni the Acropolis of the East. Nothing could exceed the lavish magnificence of Mahmoud, directed by his enlightened viziers, Abul Abbass and Ahmed Meimandi, both Persians. Mosques, bazaars, and aqueducts sprung up in all directions; and whilst his subjects, eager to emulate the prodigality of their sovereign, vied with each other in the splendour of their palaces and the beauty of their gardens, he himself wooed high heaven with the "Celestial Bride," the most costly temple yet raised in Asia to the memory of the Great Prophet of Islam.

The love of poetry and the admiration of the fine arts that distinguished many of the Eastern princes, were not wanting in the character of Mahmoud. His capital was the resort of all that was great and learned in the East. The university was crowded with students from all parts of Asia, and 9000*l.* sterling was set aside for the reward of the poets and men of letters who thronged his court, and found the patronage denied them in less favoured lands. But notwithstanding his general liberality to men of letters, his name is usually connected with an act of parsimony, in which he most worthily received the severe chastisement the pen has so often inflicted on the sword.

Having persuaded Firdousi, a celebrated poet of Persia, to undertake the completion of the Shaw Namma, or annals of the kings of Persia, a noble poem, already commenced by Assidi Toosi, a poet of great fame in Khorassan, he promised him a gold mohur (28*s.*) for every couplet he could write in praise of the ancient kings of that race. Thus urged, he wrote 30,000 couplets in rhyme; but the monarch, instead of giving him 60,000 gold mohurs (84,000*l.*), according to agreement, offered him 60,000 rupees, or 6000*l.*, as sufficient reward for a work performed with so much ease and expedition. This sum the poet indignantly refused; and retiring to his closet, penned a most bitter satire[22] of the avaricious monarch, and having sent it to him as an amusing tale, fled secretly, and took refuge with the Caliph of Bagdad, who protected him from the menacing threats of his sovereign.

Mahmoud's avarice even led him to the commission of acts more tyrannical than breaking faith with an exacting poet. Hearing that a citizen of Ghizni was possessed of much wealth, he ordered him to his presence, and reproached him for being an idolater and apostate from the faith. "O king," said the accused, "I am no apostate, but I have much wealth; take it, therefore, but do not act with injustice by robbing me of my money and good

BOOK I. 1018.

name." Enraged at his insolence, the king punished him, and confiscated his goods.

But apart from his besetting sin of avarice, Mahmoud was fond of justice, and the following well-known anecdote proves that he was even capable of magnanimity, worthy of Brutus and the days of republican Rome. On one occasion a poor subject appeared before him to complain, that having the misfortune to be possessed of a handsome wife, his domestic felicity was constantly destroyed by the visits of an omrah of high rank, who, attended by boisterous companions, turned him out of his house, beat him with stripes, and rendered his life anything but comfortable. Having heard his story, Mahmoud desired him to inform him the first time he was similarly maltreated. Three or four nights afterwards the visit was repeated; and the poor man went to the palace, as commanded, to lay the information before the king. Although Mahmoud was in the harem, he immediately arose, and seizing a sword, accompanied the petitioner to his house. When he arrived he commanded the lights to be put out, and entering alone, slew the intruder with his own hand. He immediately ordered the lights to be struck, and earnestly examined the face of the deceased, after which, saying his prayers, he called for refreshment. The man being very poor, could give him nothing but some barley bread and date wine; but having partaken plentifully, he retired to his palace. When questioned about his conduct, he said that he had ordered the lights to be put out, because he believed that none but his own sons would dare commit so open an outrage, and he feared, lest the sight of one he loved so much should stay the hand of justice. His prayers were to return thanks for having been spared the blood of his own son; but so painful had been his anxiety that for three days he had taken no water.

Although nature had given Mahmoud a frame vigorous and enduring beyond his fellows, so that few in his army could wield his mace or hurl his spear, she had failed to endow him with the beauty of person that in all ages has been valued by mankind. "I have repolished my glass," said he sadly to his vizier, "and having looked in it I see so many faults in my face that I easily overlook those of others. The face of a king should brighten the eyes of all beholders; whilst mine appears the picture of misfortune." "It is not one in ten thousand," replied the vizier, with eastern obsequiousness, "who sees your countenance; but your virtues are diffused over all."

Of the private life of Mahmoud little is known. His favourite wife was Haramnour, the daughter of his treacherous foe Elek, the Uzbek king of Cashgar, called from her beauty and dignity Mihir Schighil, the sun of beauties; but all powerful as we know the fair Uzbek to have been at the court of Ghizni[23], it is probable his domestic felicity was not altogether unruffled. It appears the inconstant warrior availed himself of the liberal ordinances of his creed to solace his leisure with other charms than those of the fair Haramnour; and that even the forbidden juice of the grapes was not altogether unknown to this otherwise strict follower of the wine-hating Prophet.

On one occasion, when in his cups, he cut off the tresses of his best-beloved mistress, and when sobered was naturally much distressed at his conduct. He refused to be comforted; and so terrible was his wrath, that none dare approach or address him. At length Hakim Ali Unseri, the leading philosopher and poet of Ghizni, addressed him in the following couplet: "On this happy day, when the tresses of your beloved are cut off, what place is there for grief? let it rather be crowned with mirth and wine, for the taper form of the cypress is best seen from the pruning of its branches." So pleased was the Sultan with this courtly simile that he immediately recovered his equanimity, and ordered the poet's mouth to be three times filled with jewels. Whether the beauty of

BOOK I. 1018. the simile also consoled the fair one for the loss of her locks, and that, in consequence, tonsure de cypre came into fashion in the hareem of Mahmoud, we are not told; but it illustrates the Eastern adage, "When the monkey reigns, dance before him;" and we see the utter impossibility of procuring impartial history from obsequious courtiers, who can always see the sun at midnight, if it is their patron's wish they should do so.

NOTES TO CHAPTER III.

[1] Urdu, in Hindostanee, is composed of Arabic, Persian, Tartar, and Sanscrit words, and was essentially the language of camps.

[2] One day he succeeded in riding down a fawn, and was conveying away his prize, when he observed the dam following his horse, and showing evident marks of distress; he was touched with compassion, and released his captive, pleasing himself with the gratitude of the mother. That night the Prophet appeared to him in a dream, told him God had given him a kingdom as a reward for his humanity, and enjoined him not to forget his feelings of mercy when he came to the exercise of power.

[3] A.D. 977. He was opposed by an allied army of Rajpoots, under the Rajas of Punjaub, Delhi, Canouje, and Kalingar; the confederate army being commanded by Jaipal, chief of Punjaub.

[4] At the battle of Lingham, "the eyes of Heaven were obscured at seeing his deeds."

[5] When Alp Arslan, the mighty lion, received Romanus Diogenes, the captive monarch of Constantinople, he asked him what treatment he expected to receive? "If you are cruel," said Romanus, "you will take my life; if you listen to pride, you will drive me at your chariot wheels; if you consult your interest, you will take a ransom and restore me to my country." "And what," said Alp Arslan, "would have been your own behaviour, had fortune smiled on your arms?" "Had I vanquished," said he fiercely, "I would have inflicted on thy body many stripes."

[6] It is related that having at great cost erected a magnificent garden near the city of Ghizni, he invited his father to visit it, expecting naturally liberal applause; instead however of praising it, the King said he esteemed the whole thing a bauble, which any one could raise with wealth; that it was not the business of a prince to raise elegant gardens and costly buildings, but the undying structure of fame which might stand for ever, to be imitated but never equalled by futurity.

[7] A.D. 997.

[8] Al Koran means "the book," or "that which should be read."

[9] Sale's Koran, chaps. v. viii. xxxvii. and xlviii.

[10] "They come! their kerchiefs green they wave,
And welcome with a kiss the brave,
Who falls in battle 'gainst a Giaour,
Is worthiest of immortal bower."

[11] No Jesuit e'er took in hand
To plant a church on barren land,
Nor ever thought it worth the while
A Swede or Russ to reconcile;
For where there is no store of wealth
Souls are not worth the charge of health.
Spain in America, had two designs,
To sell their gospels for their mines;
For, had the Mexican been poor,
No Spaniard twice had landed on their shore.

[12] Mill entirely rejects the historical accounts of the early wealth of India; but when he asserts that "it was not till the time of Akbar that gold or silver was coined for circulation in the principal parts of India, antecedently to that period small pieces of copper being the only coin," he allows his Hindoo-phobia to carry him too far. Whence came all the gold that Clive and Hastings found? the wealth that has enriched half the upper middling classes of England? The northern conquerors of India did not plant the famed pagoda tree—they came to seek it!

[13] In this golden temple was the effigy of a monster, called Matta, before whom thousands from all parts of India used to worship, and whose fury was propitiated by a small collop cut from the tongue; which, strange to say, like lizards' tails, grew again in those days!

[14] Zuleekha is the eastern name for the frail wife of Potiphar. The Bible omits all allusion to her beauty.

[15] Mounted on a white elephant, he defeated the Tartars under Ilek Khan; the battle was fought four leagues from Balkh. His elephant seized Ilek Khan, tore him from his horse, and cast him into the air.

[16] On this occasion his regular army was increased by 20,000 volunteers, calling themselves "crusaders."

[17] Canouje, from Cubja, spine; and Kanya, virgin.

[18] It is uncertain whether this was the name of the individual sovereign, or of the dynasty.

[19] The district was called Vrij, and the dialect the Vrij-basha.

[20] The real image of Chrisna was said to have escaped Mahmoud; and to have been taken to Nat'hdwarra, twenty-two miles from Oodipoor, on the banks of the Bunas: during the reign of Aurungzebe, when the sanctity of the Vrij was again violated, it was conducted to the war by Jey Sing, who consecrated to that service the heads of 100,000 Rajpoots.

[21] Ruby taken at Somnauth weighed 450 miskal, or 6lb. 8oz.; sapphire at Muttra, weighed 400 miskal. The maund on the Bombay side varies from 28lb. to 40lb. avoidupois; in either case the treasure is incredible.

[22] In his satire he says, "a raven can produce nothing but a raven;" alluding to his birth as the son of the slave of the Samanian sovereign; the lieutenant of the Caliph.

[23] See D'Herbélot, art. Meimendi.

CHAP. IV.

A.D. 1024.

THE TWELFTH AND LAST EXPEDITION OF MAHMOUD. — HE ARRIVES AT ANHULWARRA THE CAPITAL OF GUZERAT. — THE MAGNIFICENCE OF THE CITY. — THE IMPORTANCE OF THE GOD SOMA. — THE SPLENDOUR OF HIS TEMPLE. — THE ENTHUSIASTIC DEFENCE OF SOMNAUTH. — THE DEFEAT AND FLIGHT OF THE IDOLATERS. — THE IMMENSE SPOIL CONTAINED IN THE IDOL. — THE FATE OF DABSCHELIM.

BOOK I. 1024.

AL KADIR BILLA, the Caliph now reigning at Bagdad, was but a shadow of the proud sovereigns of the race of Abbass, who, 200 years before, ravaged the East, and encouraged science. His empire was confined to his capital and its immediate vicinity, and the sanctity of his lineage and the lip-service of surrounding princes was all that remained to him of the might of his ancestors. So fallen was he that when Mahmoud wrote to him, saying that "the greatest part of the kingdom of Khorassan was already under his jurisdiction, and he hoped he would desire his governors to give up the remainder," he had no resource but to submit.

To this shadow of sovereign power Mahmoud still paid a nominal subjection, and although he assumed the title of Sultan[1], King of Kings, to proclaim to the world that he had no rival, he, at the same time, with a humility that savours strongly of pride, sent a "writing of victory" to the Caliph, and was content to receive in return a doubtful title of honour, reflecting on the lowness of his birth.[2]

For three years Mahmoud rested from the labours of conquest, founding works of public utility, and adding to the wealth and luxury of his capital; his victories, celebrated in the heroic strains of the leading minstrels of Asia, and his friendship courted by embassies from all the kingdoms of the East. But his was not a nature to find lengthened enjoyment in splendid and luxurious ease; a ruthless spirit of enterprise, insatiable avarice, ill concealed under the mask of devotion, and the alluring prospect of easy victory, impelled him again to march towards the land of the Hindoo. Rapid as had been his late conquests in Hindostan, and marvellous as was the treasure he had accumulated, there was yet another region that promised victory as easy, and results even more surprising than any yet realised.

CHAP. IV.

1024.

Nearly a century before the expeditions of Mahmoud made known to the Eastern world the vast treasures of Hindostan, the accounts of Arabian merchants and voyagers had spread abroad startling accounts of the power and glory of the kingdom of Guzerat, the magnificence of its capital, Anhulwarra, and the fabulous wealth of the famed shrine of Soma, "the Lord of the Moon."

During Mahmoud's repeated invasions the truth of these reports was fully confirmed, and having now, with comparative ease, overrun and despoiled two of the great kingdoms of Hindostan, he determined to undertake the conquest of the third and most wealthy.

This, the twelfth and last expedition of Mahmoud, must be considered one of the hardiest on record. Few but this dauntless warrior would have dared the numerous dangers that threatened an advance through a country teeming with fierce and implacable foes, rendered terrible by the unknown dangers of the deserts of Marwar, the famed "region of death," to attack a sovereign whose steel-clad horsemen and chain-bearing elephants were famed to the utmost limits of India, and who could bring into the field troops as numerous as those that followed Xerxes to Europe.

At the conclusion of the rainy season of A.D. 1024,

BOOK I. 1024. Mahmoud, at the head of 80,000 chosen horse, descended from the mountains of Ghizni, and marched to the city of Moultan, on the Indus; here he supplied his troops with several days' provisions and provender for the horses; and loading 20,000 camels with necessaries for the army, he advanced through the vast deserts that flank the Rajpoot states to the capital of Ajmere. His first enterprise was only partially successful: he took and destroyed the city of Ajmere, but was unable to overcome the citadel; and, after repeated assaults, he was forced to leave it to its brave defenders. He now advanced through the arid region of Marwar, where his whole army nearly perished for want of water; but at length, after hardships that would have daunted a mind less constant, he arrived in sight of Anhulwarra Puttun, the far-famed capital of Guzerat.

Anhulwarra[3], the capital of Guzerat, situated at an equal distance between Cutch and Cambay, was the Tyre of India. It was a city of universal commerce, into which the trade of eighty-four ports continually flowed. Its population was countless, and its plenty expressed by a proverb. "Anhulwarra," says the Arabian historian, "is a sea of men, where, if you ask for water they give you milk."[4] Her king was the most illustrious prince in India, and thirty-two powerful rajas who ruled independently in their own kingdoms, acknowledged his supremacy. He was of the Jain or Buddhist faith, to whom the injunction, from the smallest insect to man thou shalt not kill, was the first and greatest commandment; and in the enumeration of his possessions we find the names of eighteen provinces, and "fourteen in which no animal life was taken."

The city was fifteen miles in circuit, and was adorned with numberless temples and colleges, palaces and public buildings, eighty-four squares, and a like number of market-places, shaded with the palmyra, the rose, the apple, the sandal-wood, the mangoe, and every kind of variegated creeper, sheltered and separated the dealers in camphor, oils, fruits, and metals, who supplied the wants of the eighteen castes that thronged its streets. Native gold enriched the kingdom; whilst the subject island of Ceylon, the land of pearls and precious stones, added its priceless products to the general wealth.[5]

CHAP. IV. 1024.

Mahmoud occupied this city without any difficulty, and so charmed was he with the profusion and novelty that there greeted his avaricious gaze, that a second time he determined to desert Ghizni, and, ruling his other provinces by deputy, to fix his seat of empire in Guzerat; and it was only the earnest representations of his courtiers, that it would be impossible to maintain a capital so far removed from his own kingdom, that induced him to abandon his design. Mahmoud had not the generosity to spare what he could not enjoy; he destroyed many of the public buildings of Anhulwarra; but in less than fifteen years it had entirely recovered its wonted splendour; and when, 200 years later, Alla the Sanguinary levelled the walls, buried the greater part of the temples under their foundations, razed the palaces, and as a last token of conquest ploughed up the ground on which they stood with asses, Komarpal, "the pillar of the Jain faith," was still one of the greatest sovereigns in India, and reigned supreme over thirty-two provinces.

It was not, however, merely to sack Anhulwarra, rich as it was, and to dethrone her kings, that Mahmoud had dared the dangers of Marwar, and the legions of Guzerat; there was yet another magnet, more powerful still, that had attracted his grasping spirit, and which promised inestimable treasures to him who had the courage to seize them. At the extreme point of the peninsula of Guzerat, now known as the island of Diu, 150 miles from Anhulwarra, was situated Puttun Somnauth or Deva Puttun, the city of the god, the most holy of all the cities of India; no spot in the world enlisted the veneration of so many millions of the human race, as Deva Puttun, the "Dwelling

BOOK I. 1024. of the Deity." Pilgrims from the most distant parts of Asia thronged this holy spot, and scarcely a caste in India but looked to Somnauth as the most hallowed shrine of its faith.

Somnauth possessed three distinct claims on the devotion and credulity of the Eastern world.[6] On this spot for forty centuries had stood the temple of Soma, the Hindoo Pluto, the incarnation of the mysterious doctrine of metempsychosis, that, venerable in the days of pagan mythology, still supplies the sole conception of a future state to one half of the whole human race. Here in all its gorgeous splendour still flourished the ancient worship of the magi; and here too was the holiest of holies, where Chrisna, the shepherd god, the Hindoo Apollo, resigned his life to the luckless arrow of a hunter.[7]

Hither, from the extreme confines of Balkh and Persia, the fire-worshippers threaded their weary way to pay their mystic adoration to the rising and the setting sun. Whilst from the most distant regions of the Carnatic and Bengal, troops of Hindoo pilgrims flocked to make oblalations under the peepul tree, where their beloved god captivated the shepherdesses with his pipe, or to bathe in the "door of bliss," the sacred pool that washed his hallowed limbs;[8] and here in the gorgeous temple of his god did the gentle votary of the Jain faith, as he carefully brushed the ground on which he was going to sit, breathe the humble prayer "that as I extend my mercy even to the ants so may thy mercy descend on me."

The enthusiasm of millions of credulous pilgrims had not failed to spread abroad exaggerated accounts of the riches of their most popular shrines; and the description of the sixty-six columns of massive gold studded with rubies and precious stones that adorned the great hall of the temple of Soma; of the chain of pure gold weighing 1200 pounds, which, extending from the summit of the principal temple to the base, supported the massive bell that summoned the pilgrims to prayer; of the heaps of diamonds and the hundredweights of pearls that loaded its coffers, were not lost upon men whose profession was one of predatory warfare. The report that on its impious altars one of the faithful was daily sacrificed to the idol, and the haughty boast of the priests, that though the other temples of Hindostan had been deserted by the gods for their excessive wickedness, this holy shrine was still under the especial protection of Soma, who with one blast of his mouth could exterminate the impious followers of Mahomed, added the stings of insult and the duty of revenge to the powerful promptings of avarice.

CHAP. IV. 1024.

The god Soma possessed the absolute disposal of the souls of all who were destined at any period to share the paradise of Brahma; he was the deity who regulated the successive transmigrations by which they were purified; and although he could not, like Pluto, cut short or lengthen the thread of human existence, he could make the transition state one of exquisite bliss or inconceivable woe.

A god who could bless the disembodied souls of credulous votaries with the sacred form of an alligator or a snake, or curse them with the despised form of a woman or a dog[9], would naturally be a deity of great importance to all who believed in him. Every Hindoo wished to stand well with the great god of Somnauth; and it can be no matter of surprise that his temple was the most splendid, and his ministering Brahmins the most pampered of all the priestly castes in India.

The Ganges, represented by a female deity, is much worshipped by the Hindoos. It is believed that it has its source in heaven, and that its waters finally return thither, after purifying the souls of men upon earth. This holy water, brought a distance of 1200 miles, was alone considered worthy to be employed in the daily ablutions of the great god of Soma. 2000 Brahmins served constantly at his shrine; whilst 500 dancing girls,

BOOK I. 1024. remarkable either for their beauty or their rank[10], and 300 barbers, ministered to the wants and solaced the leisure of these holy men. 2000 villages, with their revenues and resources, were allotted by the surrounding rajas for the sole support of these vast establishments; and it was no uncommon event for 50,000 pilgrims, from all parts of India, to be assembled at one time at the shrine of this popular idol.

The sacred portion of the city of Somnauth was one mile and three quarters round, and was defended by walls from twenty-five to thirty feet high, and about sixteen thick, faced with masonry, and surrounded by a deep fosse that was wet or dry at pleasure. For a lengthened period the Hindoo garrison, animated by the exhortations of their priests, trusting in the omnipotence of their gods, and assisted by the levies of the neighbouring Hindoo princes, successfully defended this holy spot against the scoffing soldiers of the Prophet; but at length northern vigour prevailed; and the Alla-il-Alla of the fierce Moslem drowned the Ram-Ram of the fanatical Hindoos.

The following is the account of the last and successful attack: "It was the Jooma-rat, the Sunday of Islam. In the dead of the night the green standard of the Prophet was unfurled, and entrusted to a chosen band, led by two brothers, Jaffier and Mozuffur. They reached the gate almost unobserved. A huge elephant, whose mighty head generally served in ancient days in lieu of a petard, flinched from the projecting spikes, and a camel was placed as a 'fender' to save the pioneer's head. The elephant gave a tremendous charge, the gates were burst open (and so probably was the camel), and the soldiers of the Prophet forced their way into the holy city.

Notwithstanding all his efforts, Mahmoud could not reach the shrine of Soma that night. The Hindoos, now reduced to despair, fought to the death. The Mussulmans could not penetrate beyond the outwork, and the haughty violators of Muttra and Canouje were on the point of being defeated by an enthusiastic army of priests and pilgrims; but Mahmoud, now grown grey in conquest, was equal to the occasion. Perceiving his troops wavering in every direction, he sprang from his horse, and falling on his knees in the face of the whole army, prayed to the god of Mahomed to deliver the fanatical idolaters into his hands. A life of battle had taught him that prayer without action availed little. He knew as well as the Roman traitor of old[11], that without example "a captain's orations will never make a coward a brave man." Addressing his nobles, he told them that victory or a crown of martyrdom was his choice, and taking his favourite general by the hand, he called upon them all to follow him in a charge that should secure one or the other of these glorious consummations. One more charge was made; the idolaters were driven from their walls, and a panic ensuing they took to their boats, and left their idols and their shrines to the fury of the conquerors.

CHAP. IV. 1024.

Once in possession of the city, no time was lost in securing so dear bought a prize. Pressing forward through streets encumbered with dead and flying pilgrims, the conqueror made his way to the renowned temple, whose fame had drawn him 2000 miles, and supported his courage through dangers and trials that few conquerors have overcome.[12]

Standing on a projecting rock, watered by the boundless ocean, its golden spire hailed as a beacon from afar by storm-tossed mariners and pilgrims, nothing could exceed the beauty of the site hallowed by this favoured temple. But it was not till he crossed the threshold, and his eager soldiery penetrated to the innermost shrines of the god, that he could estimate the full value of his prize.

The heart of a conqueror less fierce and relentless than Mahmoud might have experienced some feelings of awe when in a lofty hall inlaid with precious stones, the roof supported by columns of massive gold, and lighted by one

BOOK I. 1024.

lamp that reflected from inestimable jewels a mysterious light on thousands of gold and silver images, his eyes first fell on the great idol of Somnauth.

It required more than ordinary fanaticism to nerve the hand that with one blow should destroy the cherished emblem of worship, that had for four thousand years been hallowed by the prayers and prostrations of half the world; to hew, hip and thigh, the devoted priesthood, who now at the cost of their lives sought to prevent pollution to the cherished object of their faith.[13]

To Mahmoud, however, it presented nothing but the symbol of a despised creed, which it was his mission to destroy. The supernatural endowments that sanctified it in the eyes of two hundred millions of Hindoos, merely caused it to stink the more in the nostril of every true believer.[14]

The Brahmins offered ten millions sterling to save their god from destruction; but Mahmoud scoffed at their lamentations, and swore by the Koran that not for the wealth of ten thousand Somas would he appear to posterity as a merchant of idols.

The shrine and priesthood of an abhorred faith were at his feet, and both met the fate reserved for all enemies of the Prophet. Amidst the groans and supplications of an agonised multitude, Mahmoud gave orders to break in pieces their graven images; and raising the dreaded mace, which few but the monarch himself could wield in battle, he set the example in true iconoclastic style by striking off the nose of the helpless Soma. So excellent an example was not neglected by his soldiers; and in a very short time the destruction of the god was complete. The true object of the relentless zeal of Mahmoud, and the costly supplications of the priests, was now exposed. The idol was hollow, and filled with the accumulated treasures of forty centuries of votive idolatry. All the wealth hitherto acquired by the conqueror was as nothing compared with that now yielded by the prolific god. Piles of diamonds

CHAP. IV. 1024.

and sapphires, a ruby weighing upwards of 6 lbs.,[15] thousands of pounds weight of pure gold and precious stones were, to the dismay of the crest-fallen priests, brought to light by the triumphant soldiers.

The treasures extracted from this famed sanctuary alone are said to have amounted to nine millions sterling; the greatest sum ever yielded by the credulity of man to the avarice of priests.[16]

If Mahmoud imitated Cambyses[17] in himself striking down the abhorred emblem of a hostile creed, he was not less ruthless towards the shrines and their priests. He utterly destroyed this Delphos of the East; not one stone of its numerous temples were left standing on another, and fragments of the riven god were distributed over the Mahomedan world, and cast before the gates of the sacred mosques of Mecca, Medina, and Ghizni; whilst fifty thousand priests and votaries are supposed to have quaffed the fabled cup of Amreeta, that confers immortality on the Hindoo elect, to testify to the earnestness of their faith and the unsparing zeal of their foes.

For more than a hundred years the sacred city, Somnauth Puttun, lived only in the memory of pious Hindoos; robbers and outlaws alone wandered through its temples and palaces, and wolves and foxes occupied its desecrated tombs. At the end of that period, Komarpal, "the pillar of the Jain faith," rebuilt its shrines, but could not restore its violated sanctity. From the hour that Mahmoud smote the graven image of Soma, the holiest spot in India became unclean; the reverence of a hundred millions of credulous devotees passed away with that blow. Never again was the worship of the Lord of the Moon revived in that sacred spot; and deserted and despised, a receptacle for kine and filth, a globular patch of red paint, placed by loitering cow-herds, is now the only remaining symbol of the death-place of the Shepherd God.[18]

When Mahmoud had captured Somnauth, he heard that Raja Jamund, the sovereign of Guzerat, who had assisted

BOOK I. 1024. in the defence of the temple, had taken refuge in Gundala, a fort surrounded by water on all sides; thither he at once proceeded. On arriving at the spot, he found that the water was only fordable in one place, and that if caught by the flow of the tide during the passage all must perish. He was not to be daunted, but crossed with his cavalry and took the place, Raja Jamund scarcely making good his escape in a boat.

After a success so glorious and so satisfactory, alike to their avarice and their bigotry, the chiefs of Mahmoud's army, laden with spoil and wearied with victory, longed to bend their steps towards their mountain home; but the ambition of their sovereign was not bounded by the sacking of shrines and the heaping up of treasure. He loved conquest for conquest's sake, and here on the shores of the great ocean he actually meditated the subjection of the far off countries of Taprobane and Pegu.

Mahmoud returned to Anhulwarra, and in the place of the fugitive Raja Jamund, raised to the throne a Brahmin of royal lineage named Dabschelim, whose short career of sovereign power illustrates one of the most remarkable reverses of fortune that even kingly annals can furnish.

Anxious to enjoy his triumph over his former monarch, who was being conducted a prisoner to Anhulwarra, Dabschelim rode out to meet him, and made him run before his horse with a bason on his head and a ewer in his hand, intending afterwards to blind him and imprison him, according to the custom of the country, in a dark pit dug under his throne [19] where he would remain imprisoned for life, or till the death of his conqueror.[20] When some distance from Anhulwarra, Dabschelim halted, and being overcome by the heat reclined under a tree, and spreading a red handkerchief over his face, ordered his attendants to withdraw. Shortly afterwards, a vulture hovering over the place, mistaking the red handkerchief [21] for his prey, swooped upon him, and fixing in his talons, tore out both his eyes; and thus, according to the laws of the country, rendered him unfit to reign. Immediately there was a great uproar, and the imprisoned raja coming at the moment, was received with acclamations, and again declared king. Putting the basin on the head of the wretched Dabschelim, and the ewer in his hands, he drove him before him into the dungeons he had prepared, where he spent the remainder of his life.

CHAP. IV.

1024.

NOTES TO CHAPTER IV.

[1] Sultan or Soldan means βασιλεὺς βασιλεῶν, King of Kings.

[2] The Caliph sent him the title of Veli, which signifies friend and Lord, also servant and valet. It was afterwards, on the payment of a large sum, changed to *Vali,* which signifies master or commander.

[3] Anhulwarra was founded A.D. 746, and utterly destroyed A.D. 1294.

[4] The annual amount of duty paid on imposts to Anhulwarra was 250,000*l.* equal at least to one million at present. The following anecdote is told by the Arabian chronicler, in evidence of its vast population:—"One day a woman who had lost her husband went to the prince and related her misfortune. He ordered the herald to proclaim, that whoever went by the name of Kanoh, the blind of an eye, should appear at the altar of justice; when, lo! 999 persons, blind of an eye, and each bearing the name of Kanoh, appeared. The disconsolate wife went through the ranks, and yet her husband was not there, nor was he found till a second proclamation was issued!"

[5] There were gold mines at that time in Guzerat; and Ceylon, whence came all the precious stones of Hindostan, was one of its dependencies. It appears from the Sacred Historical Book of Ceylon, the Maharansi, describing the lineage of Buddha, that the island was at that time a dependency of India; it was not till A.D. 1290 that the King Vizayabahu recovered his independence and shook off the Indian yoke.

[6] There were two other sun temples at Juggernauth and Benares.

[7] "Chrisna, called Shama from his dark complexion, travelled to this Ultima Thule with his friend Arguna Yudishtra, the abdicated Lord Paramount of India, and Baldeo, and performed his ablutions at the shrine of the Lord of the Moon; he then took shelter from the noon-day heat, and slept under an umbrageous peepul. Whilst he slept a forester, mistaking the padma, or lotus-like mark on the sole of his feet, for the eyes of a deer, shot him dead."—Tod: compare deaths of Balder the Beautiful, shot in the heel with an arrow made of mistletoe, and of Achilles.

[8] Siva, or Mahadeo, was also worshipped here under the title of Swayam Náth, the "self-existent."

BOOK I. 1024.

[9] No transmigration is so dreaded by the faithful Buddhist as that into a woman or a dog.

[10] The rajas considered it an honour to have their daughters admitted.

[11] Catiline.

[12] The temple was 336 feet round, 117 long, and 74 broad. It was larger than the Temple of Sion, and yet in those days and countries the Jewish historian says "that none such had ever been built."—Tod.

[13] The idol was made of one stone 70 feet high, and, according to the Brahmins, had been worshipped on that spot four thousand years.

[14] One reason for the fierce antipathy of Mahmoud to the image at Somnauth may have arisen from the belief common amongst the Mahomedans of that time, that it was a counterpart of the idol formerly worshipped by the idolaters of Mecca.

[15] There is every reason to believe that these enormous emeralds and rubies were merely glass; according to Theophrastus, the Egyptians erected in the temple of Jupiter Ammon an obelisk of four emeralds, that is coloured glass, 40 cubits high and 4 in breadth, or 60 feet by 6 feet.

Pliny mentions another colossal statue of Serapis, or the Sun, nine cubits high, of one emerald.

Sesostris presented the King of India one of four cubits high; these must have been glass. For other particulars see Pliny, lib. xxxvii. sect. 19.

This ruby weighed 450 miskals, or 6lb. 3oz.; the largest in the Treasury of Delhi weighed 17 miskals.

[16] Alexander found in the treasury of Persia 180,000 talents of gold, about 30,000,000*l.* David took from the Moabites and Philistines 100,000 talents of gold, 1,000,000 talents of silver, which, setting the Jewish talent of gold at its stated value of 5,475*l.*, and that of silver at 342*l.*, make up the incredible sum of nine hundred millions.—Chronicles xxii.

Athenæus says that the treasures taken at Nineveh, at the death of Sardanapalus, amounted to a thousand myriads of talents of gold, and ten times as many of silver!! There were three kind of talents—The Tyrian or Eubœan talent, the Phœnician, the Jewish. It is impossible to know which is meant.

[17] Cambyses himself slew Apis the bull god, and destroyed every priest he could find.

[18] See Tod's Rajasthan.—Chrisna was the Shepherd God.

[19] Dabschelim represented to Mahmoud "that it was the custom for the kings of that country, when an enemy was in their power, to prepare for him a dark dwelling below their own royal seat, where causing him to be seated on a throne and kept closely confined, only a small hole is to be left open through which he might receive his daily food."

[20] The old Begum Somroo, being jealous of her husband's attention to one of the ladies of her court, had a pit dug under her bed in order that not a groan should escape her feline revenge, and there starved the wretched girl to death!

[21] A vulture killed Euripides by dropping a tortoise on his bald head, mistaking it for a stone.

CHAP. V.

A.D. 1026—1030.

THE PERIL OF MAHMOUD AND HIS ARMY.—HIS RETURN TO MOULTAN.—HE EXTENDS HIS EMPIRE.—ADVANCE OF THE TARTAR HORDES.—THE LAST CAMPAIGN OF MAHMOUD.—HIS DEATH.

AFTER an absence of two years and six months Mahmoud set out on his return to Ghizni, but it was only to encounter danger more terrible and destruction more imminent than any that had as yet crossed his path of conquest. CHAP. V. 1026.

A Brahmin of the shrine of Somnauth, dispossessed of his wealth and maddened at the impious desecration of all he esteemed sacred, assumed the character of a guide, and volunteered to conduct the army by a shorter route to Moultan. His services were accepted, and for three days he led them through the deserts of Scinde without water and without food. When accused of treachery he proudly confessed the ruse; and whilst enduring the terrible penalty of being flayed alive, gloried in an act that brought sudden destruction on so many of the enemies of his gods. Mahmoud retraced his steps with much labour, and one third of his army had perished before he reached Moultan. This was his last invasion of India, and with the exception of an expedition, undertaken during the next year, in which he almost exterminated the Jits[1], a nation living on the south side of the Indus, in one of the fiercest river fights on record, he never again set foot in Hindostan.

Mahmoud made altogether twelve expeditions into the devoted land of India, and on each occasion returned

BOOK I. 1026. with increased glory and wealth. He had utterly destroyed Nagracot, Tannassar, Muttra, and Somnauth,—the four most holy shrines of the Hindoos,—and pillaged Delhi, Canouje, and Anhulwarra, their most magnificent cities. He had annexed Moultan, Peshawur, and Cashmere, and had overrun Hindostan as far as Delhi and Guzerat, and the frontiers of Malwa. He did not permanently occupy any portion of these conquests, but he left terrible evidence of his power to do so at will. He proved to a rapacious world the absolute truth of the fabled wealth of India; and opened out that military road of invasion by which succeeding armies of conquerors have ever found a ready access to the fertile plains of Hindostan.

We must not suppose that, great as they were, his Indian conquests were enough to satisfy the restless ambition of the victorious Mahmoud. Notwithstanding his expeditions to that wretched country, he found time to conquer and annex the kingdom of Ghaur, a country of unequalled strength, belonging to the Soor tribe of Affghans. He defeated his father-in-law, Elich, the Usbec king of Cashgar, and took his country. He added to the kingdom of Ghizni, Seistan, between the mouths of the Indus and Persia. He conquered Irak, Georgia, and the whole of eastern Persia, and established his son in the government of Ispahan; and it was only the high-spirited letter of a chivalrous woman that induced him to spare the dynasty of Bowides, the emperor of western Persia. "During the life of my husband," wrote the Sultana-mother, when threatened with his invasion, "I was ever apprehensive of your ambition. He was a prince and a soldier worthy of your arms. He is now no more. His sceptre has passed to a woman and a child, and you dare not attack their infancy and weakness. How inglorious would be your conquest, how shameful your defeat! And yet," adds this artful lady, "the events of war are in the hands of the Almighty."

At this period the empire of Mahmoud far exceeded that of any living sovereign. He ruled supreme from Cashmere to Ispahan, and from the Caspian to the sacred Ganges. The whole Mahomedan world looked to him as its chief; and while some of his legions protected the weary march of pilgrims to their holy Mecca, others proclaimed the worship of the one God and his Prophet amidst oceans of blood thousands of miles away in the sacred cities of Hindostan.

In those turbulent times the very size of the empire constituted its chief danger. No sooner did the viceroys of provinces, themselves comprising noble kingdoms, find themselves free from the immediate control of the supreme sovereign than they immediately aimed at independence. The varied and often opposing interests of the several provinces encouraged their ambition, and prevented the centralisation indispensable to lasting empire. Already, even at the zenith of its glory, the empire of Ghizni showed unmistakeable evidence of the disruption that has limited the duration of all the great empires of the East; and the very same train of circumstances that secured the empire to the father of Mahmoud lost it to his sons.

The danger of his overgrown empire was forcibly placed before the monarch by an old woman, who came to demand redress for the death of her son, who, together with a number of merchants, was killed by robbers in the deserts of Nedubendan. In vain Mahmoud urged the impossibility of keeping order in so remote a part of his dominions. "Why, then, do you take countries," said she, "which you cannot govern, and for the protection of which you must answer in the day of judgment?"[2]

Already the rumble of that great northern torrent, that was to overrun the eastern world and sweep away all traces of civilisation from the fairest lands of Asia, was heard on the frontiers of his kingdom.

The vast deserts, extending from the borders of civilised

BOOK I. 1026. Asia far away into the northern wilds of Russia and China, have from time immemorial been the heritage of numerous pastoral tribes of Curds and Turkomans. Obliged to tend their flocks over boundless wilds, and often to contest with their neighbours the right of pasturage, these hardy shepherds are horsemen from their birth, and become warriors at an age when the youth of other nations have scarce learned to draw the bow; even their women display the hardihood and warlike skill usually confined to the stronger sex.

The first emigration of these hardy Northmen commenced at the beginning of the tenth century. Passing from their inhospitable deserts beyond the Caspian and the sea of Aral, they slowly pressed on to the more sunny regions of Persia and Samarcand. Retaining their aversion to the life of a town, and refusing to submit to the drudgery of agriculture, for the sake of supporting themselves on the "top of a weed," as they called wheat in derision, they neglected all the arts and sciences, as the signs of an effeminate race, and devoted themselves entirely to the practice of war. Totally illiterate and unable to read or write, they elected their kings by lot, and when they signed a treaty, dipped their hands in ink, and made an impression of it on paper.[3]

They embraced the creed of Mahomed as they advanced south, and gradually acquired territory and power in Transoxiana and Charizme, the seats of oriental science and learning. The declining power of the Caliphs was quite insufficient to stay the torrent; whilst their lieutenants, ever aiming at independence, welcomed with pleasure the most useful of mercenary troops; till, in less than a hundred years, their power far exceeded that of those who had encouraged their advance, and the dependence of mercenary service gave place to the haughty insolence of conquest.

Mahmoud himself had encouraged the advance of these hardy warriors, as invaluable in his endless expeditions to

India; and he discovered too late that the fierce hordes he had fostered for the destruction of his foes, sought but the opportunity to turn and rend himself. CHAP. V. 1026.

Inquiring one day of Ismael, a celebrated chief of the Seljuk tribe, who dwelt at Bokhara, what number of men he could furnish for the military service—"Send one of these arrows," replied the haughty chief, "to the camp of Seljuk, and 50,000 warriors will mount their horses; if you want more, send this arrow to the tribe of Balik, and 50,000 more will answer the summons; but if you want to know our full force, send round this bow, and, as it circulates, 200,000 horsemen will flock to your standard." Alarmed at the proximity of such powerful allies, Mahmoud attempted to remove his Turkomans into the heart of Khorassan; but it was too late. Having once tasted the delights of the pleasant regions of the south, they were loth to return again to their northern wilds. They withdrew their tribute, declared their independence, and invaded the northern provinces of Ghizni, and having defeated his general, Amir Toos, were pressing on to the capital itself, when Mahmoud, hastily collecting his troops, drove them back with great slaughter; but their retreat was like the wave of the rising storm that surges back but to return with greater fury. A few years later they appeared again in overwhelming numbers, and seized the empire with resistless might.

This was the last campaign of the great warrior Mahmoud, and his triumph was saddened by the conviction that the splendid empire he had raised with so much labour, and cemented with so much blood, awaited but his death to pass from the hands of his children.

Avarice and the lust of dominion were the ruling passions of Mahmoud, and no conqueror ever obtained more completely his heart's desire; but his latter days show that the possession of all that he had so much coveted afforded no gratification, and only added poignancy to the grief of his approaching end.

BOOK I. 1030.

A few days before his death he entered his treasury, and surveyed, with mournful eyes, the vast and varied accumulations of a life of conquest and pillage. After gazing long and earnestly on all that he had acquired with so much labour, he burst into tears, and closed the doors without distributing any portion of that wealth that was so soon to pass altogether from his possession.

The next day, reclining on a couch, he reviewed 100,000 foot, 50,000 horse, and 1300 elephants; but the dying warrior could not gaze unmoved on the companions of his dangers and the instruments of his glory: he wept bitterly as legion after legion of victorious troops passed before him, and retired in anguish to his palace, never again to show himself to his subjects. What a satire on the vanity of human ambition! He looked on "all the works his hands had wrought, and on the labour he had laboured to do, and behold all was vanity and vexation of spirit, and there was no profit under the sun."

In that gorgeous abode called the Palace of Delights, raised with the plunder of Hindoo cities, and glittering with the treasures of unnumbered shrines, the soul of the great Mahmoud was required of him, in the 63rd year of his age and the 34th of his reign.[4] He was buried by torchlight, and three miles south of Ghizni may still be seen the cupola that surmounts his grave. It is only fifteen years ago that the armies of a nation, whose name even was not then known in the East, bore back in triumph to the capital of Hindostan those world-renowned gates of sandal-wood that, torn from the temple of Somnauth by the great warrior himself, were raised by his successors to adorn his grave. To this day the priests of the Moslem faith read the Koran over the tomb of this true son the Prophet.[5]

The life of Mahmoud was one of uninterrupted warfare. He conducted in person nineteen campaigns, and was victorious in thirty sieges and battles, without once suffering defeat. His marches are some of the most surprising on record. No climate alarmed, no seasons deterred him, and he faced with equal indifference the dreary tablelands of Persia and Tartary, the mighty streams of the Punjaub, the deserts of Scinde, and the eternal snows of Thibet. Whilst on the north he held in check the rising power of the Tartars, south, east, and west he extended his empire and his faith; he seated his sons on the thrones of Balkh and Ispahan, and nominated the sovereigns of Delhi and Guzerat; he encouraged the arts and sciences, and rendered his capital the most polished and gorgeous city of the East. Altogether, when we carefully examine his exploits, we find that few of the world's conquerors have established a reputation equal to that of this Great King of the East. The Mussulman historians paint him a benefactor of the human race, a monarch who conferred happiness on the world, and reflected glory on the faith of Mahomed; whose accession illuminated the earth with the bright torch of justice, and cherished it with the beams of beneficence; whilst the Hindoos describe him as a consuming firebrand, whose only claim to immortality rests on the magnitude of his crimes; but we must remember that one is the account of those who grew rich by his conquests and gloried in his fanaticism; the other, of those whose temples he polluted, and whose cities he destroyed.

If fairly judged, he is neither better nor worse than all the other great scourges of the human race. When we carefully examine his exploits, we find that few of the world's conquerors have been more successful in war, and, without sharing the wonder of his countrymen at his virtues[6], we must acknowledge that few have eclipsed him in the arts of peace.

He was less brutal than Attila, Alaric, and others who preceded him in the realms of conquest, and his exterminating zeal for the faith of Mahomed was, a very few years afterwards, more than equalled by that of the fierce soldiers of the cross. With all his faults he was a great warrior and a sound Mussulman; whether for good or

BOOK I. 1030.

evil, no name has ever been more loudly trumpeted through the East, and, for centuries after his death, Hindoo and Persian, Tartar and Turk, recounted with awe the glories of the great Mahmoud of Ghizni.

NOTES TO CHAPTER V.

[1] The Jits, whether known as Getes, Yutes, Jits, Juts, or Jats, were at one time probably the most numerous race in India; in the fourth century they established a Jit kingdom in the Punjaub. Baber tells us that every time he crossed the Indus he was harassed by them. Nearly all the peasants of the Punjaub are said to belong to this tribe.

[2] Might we not apply the moral to our overgrown possessions in India?

[3] Some of these marks of the first Tartar Emperors were long preserved with the greatest veneration, as the most sacred relics and memorials.—Sagredo, 109.

[4] He died of stone.

[5] Mahmoud was a bigoted Sunni: the Sunnis believe Mahomedan traditions, and follow the three first Khalifs. The Sheas are followers of Ali and the twelve Imaums. The Turks adhere to the former, the Persians to the latter, form.

[6] The following epitaph, in Persian, was carved on his tomb:—"When we consider all the virtues of this great prince, we can scarcely believe he came into the world as other men."

CHAP. VI.

A.D. 1030—1040.

REIGNS OF MUSAOOD AND MODOOD.

CHAP. VI. 1030.

MAHMOUD had twin sons,—Musaood and Mohammed, —the former the eldest by a few hours. Musaood was a bold, daring youth, generous and reckless of all, save the enjoyment of the hour. Mohammed, on the other hand, was crafty and ambitious, and lost no opportunity of trying to secure the succession to the empire. No man knew better than Mahmoud the superior claims possessed by Musaood for the sovereignty of the warlike nobles of his empire, and feeling that, in spite of his predilections in favour of Mohammed, Musaood would one day be king, he asked him "how he would live with his brother after his death." "As you did with your brother Ismael, the son of Subuctugi," was the ready answer of the headlong youth; but he gave his father no cause to doubt his filial obedience, and during his lifetime employed himself in the congenial occupation of war and conquest on the northern frontier of the empire. At the time of the death of Mahmoud at Ghizni, Musaood was at his government at Ispahan, whilst Mohammed was at Gourgan, one of the maritime provinces of the empire.

Mentally and physically the brothers afforded much the same contrast as Richard of the Lion Heart and the

BOOK I. 1030.

wily and pusillanimous John Lackland. Musaood was rash, fierce, intemperate, and thoughtless; but generous to a fault, and unequalled amongst the sovereigns of his age for strength and intrepidity; his arrow could pierce the strongest mail and stay the charge of an elephant; and few of his subjects could lift his mace with one hand. He despised all the arts of diplomacy and intrigue, and trusted to the strength of his own right arm alone to secure his right to the throne. Being once told that the Court Moolah, taking advantage of his father's avowed preference for his brother, had dared to read his name first in the Khutba, or prayer for the royal family, he answered with a gay smile, "Give yourself no concern; the world is for the longest sword:"[1] a principle he was at any moment ready to maintain. Mohammed, on the other hand, was crafty, treacherous, and politic; carefully subservient to the wishes of his father, and intent only on securing his own succession to the throne.

On hearing of his father's death, Mohammed marched with all speed to Ghizni, and ascending the musnud, opened the imperial treasuries, and sought to palliate his usurpation by lavish gratuities.

When Musaood heard of this treason, he settled trustworthy governors over his provinces, and marched to Ghizni, sending word, at the same time, to his brother, that he had no desire to set aside the will of his father; that indeed his present possessions were ample for his wishes; and that he only insisted upon his right to have his name read first in the Khutba. Mohammed treated with contempt this temperate request, and marshalling his troops, marched to meet him. The gallant Musaood was naturally the object of the love of the warriors and nobles who had fought and conquered with his warlike father; and before the armies met a conspiracy was formed to seize his brother, and unite the mutinous troops with those of their legitimate sovereign.

As the ingratitude of Mohammed was greater than that of his uncle Ismael, on a similar occasion, so was the revenge of Musaood more terrible than that of Mahmoud. After executing those of the omrahs and nobles who han encouraged his brother's usurpation, he passed the "fire pencil"[2] over his eyes, and condemned him to imprisonment for life; but by one of those strange caprices of fortune that become remarkable when affecting kings, he again, at the end of nine years, regained both liberty and sovereign power; and, unchastened by misfortune, repaid with interest the punishment he had so justly incurred.

CHAP. VI. 1031.

In 1031, Musaood marched from Balkh to reduce Cutch and Mackeran, the maritime provinces of Persia; but he was soon recalled from the scene of his success to Ghizni, whence ominous reports reached him of the power and ravages of his fierce neighbours the Turkomans. These warlike emigrants, introduced by Mahmoud into his territory to assist in his Indian wars, were rapidly changing their ancient character for one more noble and more destructive. The shepherds were converted into robbers, the robbers into armies of conquerors, till gaining confidence with success they soon dared to measure their strength with the proudest sovereigns of Asia.

The haughty Musaood could not be induced to look upon them as an enemy more formidable than the wild tribes of the vast desert. He was ignorant of their power, and would take no means to resist them. In vain his omrahs in Khorassan urged that his enemies, "although at first but a swarm of ants, were now little snakes, and, unless instantly crushed, would acquire the venom and magnitude of serpents." He did not condescend to march against them in person, and contented himself with receiving a feigned submission from the chiefs, in which they declared "that they were the king's servants, and not at all desirous to disturb anybody but

BOOK I. 1032.

his enemies; they merely desired an annual subsidy to enable them to live at home without plunder, or to be led out to war that they might exert their skill in what they reckoned their only profession." But this humility was simulated. Everywhere they appeared in arms. One after another his generals were defeated and driven back, till Samarcand, and the vast regions beyond the Oxus, were for ever lost to his empire.

But notwithstanding the growing powers of his Turkoman neighbours, the empire of Ghizni at this period extended from the Indus to Ispahan; its capital was the most magnificent in the East; and seated on a golden throne studded with jewels, and canopied with a crown of pure gold weighing more than a ton[3], suspended by a golden chain, its sovereign was still the richest in the known world.

In the year A.D. 1032, Musaood conferred the ensign of royalty upon his eldest son Modood, and sent him to the government of Balkh, whilst he himself marched to Hindostan; and having harried the country from Attock to within forty miles of Delhi, fixed his second son Mugdood on the throne of Lahore. In the mean time the ominous shadow of Turkoman invasion that for years had been creeping over the kingdom of Ghizni, again assumed definite proportions; the mighty host that had been again and again broken and scattered by the strong hand of Mahmoud, burst at length with resistless fury on the kingdom of his son.

In 1030, Togrul Bey, the son of Michael, the son of Seljuk, was chosen sovereign by lot[4], and invested with the insignia of royalty in the city of Nishabur, the capital of Khorassan. "It would be superfluous," says the great historian, "to praise the valour of a Turk;" and the ambition of Togrul was equal to his valour.

Nothing could withstand the fierce onslaught of this desert prince, backed by a nation to whom war was more an occupation than a trade. Almost without a struggle he drove back the generals of Musaood, deprived him of the eastern provinces of Persia, and pressed hard on his Indian possessions. In the west he annihilated the dynasty of the Bowides, and transferred the sceptre of Irak, from the Persian to the Turkish nation, whilst by the conquest of Persia he approached the Roman country, and "the shepherd presumed to send an ambassador to demand tribute of the emperor of Constantinople."[5]

Convinced at length of the magnitude of the danger that threatened his empire, Musaood returned in haste to Ghizni, and collecting all available troops, marched to Balkh to meet Togrul in person; but such was the insolence of the enemies he had despised, that, no sooner had he quitted his capital, than Tiggi, a renowned partisan of the Turkomans, advanced by forced marches from Khorassan to Ghizni, and met with no repulse till he had rifled the king's stables and grossly dishonoured the capital.

At the approach of Musaood, Togrul retired towards Khorassan, whither he was followed by Musaood, who spent the spring of A. D. 1038 in the city of Nishabur. At length, after several unsuccessful attempts at a compromise, he marched against his wary foe who awaited him at Zendecan[6], a small town of Khorassan, two days distant from Maru. The first onslaught of Musaood was successful, and the Seljuki were driven back; but having carried the pursuit too far, his troops were suddenly surrounded, and after a gallant resistance defeated with great slaughter. Well did Musaood bear the name of Rustum[7] on this fatal day, and never did monarch display more daring and prowess in defence of his throne; but it was in vain; deserted by his troops, all lost but his honour, he was at length forced to fly to Ghor, whence he retired to Ghizni.

The victory of Zendecan was attended by the most important results throughout the length and breadth of Asia. It terminated, almost without a struggle, the dynasty of

BOOK I. 1038. the Abbasside Caliphs[8], and placed the shepherd kings on the throne of Bagdad. The Caliph was deprived of all secular power, and, like the Pope of Rome, retained only his spiritual supremacy, while Togrul was appointed temporal vice-regent of the Moslem world.[9] Dispirited by his defeat, shorn of his magnificent possessions beyond the Oxus, and threatened in his very capital by the mountain Affghans, Musaood, formed the resolution of abandoning Ghizni, and retiring with his treasure to Lahore. Leaving his son Modood to defend Balkh, and despatching Mugdood to Moultan, he commenced his melancholy march towards his Indian provinces; not as of old, for the sake of conquest and rapine, but to seek a refuge his race could scarcely claim from the princes of Hindostan.

The hand of destiny fell heavily on the fallen Musaood. On the banks of the Ghelum his slaves and soldiers mutinied and rifled his treasure, and, dreading the results of their treachery, seized and delivered him to his blind brother, Mohammed. The revenge of Mohammed was not bloody, but was more galling than death to the proud soul of his brother. Musaood was confined in the castle of Kirri, and denied the retinue and luxury due to his rank. On one occasion, being in want of the necessaries of life, he sent to request some money from his brother, who returned an insulting message with the pitiful sum of 500 dirms. "O wonderful! O wonderful cast of Providence," said Musaood, on receiving it. "O cruel reverse of fate. Yesterday was I not a mighty prince, three thousand camels bending under my treasure? To-day, I am forced to beg the mere mockery of my wants!" But his kingly dignity did not desert him. Borrowing 1000 dirms from his sorrowing attendants, he gave them as a present to the messenger, telling him, at the same time, to take back to his brother the paltry sum, which could only have been proffered in derision.

Incapacitated by his blindness from exercising sovereign power, Mohammed raised to the throne his eldest son,

Ahmed, a prince of fierce and implacable nature, who, without seeking his father's consent, went to Kirri, and slew his uncle Musaood with every adjunct of cruelty and insult.[10] CHAP. VI. 1040.

Mohammed wept bitterly when told of his brother's death, and wrote to Modood to disown the deed; but tears did not stay the hand of Modood. Marching from Balkh to Ghizni, he received the homage of his capital, and immediately advanced against Ahmed, whom he defeated and took prisoner. The revenge of Modood was very terrible: he slew every soul belonging to the family of his uncle, with the exception of Abdul Rahim, who alone had shown tenderness to the fallen Musaood in his captivity.[11] Musaood reigned nine years; he was a brave prince, and generous; but was indolent, and wanting in the sustained energy necessary to empire in those turbulent days. Deprived of the vast regions of Transoxiana, Khorassan, and eastern Persia, and prevented by the state of his northern frontier from adding to his Indian possessions, the power of Musaood was latterly restricted to the mountainous regions of Cabul and Zabulistan, and the maritime states of the Indus and Persia; and during his reign the mighty empire of Mahmoud, that overshadowed the Eastern world, showed symptoms of that decline from which no power ever rallies.

After the death of his uncle and cousins, Modood had no relative to fear but his brother, Mugdood, who, according to the custom of his race, immediately prepared to contest the succession to the throne. Advancing from Moultan, at the head of an array of native and foreign levies, he rapidly reduced the whole country, from the Indus to the sacred city of Tannassar, whence he marched to meet Modood near Lahore. The Indian levies of Mugdood far outnumbered the troops of Ghizni. The omrahs of Modood's army were dispirited and preparing to desert, when treachery preserved the crown to the eldest son of Musaood. The rival armies were already in sight of

BOOK I. each other, when Mugdood and his general were both assassinated by an unknown hand.

1040. Modood returned to Ghizni, and having married a princess of the Seljuks, these turbulent neighbours nominally submitted to his rule, and resigned the provinces they had occupied beyond the Oxus.

NOTES TO CHAPTER VI.

[1] Or, "concern not yourselves when swords are truest, we may write what follows."

[2] Royalty was always blinded with a red hot needle drawn across the pupil.

[3] The crown weighed 70 maunds, each maund weighed 37 lb. avoirdupois, which gives a weight of 2,590 lb.

[4] The names of the candidates were written on arrows, which were drawn from a quiver by a child. Darius Hystaspes was chosen by the neighing of a horse. In A.D. 700 the Polish Diet being unable to nominate a successor to the throne, they erected a pillar in a large plain, and, fixing a starting-post, decreed that whatever candidate should first reach the pillar, on a certain morning, should be king; many ran for such a plate, which was won by Lescus, who shod his horse with iron, and strewed the ground with little iron spikes. However, being discovered, he was skinned alive. (The same cruel device was tried with Blink Bonny at Goodwood two years since.)

[5] See Gibbon.

[6] Famous for the production and manufacture of cotton.

[7] Rustum was the great hero of Persian romance, immortalised by Ferdousi in the Shah Namma; Musaood for his gallantry was christened Rustum II.

[8] It had lasted 281 years.

[9] See D'Herbelot.

[10] It was long believed he threw him down a well.

[11] During the captivity of Musaood, Abdul Rahim went with his brother Reiman to see him, when the latter insultingly pulled off his uncle's cap and threw it from him; Abdul Rahim immediately replaced it on the king's head with much respect, chastising his brother for his mean and barbarous behaviour.

CHAP. VII.

A.D. 1044—1186.

THE PRINCES OF INDIA COMBINE TO SHAKE OFF THE MUSSULMAN YOKE.—THE DEATH OF MODOOD AT GHIZNI.—THE REIGNS OF IBRAHIM, MUSAOOD, BYRAM, AND CHUSERO I. AND II.—THE DESTRUCTION OF GHIZNI BY ALLA.—THE DYNASTY OF MAHMOUD FINALLY EXTINGUISHED.

CHAP. VII. 1044.

THE Hindoo princes of India, who had received nothing but insult and dishonour from their northern conquerors, were not slow to perceive the inroad the domestic quarrels of its princes, the revolt of the principal governors, and the unceasing encroachments of the Seljuk Turkomans had made in the power of the Ghiznian empire, and they were not loath to take advantage of it. In the year 1044 they made a combined attempt to shake off the Mussulman domination.

Besuldeo, the Pillar of Victory, King of Delhi, availed himself of the credulity of his subjects, to arouse their enthusiasm; he pretended to have seen a vision, in which the great idol of Nagracot, carried away by Mahmoud, appeared to him, and warned him that now being revenged on Ghizni, he intended to return to his former abode, and charged him solemnly to meet him there.

Besuldeo assembled an immense army of credulous fanatics, and being joined by the Chohan king of Ajmere, attacked and took Tannassar and other towns, and after a siege of four months retook Nagracot. Besuldeo had secretly brought with him from Delhi, an idol of the

BOOK I. 1044.

exact shape and size of that seized by Mahmoud; and the night before his triumphant entry it was secretly introduced by the Brahmins, and placed in the chief square of the city. In the morning when it was discovered, the enthusiam of the multitude knew no bounds, the return of the idol from Ghizni, was hailed as a token that the gods themselves had at length determined to drive the barbarians from the land of virtue.

Taking advantage of this signal evidence of the favour of their deities, a religious war was immediately preached by the Brahmins, throughout the Indian territories of Modood. From one end of Hindostan to the other, the native princes took heart, and allied themselves to the Kings of Delhi and Ajmere; thus reinforced, Besuldeo proceeded from victory to victory, till the Punjaub was overrun and Lahore itself invested.

After a gallant defence of seven months, the garrison of Lahore saved themselves by a desperate sortie, and the Indian troops retired, after the first successful campaign ever waged against their Moslem oppressors.

Notwithstanding his continued reverses on the side of India, Modood was everywhere successful in the north; the Seljuks, who had broken faith and advanced on Balkh, were repulsed with great slaughter, and the Kizzlebashes of Candahar forced back to the confines of Persia.

Modood died of a liver complaint at Ghizni, after a reign of nine years; during which he displayed average ability, and more than usual virtue.

The crimes that almost invariably attend the death of one Asiatic sovereign, and the accession of another, are familiar to all readers of Eastern history; the only right to the succession that was never questioned, was that of the strong over the weak; and he who had the will to seize and the power to hold, could dispense with all legal right to the throne. "Make me King to-day, and kill me to-morrow," said a Prince of the Ommiades, when urged to take part in a conspiracy that was to place the crown on his head; and the musnud was but a short step from the grave to the greater number of the sovereigns of Ghizni. During the next nine years four sovereigns sat on the throne of Mahmoud, and all from the child, "whose nurse was rocking him to sleep after his rice and milk," to the tyrant carousing after some deed of blood, paid with their lives the penalty of their royal birth.

Modood was succeeded by his infant son, who was murdered after six days by his uncle Ali. Ali reigned two years and was deposed by Reshid, a son of Mahmoud, who, after forty days of intolerable cruelty, was assassinated by his omrahs, and Feroch Zaad, a son of Musaood, chosen by lot to succeed him.

Feroch Zaad died after a comparatively peaceful reign of six years, and was succeeded by his brother Ibrahim. During this troubled period of fifteen years, Nagracot was again taken by the Moslems, and the Hindoos driven back; but with this exception the territory left by Modood was not extended by the sovereigns of Ghizni.

The reign of Ibrahim presented an exception to this era of turbulence. He was an austere prince, delighting in learning and the arts of peace; he added two months to the Ramadan, which he observed with the greatest care; he was famed throughout the East for his caligraphy [1], and copies of the Koran in his own handwriting, may still be seen in the sacred mosques of Mecca and Medina.

His historians informs us that, "in the flower of his youth, and amid a paradise of pleasure, he had conquered all the sensual appetite;" but he had nevertheless thirty-six sons, and forty daughters by the ladies of his harem [2]; all of whom he gave in marriage to learned and religious men. Can we wonder that with such rewards Ghizni was esteemed the Utopia of philosophers and divines? Ibrahim contracted a marriage for Musaood, the eldest of his thirty-six sons, with the daughter of Mallek, sovereign

BOOK I. 1098. 1114.

of the Seljuks, and concluded a treaty, ceding to the Turkomans all the countries they had seized on the northern frontier, on condition they observed a strict peace.

He was a just prince, and the following anecdote speaks well for his humanity. "One day seeing a prisoner carrying a heavy stone, his pity was awakened, and commanding him to throw it down, he gave him his liberty. The stone remained in the public thoroughfare, and so strict was the law, that none dare remove it. One day a courtier's horse having stumbled over it, he took the opportunity of requesting that it might be removed. 'I have commanded it to be thrown there,' answered Ibrahim, 'and there it must remain, as a memorial of the misfortunes of war, and my own pity; for it is better for a king to be obstinate, even in his inadvertences, than to break his royal word.'"

Ibrahim reigned thirty-one years, and was the contemporary of Togrul Beg, Alp Arslan the Valiant Lion, and Mallek Shah, the three greatest sovereigns of the Seljuk Tartars. Seventy years had elapsed between the death of Mahmoud and that of Ibrahim, during which the Ghiznian empire rapidly declined towards the north, and made but little progress in the direction of Hindostan.

Musaood II. succeeded his father Ibrahim, and walked in his steps. He despatched an army across the Ganges, and carried his conquests farther than any sovereign since the days of the great Mahmoud. Owing to the dangerous proximity of the Seljuks he removed his court to Lahore, which thus in a manner became the capital of the empire. He reigned sixteen years, during which his country flourished, and his subjects had comparative peace.

Musaood II. was succeeded by his son Shere, who was almost immediately assassinated by his brother Arsilla; but fratricide soon met its own reward. Byram, a younger brother, fearing a similar fate, fled to his uncle Sinjur, chief of the Seljuks, who, espousing his cause, marched to Ghizni, and defeating Arsilla under its very walls, placed Byram on the throne. Byram made two expeditions to India to chastise Balin, viceroy of Lahore, who was aiming at independent sovereignty. He was victorious on both occasions, and on the second his troublesome enemy was effectually disposed of by being engulphed with his whole family in a quagmire.

But there were other lieutenants of the Ghiznian empire equally ambitious with the viceroy of Lahore; and it was the cruelty displayed by Byram in the punishment of one of these rebellious princes that caused the final overthrow of the family of Mahmoud.

The mountainous kingdom of Ghor was still nominally a province of the Ghiznian empire. It was conquered and annexed by Mahmoud, but continued to be ruled in his name and that of his successors by hereditary princes of the Soor tribe of Affghans. Its inhabitants laid claim to the highest antiquity of race, and affected a superior sanctity on the score that they were specially converted by Ali himself, the son-in-law of the Prophet. Cuttub, the reigning prince of Ghor, had married the daughter of the rebel Balin, and was probably an abettor of his treason. Under the garb of friendship, Byram invited him to Ghizni, and when there treacherously poisoned him.

Sief, the brother of Cuttub, immediately collected a large army, and attacked Ghizni. Byram was driven from his kingdom to the borders of India, and Sief was by the consent of the people crowned in his stead. But during the winter months Byram returned with a large army, and being assisted from within soon regained his capital.

Sief was taken prisoner, and barbarously tortured and slain, whilst his vizier Mujud, a Syed, or lineal descendant of the Prophet, was impaled alive.

Alla, the brother of Cuttub and Sief, who then commanded in Ghor, advanced to avenge his brothers and the holy Syed; and in the year 1152 Byram was a second

BOOK I. 1155.

time forced to fly to India, where he soon died, after a disastrous reign of thirty-five years.

Ghizni was at this period without doubt the most highly-adorned city of the Eastern world. The mosques, the gardens, the bazaars, aqueducts and palaces constructed and enriched by the golden harvests of a century of successful pillage of the wealthiest region in the world, had inspired the song of many an Eastern poet, and raised the envy of the splendid vicars of the Prophet themselves. But the fierce soul of Alla, called from his ferocious disposition the "Burner of the World," experienced no spark of tenderness for the luxurious capital of the murderers of his race. For six days was this fair city and all it contained given over to the ravages of the fierce mountaineers of Ghor, and on the seventh the fury of the flames and the immensity of the ruins alone bore witness to its former magnificence and extent.

There was one refinement of cruelty attending the destruction of Ghizni that only an Eastern despot could have conceived and a merciless soldier have executed. A number of the first citizens of Ghizni were marched in chains to the city of Ghor, a distance of 250 miles, each with a bag of clay round his neck, which, at the end of their melancholy journey, they were compelled to mix with their own blood to compose the mortar for a tower that was to celebrate the destruction of their capital.

Alla defiled the very graves of the royal family of Ghizni; but in consideration of the valour of Mahmoud and Musaood, and of the sanctity of Ibrahim, he spared their tombs from desecration.

He returned to Ghor, leaving ruin and desolation where all had hitherto been splendour and luxury. He completed the conquest of the northern provinces of the Ghiznian empire, and attacked and took Herat and Balkh, but was in his turn defeated by Sinjur the Seljuk, and with difficulty escaped with life. He died in A.D. 1155 three years after the fall of Ghizni. His son succeeded him, but was killed by the Turks in less than a year, and his successor, Yeas, appointed his brother Mohammed the governor of his Indian provinces.

Chusero, the son of Byram, had, in the mean time, retreated to Lahore, and ruled there over the Indian provinces of Ghizni in comparative peace. He attempted to regain his capital, but was defeated by the Turks or Moguls, who, on the return of Alla to Ghor, had occupied the city. Chusero reigned seven years, and was succeeded by his son Chusero II.

Shahab Mohammed, appointed by his brother Yeas King of Ghor, governor of his Indian provinces, was a warrior of the temperament of the great Mohammed of Ghizni. War was his occupation and delight, and during a period of twenty-five years his sword scarcely knew its scabbard. He conquered the valley of Peshawur, together with Moultan [3], and all the provinces of the Indus; and twice he besieged Chusero in his capital of Lahore without success, but the third time he effected by treachery what his arms were unable to accomplish.

On one of the preceding expeditions, Chusero had delivered his son to Mohammed as a hostage for his good behaviour; and this circumstance was now turned by the crafty Prince of Ghor to the final destruction of the family of Mahmoud. Giving out that having every confidence in the good faith of Chusero, he intended to turn his arms against the Seljuks, he sent back his hostage with a magnificent retinue by short marches to Lahore; whilst Chusero, anxious to embrace his son, advanced by long marches to meet him. In the mean time Mohammed, with 20,000 horse, made a circuit, and marching with incredible speed, got between Chusero and his capital.

This happened in A.D. 1186; and a few months later Chusero, with all his family, were put to death, and the dynasty of Mahmoud for ever extinguished. This dy-

BOOK I. 1186.

nasty lasted altogether 189 years, during which period eleven sovereigns reigned at Ghizni and two at Lahore. Mahmoud was the only great monarch of his race; and from the hour of his death the empire he had acquired with so much labour and blood began to fall away from his descendants. In less than 150 years scarcely an acre of the mighty empire extending from Delhi to Ispahan inherited by Musaood, remained to Chusero.

The growing power of the great Turkoman race first shook the foundations of the Ghiznivite empire; but the final ruin was caused by internal disruption and weakness. During this period innumerable warlike expeditions were made to Hindostan, but no warrior of his race ever penetrated so far as Mahmoud; and though in the Punjaub, and the provinces on the Indus, where the conquerors had established themselves in force, the customs of more northern climes were blended with those of India; — the tapering minarets of Islam replaced the massive temples of the Hindoos, and the classical Sanscrit retired before the forcible but more barbarous Hindostanee;—Moslem influence was entirely confined to these regions; and even the taking of Canouje by Mahmoud caused as little anxiety to the southern population of Hindostan as the conquest of Geneva by the Saracens in the tenth century did to our own skin-clad countrymen.

The same year that witnessed the ruin of the Ghiznivite dynasty saw also the fall of the Seljuks, who had caused it. The power of the Seljuks endured little more than sixty years; but during that short period the valour and martial prowess of Togrul, Alp Arslan, and Mallek, prostrated all Asia at their feet. The rapid growth of their power was the cause of their speedy decline; and the impossibility of maintaining order over boundless regions, and restraining the ambition of princely viceroys, caused their ruin, as it had done that of almost every eastern empire that had preceded them. The lieutenants of Sinjur, the son of Mallek, the fourth sovereign of the

Seljuks, contended amongst themselves for supremacy, and divided the empire. CHAP. VII.

In England thirteen and in France six sovereigns were contemporaries of the Ghiznivite dynasty, whilst, during the same period no less than thirty-seven popes ascended the chair of St. Peter. Four successive dynasties usurped the throne of England; and it was the spirit of her people alone that saved her from humiliation as supreme as that attending the ruin of the last sovereign of the house of Mahmoud. A consideration of the following short chronological data will show that if India had cause to groan under cruelty and oppression, the condition of the other portions of the known world was but little better:— 1186.

A.D. 1002. Great massacre of Danes by Ethelred of England.
1018. Normans invade Italy.
1039. Macbeth murders Duncan and usurps the crown of Scotland.
1043. The Turks subdue Persia.
1055. The Turks overthrow the Caliphs.
1058. Saracens driven out of Sicily.
1061. Rise of the rival factions of Guelphs and Ghibellines.
1095. Institution of Order of Knights of Jerusalem.
—— First Crusade of Peter the Hermit.
1098. Crusaders take Antioch.
1099. Jerusalem taken by Godfrey of Boulogne.
1139. Saracens driven out of Portugal.
1147. Second Crusade of St. Bernard.
1187. Jerusalem taken by Saladin.
1189. Third crusade of Richard I. and Philip Augustus.

NOTES TO CHAPTER VII.

[1] He was almost a contemporary of our own Henry Beauclerc.

[2] This was a fair family; but Ibn Batuta mentions a story of an Abyssinian prince that quite throws Ibrahim in the shade. A noble of Abyssinia appeared at court, and presented to his sovereign eighty sons all fit to carry arms. The king received him graciously, and inquired how many more he had: "No more," replied the noble. "No more!" exclaimed the sovereign in a rage. "Out of my sight, calf; are there no women in my dominions?" Muley Ishmael, of Morocco, is said to have had 700 sons, who ap-

BOOK I. 1186.

peared on horseback as warriors in the army of their father, so notorious for his cruel ferocity.

[3] Mohammed obtained the city of Adja by stratagem. He sent a private message to the raja's wife, promising to marry her if she would make away with her husband. She thanked him for his kind offer of matrimony, but excused herself on the score of being too old, adding, however, that she had a very beautiful daughter, who would be most happy to become his bride; and if, as a marriage portion, he would bestow on her the territory of Adja she would soon find means to dispose of the raja. Mohammed made a feint of accepting the conditions, he married the daughter and enrolled her amongst the faithful; the raja was poisoned, and the faithless wife received her due reward, by being carried off to Ghizni, where she soon after died in prison.

CHAP. VIII.

A.D. 1191—1193.

MOHAMMED OF GHOR INVADES HINDOSTAN. — IS DEFEATED BY PITHOWRA. — THE INTERNAL DISSENSIONS OF THE GREAT PRINCES OF INDIA. — THE QUARREL BETWEEN PITHOWRA AND THE KING OF CANOUJE. — PITHOWRA CARRIES OFF THE DAUGHTER OF JEICHUND, AND RETREATS TO DELHI. — THE FALL OF DELHI, AND THE DEATH OF PITHOWRA AND HIS FOLLOWERS.

CHAP. VIII. 1152. 1156.

THE mountain region of Ghor, situated midway between Cabul and Balkh, was the nursery of the fierce Affghan races who, for five centuries, furnished the greater number of the monarchs of Hindostan. Possessing the main channel by which the wealth of Ind flowed from the banks of the Indus to the great cities of Balkh, Bokhara, and Samarcand, the Affghans were a race of warrior merchants who, by turns, monopolised or taxed the overland trade through their dominions.

We have seen how Ala, the "Burner of the World," destroyed the fair city of Ghizni. His triumph was short. The following year he was attacked and taken prisoner by the Seljuk Turcomans, and his capital pillaged. He was soon restored to liberty, when his conquerors in turn succumbed before the fierce onslaught of a more northern race of warriors.[1] He did not long survive his captivity, and died after a turbulent reign of four years.

He was succeeded by his son, Seif, who was assassinated by one of his chiefs in less than a year.

BOOK I. 1186. 1191.

Gheias, his cousin, immediately mounted the throne, and associated his brother, Mohammed Shabab, with him in the government. Gheias appears to have been an indolent prince, taking his ease at Herat and Ghizni, and only occasionally rousing himself to take part in the unceasing wars that constituted the occupation of his brother.

We have already seen how Mohammed of Ghor, after two unsuccessful invasions, finally captured Lahore, the last stronghold of Chusero, and utterly extinguished the last sovereign of the fallen house of Mahmoud.

There was now no Mussulman power between Mohammed and the wealth of India, and he lost no time in clutching the prize that lay within his grasp; and in A.D. 1191 he advanced into Hindostan, and invaded the kingdom of Ajmere.

Delhi and Ajmere were, at this period, united under Pithowra, chief of the Chohans, the most ancient of the princely races of Rajpoot. He was their Paladin, described by their poets as "an autumnal moon, for an ornament to the tribe of the Chohans." Under his banner fought all that was brave and noble in Hindostan. The two armies met on the banks of the Sirsutti, fourteen miles from Tannassar, and about eighty from Delhi. The contest was long and fierce; but at length the native powers gained the advantage, and the Moslems were forced to give way. Desperate at the prospect of defeat by a foe he was accustomed to despise, Mohammed displayed the devotion that had saved his great predecessor in conquest on a similar occasion. Conjuring his omrahs in the name of the Prophet to follow him to glory or death, he headed a fierce charge, and singling out the King of Delhi, engaged him in mortal combat.

Well did Mohammed sustain the hereditary valour of his Affghan lineage. Although only on horseback, he attacked the war elephant of Pithowra, and such was his unequalled strength, that, with one dash of his spear, he

CHAP. VIII. 1191.

drove out three of the back teeth of that enormous animal[2]; but his gallantry was in vain, Pithowra wounded him with his lance, and he was only saved from destruction by the devotion of his servants. His army was scattered and pursued a distance of forty miles, whilst he was carried, almost insensible, to Lahore.

When he recovered, he disgraced those omrahs who had sought safety in the speed of their horses, by obliging them to walk round the city with the nosebags of their chargers fastened round their necks; at the same time giving them the choice of eating the fodder, or of having their heads struck off. Mohammed returned to Ghor, and afterwards to Ghizni, where he consoled himself for his defeat by the voluptuous enjoyment of every Eastern luxury. In the mean time the dissensions of the great princes of Hindostan were involving them in a struggle which eventually consummated their own ruin, and established Moslem rule in the most ancient capitals of India.

The Mussulman power had hitherto made itself felt in the north of Hindostan, more by repeated inroads than by actual occupation; and although numerous kingdoms acknowledged its rule, and the coin of many cities was stamped with the name and titles of the descendants of Sultan Mahmoud, the head of the state still resided at Ghizni and Lahore.

Delhi and Canouje had more than once fallen a prey to the rapine of the invaders, or been ransomed by the wealth of their citizens; but in the year 1195 they fell permanently into the hands of the Mussulmans, and the crescent and green flag of Islam waved over these capital cities of Hindostan, there to remain until finally lowered before the cross and bayonet of the Christian.

As I before mentioned, Hindostan was, at this period, divided into the four kingdoms of Canouje, Delhi, Mewar[3], and Anhulwarra or Guzerat. Of these, Canouje and Delhi were the most powerful. When the last of the family of the craven Korrah, who abandoned his kingdom and

BOOK I. 1191. his creed at the bidding of Mahmoud of Ghizni, was destroyed by the indignant princes of Hindostan, his capital was vacant to become the prize of the most daring. Jya Chandra, chief of the Rahtore Rajpoots, "conquered by his own arm the unequalled kingdom of Canouje," and his descendant, Jeichund, now sat on his throne. The kingdom of Delhi owned the sway of Pithowra, the renowned chief of the Chohans. The latter claimed supremacy over all the countries westward to the Indus, embracing the land watered by its arms, from the foot of the Himalaya to the Aravulli chain; and numbered amongst his one hundred and eight great vassals many of the subordinate princes of India.

The territory of Jeichund extended north to the foot of the Snowy Mountains; eastward, to Benares, across the Chumbul to Bundelkund; on the south, it met Mewar. Both Chohans and Rahtores were Rajpoots of the purest descent; and, in order clearly to understand the romantic tale that terminated their dominion in Hindostan, it is necessary to examine the history of this noble and chivalrous people.

Probably no family of the human race ever possessed so liberal a portion of that essence of reckless daring, called chivalry by poets and romancers, as the Rajpoots of India. They were, in all probability, of Indo-Scythic origin, and exulted in an unbroken line of male ancestors for 1300 years. They worshipped the sun, the horse, and the sword, and believed in a hero's heaven (called Suratoca), that combined all the luxuries of the paradise of Mahomed with the strife and feasting of the Walhalla. War was the breath of their nostrils, and, except a death by disease, no condition of existence carried with it greater terrors than a life of peace.[4] The slightest cause furnished them with the means of avoiding either alternative. Where all were anxious to fight, the heedless twirl of the moustache, or an idle word spoken in jest, were sufficient to cause the deadliest wars; and whilst one fierce warrior undertook a campaign, solely to recover the plume of his helmet lost in a former battle, where his monarch fell, another, finding himself sinking, and, unfortunately, at peace with all his foes, sent word to one of them to beg him, as a great favour, for one more battle, in the midst of which his soul might part in peace.[5]

Exulting in the purity of their descent, they valued the honour of their women far above life or lands. No insult was more dreaded, than that offered to a wife or mistress; and no revenge so sweet as that enjoyed by the successful warrior, beloved by the wives of his conquered foes. Every Rajpoot expected of his wife the voluntary sacrifice of the Sati, when he was removed to the realms of death; and never hesitated to insist upon the forced one of the Johar[6], when the fortune of war threatened to place them in the hands of their enemies. Their first law was "to get land;" their greatest crime a forgetfulness of favours. In pursuit of the former no war was too unjust, no dangers too great; and 60,000 years in the lowest hell was the doom assigned to those who violated their faith or forgot a favour.

The narration of events that delivered Delhi and Canouje over to the Mussulmans, is one of the most charming romances in history. The pages of Froissart and Amadis de Gaul do not contain more stirring tales of heroism; and never did the brain of a Quixote conceive or the arm of a Cid carry out more desperate acts of daring enterprise.

In the centre of Hindostan, amongst a dusky race of warriors at that time unknown in Europe, we are startled by an episode of real life, displaying deeds as fearless, and devotion as complete, as any that could be found amongst the chosen band of Europe's chivalry, at that very time time besieging Askalon under Richard of the Lion Heart.

Jeichund, the monarch of Canouje, was probably at

BOOK I. 1191. that period the most powerful, as he was the most liberal, of all the sovereigns of India. Adventurers of all nations and religions found employment in his service; and master of all the wealth and resources of hitherto unrifled Bengal, he could bring into the field an army numbering 80,000 men in armour, 30,000 horse covered with quilted mail, 300,000 infantry, 200,000 bowmen and axemen, besides a cloud of elephants bearing warriors.

His historians relate, that he overcame many neighbouring sovereigns, making eight tributary kings prisoners; that he twice overrun the kingdoms of Anhulwarra and Guzerat, and extended his conquests north of the Nerbudda, into the heart of the Deccan.

He shared with the gallant Pithowra the glorious victory where the northern legions of the King of Ghor were driven like chaff before the troops of Hindostan, and the Nilab or blue water, changed its name to Soorchab or red, from the blood of the slain; at length, in the fulness of his pride, he determined to have divine honours paid him in the rite of Soenair or Feast of Rajas, a distinction involving the most august ceremony, and considered as a virtual assumption of universal power.

The celebration of this feast had only been recorded in fable, and had generally been attended with disaster, so that no dynasty of India, since the days of the Pandus or early monarchs of the country, had dared to revive it. Not even the mighty Vicrama, who introduced his own era, had the audacity to attempt what the Rahtore determined to execute.

All India was agitated by the reports of the magnificence of the preparations for this sacred rite, in which every office, down to the scullions of the banquet hall, must be performed by Rajas; and invitations were despatched to every prince, desiring him to assist at the pompous festival, which was to conclude with the nuptials of the Raja's only daughter, who, according to the custom of those days, would select her future lord from the assembled chivalry of India. CHAP. VIII.

The Rajpoot bard dilates on the revelry and magnificence of the scene; the splendour of the Yug-Sála, or Hall of Sacrifice, surpassing all powers of description, in which were assembled all the Princes of India, save Pithowra Lord of the Chohans, and his brother-in-law Samarsi of Cheetore, who scorned this assumption of superiority of the Raja of Canouje. Pithowra was at one time, indeed, making preparations for the journey; but he was reminded that the empire by right belonged to the Chohan dynasty, and consequently that a Rahtore was not qualified to insist upon such a sacrifice. These words kindled the flames of resentment in the heart of Pithowra, and he refused to set out on his journey. 1191.

No sooner was the disaffection of Pithowra known at Canouje than Jeichund wished to march at once on Delhi, and compel him at the sword's point to be present at his coronation; but time was short, and the Brahmins urgent, and he listened to those who counselled discretion as the better part. The sums of money expended on these more than regal festivities were enormous; and the priests, who were alarmed lest accident should interfere with their golden harvest, soon hit upon a plan, by which the celebration might be conducted in perfect order, notwithstanding the absence of the contumacious Raja.

According to Hindoo law, the presence of Pithowra, and his brother-in-law Samarsi, of Cheetore, was absolutely necessary to the proper observance of the ceremony of supreme inauguration; but, as in the particular case, they could not produce the originals, it was wisely determined that their effigies made of gold would answer the same purpose. Images were accordingly made, and the most servile posts assigned to them; that of the king of the Chohans being porter of the hall, the most humiliating office a high-caste Hindoo can perform.

Pithowra's whole life was one succession of feats of

BOOK I. 1191.

arms and gallantry; seven times had he defeated the kings of Ghor and Ghizni, and seven times carried his arms to the gates of Lahore. His lineage was the highest of the whole company; no wonder that the blood inherited from a long line of heroes boiled in his veins at so public an insult; and he swore by every god of the Hindoo calendar[7] that he would be avenged.

Accordingly, having disguised himself, and selected 500 picked warriors, he proceeded secretly to Canouje, a distance of rather more than 200 miles, with the full determination of making the Rahtore smart for his contemptuous treatment of a Chohan. When he arrived at Canouje he mixed with the crowd that a celebration of any kind will always collect in an Indian city; and watching his opportunity, attacked the palace in the height of the festival, seized his golden image, and after committing great slaughter, cut his way back in triumph to Delhi.

Whatever might have been the subsequent result of this daring insult to the great Raja in his own capital, thus bearding the lion in his den, the immediate catastrophe was accelerated by a domestic complication that was probably as unexpected as it was untoward.

In all ages and quarters of the world women have admired valour and adored heroes; and although history does not endorse the assertion, that " none but the brave deserve the fair," it yet establishes the fact that at any rate they always succeed in obtaining the favours of the softer sex. From the earliest mythological days of Mars and Hercules to the present, it has always been the right of valour to be beloved by beauty; and the pages of history justify and even applaud many a fair dame who has quitted her legitimate spouse, for no other reason than that she had found a braver lover.[8] And even amongst good Christians the right of repudiating a husband of negative spirit for a lover of positive and illustrious valour has been asserted and exercised[9] without disgrace.

CHAP. VIII. 1191.

In the days of Rajpoot chivalry, knights and princes strove in full court for the prize of beauty, and the successful hero received publicly the garland of marriage at the fair hands of the object of their contention. And it was usual on these occasions of the Feast of Rajas for the most beautiful of the daughters of the monarch to grace with her choice the hand of some friendly prince. Had the daughter of Jeichund observed this practice, undoubtedly all would have been well; but unfortunately for her peace of mind she had heard of Pithowra; his many victories over the enemies of her faith had long been the theme of native bards, and probably his last daring inroad into her father's palace, when he carried away the image through which he had been insulted, had been freely canvassed and heartily approved in the secret recesses of the ladies' chamber.

She became desperately enamoured of the gallant Raja, rejected her father's choice of a husband, and as a reward for her unheard-of disobedience was separated from her more docile lady friends and confined in a separate palace.

"Love sought is good, but given unsought is better;" and Pithowra had now a double motive for action — love and revenge. He determined to enjoy both or perish in the attempt — to spoil the sacrifice and bear away the fair of Canouje from its halls, though beset by all the heroes of Hind. The first object was to set the dusky beauty free; and with characteristic daring he adopted the bold and apparently impracticable plan of communication with her in person.

At Pithowra's court at Delhi, were one hundred Samants or Paladins, the pick of India's chivalry, whose swords had never flashed in vain against the legions of the north, and who like the knights of the round table were sworn to a life of daring and adventure.

Willingly did they undertake to second the chivalrous frolic of their sovereign, and bravely did they redeem

BOOK I 1191.

their pledge. Having assumed various disguises, they accompanied Pithowra who, in the character of a servant, journeyed in the suite of the great Rajpoot bard Chund, to the capital of Canouje.

Once arrived at the royal palace of Jeichund, the danger and difficulty of the undertaking only commenced. The seclusion of high-caste Hindoo women was not probably so strict as at present, but still their separation from the outer world has always been very close. This selfish treatment of the fairest part of the creation has recoiled on their oppressors; it has rendered deceit necessary, and vastly increased the aptitude for intrigue common to all Eastern ladies.

Love is but a dull stream without shoals and rapids; and Pithowra, like a true knight, only courted the rose the more for the thorns that surrounded it: love, especially that which is forbidden, is a science freely discussed, and carefully studied in the East. The difficulty of meeting, and the necessity of making the most of the fleeting opportunities that do occur, have sharpened to a remarkable degree the apprehension of both sexes; and watched and guarded as they are, and apparently unapproachable, Eastern ladies have the reputation of being the greatest flirts and most successful intriguantes in the world.[10] Such as they are now, they were probably in the days of Pithowra. Love does not change much, it is protean in form, but uniform in nature; it has ruled the world, and laughed at locksmiths, from the beginning of the chapter to the present time. "The fox knows a great deal," says the old Spanish proverb, "but a woman in love knows more," a fact that the Rahtore beauty determined to illustrate.[11]

Here in a royal palace in the very centre of the capital of his most deadly enemy, whose pride and power he had publicly insulted, surrounded by foes, any one of whom would have risked much to take his life, did this daring lover of Hindostan carry on a communication with the lady of his affections. As may be imagined, such devotion did not wait long for its reward. Vines and young women are hard to keep, and the princess who might perhaps have successfully resisted her own love, was powerless against that which she inspired. It was not long before she found an opportunity to join her royal lover, with whom she fled towards Delhi.

Pithowra bore off the prize in full day. A desperate running fight of five days took place; and bravely did his paladins defend their lord. Insensible apparently to their own mortality, they stood one before the other, and with their lives opposed the troops of Jeichund.

Pithowra and his bride reached Delhi in safety, but nearly all his bravest warriors were left dead on the road. In the words of the bard, "he preserved his prize, and gained immortal renown, but he lost the sinews of Delhi." Arrived in his luxurious capital, surrounded by brave and devoted troops, who kept his enemies at a distance, the fate of the great Triumvir overtook Pithowra. He yielded himself to the agreeable society of his young bride, and neglected to prepare himself for the day of retribution which his repeated insults towards his powerful rival rendered inevitable. Fierce and constant were now the contests on the Cali-nadi or Blackwater, the boundary stream that separated the kingdoms of Delhi and Canouje; but it was not till Jeichund called in the assistance of Cuttub, the successful general of Mohammed of Ghor, that Delhi was taken, and Pithowra and Samarsi, with all the heroes of Delhi and Cheetore, met a glorious death on the banks of the Cagger.

BOOK I.
1191.

NOTES TO CHAPTER VIII.

[1] The tribe of Euz, Turks long settled in Kipchak.

[2] This is simply impossible; but it serves to illustrate the exaggerated tone of native historians.

[3] Mewar — a corruption of Medza-war — the central region extending from the kingdom of Delhi to Guzerat.

[4] They were essentially what the Spaniards style "Hombre de Bigotes."

[5] Nothing a Rajpoot dreaded so much as dying by disease. In 1475 disease seized Rawul Chachick, raja of Jessulmere, after a long course of victorious warfare, in which he subdued various tracts of country, even to the heart of the Punjaub. In this state he determined to die as he had lived, with arms in his hands; but having no foe near with whom to cope, he sent an embassy to the Langa Prince of Mooltan, to beg as a last favour the jood-dan, or "gift of battle," that his soul might escape by the steel of his foeman, and not fall a sacrifice to slow disease. The Prince, suspecting treachery, hesitated, but the bhatti, messenger, pledged his word that his master only wished an honourable death, and that he would only bring 500 men to the combat. The challenge being accepted, the Rawul called his clansmen around him, and recounted what he had done; seven hundred select Rajpoots who had shared all his victories immediately volunteered to take the last field and make oblation of their lives with their leader; previous to setting forth he arranged his affairs, and appointed his sons to separate portions of his kingdom. Meanwhile Rawul Chachick marched to Dhooniapoor to part with life. When he heard that the Prince of Mooltan was within four miles his soul rejoiced; he performed his ablutions, worshipped the sword and the gods, bestowed charity, and withdrew his thoughts from this world. The battle lasted two hours, and Rawul fell, with all his kin, after performing prodigies of valour. 2000 Khans altogether fell beneath their swords; after the battle the king returned to Mooltan.

Menu commands: "Should the king draw near his end through some incurable disease, he must bestow on the priests all his riches accumulated from legal fines, and having duly committed his kingdom to his son, let him seek death in battle, or, if there be no war, by abstaining from food."

[6] Sati was self-sacrifice after the death of the husband, Johar during his lifetime.

[7] There are three hundred millions of them!

[8] See the lives of Chelidonis and Acirotatus.

[9] In the fifth century, Basina, wife of a king of Thuringia, left her husband and repaired to Childeric, King of France, telling him she did so because he was a braver man; and adding that had she known a braver man than him, she would have gone to him to the uttermost parts of the earth; but she did a more remarkable thing than this—she actually reconciled her two husbands!

[10] Some idea of the perfection to which the means of secret communication has been brought by the fair denizens of the Eastern harems, may be gathered from the following in Lane's "Arabian Nights":— CHAP. VIII. 1191.

A lover sent his love a fan, a bunch of flowers, a silk tassel, some sugar-candy, and the chord of a musical instrument. She returned for an answer a piece of aloe plant, three black cumin seeds, and a piece of a plant used in washing.

Explanation:—"Fan" (wanted to pay her an evening visit); "bunch of flowers" (that he wished it to be in her garden); "silk tassel" (hoped they should have wine); "sugar-candy" (* * *); "chord of musical instrument" (that they would be entertained with music)."

Answer:—"Piece of aloe plant," (patience); "three cumin seeds" (time for three nights); "plant used in washing" (that she was going to the bath and would take that opportunity of seeing him).

[11] Mucho sabe la zorra, pero sabe mas la dama enamorata.

CHAP IX.

A.D. 1194—1235.

MOHAMMED RAISES FORCES FOR A CRUSADE AGAINST INDIA. — DEFEAT AND DEATH OF JEICHUND. — MOHAMMED TURNS HIS ARMS AGAINST BENGAL. — THE FALL OF BENARES. — HE RETURNS TO GHIZNI. — HIS DEATH BY ASSASSINATION. — CUTTUB-UL-DIEN FOUNDS THE SLAVE DYNASTY A.D. 1205. — HE IS SUCCEEDED BY HIS SON, WHO RESIGNS THE SOVEREIGNTY TO ALTUMSH, HIS SON-IN-LAW, WHO GREATLY EXTENDS THE EMPIRE. — THE FIERCE CAREER OF GENGHIS THE SHEPHERD KING.

BOOK I. 1194.

THE conquest of Delhi by his lieutenant, Cuttub, A.D. 1193, raised the emulation of Mohammed, and the year following he roused himself from his repose and preached a crusade against India, a watchword to which in those days warriors sprang ready armed from the ground.

Raising a magnificent force of 100,000 horse, recruited from Turks, Persians, and the fierce Affghans from the mountains of Ghor and Ghizni, he crossed the Indus, and marched to Peshawur. Never probably was such a splendid army of mercenaries ever marshalled against the devoted land of India; nearly every warlike nation of Northern and Central Asia furnished her warriors for this grand effort of spoliation; and the glitter of their armour of gold and silver, the tramp and neighing of the steeds, and the fierce energy of Mohammed himself, has furnished many a tale to the poets and troubadours of the East.

When questioned by one of his omrahs, regarding the destination of this noble force, Mohammed answered:

"Know old man, that since the time of my defeat in Hindostan, notwithstanding external appearances, I have never slumbered in ease, or awaked but in sorrow and anxiety. I have, therefore, determined, with this army to recover my lost honour from those idolaters or die in the noble attempt."

CHAP. IX. 1194.

He united his troops with those of Cuttub, who met him with 50,000 horse, and advanced to Canouje, where he encountered the host of Jeichund, numbering 300,000, and including in its ranks no less than 150 princes, who had all sworn by the Ganges to destroy their enemy, or quaff the cup of martyrdom; but "notwithstanding their sounding threats, their rank-breaking elephants, war-treading horses, and bloodthirsty soldiers, Mohammed surprised their camp in the night, when this mighty army once shaken, was lost in its own ruins, and recoiled like a troubled torrent from the bloody plain."[1] The native army was routed with immense slaughter, and Jeichund himself met a congenial death in the sacred Ganges.[2] Canouje was taken and sacked; and thus the proud capital of thirty generations of mighty sovereigns sank for ever to the condition of a third-rate city under the Moslem conquerors.

Canouje never revived; and during many centuries the extent of its ruins and the glowing relations of bardic chroniclers have alone attested its former magnificence. But although the Rajpoot capital was destroyed, her sovereign and her bravest slain, the sons of those who had made her famous in story, still remained, and perpetuated in a distant land the noble qualities that had gained for them the palm of Indian chivalry. Sioje or Sivaji, the nephew of Jeichund, retired to Marwar[3], which then included the district from Sutledge to the ocean, with a handful of retainers, and took service with a petty chieftain of the desert. In less than four centuries we find the descendants of these exiles of the Ganges, occupying nearly the whole desert, having founded three

BOOK I. 1194. capitals, studded the land with feudal strongholds, and capable of bringing into the field 50,000 men, "the sons of one father," to combat the emperor of Delhi.[4]

After the victory of Canouje, Mohammed turned his thoughts to the conquest of Bengal, hitherto exempt from Moslem invasion. During the next year he took the holy city of Benares, the most ancient seat of Brahminical learning, and the fountain head of that subtle philosophy with which the priestly caste had for four thousand years delighted to confound the reason of their followers.

Benares is the sacred spot where the supreme himself is supposed by orthodox Hindoos to spend three hours of every day, reclining during the other nine on a large rock of black marble, under an aged peepul tree, in a little court inside the fort of Chunar. The sanctity of Benares dates back to the days of fable. In very ancient days, ages before history has any record, Siva the Destroyer, the most sovereign person of the Hindoo Trinity, built this wonderful city of the purest gold, added temples of precious stones, and called it Casi[5], or the Magnificent; but in course of time, in consequence of the wickedness of the people, he turned it into stone; and lately its wickedness has so increased that the indignant god is still further displaying his anger, by converting the stone edifices into huts of mud and thatch.

But Benares had more urgent claims than those of sanctity or antiquity, on the attention of Mohammed. Its temples, yet unrifled by the fierce soldiers of the north, were said to be the richest in the world; it was a city of priests, and out of a population of 600,000 souls, 80,000 were officiating Brahmins.

Mohammed encountered but little opposition: at the first attack the Raja was defeated and slain, the city was taken, the shrines pillaged, and the priests put to the sword.

It is recorded that after the victory, Cuttub presented

Mohammed with 300 elephants, who all fell down on their knees to him at the same moment, with the exception of one white one, which refused to kneel, and nearly killed its driver.[6] Mohammed returned this elephant to Cuttub, who rode it till his death; when the affectionate animal pined away with visible sorrow, and died the third day. CHAP. IX. 1194.

A thousand temples were pillaged and destroyed in Benares alone, and the accumulation of treasure was enormous. The army returned to Ghizni, and when Mohammed at the head of his victorious legions, followed by 4000 camels laden with the spoils of many cities, wound through the plains that lay at the foot of his mountain capital, those ancients amongst the crowd that thronged the ramparts, who remembered Ghizni in her pride, grew young again as they gazed on a sight that recalled to their memories the grandeur of their once unequalled city; and warmed into eloquence, as they recounted to their children's children, the stories they had listened to in their youth, of the fabulous wealth and glory of the first and greatest Sultan of their race.

Mohammed of Ghor actually possessed supreme authority in the Indian provinces of Ghizni for thirty-two years, though during twenty-nine years of this his brother, Yeas-ul-Dien, was nominal sovereign of the empire. He owed a great portion of his conquests to the talent and vigour of his slaves Cuttub and Eldoze.

According to the custom of the East, Mohammed bought and adopted slaves, whom he selected for the indulgence of a whim or their own merit. This traffic was unchanged since the patriarchal days, when Potiphar bought Joseph to look after his business.[7] The number of slaves thus purchased, who in those turbulent days attained supreme authority in the East, is very striking; and in India especially they founded a dynasty of slave kings.

Mohammed made nine expeditions to India, and re-

BOOK I. 1205. 1211.

turned laden with spoil seven times. He left a treasure, the account of which is incredible to northern imaginations, but which all Eastern authorities corroborate. He was cruelly assassinated by the Gickers or Jits when camped on the banks of the Nilab, the scene of his former defeat by Pithowra.

Mohammed left but one daughter, and at his death the empire was divided among his slaves. Eldoze kept possession of Ghizni and the northern provinces; Nasir Kubachi ruled Mooltan and Scinde; whilst Cuttub remained in Hindostan, and established his seat of empire at Lahore.

Cuttub, called the Polestar of Religion, mounted the throne of Lahore A.D. 1205. He was the founder of the dynasty of the slave kings, and was the first of the Mahomedan monarchs who from choice established his capital in India. He was a glorious soldier, and victory attended his arms from one end of Hindostan to another; he reconquered Malwa, Guzerat, and Ajmere, embellished Delhi, and built the famous Cuttub minar, on the ruins, and with the remains, of twenty-five Hindoo temples. With empire constantly within his grasp, Cuttub never for a moment forgot his duty to his patron and governor Mohammed of Ghor, and during his lifetime never aimed at independent sovereignty. Like him, his actual reign was of short duration, although his influence and power were exercised during more than a quarter of a century. He was killed at Delhi by a fall from his horse when playing at ball.

Cuttub possessed in its greatest perfection the Eastern virtue of generosity. Long before he ascended the throne, he was celebrated as the "bestower of lacks;" and for centuries after his death, when a prince was marked for his liberality, his subjects said, "he is as generous as Cuttub."

Cuttub was succeeded by his son Aram; but he was a weak prince, and unable to control the fiery omrahs of the school of his father and Mohammed of Ghor. Nasir, a slave of Mohammed, rebelled, and appropriated Scinde, Moultan, and other places, whilst Mohammed of Chilligi, another slave, possessed himself of Bengal. Several other princes declared their independence, till at length his nobles finding the kingdom dwindling to a mere province, compelled him to resign the sovereignty to Altumsh, the son-in-law and adopted son of Cuttub. 1211.

Altumsh was one of the most famous of the dynasty of the slave kings, and his history will illustrate the capricious fortune that for some centuries regulated the destinies of the monarchy of Hindostan. He was the favourite son of a great chief in Tartary, but, like Joseph, incurring the jealousy of his brethren, they stripped him one day out hunting, and traded him away to a company of slave merchants, who sold him to a prince of Bokhara, in whose household he received a liberal education. At the death of this prince he was again exposed for sale, and bought by a merchant who carried him to Ghizni. Here the Emperor Mohammed of Ghor heard of his beauty and talents, but could not agree with the merchant about the price; he was therefore taken back to Bokhara, as none dare bid against the king. At length Cuttub obtained his sovereign's permission to complete the purchase, which he did for 50,000 pieces of silver. Altumsh rapidly rose in the household of Cuttub, till, at length, having married his daughter, he was created captain-general of the empire; and when the incapable Aram was deposed, he was unanimously elected to the throne. In his more able hands, the empire was again united, and the rebel governors were successively defeated.

Eldoze, the most powerful of these ambitious vassals, who at the death of Mohammed had revolted, and established his authority in the northern provinces of the empire, was defeated during an advance he made into Hindostan; and being taken prisoner, soon died. Not content with having established his authority, Altumsh soon began to extend it. Bengal, Bahar, and the provinces

BOOK I. 1235.

of Sewaulik, were in turn reconquered and annexed: the strong fortress of Gwalior was reduced after a siege of twelve months, and in the next year the wealthy province of Malwa, was brought under the rule of the King of Delhi.

In the city of Oojein, in Malwa, Altumsh destroyed one of the few holy places remaining to the persecuted priests of Brahma. The temple of Maha Kali, the great god of death, was one of the most magnificent in Hindostan: built on the exact plan of that of Somnauth Puttun, it was surrounded by a wall 100 cubits high, and its construction had occupied the space of 300 years. Its founder was Bicker Majit, the most revered of all the ancient monarchs of India; the date of whose death was even in the days of Akbar, the most popular era of the natives of Hindostan.

The temple was razed to the ground; and the idols of the great king and of the god of death taken to Delhi and broken at the door of the great mosque. Altumsh was an enterprising, able, and good prince, and died in his bed, A.D. 1235, after a signally prosperous reign of twenty-five years. In the mean time the Ghorian dynasty, west of the Indus, was overthrown by Mohammed, sultan of Charizm, who thought himself invincible. He had subdued Persia, Khorassan, Bactriana, Cabul, Ghizni, Ghor, Transoxiana, and Lahore, and (in Eastern parlance) reigned over a hundred nations. But his vainglory tempted him to dare the power of Genghis Khan, at that period ravaging Northern Asia. The prodigious armies of these great conquerors met on the plains of the Jaxartes, Mohammed was defeated, and it is said, 350,000 men were slain. Mohammed escaped with difficulty, and was soon after assassinated on an obscure island in the Caspian Sea. His son, Jebal-Eddin, attempted to retrieve his father's defeat, but was forced back by the legions of Genghis to the banks of Indus. Here he made a glorious stand; but finding victory hopeless, he forced his horse into the river[8], and reached the other bank in safety. At this moment Genghis reached the bank, and several of his officers wished to pursue him, but he would not permit them: the daring courage of Jebal-Eddin excited his admiration, and he exclaimed with enthusiasm, "Happy the man who can boast of such a father!" Jebal-Eddin took temporary refuge in India; but was soon afterwards assassinated in Kurdistan. CHAP. IX. 1235.

It was in the thirteenth year of the reign of Altumsh, that Tamugin, better known as Genghis[9], Khan of Khans, mighty monarch of the pastoral world, lord of many millions of shepherds, swept across the dark page of Asiatic history with a fiery glare, that, like a flash of heaven's artillery, startled and appalled the world, and brought sudden destruction upon all who chanced to be in its course. In the year A.D. 1227, the very year in which St. Louis headed his ill-fated crusade to the Holy Land, this colossus of the history of blood, who pretended, like Attila, to have received a Divine commission to conquer the world, stalked like the destroying angel at the head of his Scythian and Tartar hordes, through all the fairest regions of Central Asia and Persia and China.

No name is written on the page of history in characters so fierce and bloody as that of this chief of the pastoral millions of Central Asia. From the time when seated upon a black sheepskin, according to the ancient custom of these shepherd warriors, he was proclaimed chief khan of all the Turkoman races, until the day of his death, twenty years after, on the frontiers of China, his career was one unceasing course of bloodshed and destruction. Upwards of 14,000,000 of human beings are supposed to have been slaughtered by Genghis during the last twenty years of his life. From the shores of the Caspian to the frontiers of China, and from Indus to the Pole, this "prince of the power of the sword," and his fierce soldiery, made good the cruel boast of the greatest warrior of their race, that their horses could gallop without stumbling

BOOK I. 1235.

over ground where populous cities had once stood, and wiped away, without remorse, from the fair front of nature, the fertility and civilisation that five centuries have not been able to renew.[10] By his own countrymen he was supposed to have had a Divine origin[11], for the singular reason that his family could only be traced back ten generations; but by the millions who cowered and perished under his smiting scimitar, he was accounted a scourge of God, a demon of wrath, sent to depopulate the world. No wonder that amongst the ignorant heathens of those countries, a supernatural birth was attributed to such a monster: he was said to have come into the world with congealed blood in his hands; and the milk of wild beasts[12] was reported to have matured the savage spirit, that delighted to shed the blood of his fellow-creatures, as it were water, and who habitually quenched his thirst in a goblet made from the skull of his former sovereign.[13]

So rapid were his marches, and so unexpected his onslaughts, that it was the common belief of his terrified victims, that his horses had wings; and that, like the famed steeds of Dardanus, they were so swift, that in running they did not bow down the ears of standing corn.

Knowing no God[14] but his own will, no pleasure but the destruction of his kind[15], he was swift to shed blood, and scoffed at all learning and religion as equally vain. He littered his horses with the leaves of the rarest library in Asia; burned the Bible with every possible mark of contempt, and cast the Koran under his horses' feet in the centre of the holy mosque of Bokhara.[16]

Genghis was indeed the savage scourge of the human race, sent apparently with no object but to bite[17] the world, and bring destruction and woe on its inhabitants, slaying even more than the curse of God himself, at the head of his 500,000 Huns.

Flushed with the subjugation of the great kingdoms of Central Asia and Persia, this fierce warrior crossed the Indus, and penetrated as far as the Dooab[18]; but could not spare time to complete the conquest of Hindostan. The far distant land of Cathay was his object, and heedless of the golden prize that lay at his feet, he passed India in his relentless course, bent only on shedding the blood of the hated Chinese.[19] 1235.

The history of Genghis gives us a curious glimpse of the civilisation[20] and social laws of the Moguls at their transition state from barbarism to comparative civilisation. Their code of laws was formed entirely to meet the requirements of a military people. It recognised but two punishments, bastinado and death, by which every crime against the person or state was judged. The number of blows extended from seven to seven hundred; and so universal was the application of this punishment, and so strong the patriarchal right of this desert-born race, that even princes commanding armies could be punished with stripes at their fathers' desire.

Genghis Khan was one of the greatest conquerors of history; his sword was never in its scabbard; and the empire he bequeathed to his son extended 1800 leagues from east to west, and more than 1000 from north to south. Rivalling his great prototype, Alaric, in the magnificence of his conquests, he eclipsed him in the splendour of his obsequies. The assistance of Nature herself was invoked by trembling man to hide the bones of conquerors whose relentless career caused them to be viewed as more than mortal. A river was diverted from its bed to afford a safe resting-place for the body of Alaric[21], whilst, far away on the borders of China, a mountain[22] was raised over the remains of Genghis Khan, and a forest planted, to exclude for ever the footsteps of man from his grave.

But although Genghis passed away like an evil dream, his was the portentous shadow that gave warning of the coming event.

The lustful eye of Mogul conquest had fallen on the land of India, and the first stepping-stone was laid for the great invasion effected by Timour some 150 years later.

BOOK I. 1235. From that day the Mogul soldier was an institution of the country; and more than once during the succeeding century did these warlike mercenaries, after obtaining a like dangerous power, suffer the same extermination as the Mamelukes and Janissaries of later days.

NOTES TO CHAPTER IX.

[1] Ferishta.

[2] His body was identified for the funeral pyre by a set of artificial teeth that were fastened in with gold wedges and wires.

[3] A corruption of "Maroo-war," the region of death.

[4] See Tod's Rajasthan.

[5] Casi, splendid, magnificent; ancient name of Benares.

[6] This is the only white elephant mentioned in Indian history, except the one that carried Mahmoud against the Usbeks, and that ridden by Warren Hastings.

[7] To this day in Egypt slaves are considered most trustworthy; witness the commendation bestowed on an official by Mehemet Ali: "This is a man of excellent antecedents: *he was bought!*"

[8] At Attock the Indus is only 260 yards broad, but it is very deep and rapid; and in great floods reaches the top of a bastion thirty-five or forty feet above the ordinary level.

[9] Genghis or Zingis means "most great."

[10] Such was the civilisation of Central Asia at this period, that, according to Abulfeda, the streets of Samarcand were paved, and the water conveyed to the city in leaden pipes.

[11] His birth was attributed to the immaculate conception of a virgin.

[12] Le Dieu Mars m'engendra d'une fière Amazone, et je sucai le lait d'une affreuse lionne.

[13] He carried about the skull of the Khan of the Keraites, known in history as Prester John, chased in silver. Pope Sixtus diverted himself with having had the power of cutting off the head of an earl, the Count di Popoli; but he nearly burst with envy when he heard of Queen Elizabeth's superior happiness and power in being able to cut off a crowned head:—"O beata femmina, che ai gustata il piacer de far saltare una testa coronata." Oh, happy woman, who has tasted the pleasure of cutting off a crowned head.—How he would have envied Genghis decapitating a king and drinking out of his skull.

[14] Genghis and followers were all strict Deists.

[15] Genghis one day asked one of his generals what, in his opinion, was the greatest pleasure of man? "To go hunting," said he, "on a spring day, mounted on a fine horse and holding a falcon on your wrist, to see him pull

down his prey." "No," said Genghis, "the greatest enjoyment of man is to conquer his enemies; to drive them before him; to snatch from them all they possess; to see the persons dear to them with their faces bathed in tears; to mount their horses and carry away captive their wives and daughters." CHAP. IX. 1235.

[16] Bokhara at this period was the greatest seat of learning in the East; students flocked from all parts to her famed university, which equalled the renowned Academy of Sciences in Samarcand.

[17] "Teeth hadst thou in thy head
When thou wast born, to signify
Thou camest to bite the world."—*Richard III.*

[18] See M. Petit de la Croix.

[19] Genghis made the great canal of China, in order that the treasure of that country might reach him without loss attending the long sea passage.

[20] One law ordered adulterers to be punished with death; but the inhabitants of Kaindu, who, from remote times, had been accustomed to resign their wives to the strangers who visited them, retiring from their own house during their stay, representing to the Tartar Prince the hardship to which this new enactment would subject them, by preventing the exercise of their accustomed hospitality, they were relieved by special exemption from the oppressive operation of this law.

[21] The waters of the Busentiris, a small river that flows round Constantia, were diverted from their course, and the gorgeous sepulchre of Alaric raised in the centre of its bed. The waters were then restored, and the last resting-place of the scourge of God hidden for ever from the gaze of man. To make this more certain all who assisted at the funeral were killed.

[22] Burkhan Caldin is the name of this enormous artificial mountain; the Chinese call it Han to this day.

CHAP. X.

A.D. 1236—1286.

SULTANA RIZIA ASCENDS THE THRONE AT DELHI. — HER SHORT REIGN AND CRUEL DEATH. — SHE IS SUCCEEDED BY THE FOLLOWING KINGS:— BYRAM II., MUSAOOD IV., MAHMOUD II., BALIN, AND KAI KOBAD, WITH WHOM ENDED THE DYNASTY OF THE SLAVE KINGS.

BOOK I. 1236. FEROSE succeeded his father Altumsh, but he was a weak wicked prince, and within a year the lovely Sultana Rizia, his eldest sister, was raised by the unanimous voice of the omrahs in his place; and for three years the Imperial Musnud at Delhi was occupied by a woman. She was a woman of considerable energy and genius, and twice during his lifetime her father had entrusted his kingdom to her care. "Know," said he to his omrahs, "that the burden of power, too heavy for my sons, though there were twenty of them, is not so for the delicate Rizia;—she has in her more spirit than them all."

Her beauty is described by her vizier, Mulak Junede, as "sufficient to ripen the corn in the blade;" and he adds, "she could revive with a look her dying friends, or render helpless her most powerful foes;" but "woe to the land where a minor rules, or a woman bears sway," says the Hindoo bard Chund; and certainly, in this instance, the feminine attributes of the heart of the Sultana, quite outbalanced the masculine qualities of her head; the injudicious elevation of an Abyssinian slave, to the command of her armies, roused the indignation of the nobles of her court, and she and her paramour were deposed and subjected to a cruel death.

1236. During the succeeding twenty years, the history of Hindostan is one unbroken chain of plots and counterplots, invasions and massacres, amidst which the Mussulman power rose and fell, according to the talent or enterprise of the individual occupying the throne.

Bengal and Behar acknowledged Mahomedan governors; the currency of the country was inscribed with the name of the Sultan of Delhi, and the faith of Mahomed asserted its right to the position of the dominant religion of Hindostan.

The country was a prey to unceasing rapine, and districts of the utmost fertility were depopulated and reduced to the condition of primeval deserts. Everywhere the native Rajas and Mussulman nobles, taking advantage of the general disturbances, sought to enrich themselves at the expense of their neighbours; and the wretched ryots, totally unprotected, found untilled lands the only protection from extortion and pillage. Many of the most populous districts of Hindostan were thus impoverished and depopulated, and the miserable inhabitants driven to the forests and jungles, there to eke out a starving existence till better days should come.

In the mean time the Hindoo Rajas, still cherishing their enmity to the faith of their conquerors, acquired much of their military science, and rebelled on every practicable occasion.

As the present sketch does not profess to be a careful relation of the annals of crime, the reigns of some of the Princes of India, will detain us but a short time. Sultana Rizia was succeeded by her brother, Behram Shah, a weak and cruel sovereign, the puppet of a crafty vizier, who dethroned him and threw him into prison, where he died after a miserable reign of two years. He was succeeded by Musaood, son of Ferose Shah, the eldest son of Altumsh, who soon gave himself up to wine and

BOOK I. 1244. women, and exercised various modes of cruelty, injustice, and oppression, dispensing with all counsel, and placing the way of ruin before him.

At length the omrahs bound up their loins of hostility against him, and the remainder of his life was spent in imprisonment; he was a weak and foolish prince, a slave to his pleasures, and without firmness of mind to entertain one commendable virtue. He was succeeded by Mahmoud II., the adopted son of Cuttub. Mahmoud's early years were passed in confinement in Bengal, till he was liberated by his nephew Musaood, and here he acquired those singular habits, that make him an exception to the usual run of royal personages. During his imprisonment he despised the Emperor's allowance, and wrote for his livelihood; he became one of the best scribes of the day; and an anecdote related of his talent, indicates a kindness of nature, and consideration for the feelings of others, that sovereigns do not always extend to unfriendly critics. One day having requested an omrah, of some literary reputation, to inspect a Koran of his writing, the omrah pointed out a word which he said was wrong. Mahmoud looked at it, and smiling, drew a circle round it; but on the omrah's departure he began to erase it, and restore the word. On being asked why he did so, he said he knew the word was originally right, but he thought it better to erase it from the paper, than hurt the heart of a poor man by bringing him to shame.

In his domestic character he rather resembled our James I. Contrary to all customs of Eastern princes, he had but one wife, whom he obliged to perform every homely duty of housewifery; and when one day she complained she had burned her fingers in baking his bread, and desired he would allow her a maid to assist her, he rejected her request, saying he was merely a trustee for the state, and that he was determined not to burthen it with needless expenses. He therefore exhorted her, in the most aggravating manner, to persevere in her duty with patience, assuring her that God would reward her in the end.

CHAP. X.

1265.

In these days the kings of Delhi kept on foot enormous mercenary armies; and the vizier of Mahmoud went out to meet the ambassador of Hoolagoo, the grandson of Genghis Khan, at that time Emperor of Persia, with 50,000 foreign horse; 200,000 infantry were drawn up in files along the road, with 3000 artillery chariots, and 2000 war elephants in the intervals. All these troops performed their most skilful evolutions before the Mogul.

Mahmoud was a beneficent sovereign. He settled the countries of the Punjaub and Moultan; severely chastised the Jits, and revived much of the influence of Cuttub and Altumsh. He died naturally A.D. 1265, after a reign of twenty-one years.

Mahmoud was succeeded by his vizier Balin, or Balaban, who walked in his steps, and raised the renown of the slave kings for power and justice to the highest pitch it had hitherto attained.

The history of Balin would not appear strange amid the fanciful tales of the "Arabian Nights," and proves, amongst a hundred other instances, that fiction, however startling, is often equalled by unquestioned reality.

The Sultan Altumsh, or Shams Oddin, perpetuated the custom of Mohammed of Ghor, and, in fact, all Eastern monarchs of importance, of recruiting the officers of their army and household from the slave markets of the northern and western kingdoms of Asia. On one occasion he sent a merchant to purchase slaves from Bokhara and Samarcand. He returned with one hundred youths of all kindreds, and nations, and colours, who all pleased him, except Balin, whom he rejected on account of his despicable appearance. On hearing the cause of his rejection, Balin thus addressed the Emperor: "Lord of the world! why have you bought all these slaves?" The Emperor smiled, and said: "For my own sake." "No

BOOK I. 1265. doubt," replied the youth. "Buy me, then, for God's sake." "I will," said the Emperor, who accepted him and placed him amongst the rest; but on account of his mean appearance, he gave him a situation amongst the cup-bearers. By talent, valour, and intrigue, Balin gradually rose till he became a general, and afterwards vizier; and Mahmoud, leaving no sons, he ascended the throne of Delhi, by the universal desire of the princes and nobles of his kingdom.

He was a magnificent sovereign, fond of show and regal pomp. His state receptions, his chain elephants, his horse guards, consisting of 1000 noble Tartars in splendid armour, were long famous in Hindostan. The following is Ferishta's account of his magnificence:—"Such was the pomp and grandeur of the royal presence, that none could approach the throne without terror. The ceremonies of introduction were conducted with much reverence and solemnity, and everything disposed so as to strike awe and astonishment into the beholders." Nor was Balin less magnificent in his cavalcades. His state elephants were caparisoned in purple and gold; his horse guards were mounted upon the finest Persian steeds, with bridles of silver and saddles of rich embroidery; five hundred chosen men in rich livery, with their drawn swords upon their shoulders, ran proclaiming his approach, and clearing the way before him; the omrahs following according to their rank, which was decided by their equipages and attendants. The monarch, in short, seldom went out with less than 10,000 men, which he used to say was not to gratify any vanity in himself, but to exalt him in the eyes of the people. He was a man in many ways especially fitted for the kingly office. Under him the court of Delhi became famous for justice and wise government, and his alliance was courted by the kings of Persia and Turkey.

The fierce course of conquest and destruction, of Genghis Khan in Asia, produced an effect on the empire of India as unexpected as it was beneficial. The sovereigns of Central Asia and the frontiers of Persia, expelled at once from their thrones and country, sought refuge in the shadow of the imperial court at Delhi. And during this reign twenty sovereigns, including those of Khorassan, Persia, Roumelia, and Syria, partook of the imperial bounty and attended the court of Balin. They had princely allowances and palaces, and on public days were ranked before the throne. The court of Balin was considered the most magnificent and polite in the world. He was a great moralist, and punished severely all who indulged in wine, women, and play. He was free from grasping ambition; and when urged to reconquer Guzerat and Malwa, that had shaken off the yoke imposed upon them by Cuttub, he refused, saying, the Mogul Tartars had become so powerful in the north, having conquered all the Mussulman princes, that he thought it better to secure what he possessed against those invaders, than weaken himself by foreign wars, and leave his own country unguarded. Balin died in 1286, after a reign of twenty-two years: his advice to his son was worthy the wise king of Israel; but like him he fell lamentably short of his own precepts. He told him, that he himself had spent a long life in the administration and government of kingdoms, and by study and experience had acquired some knowledge which might be of service to him after his death; that in the course of nature this occurrence now hastened apace, he therefore desired he would lend him the ear of attention, and treasure up his maxims in his mind. "When you shall ascend the throne," said he in conclusion, "look upon yourself as the deputy of God; have a just sense of the importance of your charge, and permit not any uneasiness in yourself to sully the lustre of your exalted station, and let not avaricious and low-minded men share your esteem, or bear any part of your administration. Let your passions be governed by reason, and beware of giving way to your rage: anger is dangerous

BOOK I. 1286. in all men, but in kings it is the weapon of death. Let the public treasure be expended in the service of the state, with that prudent economy, yet benevolent liberality, which reason will dictate to a mind always intent on doing good. Let the worship of God be inculcated by your example, and never permit vice and infidelity unpunished to hold up their face to the day. Be ever attentive to the business of the state, that you may avoid the imposition of designing ministers. Make it your study to see them execute your commands without the least deviation or neglect, for it is by them you must govern your people. Let your judges and magistrates be men of capacity, religion, and virtue, that the light of justice may illuminate your realms. Let no light behaviour, either in public or private, detract from that important majesty which exalts the idea of a king; and let everything around you be so regulated as to inspire that reverence and awe, which will render your person sacred, and contribute to enforce your commands. Spare no pains to find men of genius, learning and courage; you must cherish them by your beneficence, that they may prove the soul of your council, and sword of your power. Throw not down a great man to the ground for a small crime, nor entirely overlook his offence. Raise not a low man too hastily to a high station, lest he forget himself, and be an eyesore to men of superior merit. Never attempt anything, unless it is through necessity, but having once determined upon a measure, let your perseverance be never shaken by doubt, nor your eye ever deviate from the object: for it is better for a king to be obstinate than pusillanimous, as in the first case he may chance to be right, in the latter he is always sure to be wrong: nothing more certainly indicates the weakness of a prince, than a fluctuating mind."

What sentiments can be nobler? Yet this man was cruel in the extreme; and it was with the utmost difficulty the cadis and muftis and other civil and religious officers could prevent his impaling alive all the prisoners he took in a predatory expedition to Bengal; he put to death every one of the relations and principal adherents of the rebel Tughril; sparing neither women nor children, and even massacred a hundred fakeers, because they had received alms from him. When Balin was sick with his last fatal illness, he sent for his son Kera from Bengal, in order that the omrahs might swear fealty to him as his successor; desiring him at the same time to remain with him, and send a trusty governor to his province. Instead of obeying him, however, Kera, who it appears disliked the form and ceremony of his father's court, returned to his kingdom without his permission; which so enraged Balin, that sending for Kera's son, Kai Kobad, from Moultan, he appointed him his successor; and exacted a solemn promise from his omrahs that they would exclude his undutiful son, and support the claims of his grandson. When Kera heard of his son's usurpation at Delhi, he immediately marched from Bengal to recover his rights; but the die was already cast; and according to the custom of Hindostan, Kai Kobad, once seated on the musnud, was considered the rightful possessor of the kingdom.

CHAP. X. 1286.

This illustrates a peculiarity in the succession to the throne of Hindostan, that was unknown in any other country.

"It is a singular custom in Hindostan," says the Emperor Baber, writing 200 years later, "that there is little hereditary descent in succession to the sovereignty. There is a throne attached to the king; there is in like manner a seat, or station, assigned for each of the emirs, viziers, and soubahs. It is that throne and these stations alone which engage the reverence of the people of Bengal; a set of dependants, servants and attendants are annexed to each of these situations. When the king wishes to dismiss or appoint any person, whosoever is placed in the seat of the one dismissed is immediately attended and obeyed by the

BOOK I. 1286.

whole establishment of dependants, servants and retainers annexed to the seat which he occupies; and this rule obtains even as to the royal throne itself."

Whoever kills the king, and succeeds in placing himself on that throne, is immediately acknowledged as king; all the emirs, viziers, soldiers and peasants, instantly obey and submit to him; and consider him as being as much their sovereign as they did their former prince, and obey his orders as implicitly.

We have remarked that usurpation was the rule not the exception amongst the princes of Hindostan; the lawful heir seldom obtained his birthright without bloodshed, and never maintained it without a contest.

In the course of incessantly recurring revolutions, in which the sceptre was constantly changing hands, the rajas and omrahs would naturally desire some more stable object of their loyalty than the shifting puppets who in turn occupied the throne, and would imperceptibly fix their affections on the paraphernalia of sovereignty rather than on the sovereign himself. This feeling was shared by the natives in general; and hence gradually sprang up a kind of loyalty, that varied from that of every other people in the world; inasmuch as the emblems not the person of royalty were the objects of their homage. Delhi came by degrees to be considered the seat of empire; the possession of the musnud constituted the sole right to command; and whoever could secure the former, and occupy the latter, whether Hindoo or Mussulman, Affghan or Mogul, exacted for the time being the loyalty and respect of the millions of Hindostan.

The musnud and umbrella of empire were to the natives of Hindostan what the colours are to a regiment, and the monarch for the time being was looked upon in the same light as the officer who bears them, honoured by, instead of honouring, the temporary post. The great offices of the state were engrossed by omrahs and nobles, whose right of tenure was hereditary. Their functions

CHAP. X. 1286.

were inalienable, and their duty was to render homage to the occupier of the throne without any indiscreet inquiry of how he came there, or whence he derived his divine right.

The loyal creed of Hindostan was comprised in these few words: "We are faithful to the throne, and whosoever fills it exacts our obedience and respect." Owing to the indifference of the masses, all revolutions were naturally confined to the court itself; the combatants were generally confined to a few leading rajas about the capital; and the great mass of the people did not interest themselves in the numerous struggles that in no way influenced their lot.

Kai Kobad was a youth who, contrary to the example of his father, "delighted in love, and in the society of silver-bodied damsels with musky tresses." His example was eagerly followed by all classes, till Delhi became a bye-word for every kind of immorality; magistrates were drunk in the public streets, and riots were heard in every house. In the mean time the rival parties at court — the Tartars, and the Chilligies, a fierce and savage race of Affghans, contended for the supreme power. The former being the most powerful with the king proscribed the Chilligies, the first on the list being Ferose, their chief; but he came of too warlike a race to allow himself to be defeated without a struggle. He slew at the door of his tent the treacherous Tartar who came to invite him to the king's presence; and his purpose once declared his sons attacked the Tartar camp, and carried away the king's infant son prisoner. In the mean time the intemperance of Kai Kobad brought on paralysis, in which helpless state he was cruelly beaten to death with a cudgel by a Tartar omrah, whose father he had unjustly slain, who wrapped him up in his bed clothes, and threw him into the river. Thus perished the last of the slave kings after a reign of three years. With his murder, and that of his son, ended the dynasty

BOOK I. 1286. founded by the slaves of Mohammed of Ghor, which had possessed the throne of Hindostan during the space of eighty-one years. It was founded by Cuttub A.D. 1205, and extinguished A.D. 1286. It numbered ten sovereigns, of whom only three died without violence.

CHAP. XI.

A.D. 1287—1316.

THE REIGN OF THE BENEVOLENT FEROSE.—HE IS SUCCEEDED BY HIS NEPHEW ALLA IN 1295.—THE STATE OF THE SOUTHERN PART OF INDIA AT THAT PERIOD.—THE EXPEDITIONS OF ALLA INTO THE DECCAN.—THE SACKING OF CHEETORE: HIS DEATH IN 1316.

CHAP. XI. 1287.

No sooner was Kai Kobad dead, than his infant son was destroyed, and Ferose mounted the throne at seventy years of age; had he been younger or his mercy been tempered with more vigour, India would probably have advanced with rapid strides, on the road of civilisation, "such is the might of kings," and so great are the blessings which it is in the power of a wise ruler to impart.

But Ferose was old, a long life had taught him the vanity of man's severity, and he was unwilling to shed the blood, even of his foes. "I am old," he said, when urged to revenge himself on his enemies, "and wish to go down to the grave without shedding blood."[1] "Evil for evil," he used to say, "was easily returned, but he only was great who could return good for evil;" when urged to attempt a siege, that must have cost many lives, he refused, saying that "being on the brink of the grave," he was "unwilling to entail the curse of widows and orphans, on the reign of a few years."

But the policy of ruling without bloodshed, was one that possessed no value in the eyes of the fierce omrahs

BOOK I. 1295.

of his court, who, cradled amidst scenes of blood, and nurtured in the palaces of tyrants, regarded mercy as a sign of weakness, and the shedding of blood the rightful attribute of kings. "Clemency," says the Mussulman historian, "is a virtue that descends from god; but the degenerate children of India did not deserve it." One act of severity alone marked the reign of Ferose, but that was of a nature that, since the murder of Syed Mujud, the minister of Seif at Ghizni, was without parallel in the history of India. The Syed Molah, or chief priest, a celebrated dervish, plotted against the king, and was by his orders trodden to death by an elephant. Prodigies marked the death of the saint, and no rain falling during that year, whole districts were depopulated.

Ferose was not wanting in energy, and conducted his foreign wars with vigour and success; he conquered his enemies as much by his generosity as by his military capacity. During his reign the Mogols under Hoolagoo, the grandson of Genghis, invaded India in great force, but were defeated with much slaughter near Moultan. Ferose received those who deserted or were made prisoners into his service on their becoming Mussulmans[2], and assigned them land, where they erected the city of Mogul-poor; Hoolagoo himself was honoured with the hand of Ferose's daughter. But notwithstanding this vigour and even occasional severity, Ferose was too humane for the age in which he lived, and for the nation he governed; and when after a disturbed reign of eight years, he was assassinated by his nephew Alla, he left a name for clemency, and a love of mercy, that gilds the memory of but few Eastern monarchs. Alla, the nephew and murderer of the good Ferose, known only to the Hindoos by the name of the "Sanguinary," was the greatest sovereign that had appeared in India since the days of Mahmoud of Ghizni. As illiterate as the great founder of his faith himself[3], he was as enterprising and bloodthirsty as any of the descendants of the fierce race of

Ali. The murder of his uncle was necessarily followed by that of his kindred, and after a judicious extirpation of the lineal heirs of his predecessors, he turned his projects to self-aggrandisement and foreign conquest. In his person Alla united the ambition of Alexander and of Mahomed, and nothing would satisfy him but giving his subjects a new creed and making the conquest of the world. He struck coins in the name of Alexander II., and entertained serious thoughts of setting up for a prophet and founding a new religion.

The history of India has hitherto been almost entirely confined to that part of the peninsula known as Hindostan proper, and the countries west and north of the Indus. It is in the reign of Alla that we are first introduced to the magnificent regions lying south of the Nerbudda, a country almost as extensive as Hindostan itself. The native Hindoo Rajas of the Deccan had as yet entirely escaped the attack of the Mussulman conquerors of Hindostan; and although we occasionally find, in the historic narration of the conquests of Alla and others, that certain kingdoms south of the Nerbudda already acknowledged Mussulman rulers, these were merely individual adventurers whose superior energy and fortune had raised them to a throne.

During the reign of Ferose, Alla was governor of the districts of Hindostan, bordering on the frontiers of the Deccan, and so attractive were the accounts of the wealth of the shrines, and the splendour of the cities of those southern regions, that having gained the consent of the Sultan at Delhi, in 1292 he crossed the Nerbudda with a body of horse to pillage, and to slay, in the approved fashion of his nation and his creed.

After a meandering march of two months, during which he visited in simulated friendship, the courts of many rajas, and spied out the wealth of their kingdoms, he suddenly attacked the rocky citadel of Dowletabad, which was then, as now, one of the strongest hill forts of the Deccan.

BOOK I. 1292. Complete success crowned this his first attempt, and the treasures and jewels of the Raja Ram-deo rewarded his adventurous attack. It was when encamped near Dowletabad, that the scornful Moslems first became acquainted with the mighty excavations of Ellora and Adjunta; in these gloomy chambers were assembled every god of the Hindoo calendar; here, with all the hideous paraphernalia of heathen worship, were celebrated the bloody rites of the relentless Siva, and raised high amongst its rival gods, might still be seen the idol of the already discarded deity Buddha.[4]

The excavations of Ellora and Adjunta may even in their decay be considered the most extraordinary monument of human labour and ingenuity in India; at the time of their completion, when the bewildering minutiæ of the paintings and sculptures were uninjured, they were probably amongst the wonders of the world.[5] These temples are no longer considered sacred by the Hindoos, or at least are not regarded with any great reverence; both the date and the cause of their disgrace are unknown; but it is supposed that the multiplied representations of the despised Buddha are displeasing to the orthodox Hindoo.

Alla retained such golden recollections of the treasures of the Deccan, and was so anxious to enrich the Mussulman, at the expense of the Hindoo capital, and to transport to the mosques of the true believers of Hindostan, the spoils of the temples of the infidel, that as soon as he had comfortably disposed of his relations, and seated himself on the throne, he despatched his general, Cafoor, across the Nerbudda, with orders to penetrate far south, into the kingdoms of the Carnatic and Mysore.

Little, if any, authentic record remains of the early history of the southern portion of the peninsula of Hindostan; but the immense wealth possessed by the rajas and their priests, when we first hear of them through the Mussulman historian, the size and splendour of their cities and palaces, the number of their priesthood, and the wealth of their shrines, establish the fact of their prosperity beyond a doubt; and the vast number and startling size of the unequalled tanks and works of irrigation, both in the Carnatic and in the island of Ceylon[6], proves their inhabitants to have been an enterprising and enlightened people.

The great accumulation of treasure, found by the conquerors in the possession of the rajas and priests, cannot be altogether accounted for by the hereditary tradition of the country, that applauded no act of a sovereign so highly as the collection of treasure, and esteemed none so disgraceful as its dissipation. Neither sovereigns nor priests[7] can accumulate wealth from a needy people; we may therefore naturally conclude that the population of southern India had for generations been wealthy; and judging from the analogy of history, we may fairly attribute to a peaceful rule and developed resources, the undoubted existence of their prosperity at the period of the invasion of Cafoor.

The tablelands of the southern part of the Deccan, and of Mysore, and the burning plains of the Carnatic, presented probably the Hindoo type of language, caste, and religious worship, in its pristine purity. In the plains and valleys of the south, the institutions of caste, older than tradition itself, had taken deep root, and flourished like the sacred banyan tree; and the triple worship of the Hindoo Trinity waxed mighty on the deception of priestly craft, and the simple credulity of the multitude.

We have a very distinct account of the condition of the southern portion of the peninsula of Hindostan, from the pen of Ibn Batuta, a native of Tangiers, who travelled through that country about thirty years later, during the reign of Mohammed Tughlak.[8] He describes Dowletabad as a rich and fruitful region, inhabited by a religious and peaceful population, skilful in the application of watermills to irrigate their orchards, and under whose careful

BOOK I. 1295.

cultivation the vine and pomegranates bore fruit twice in the year. Madura and Biyajanagur, we learn, were cities of unequalled splendour, exceeding Delhi and Canouje in magnitude and Milan in elaborate beauty, thronged by prosperous citizens, skilled in every art and profession, and possessing, amongst other civilised comforts, good bedsteads and neat gardens.

The roads of Malabar, he tells us, were well shaded, and at each half-mile was a house of wood fitted up for the accommodation of weary travellers; wells were equally numerous, and an infidel attended at each to give drink to the passers-by.

During a journey of two months through these favoured and peaceful regions, he did not see a space free from cultivation; everywhere he found gardens with houses placed in the centre, and surrounded by wooden fences to separate them from each other. A man was put to death for stealing a nut, or a grain of seed; and as may be easily imagined under so severe a code of laws, thieves were unknown; and none but the rightful owner would attempt to touch even the fruit that had fallen from the tree. No beasts of burden were seen from one end of the country to another, or any horses but those belonging to the king's stables. The people of this country paid tribute to the King of Hinaur, who was feared for his power by sea, and attacked and pillaged every vessel that passed without paying him tribute. There were few Mussulmans at that time in the south; but already a daring race of Arabs, most of whom had committed the Koran to memory, had established themselves on the coast of Malabar, and carried on a fierce war for the faith by sea.[9]

The trade of the west coast of India appears to have been very considerable. Cambay, Surat, Goa, and all the ports of the Concan were inhabited by foreign merchants, who traded with the Persian Gulf and the Red Sea;

whilst Calicut, Hinaur, and other harbours of Malabar, were thronged by large Chinese junks[10], commanded by great nobles, and manned with a thousand sailors and soldiers, who exchanged the silks and porcelain of the Celestial Empire for the pepper and gems of Malabar.

Rumours of fierce invaders from the snowy regions of the north, of the worship of a strange god, of kingdoms depopulated, and dynasties overthrown, would naturally reach the courts of the far kingdoms of the south; but as yet it was only the shadow of war that caused them disquiet: the reality was far off, and they knew only of the massacres and sacrileges of northern India by report. No hostile army had yet spurned their priests, and hewn in pieces their gods; but these days of peace and security were at an end. Already legions of fiery Moslems were devastating their fields and violating the sanctity of their homes: for the first time in history they saw their rajas slain, and their holiest temples destroyed; bitter indeed was the first draught of foreign conquest quaffed by the inhabitants of southern India during the reign of Alla the Sanguinary.

The expedition of Cafoor was crowned with perfect success; and booty to the amount of one hundred millions sterling was said to have been carried back to Delhi. At this period the natives of the Carnatic wore no bracelets, rings, bangles, or any ornaments that were not of gold; and so great was the abundance of the precious metal, that the soldiers of Alla scorned to cumber themselves with any inferior kind of booty.

The scattered and exaggerated accounts of the Carnatic, that about this period began to reach England, probably originated the vision of the golden land of Tapingo, which the enthusiastic dreams of Columbus pictured far away on the shores of Cathay; and certainly the profusion of the precious metals, amongst a people who lined their temples and the palaces with beaten gold,

BOOK I. 1300.

and scorned even a currency of the baser metals, can only be equalled by the narratives of the companions of Pizarro of the golden treasures of the Incas of Peru.

Cafoor pushed his depredations as far as Seet Bundar Ramessar, a post on the Coromandel coast, opposite Ceylon, and a celebrated place of Hindoo pilgrimage. Thousands of idols were torn from the shrines, where, for countless centuries, their mysterious presence had awed the people and enriched the priests; and in the capital of the Carnatic, on the site of one of the holiest temples of the south, was raised a mosque, from whose minarets the adan of the mueddin, ringing out clear and high, was heard night and morning, summoning the faithful to prayer, and under whose dome the worship of the one God and of his Prophet was for the first time celebrated in the sight of the wondering idolaters of Brahma.

Whilst Cafoor was ravaging the happy regions of the south, Alla himself, in A.D. 1300, invaded Guzerat, and utterly destroyed the cities of Anhulwarra and Somnauth, (rebuilt by the Jain sovereign after the conquest of Mahmoud), levelling every building to the ground, and ploughing up their very foundations with asses, as a sign of supreme humiliation. From thence he turned his destructive legions against Rajpootana, the land of the descendants of Sivaji, the nephew of Jeichund, the last Hindoo monarch of Canouje. Rajpootana is a mountainous territory of considerable extent, situated at the western extremity of the magnificent plain watered by the Ganges and the Jumna. It is chiefly marked by the long range of the Aravulli Hills, which, beginning on the frontiers of Guzerat, extend north-north-east to the borders of Delhi; on the western side, it descends to the districts of Mawar, whose arid plains are gradually confounded with the Great Desert; on the east, it slopes down into a prolonged tableland forming the district round Ajmere and the territories of Mewar and Jeypore. Although bordering so closely on the Mussulman dominion in Hindostan, the inhospitable nature of the soil, and the warlike character of its inhabitants, had entirely saved it from molestation; and almost within hail of the capital the Rahtore Rajpoots had maintained inviolate their territory, their caste, and their peculiar institutions.[11] CHAP. XI. 1300.

The story of the two sieges of Cheetore by Alla, as told by Col. Tod, is one of the most romantic that adorns the annals of even this land of romance. Lakumsi, a minor, was at this time sovereign of Cheetore, and Bheemsi, his uncle, was protector; he had married Pudmani (a name signifying singularly beautiful), the daughter of the King of Ceylon, whose matchless beauty forms to this day the inspiring theme of the bards of Hindostan. In his luxurious harem at Delhi, the imagination of Alla had been inflamed by the description of the unequalled beauty of this houri of Cheetore and he determined to become the possessor of such a prize. He marshalled an army for the conquest of Rajpootana, and after a weary march of several months encamped under the walls of Cheetore; and demanded as the price of his retreat the hand of the fair princess. But the Rajpoots of those days esteemed the honour of their women far above all earthly considerations, and his terms were indignantly rejected; for several months he continued the siege without success, and at length finding success hopeless, he modified his demands to a mere sight of this extraordinary beauty; a gratification he was only permitted to enjoy by the refraction of numerous mirrors. Relying on Rajpoot honour, he entered Cheetore slightly guarded, and having contemplated the reflected charms of Pudmani, he set out on his return to his camp; unwilling to be outdone in generous confidence, Bheemsi accompanied him back to the front of the fortress, where, with unequalled deceit, Alla had prepared an ambush, and seizing Bheemsi, hurried him off to his camp, and made his liberty dependent on the surrender of his wife. No sooner did the news reach Cheetore, than Pudmani

BOOK I. 1300. expressed her consent to the terms, and having taken counsel with her kinsfolk, a plan was devised by which her honour might be saved, and the bad faith of Alla deservedly punished: intimation was sent to Alla that the day he withdrew from the trenches, Pudmani would surrender herself to him; but a stipulation was made, that she should be accompanied by a fitting band of handmaids, and strict orders were to be issued to prevent curiosity from violating the sanctity of female decorum and privacy. On the day appointed, seven hundred litters accompanied her to the royal camp; each was borne by six armed soldiers, disguised as porters, and contained a knight of Cheetore; the litters were deposited within the royal tents, and half an hour was allowed for the parting of the husband and his lovely wife. At the termination of the interview the former was placed in a litter to be taken back to the city, whilst the greater number of supposed handmaids remained to accompany their queen to Delhi.

The treachery of Alla hastened the result of the stratagem; for upon his endeavouring to prevent the return of Bheemsi, the Rajpoot warriors sprung ready armed from their litters, and attacked the Patan troops. A fierce and bloody contest ensued; a fleet horse conveyed their chief to Cheetore, and Pudmani was saved at the expense of the lives of nearly every knight and noble of Cheetore. The account of this siege affords a touching illustration of Rajpootni devotion, and of the lofty heroism that enables a wife to brave the bitterest death to preserve her husband from dishonour, and to gaze with emotions of deep joy upon the appalling rite of the suttee that is to reunite her in the warriors' paradise to the beloved object of her earthly devotion.

Amongst the fallen was Gorah, the uncle of Pudmani. When his nephew Badul, a stripling of twelve, returned with the survivors from the camp of Alla, the wife of Gorah questioned him about his uncle's conduct, ere she performed the last rite of suttee. "He was the reaper of the harvest of death," said Badul. "I followed his steps as the humble gleaner of his sword; on the gory bed of honour he spread a carpet of the slain: a barbarian prince his pillow; he laid him down, and sleeps surrounded by his foes." Again she said, "Tell me, Badul, how did my love behave?" "Oh mother! how further describe his deeds, when he left no foe to dread or admire him." She smiled farewell to the boy, and adding, "My Lord will chide my delay," sprang into the flame.

The Rajpoot capital is described as having been sacked three times and a half during Mussulman rule in India; this was the half sack of Cheetore, as though the city was not taken the flower of the nobility fell.

A few years later Alla again turned his arms against the Rajpoots, and on this occasion occurred the first saka, or sack of Cheetore the Immaculate. The defenders of Cheetore, weakened by his former onslaught, were unable to cope with the fresh legions of the steel-clad Khorasanes and Koreishis of Alla's army, who rolled on like the clouds of Bhadoon, and the city was taken.

The following legend describes its fall. "The child Lakumsi was dead, and Bheemsi was now sovereign; one night, after an arduous day, he was laying on his pallet pondering on the danger of his beloved country, when he was aroused by a voice exclaiming, 'I am hungry!' and his blood froze, as he recognised between him and the camp the form of the guardian goddess of Cheetore; 'not satiated,' exclaimed the Rana, 'though 8000 of my kinsmen were late an offering to you?' 'I must have regal victims,' answered the goddess; 'and if twelve who wear the diadem bleed not for Cheetore, the land will pass from the line.' Having said this she vanished. Next day he recounted his vision to his chiefs, who treated it as a disordered fancy; he commanded their attendance at midnight, when again the form appeared, and repeated the terms on which alone she would remain

BOOK I. 1300. amongst them; 'though thousands of barbarians strew the earth what are they to me? On each day enthrone a prince, let the emblem of royalty proclaim his sovereignty, and for three days let his decrees be supreme; on the fourth let him meet the foe and his fate, then only will I remain.'"

The Rana had twelve sons, and after a generous contest for priority, the eldest was proclaimed sovereign; for three days he reigned supreme, on the fourth he fell in battle; each in turn followed his noble example, and each in turn on the fourth day met his fate, until all but the youngest were slain. One more victim only was required; calling his chiefs around him, the Rana said, "Now I devote myself to Cheetore." No power could turn him; a chosen band was sent to cut a road through the enemy's ranks, and deposit his surviving son in safety; this being done he gave orders for the johur, or self-immolation of the women, the last refuge of conquered Rajpoots, in which thousands of the wives and daughters of Cheetore, including the fair Pudmani, died; the Rana then put on his saffron robe, the emblem of sacrifice, and set out with his chosen followers to meet a certain death.

Alla remained several days in Cheetore, sacking and destroying all the magnificent buildings of the Rajpoot capital. Of all the works of a highly-refined race, the palace of the noble Bheemsi and his spouse Pudmani alone escaped destruction. After the sack of Cheetore Alla turned his arms against the neighbouring state of Jessulmere; for eight months the capital held out against him; the blockade was perfect, and the privations of the besieged were terrible. When their sufferings were beyond endurance, Moolraj, the Prince of Jessulmere, assembled his nobles and thus addressed them: "We are the sons of the free, the blood of the Rhatore runs in our veins; shall we see our homes defiled, and our women dishonoured by a barbarian foe? For eight months we have defended our dwellings, but our supplies are expended, and there is no passage for more; what is to be done?" The chiefs replied, "There is but one refuge left, and that is the johur. We must immolate the females, destroy by fire and water whatever is destructible, and bury what is not, then open wide the gates, and, sword in hand, rush upon the foe, and thus obtain heaven." CHAP. XI. 1300.

Moolraj and his chiefs repaired to their palaces, and told the women their decision, and desired them to prepare to meet them in heaven.[12] Smiling, the queen replied, "This night we shall prepare, and by to-morrow's light we shall be the inhabitants of paradise."

The night was spent in preparations, and next morning, at the royal gate, were collected the young, those under sixteen, the middle aged, and those over forty; they bade a last farewell to their friends; the johur commenced, and 4000 females, from infancy to old age, surrendered their lives, some by the sword, others by fire; no one feared to die; every valuable was destroyed, and not the worth of a straw was preserved for the foe; three thousand eight hundred warriors with their faces red with wrath died with their chiefs.[13]

Whilst Alla was razing to the ground the fairest cities of Rajpootana and Guzerat, and his evil genius, Cafoor, was pillaging and devastating the fertile kingdoms of the Carnatic, a small cloud arose in the north-west, which, increasing in size and portent as it rapidly advanced, at last broke on the frontiers of his empire with a fury that threatened to carry all before it.

Ever since the passing ravages of the Great Khan, bands of fierce and hardy Scythians had continually been pressing down from the north of Asia and locating themselves on the frontiers of India, where, having embraced the creed of Mahomed, they were in large numbers added as mercenaries to the armies of the Sultan of Delhi.

Encouraged by partial success, and inflamed by the account of the wealth of Hindostan, in the year A.D. 1292, Cutterlich, son of the King of Transoxiana, crossed the

BOOK I. 1300. Indus with 200,000 horse, and almost reached Delhi. He was defeated by Alla, and Ziffer his general, at the head of 300,000 horse and 700 elephants. Ziffer pursued them a distance of thirty-six miles; but having at length outstripped his own troops he was surrounded by the Moguls, and after deeds of extraordinary valour, slain. When offered life and honour if he would yield, he replied, "he knew no greater honour than to die in discharging his duty." The terrible slaughter of the Moguls on this occasion caused the name of Ziffer to become a terror to their nation. And for centuries after, when his horse started or was unruly, the Mogul soldier would ask him if "he saw the ghost of Ziffer?"

The slaughter of the Moguls was very great, and for thirty miles the land was dyed with their blood. But notwithstanding their defeat and destruction many thousands of these hardy adventurers remained in Hindostan, where their northern energy and military character soon gave them great power over the enervated Affghans, who then ruled that country; but in the year 1300, in consequence of the discovery of a supposed plot to destroy and partition his kingdom, Alla gave orders for their extermination, and in one day the corpses of 15,000 Moguls cumbered the streets of the capital. Little did the timid citizens of Delhi, whilst gloating over the agonies of thousands of their enemies, brought to the capital to be trodden under foot like grasshoppers or dashed against the walls and dismembered by fierce elephants, imagine how soon the tables would be turned, and a like destruction come upon themselves; that e'er a hundred years had passed, terror and suffering should be the portion of their race; that a hundred of their descendants should flee before one of those they were now so ruthlessly slaying; that at the tramp of the Mogul panic should seize the city; "that a man should rise up at the voice of a bird, and fear should be in the way, and mourners go about the streets."

The able and unprincipled Alla was now growing old; the angel of death was close on his track; and cruel and ruthless as he had occasionally been he yet exhibited during the last years of his reign a solicitude for the welfare of his subjects that was rare in his age and country. Having summoned the great omrahs of his nation together, he took council with them; not this time how to enlarge his dominions, but how to increase the wealth and prosperity of what he already possessed.

According to the Persian historian, he was completely successful. The empire, says Ferishta, never flourished so much as in this reign; order and justice travelled to the most distant provinces, and magnificence raised her head in the land; palaces, mosques, universities, baths, and all kinds of public and private buildings seemed to rise as if by the power of enchantment; neither did there in any age appear such a concourse of learned men from all parts; forty-five, skilled in the sciences, were professors of the universities. Robberies and thefts, formerly so general, were now almost unknown. The traveller slept secure upon the highway, and the merchant carried his goods in safety from Cashmere to the Carnatic, and from the sea of Bengal to the mountains of Cabul.

Although through life a slave to intoxication, Alla discarded the vice in his old age. Edicts were issued forbidding the use of wine or strong drinks, under any circumstances whatever; and he coupled the pleasure of tippling with the pain of instant decapitation.

He himself set the example of total abstinence to his subjects, by emptying his cellars into the streets; in this he was followed by all ranks of his subjects, so that for days the common sewers of Delhi flowed with wine. He was an enterprising sovereign, and only abandoned his plans of universal dominion from the conviction, to use his own words, "that there were in the world many heads as hard as his own." He numbered his cavalry and found he had 475,000; to each man he paid from 80 to 240

BOOK I. 1300. rupees, according to the value of the horses and accoutrements, whilst his household servants amounted to 17,000.

The character of Alla was very equally balanced between good and evil; the man and the beast equally divided his nature: the resultant of these two opposing forces often compelled him to a middle course, under which, during a reign of twenty-one years, his subjects flourished and his empire attained prosperity.

Perfectly illiterate when he mounted the throne, he not only educated himself, but obliged his subjects to follow his example; he was so sensible of the disadvantages he laboured under, by his ignorance of letters, that he applied himself privately to study, and notwithstanding the difficulty of acquiring the Persian manner of writing, he soon read all addresses, and made himself acquainted with the best authors of his language. After he had proceeded so far as to be able to hold part in learned discourses, he encouraged literary subjects, and showed particular favour to all the eminent men of the age.

The great axiom of his internal policy was, that religion had no connection with civil government, but was only the business or solace of private life, and that the will of a wise prince was better than the variable opinions of bodies of men. He ordered a tax of half the real annual produce of the lands to be raised over all the empire, and to be regularly transmitted to the exchequer. He appointed officers to superintend the collectors, who were to take care that no more should be required from the farmers than was in proportion to the estimate which they had given in of their estates; and in case of neglect or disobedience the superintendents were obliged to refund the overplus and to pay a fine for the oppression. The farmers at the same time were confined to a certain proportion of land, and to an appointed number of servants and oxen to cultivate the same. No graziers were permitted to have above a certain number of cows, sheep, and goats, and a tax was paid out of them to the government. So strictly did the emperor look after the behaviour of the collectors and other officers of the revenue, that many of them who formerly kept great retinues were obliged to dismiss them, and to have all the menial offices of their families performed by their wives and children. Neither were they permitted to resign their employment till they found others as capable as themselves to execute the duties of their offices. These regulations were good, but they were arbitrary and severe. A murderer from his youth and a robber on the grandest scale, he yet suppressed theft throughout his dominions, and rendered life and property as secure in the thirteenth century as at present. In the year 1316, after a reign of twenty years, Alla gave up that life which like a comet had alternately inspired the terror and the admiration of his subjects; but not without suspicion of having been poisoned by his infamous favourite Cafoor.

NOTES TO CHAPTER XI.

[1] Contrast the following dying injunctions of the King of Israel: "Moreover, thou knowest also what Joab, the son of Zeruiah did to me. Do therefore according to thy wisdom, and let not his hoar head go down to the grave in peace. And, behold, thou hast with thee Shimei the son of Gera, &c., &c. Now therefore hold him not guiltless; for thou art a wise man, and knowest what thou oughtest to do unto him; but his hoar head bring thou down to the grave with blood."

[2] The followers of Mahomed never call themselves Mahomedans, as too familiar; but Mussulmans resigned, or muminians believers: thus they never call us Christians but Nazarenes or Nessora.

[3] The Great Prophet could neither read nor write, and all his writings were done by dictation, and many of them scratched on the bones of animals.

[4] Buddha was received into the Brahminical Pantheon, as one of the Avatars of Vishnu, but orthodox Brahmins disliked him, and he is now looked upon as an impostor in the temples of India.

BOOK I. 1291.

[5] One pagoda, 100 feet high and 500 feet in circumference, hewn out of the solid rock, of a sugar loaf form, was sculptured so as to represent fine lace, and was separated from its parent rock by an excavated area of several hundred feet.

[6] Ceylon was at this time ruled by Tamuls from the Malabar coast, and it is probable that all the tanks in that island are their work.

[7] An old Italian proverb about the greediness of the priests of Italy, already quoted, applies with full force to those of India; and to the four things mentioned by Solomon as being never satisfied, Brahmins might certainly be added.

[8] Ibn Batuta left Tangiers in A.D. 1324, and travelled to Delhi. When he arrived at the court of Mohammed, the vizier gave him 2000 dinars to have his clothes washed; not probably before they wanted it. He travelled through the greater part of Hindostan, the Deccan, Guzerat, and Malabar.

[9] Probably the ancestors of the present race, called Moplas, the most determined and energetic of all the inhabitants of India.

[10] Ibn Batuta tells us some of the junks had as many as 600 sailors and 400 soldiers. The commander was a great emir. In the large ships they sow garden herbs and ginger, which they cultivate in cisterns made on purpose, and placed on the sides of them. In these, also, are houses constructed of wood, in which the officers lived. "Generally speaking," says Ibn Batuta, "the Chinese are the richest people in the world."

[11] Tod.

[12] The sacrifice by which the women perform suttee before their husband's death is called the sohag or johur.

[13] This saka took place A.D. 1295. See Tod's "Rajasthan."

CHAP. XII.

A.D. 1321—1387.

THE REIGNS OF MUBARICK AND CHUSERO.—THE REIGN OF GHAZI TOGHLAK. —MOHAMMED III. TWENTY-SEVEN YEARS.— FEROSE III. THIRTY-NINE YEARS.

CHAP XII. 1321.

THE rapid decay of the Affghan rule in Hindostan dates from the death of Alla. The character of his immediate successor, Mubarick, was too infamous to deserve even the most passing mention in history; stained by every vice that can debase human nature, the most brutal deeds of Rome's worst emperors are eclipsed by his fiendish freaks. He beat to death the principal of the preachers, who was the keeper of the jewels, because he had been outwitted by some Hindoos; and some omrahs who spread the report of his death, which in those days was sufficient to have caused a revolution, were by his orders buried alive. They had buried him alive in jest, he said, but he would bury them alive in earnest. After a disgraceful reign of five years, he was assassinated by his minion Chusero, or Hasan, and the government of Hindostan passed from his hands into those of a monster as brutal as himself.

Chusero massacred all that remained of the race of Alla; but, at the end of five months, was defeated and slain by Ghazi Toghlak, the Patan governor of Lahore (a former slave of the emperor Balin, and son of a Jit woman), who was by the unanimous voice of the omrahs

BOOK I. 1321.

desired to mount the throne: the story is thus told. The day after the defeat of Chusero, Toghlak mounted his horse, and entered Delhi in triumph. When he came in sight of the royal palace, he began to weep, saying with a loud voice, "O ye subjects of this great empire, I am no more than one of you who unsheathed my sword to deliver you from oppression, and rid the world of a monster; my endeavours, by the blessing of God, have been crowned with success; if, therefore, any of the royal family yet remain, let them be brought that justice may take place, and that we his servants may prostrate ourselves before his throne. But if none of the race of kings have escaped the bloody hand of tyranny and usurpation, let the most worthy of the illustrious order be elected among you, and I shall swear to abide by your choice."

The people cried with one voice that none of the princes were now alive; that as he had shielded them from the rage of a tyrant, none was more worthy to reign than himself. Then, seizing him in a manner by violence, they placed him upon the throne, and hailed him by the title of Ghazi, King of the World. Under the fostering care of this excellent monarch a transient prosperity again spread over Hindostan, but it was of short duration; he was killed, after a reign of four years, by the falling in of a wooden pavilion, prepared by his son, Mohammed, to do him honour, and so contrived, that as soon as the throne in the centre should be pressed, the whole edifice fell to pieces.

Mohammed III. was a monster who walked in the footsteps of Alla the Sanguinary, and during twenty-seven years scourged the land of Hindostan. His reign, begun with parricide, was one continued course of bloodshed and cruelty. He took it into his head that he should be better served by those of low estate than by nobles, and accordingly he promoted a singer, a gardener, a weaver, a slave, and others to be omrahs, forgetting the advice of the sage, that he who exalts the head of a beggar, and hopes great things from his gratitude, inverts the nature of things, and nourishes a serpent in his bosom, &c.

Under this atrocious monarch, all the conquests of Alla were lost, and the empire of the Sultans of Delhi dwindled away to its former limits.

The heart of a tyrant is ingenious in devising fresh means of torture for his subjects ; but it required an Eastern training in the school of Alla and Mubarick to conceive that perpetrated by Mohammed.

Being much irritated by the rebellion of the inhabitants of Delhi, and particularly so at a letter they had written complaining of his exactions, he ordered the inhabitants to quit the city, and proceed to Dowletabad in the Deccan, distant forty days' journey. Upon some hesitation being evinced, he made a proclamation, that any person whatever, being an inhabitant of the city, and found in any of its houses or streets on a certain day, should receive immediate punishment. All left their homes ; but the king's servants finding a blind man in one of the houses, and a bed-ridden one in another, he commanded the former to be projected from a catapult, and the latter to be dragged by his feet to Dowletabad : but his limbs dropped off by the way, and only one of his legs was brought to the city and cast into it, to fulfil to the letter the order that every man should go to that place.

After years of desperation and suffering, when the greater number of those who had been thus forced from their homes and property into a strange land, and amongst a people who knew them not, had perished of hunger and want, he allowed the miserable remnants to return to Delhi, to find their noble city tenanted with beasts of prey, and their fertile fields barren wastes.[1] If Mohammed eclipsed Nero in ferocity, he at least equalled him in folly. The farce of installing a favourite

BOOK I. 1324.

horse in the consular dignity was quite exceeded by a freak of the monarch of Hindostan. During one of his marches in the Deccan, he was seized with a violent toothache, and having endured its extraction, he ordered it to be buried with much solemnity at Beir, and a magnificent mausoleum to be raised over it, where it still remains, a startling monument of human vanity and folly. Truly, " man, proud man, drest in a little brief authority, like an angry ape, plays such fantastic tricks before high heaven as make the angels weep."

In the north the hardy Moguls, undaunted by their repeated repulses, and still forced on by increasing numbers in their rear, kept continually pressing down on the fertile plains of Hindostan; whilst in the south the whole of the Deccan, with the exception of Dowletabad, threw off the Mussulman yoke; and the Hindoo population of the Carnatic and Mysore, dismayed by a report assiduously spread by the priests that the Mahomedans had formed a plan for the forcible conversion of all the worshippers of Brahma, rose *en masse*, and massacred or expelled every follower of the Prophet from their country.

For some years, the Deccan was almost entirely freed from Mussulman rule; and the city and fortress of Dowletabad constituted the sole remaining possession of the Sultan of Delhi south of the Nerbudda.[2] To meet the emergencies of his tyranny and prodigality Mohammed tripled the already grievous imposts on the people; but he overstrained the endurance, even of the patient ryots of Hindostan. Whole provinces were abandoned and became desolate, and the wretched inhabitants sought in inhospitable jungles and in a life of rapine a relief from exactions that were intolerable. But Mohammed was not to be thus baulked of his victims. Surrounding the districts where his wretched subjects had thus sought shelter with a cordon of his troops, as if for a great hunt, he gradually

1351.

contracted the circle, and destroyed all within it like wild beasts. This was repeated, till throughout whole provinces, once populous and fertile, man was exterminated, and the wild beasts of the forest resumed primæval sway. But with all his atrocious attributes Mohammed possessed qualities that have made his name famous in Indian history. Brave and skilful in all warlike exercises, his ambition was unbounded, and universal empire his aim. He made war on the grandest scale, and the Deccan, Persia, and China were by turns the objects of his cupidity and the graves of his armies.[3] He was a magnificent patron of learning, and the professors of philosophy, logic, and physic enjoyed at his hands a profusion never before equalled. His writings were numerous, and remarkable for elegance and vigour, and his memory was so extraordinary as to favour the belief that he knew the Koran by heart. He built almshouses and endowed hospitals, and himself attended the sick in order to study the symptoms of disease. But with all these brilliant attributes his heart was cruel as the grave; he spurned all laws of justice and humanity; he found pleasure in contemplating human suffering; and the misery of his subjects was by turns a subject of indifference or delight. At length, after a reign of twenty-seven years, during which time, says his historian, he laboured with no contemptible abilities to make himself detested by God and abhorred by all men, Mohammed died of eating too much fish at the termination of the feast of Mohurrum: fit ending for a monster cursed with such passions and instincts.

In Ferose III., the nephew of Toghlak and successor of the worthless Mohammed, one bright gleam of light burst through the murky atmosphere of imperial crime, and for nearly forty years illumines the departing glory of the Affghan dynasty. Ferose III., although of the most warlike tribe of the adventurous race of Affghans, was no warrior. He was a man of peace. The lust of conquest was un-

BOOK I. 1351.

known to him. He knew that "he that loveth silver shall not be satisfied with silver," and that "silver and gold and the peculiar treasures of kings and of the provinces do not bring happiness." And during a reign of thirty-seven years he sought in the arts of peace, in the cultivation of science, and the improvements of agriculture, the means of restoring that happiness and prosperity to his people which the ceaseless wars of his ancestors had banished from the kingdom.

The mosques that he built, and the gardens he laid out, the schools he endowed, the caravanserais and the hospitals, the baths and the tombs, the fifty canals and the hundred bridges, the hundred palaces and the hundred and fifty wells with which this enlightened monarch enriched and developed the resources of his kingdom, have most justly earned for him the enthusiastic commendations of historians. The good works of the enlightened Ferose did not pass away with the life of him who constructed them. The canal, a hundred miles in length, with which he connected the Sutlej and the Jidger, the seven splendid sluices at the Hissar Ferozebad, the gigantic cutting destined to irrigate and enrich the parched deserts of Sirhend and Loodiana, still remain to testify to his enlightened rule, and to indicate by evidence that cannot lie, by fertile lands and populous districts, how different might now be the condition of India had his successors followed in his steps.

The inestimable blessings of irrigation which science has conferred upon the plains of Lombardy, China, and the Carnatic, and by which nature has through all time enriched the Delta of Egypt, Ferose provided for many of the parched regions of Hindostan. The magical effect of an arctic spring, succeeding the dreariness of an eight months' winter, is not more startling than the progress and amelioration which follow any works of irrigation in India. Thousands of acres, that had before only produced one scanty harvest, now sent forth two abundant ones. Hundreds of thousands of inhabitants flocked from regions less blessed to those fruitful abodes of plenty; and soon the banks of the canals were lined with villages, the fruitful plains covered with cattle, and the name of the beneficent Ferose blessed by the lips of thousands of prosperous subjects.

Ferose levied a tax of a tenth of the produce of the land fertilised by the canals, which, together with the revenues of other districts newly brought into cultivation, he applied to charitable uses. Such was the example of philanthropy and enlightened policy, set by an Eastern autocrat, in the age that saw the Turks first enter Europe, and the rival Popes leave Avignon; in which Nicola Rienzi, last of Romans [4], galvanised into spasmodic life the scarcely animate remains of the queen city of the world.

Finding the infirmities of age pressing hard upon him, Ferose abdicated the throne in favour of his son Mohammed; but he lived to resume the reins of authority on the expulsion of that prince by the dissatisfied omrahs, and at their advice, to place his grandson, Toghlak, on the throne. He expired A.D. 1387, at the age of ninety-one, in the thirty-seventh year of his reign.

Nearly five hundred years have elapsed since Ferose reigned over a tenth of the territory we now possess. For the last fifty years the resources and revenues of the entire peninsula of India have been in English hands. In that period science has advanced with a bewildering rapidity that dwarfs in the far-off distance the mightiest intellects of the preceding generation, and the history of the world may be searched in vain for any corresponding progress of the human race. During these many years of almost universal amelioration, what has England done to enrich India, or even to maintain undiminished existing sources of prosperity?

Will the unprejudiced historian deny that the Affghan sovereign of that day was wiser in his generation, more

BOOK I. 1387.

philanthropical in his principles, more liberal in his plans and labours, and more worthy of the love of his subjects, and of the blessings of their children's children, than the body of merchant princes, who, satisfied with self-praise, have viewed with apathy, if not aversion, all plans for the improvement of India, and watched without shame the gradual decay of those wondrous monuments of industry and civilisation, over whose destruction even time still lingers, that provided water for a parched-up land, and converted arid wastes into some of the noblest provinces of the world.

The Lotos placed aloft in the thousand temples of India and Egypt demonstrates the strong traditional veneration for the aquatic element amongst a people who know no other want. Can we, in thus cruelly ignoring the great instinctive worship of our subjects, deny that we have deserved the enmity of millions of the present generation, or expect to escape the contempt of those who are to come.

Those who carefully and without prejudice will examine the present condition of public works in India, must acknowledge that the millions of India have more reason to bless the period of thirty-nine years passed under the Affghan Ferose, than the century wasted under the vaunted influence of the Hon. East India Company's rule.[5]

But even the beneficent rule of Ferose was unable to stay the march of corruption, and while he was doing his utmost to ease the burdens and improve the condition of his subjects, destiny, with her unswerving step, was completing the downfall of the Affghan dynasty.

The various northern races who had settled in the warm regions of Hindostan and founded the Mussulman empire, had, like all exotics, drooped, and lost their energy on a foreign soil. The Hindoo rajas no longer trembled before the fierce energy of the Moslem omrahs.

In many parts of the empire the flag of revolt was raised; the wealthy provinces of Bengal asserted their independence, and again the dominions of the haughty monarchs of Delhi dwindled to decay. CHAP. XII.

Mahmoud, the grandson of Ferose, was the last sovereign of the Affghan race that sat on the throne of Hindostan; and diminished as his ancestral empire had now become, he was not long allowed to enjoy it unchallenged. He had omitted the first and most necessary step for the secure possession of an eastern throne, in not destroying all the males of his family. He was opposed by Nuserit, another grandson of Ferose, and for a time the plots and counterplots and bloody contests of these candidates for sovereignty, who held their rival courts in Delhi, equalled those then raging between the Orsini and the Colonna in the streets of the Holy City itself. Their bitter contention received the quietus that generally attends disputes of that nature; whilst they were striving for the shadow, the substance was seized by one stronger than either; during their domestic strife, the crafty minister of Mahmoud, giving each of the rival claimants a shell, kept the pearl of possession for himself. 1393.

The sure sign of desolation exhibited by a kingdom divided against itself, like the death struggle of an animal in the great pampas of South America, soon attracts birds of prey, from regions far out of sight, to share the feast of corruption. Fierce animals, natural enemies at other times, on these occasions unite in making common cause to despoil a defenceless carcass.

Two hundred years before, the disunion of the Hindoo rajas, caused by the romantic enterprise of Pithowra, brought the Affghan to Delhi; and in turn their own dissensions attracted a foe more fierce and powerful than they.

BOOK I

1393.

NOTES TO CHAPTER XII.

[1] Ibn Batuta, who travelled in Hindostan during this reign, describes Delhi as "the greatest city in the world with the fewest inhabitants."

[2] The famous mosque of Delhi was originally a Hindoo temple.

[3] He sent an army of 370,000 horse, according to Ferishta, to Persia, but was obliged to disband them for want of pay.

He penetrated the Himalayas with 100,000 horse for the invasion of China, but was opposed by a Chinese army he dared not encounter; his troops perished through fatigue, famine, and disease, and scarcely a man survived to describe the disaster.

[4] Then turn we to her latest Tribune's name,
From her ten thousand tyrants turn to thee,
Redeemer of dark centuries of shame,
The friend of Petrarch, hope of Italy,
Rienzi! last of Romans!

[5] The magnificent works of irrigation left by the native princes of the Carnatic, in fourteen districts alone, represent a capital of fifteen millions! one of them is capable of supplying water for agricultural purposes to thirty-two villages for eighteen months. The following extracts from Colonel Cotton's report on public works of Madras show their present condition:—"So generally indeed have I found the works in a defective state, that I believe I may say that nearly all the tanks in the country, and nearly all the channels water less than they did; many only one-fourth, and great numbers from one-half to three-fourths." Again, in p. 6 of the same report. "The extent of irrigation may be judged from the fact, that in fourteen of the chief ryotwar irrigated districts, the number of tanks and channels considerably exceeds 43,000 in repair, besides 10,000 out of repair."

So that under the vaunted rule of England the natives of India have altogether lost one-fifth of the magnificent works of irrigation left them by their ancestors, and only derive one-half the former advantages of those that remain!

The fact is damning, indeed, when we consider that this has occurred in a land where the actual existence of millions depend upon the artificial supply of water; and that we had not to provide, but merely keep in repair, existing means of irrigation.

CHAP. XIII.

THE REIGN OF TIMOUR THE TARTAR, ALSO CALLED TAMERLANE. — HE INVADES INDIA, AND MAKES HIMSELF MASTER OF DELHI, THE CAPITAL OF HINDOSTAN. — HE DEFEATS BAJAZET, THE OTTOMAN EMPEROR. — HIS DEATH.

CHAP. XIII. 1398.

THE spectacle exhibited by the Affghan dynasty tottering to its fall did not long escape the notice of a conqueror more ambitious than Genghis and more ruthless than he of Ghizni, who, after a flight of uninterrupted conquest, was hovering over the banks of the Indus watching an opportunity to bury his talons in the tender flesh of Hindostan.

In the year 1398, very nearly 400 years after the invasion of Mahmoud of Ghizni, Timour the Tartar, at the head of a mighty army of Mogul horsemen, crossed the Nilab at Attock[1], and joined one of his grandsons who had already laid siege to Moultan.

From the earliest age at which the human mind displays its natural instincts, Timour[2], surnamed Leng from his lameness, aimed at universal empire. His father, of the noble tribe of Berlass, was hereditary chief of Kesh, the Green City, in the fruitful plains near Samarcand[3], and his mother was the fourteenth in lineal descent from Genghis, the great Khan.

The career of Timour commenced at the age of thirteen; at that of thirty-five he was at the Couraltai, or general diet, held on the plains of Akiar, close to his native city,

BOOK I. 1398. proclaimed lord and irresponsible monarch of the boundless regions and unnumbered millions of Central Asia.

The first twenty years of his life were passed in trials and hardships that would have broken the spirit of one less determined; but months and years of suffering and privation were unable to daunt the buoyant courage of the young Tartar, fostered in a superstitious age and community, by the sanguine predictions of the professors of the dark science of astrology: he was told that at his birth the planets quitted their orbits: and the title of Sahib Keraun, Lord of Auspicious Conjunctions was bestowed, on the young prince, whose wonderful destiny could change the eternal laws of heaven itself. But although Timour knew how to avail himself of the credulity of a superstitious age, his was not a mind to be warped by the worthless flattery of courtiers or the interested predictions of soothsayers. "I confide," said he, "in the assistance of the Almighty, who has never abandoned me; what avails the triplicity or conjunctions of the planets to me who never delay one moment the execution of my projects, when I have taken sufficient means and precautions to bring them to perfection?"

"The noise of a whip, and the noise of the rattling of the wheels, and of the prancing horses, and of the jumping chariots,"[4] the shouts of victory, the groans of the dying, the flames of cities, and the smell of death should herald the approach of the great Timour Beg on the stage of history. Every battle of the warriors, we are told, is with confused noise, and garments rolled in blood; but those of Timour were indeed with burning and fuel of fire.

Emerging from the dread city of Samarcand, that, standing in the very centre of the old world[5], has, apparently, in all ages been the capital of the empire of death, whence Azrael has, in his own season, sent forth on his bloody mission so many of the great scourges and conquerors of mankind, Timour[6], the destroying prince, willing servant of such a lord, had already overrun and depopulated half of

Asia. Iran and Persia, Georgia and Khorassan, the frontiers of China and Eastern Tartary had all in turn felt the power of his sword. The shores of the Caspian had been invaded, the tributary provinces of Russia occupied, and Moscow itself had trembled at the approach of the Mogul.

The invasion of Hindostan was merely an episode in a life of conquest, the passing whim of the victor of thirty-five campaigns, and from whose brow already flashed the glories of a score of conquered crowns. Arrived on the frontiers of India, Timour saw his opportunity, and thus cheerfully explained his views to his emirs: "Fortune, my dear friends, furnishes us with such happy conjunctions that she seems to offer herself to us and invite us to lay hold of the favourable opportunities which present themselves; for, as we have already seen Iran and Touran, and almost all Asia, under our command, she now shows us India, through the disorders of the princes who govern it, opening its gates to receive us. My name has spread terror throughout the universe, and the least motion I make is capable of shaking the whole earth, it is therefore time to attack the people of India, where, having overcome what opposes our designs, we shall oblige this kingdom to acknowledge no other sovereign but me. What think ye, my dear friends, who are the companions of my victories, of this great enterprise. Speak all in general and every one in particular your opinions of this proposal, which appears reasonable since fortune has not yet withdrawn her protection from us." They answered that the order of the emperor was a law to all men, and more particularly so to those who were his slaves; that wherever he should set his feet there they should be ready to lay their heads. Thus encouraged, he girded up his loins, and crossed the Attock, and began destroying the temples of India and giving currency to the Mahomedan religion in that country.

BOOK I. 1399.

Little more than five months was occupied by Timour in the invasion of Hindostan; but they were months of blood. Never, in his former conquests, had the fatal scythe of this colossus of blood reaped so heavy and unresisting an harvest of human life, or his destroying troops more fully exemplified the truth of the brutal boast of the devastating Alaric, that "thick grass was easier to cut than thin."[7] When the angel of death wishes "to sup full" of horrors he animates the soul of a conqueror or a fanatic. Nature, in her most avenging mood, is merciful compared to destroying man. No plague, no earthquake, no convulsion of nature, but that of the great flood itself, ever sent to their last account more of the human race in a few short months than did the swords of Genghis and Tamerlane and other fell destroyers of their species.[8]

Advancing steadily day by day by regular marches of thirteen miles, the country on either side bright with burning villages, his camp cumbered with captives and plunder, devastating like a flight of locusts, and leaving scarce a wreck behind, butchering from a love of blood, and destroying from a barbarous hatred of refinement, the exterminating legions of Timour approached the capital of Hindostan.[9] All the noble works that adorned her gorgeous cities were destroyed; and of all the teeming millions that inhabited her plains, the holy race of the Syeds [10], the lineal descendants of the great prophet of Mecca, were alone found worthy of mercy. In the great temple of Kukel, Timour broke the idol with his own hands; and when asked by the Brahmins to spare their god, he fiercely answered, "I will break your gods to give them an opportunity of performing a miracle by healing themselves."

Encamped before the city of Delhi, Timour gave orders for the prelude of the most frightful tragedy that even his mind, fertile in conceiving deeds of blood, had yet devised. On the 31st December, 1398, was perpetrated, in cold blood, one of the most appalling massacres that disfigure the bloody pages of Eastern history. In comparison with it, the murder of the innocents, the slaughter of St. Bartholomew's day, the blind fury of Attila and his Huns, the destruction of the Jews at Malaga, or of the Saracens in Jerusalem, sink into insignificance, and almost shine forth as deeds of mercy. The camp of Timour was full of prisoners, and fearing that, in the event of any reverse, they would rise against him, he commanded that all captives above fifteen years of age should be put to death, adding, that any who hesitated or refused to execute his command should themselves be slain, and their wives, children, and effects be given to whoever should inform against them. As soon as this diabolical command was made public, it was put into execution, and in less than an hour a hundred thousand Indians [11], according to the computation of the Mussulman historian, were put to death. So universal was this massacre, that Moulana Masareddin Amor, one of the most reverend doctors of the court, who could never consent so much as to kill a single sheep, was constrained to order fifteen slaves whom he had in his house to be slain.

Timour afterwards ordered that one soldier out of every ten should keep watch over the Indian women and children.[12] We stand amazed at the inhuman cruelty of the mind that could devise, and the ferocity of the hands that could execute, such a deed of blood. No excitement, no feelings of revenge prompted this wholesale atrocity: it was merely an act of deliberate policy, designed and executed with the indifference of the sportsman who ferrets his rabbits when they have become too numerous.

It was, moreover, the act of the man who tells us himself, that in his youth he had made a vow never wilfully to injure any creature, and that when he did so he was sorry for it; that, having one day unintentionally

BOOK I. 1399. trodden on an ant, he felt as if his foot had lost its power. If such was the treatment of those who had yielded, what would be the anticipated fate of those who presumed to defend their children and their gods?

"God," says the Persian historian, "was angry with the people of Hindostan, and he gave them Mohammed, a prince as unfit for the age in which he lived as he was unworthy of better times." Gathering from the terror of his subjects the obedience he could not exact in more peaceful times, and supported for once both by Mussulman nobles and the native rajas, this miserable monarch struck one blow for the birthright that had descended to him through twenty-two sovereigns of his race, and on the plains before Delhi made one gallant effort to defend his people and his throne; but the Affghan soldiers of Mohammed's armies were exotics. A long residence under the scorching sun of Hindostan had left them little of the ancient vigour of their race. Their creed and their love of display were all that remained to connect them with the fierce warriors who overran India under the monarchs of Ghor and Ghizni. They could not cope with their compatriots fresh from the invigorating plains and mountains of the north. Even the terrible aspect of the long lines of turreted elephants failed to awe men who had conquered every foe from the Indus to the Mediterranean Sea.[13] The elephants, terrified by fire-arms, were forced back on the foot soldiers. The army was driven with great slaughter into the city, and, according to the historian, "in a short time the field was covered with elephants' trunks, and the heads and bodies of the slain." Mohammed sought safety in flight, and the devoted inhabitants of Delhi capitulated under the vain promise that their lives should be spared.

Timour pitched his tents outside the city, and for several days carefully abstained from any attempt at pillage. Whether he ever intended to exercise the rare virtue of clemency, we can never tell: the man whose hands were still red with the blood of 100,000 prisoners; who at Bagdad, the abode of peace, could erect a pyramid of 80,000 human skulls, and at Aleppo could converse with perfect calmness on general questions of philanthropy, whilst the streets ran deep with the innocent blood shed by his licentious soldiers, cannot be credited with any great amount of consideration for a few hundred thousand more or less helpless women and children. He himself, both in the commentaries on his life and by the pen of his secretary, asserts his indignation at the want of faith exhibited by his troops. It is probable that his thoughts were more embittered by the sense of the immense booty the wanton barbarity of his soldiers had sacrificed, and by their individual exactions, which defrauded his treasury, than by any maudlin regrets for the thousands of lives they had destroyed. It would appear from some of the numerous accounts of this invasion that the women of his court were the unwitting causes of this massacre; that again, in the revolving circle of events, woman's curiosity brought woe into the world; and that, for a second time in the space of three hundred years, a woman was the teterrima causa of the destruction of Delhi.

Timour, mistrustful of the fierce nature of his troops, was encamped outside the city; but this did not at all suit the curiosity of the sultanas of his court, who, wishing to see the rarities of Delhi, and especially a famous palace adorned with a thousand pillars, built by an ancient king of India, went under a strong guard into the city, and, the gates being left open, upwards of 15,000 soldiers entered at the same time. Whether this was the accidental or intentional cause of the subsequent slaughter does not much signify. No sooner did these savage barbarians, brutalised by bloodshed and inflamed by fanaticism, make their way into the city, than deeds of rapine and murder, of which history, alas! has but too

BOOK I. 1399. many, were enacted throughout the city, and scenes of indescribable horror, like those that during the late mutiny made the blood of Englishmen run cold in their veins, were there enacted on a larger scale, and with greater numbers.

It was not then the extermination of a few hundreds by as many thousands; it was not so many curs worrying a sick lion; but it was the fury of thousands of the strong against tens of thousands of the helpless,—of a pack of ravening wolves amongst a fold of sheep.

The inhabitants of the city were ten to one to the Moguls, and at first they rose against their invaders; but undefended by their elephants, deserted by their sovereign and leaders, they were no match in street warfare for their hardy foes. Their desperate courage was soon cooled in their own blood[14]; abject terror paralysed the native mind; all opposition ceased, and "a lion amongst a herd of neat" did not lord it with more ferocity than did the Mogul amongst the Hindoos of Delhi. Hundreds were pillaged and driven by one man; and the same scenes of universal prostration and helpless agony, of brave men paralysed by fear and driven like sheep to the slaughter, that a few years later marked the career of the conquering bands of Cortes and Pizarro amongst the gentle aborigines of Mexico and Peru, were daily enacted in the streets of Delhi.

Fifteen days only were passed by the conquerors at the capital; but during those days the city was a shambles. There was a multitude of slain and a great number of carcases. The demon of destruction raged abroad unfettered; and the "mailed Mars did sit up to his ears in blood." The air resounded with the shrieks of the innocent and the helpless: every street ran with blood, and every house was the scene of some infernal barbarity or insolent exaction. On the 4th of January, 1399, Timour erected his standard on the walls, and, going in person to the gates of the capital, seated himself on the ancient musnud of the sultans of Delhi. Surrounded by scenes of bloodshed that would have blanched the cheek of one less steeled to sights of misery, the haughty Timour received the homage of suppliant princes, and decided the fate of prostrate kings. Here, in token of submission, were presented two white parrots that for seventy years had been handed down from one sovereign to another as emblems of supreme empire. Tame elephants and rhinoceroses were brought to kneel before him, as they had been in the habit of doing to the Indian sovereigns, uttering great cries as if imploring mercy; and whilst his pampered steeds, fed on bread and butter and sugar, and bowls of milk and rice[15], were stalled in the palaces of kings, and his rude soldiery quartered in pleasant gardens that till then had known only the footfall of the slippered denizens of the zenana, his architects took designs of the great mosque as a model for the one to be erected to the god of Mohammed at Samarcand.

Tamerlane never meditated a permanent settlement in Hindostan. His emirs, nurtured and hardened amongst the snows and frosts of Central Asia, dreaded the effects of the sultry heats of India: their children they feared would degenerate into a race of Hindoos. Moreover, Timour could brook no rival, however distant; and when Bajazet, the Ottoman conqueror, cast down the gage of battle for the prize of universal sovereignty, the lame Timour displayed no want of alacrity in picking it up.

Hastily quitting the deserted streets and smoking ruins of Delhi, Timour made a rapid detour of fire and sword through the country of the Upper Jumna. In seventy days from leaving Delhi he crossed the Indus on his return to Samarcand, and during one month of that period he is said to have gained twenty-seven battles and reduced seven castles of great strength. The rapidity of his marches appear incredible[16]; and hard indeed did he labour in his vocation of shedding blood.

But although his presence passed away like a hideous

BOOK I. 1399.

dream from the land of Hindostan, the merciless acts of his fierce soldiery were long remembered as the work of some mighty storm that had destroyed the land; not a family or an individual but had some separate tale of horror to haunt his sleeping and terrify his waking hours. The history of those fifteen days were written in letters of blood that fifty years could not obliterate. For generations the memory of the great Beg was a tower of strength to the invading Moguls; and his name a Medusa's head that paralysed the strongest arms and turned into stone the boldest hearts of Hindostan. Years after the mighty conqueror was summoned to give his last account of his merciless career, the haughty words and ferocious gestures, the thick fingers and long legs, the flashing eyes and piercing voice of this man of blood were described with faltering tongues and blanched cheeks by the dusky matrons of Delhi.[17] What the name of Richard of the Lion Heart[18] was to the Frenchmen of the days of the crusades, that of the Black Douglas[19] to the border nurses of England, or that of Dhannagee Jodow, the great Mahratta, to the later races of the Moguls, that for centuries was the name of the lame Timour to the still terrified natives of Hindostan.

Timour remained but a short time at Samarcand, whence, with an army thirteen miles in breadth, he extended his conquests westward through Persia and Armenia, till the Mogul and Ottoman powers clashed in the neighbourhood of Erzeroom, and Bajazet and Timour met face to face on the field of Anjonia.

The haughty tone of the correspondence of Bajazet and Tamerlane getting more inflated and insulting as they approached each other, reminds us of the almost fabulous pride of Attila or Xerxes.[20] Such missals, although professedly written to unite the two great Mussulman powers in the laudable purpose of extirpating Christianity throughout the world, could only have the effect of increasing the mutual jealousy of the rival sovereigns. The contact of flint and steel was not more certain to cause fire than the meeting of two such spirits to end in battle. They fought on the fields of Anjonia; but the result had been foreshadowed in the past campaign, in which Timour had, in seven days, reduced a fortress that had occupied the sultan seven years. The personal valour and chivalrous bearing of Bajazet could stand no chance against the overwhelming power and irresistible energy of such a warrior. CHAP. XIII. 1399.

Timour triumphed with great slaughter; and while he and his secretaries boast of his clemency, history disfigures his victory with indiscriminate massacre, and a captive monarch in an iron cage.[21] Towards the close of his career the conquering Timour returned to his capital to celebrate the marriage of his six grandsons, and to hold high festival amongst the khans and kings of his mighty empire. Possessor of twenty-eight crowns, and lord of the Eastern world, Timour was indeed one who, like the great Triumvir, could afford "to give a kingdom for a mirth;" and for two months Samarcand became the scene of the most gorgeous barbaric festival probably ever held.

Universal dominion, the spoils of unnumbered conquests, the offerings of a prostrate world, combined to render this one of the most magnificent pageants ever seen. During this festive season the dread gates of the Green Palace[22] were closed, and the Turquoise Gates and Porcelain Pavilion open to all comers. The heart-delighting gardens of the imperial palace ran with karmiz[23], hippocras, brandy, wines, and other liquors. The wood of several large forests was cut down to dress the victuals of the banquet, which lasted two months. That joy might be universal, and liberty untrammelled, the crier read a proclamation as follows: "This is the time for feasting, pleasure, and rejoicing. Let no

BOOK I. 1399. one complain of or reprimand another; let not the rich encroach on the poor, or the powerful on the weak; let none ask another why have you done thus?"

"The orders of the state, the nations of the earth," says the haughty chronicler of those days of Eastern triumph, "were marshalled at the banquet; neither were the ambassadors of Europe excluded; for even the smallest fish[24] have their place in the sea."[25] From that day no man was allowed to drink wine. Soon after this august celebration of universal dominion the great conqueror was summoned to his account. Stretched on the bed of death Timour calmly awaited the fate he had so unmercifully spread through the world. "At night, between evening prayer and bed-time (that is about eight o'clock), he several times made profession of his belief, "There is no other god than God;" then he gave up his soul to the angel Azrael, who called him in these words: "Oh soul, that hopes in God, return to thy Lord with resignation. We belong to God and must return to Him." Although Timour never exercised any absolute authority in Hindostan, those rajas and governors who had submitted to him continued to rule in his name. The money of the capital was stamped with his image, and the name of the mighty Beg was still invoked in the mosques, and cursed in the temples of Hindostan.

No sooner had the Moguls departed than, unwarned by the past, old animosities were rekindled, and the several claimants revived their pretensions to the throne; but after two or three years of intestine war and domestic treachery, the miserable Mahmoud was left sole monarch of his decimated capital.

Crushed and ruined as Delhi now was, her empty streets and dilapidated palaces formed a fitting abode for the diminished grandeur of the monarchs of Hindostan. The fierce inroad of Timour had swept away the existing landmarks, and shaken to its very centre the rickety fabric of the slave dynasty; and it needed only the subsequent flight of Mahmoud, and the suicidal discord of his nobles, to bring it headlong to the ground. CHAP. XIII. 1414. 1447.

Taking advantage of the utter disorganisation that overspread the country, nearly all the rajas had asserted the independent sovereignty of their provinces; and one by one the wealthy districts of Oude, Canouje, Guzerat, and Malwa, started into kingdoms under the nobles of Mahmoud, or the lieutenants of Timour.

For ten years after the invasion of Timour, Mahmoud survived, the puppet of an ambitious vizier, and the victim of unnumbered plots: fit representative of the fallen glories of his race. His reign lasted twenty years, and was one of the most disastrous that India had yet seen. "God was angry with the people of Hindostan," says the Persian historian, "and he gave them Mahmoud, whose only virtue was, that his folly made him insensible to those shocks of fortune which abilities much greater than his could not perhaps avert."

At the death of Mahmoud the capital was seized by Chizor Khan, a Syed or lineal descendant of the Prophet, —the highest and most venerated caste, that gives the possessor a peculiar sanctity in the eyes of all men. His father had been a powerful omrah at the court of Ferose, and was by him appointed viceroy of the Punjaub. Chizor was succeeded by his son Chizor, whose right was established by Timour.[26] The dynasty of the Syed lasted thirty-six years; and during that period the kingdom of Delhi was nominally a province of the mighty empire of the Moguls. Coins were struck, and the Khutbah read in the names of Timour and his sons; and a yearly tribute sent to Samarcand. During the reign of Alla, the last of the Syeds, the territory of the kings of Delhi was at its minimum, and consisted merely of the district immediately surrounding the capital. Four of this holy race, neither better nor worse than the ordinary occupants of the throne of Hindostan, succeeded in rais-

BOOK I. 1450.

ing the umbrella of empire above their heads; but the fourth (Alla II.)[27] could not endure the cares and duties of an Eastern throne, and in 1450 abdicated, either by choice or compulsion, in favour of Beloli, an Affghan of the Lodi tribe,—a great feudal chief, who had been adopted by his father Mohammed V.

From their geographical position, the Affghans profited more that any other nation by the overland trade of India; and the wealth and power thus acquired by their princes, was one of the chief reasons of their lengthened supremacy in Hindostan. The tribe of Lodi was especially enriched by it; and for many generations the family of Beloli had been amongst the most powerful of the northern feudatories of Hindostan. His grandfather was viceroy of Moultan, his father governor of Lahore, and his uncle Islam, who ruled at Sirkind, retained 12,000 warriors of his tribe at his own expense.

There was something portentous in the birth of Beloli; and from his early youth the chance words of a madman directed his thoughts to the throne. His mother was killed by the fall of a house a few days before her confinement was expected, and Beloli was saved by the Cæsarian operation performed by his own father. One day when yet a child he went with his companions to visit a famous dervish, who, amongst other disconnected ravings, called out, "Who will give me 2000 rupees for the empire of Delhi?" Beloli answered, that he had only 1600 rupees in the world, but was ready to part with them at that price. The dervish accepted the money, and laying his hands on Beloli, saluted him king. Beloli silenced the ridicule of his companions, by saying, that if the thing came to pass, he had made a cheap purchase; if not, the blessing of a holy man could do him no harm.

He reigned thirty-eight years, and was succeeded by his brother Secunder: during his reign religious persecution, that had ceased many years, was revived in Delhi. A Brahmin being abused by a Mahomedan for his idolatry, answered that he esteemed the same God to be the object of all worship; and therefore believed the Mahomedan and Hindoo religions to be equally good. For the impiety of this answer he was summoned before the judge, and the affair making some noise, Secunder called together all the Mahomedan doctors of fame in the empire to decide the cause; after much weary argumentation they pronounced the liberal judgment, that the Brahmin should be forced to turn Mahomedan, or be put to death: he refused to apostatise, and died a martyr to the faith of his ancestors. This act was followed by a general destruction of Hindoo temples, and the erection of mosques in their stead; but the religious persecution was entirely confined to the territories of Delhi, which at that time were fortunately very limited.

Secunder abandoned Delhi, and moved his court to Agra, which thus for the first time became the capital of the sovereigns of Hindostan. He reigned twenty-four years, and was succeeded by his son Ibrahim, a haughty, tyrannical prince, whose cruelty and inefficiency paved the way for the advance of Baber, by whose victorious arm he fell on the fatal field of Paniput, after a disastrous reign of twenty years; when Delhi, and all that remained of the great Mussulman empire of India, finally fell into the hands of the descendants of Timour, A.D. 1526.

NOTES TO CHAPTER XIII.

[1] Attock, 600 miles from Delhi, signifies "Forbidden," strict Hindoos being forbidden to cross it.

[2] Timour means iron.

[3] The valley of Samarcand was one of the four paradises. Damascus, Obolla in Chaldea, and Schab Bowian in Persia, were the three others.

BOOK I. 1526.

[4] Naham, ch. iii. v. 2.

[5] The circumference of a circle, described from a centre at Samarcand, with a distance at Madras, will pass through Cairo, Constantinople, Moscow, and Madras, and comprise a considerable part of Tartary and China.

[6] A name given him in India. The destroyer of Astracan, Carizme, Ispahan, Bagdad, Aleppo, Damascus, Brousa, Smyrna, and a thousand other places.

[7] When Alaric heard that thousands were daily dying in Rome, he retired, saying he was sorry for it, as "thick grass was easier cut than thin." When asked what he would spare, he said, "Perhaps their lives."

[8] Cæsar is said to have killed a million; Mahmoud II. three millions; Genghis is said to have killed fourteen millions; and Bartholomœus a Casa, a Spanish bishop, says his countrymen, in forty-two years, urged by the love of gold, but ostensibly in the name of religion, destroyed upwards of twelve millions of men in South America.

[9] The march occupied two months.

[10] Syeds. See Ali Hassan and Hossein.

[11] These numbers must be exaggerated.

[12] On occasion, this strange conqueror could show equal generosity. After the defeat of Bajazet, A.D. 1403, as he was passing through Ardebyl, on the way home, he was visited by a celebrated Mussulman saint, called Shykh Sudder Addyn Seffy, and, at the termination of the interview, the emperor asked him "What he could do for him?" The saint replied, "Liberate your captives." The emperor answered, "I not only liberate them, but give them to you." He did so; and these persons, amounting to 40,000, became devoted adherents of the saint, who was a descendant of Ali, and head of the Syeds. The fact was, human life possessed no value in his eyes; and it made no difference to him whether he gave away 40,000 prisoners or killed them.

[13] An amusing anecdote is related in Timour's biography of this action. The Mogul soldiers were not much disturbed about the Indian army; but as they had never seen any elephants before, they ignorantly imagined that arrows and sabres had no effect on the bodies of these animals; that they were so strong that they could overthrow trees only by shaking the earth as they passed along; that they could shove down the strongest buildings; and that in battle they would toss both horse and horsemen to a vast height in the air. This dispirited many, so that when the posts were fixed for the officers and lords of the court, Timour, who always showed respect to the men of learning about him, civilly demanded of them what posts they would choose. Several of these doctors, who were always near Timour's person, being frightened at what they had read and heard of the elephants, answered immediately: "If it please your Majesty, we choose to be near the ladies." See history of Timour by Cherefedin Ali of Yezd, his contemporary, translated by M. Petit de la Croix.

[14] Dow from Ferishta.

[15] Human flesh, the food of the mares of Diomed, would have been nourishment more suited to the steeds of such a warrior as Timour. The horses of warriors have, in all ages, received the greatest care from their lords when living, and not unfrequently shared the honour of his grave when dead. The anxious Andromache appears to have bestowed more exciting food than bread and butter on the horses of Hector:—

"For this, high fed, in plenteous stalls you stand,
Served with pure wheat, and with a female hand;
For this my spouse, of great Acteon's line,
So oft has steeped the strengthening grain in wine."

Selim, the son of Solyman the Magnificent, gave his horses some powder to snuff up at his father's death, in order that they might weep as well as his relations.

[16] He marched 100 miles from Adjodin to Ballinigi in one day. On the 5th September, 1393, he marched eighty miles without a halt, swam the Tigris, and took Bagdad. Turkomans have been known to march 1000 miles in ten consecutive days.

[17] He was corpulent, tall, had a large head and ample forehead; his countenance was agreeable and complexion fair; long beard; strong and well-limbed; broad shoulders, thick fingers, and long legs. Amazing constitution, but maimed in one hand and lame in one leg; eyes full of fire, voice loud and piercing.

[18] "Qu'as-tu? Vois-tu le Roi Richard?" was the common expression of a Frenchman, of the days of the crusades, when his horse started.

[19] "Dost see the Black Douglas?" was the cry of English nurses in the days of Robert the Bruce to children who required a bogie, at present specified as the policeman up the street, to quiet them. Dhunnagee Jodow was a famous Mahratta chief in the seventeenth century. He was perpetually harassing the camp of the Moguls, and the mere rumour of his approach was sufficient to put the largest number of them to flight. When a horse refused to drink, it was a common saying amongst Moguls: "Of what are you afraid? One would suppose you saw Dhunnagee in the water."

[20] The message Attila sent to the Emperor of the East and West was delivered in these words by his ambassador: "Attila, my lord and thy lord, commands thee to prepare a throne for his immediate reception." Xerxes wrote to Mount Athos: "Thou haughty Athos, that liftest up thy head to the skies, presume not to oppose my labourers with stones, through which they cannot hew, or I will tear thee from thy foundations, and cast thee into the sea." The same spirit prompted him to order the Hellespont to receive 300 lashes for destroying his bridges, and made Cyrus divide the river Gyndes into 360 courses for drowning one of his sacred horses of the sun.

[21] When Bajazet was conducted to Timour he regarded him attentively, and perceiving that he was blind of an eye, he burst out laughing. "You laugh at my disgrace, Timour," said Bajazet, haughtily; "but remember it might have happened to you equally as it did to myself. God is the disposer of events, and it is He who distributes them." "I do not doubt it," answered Timour, with equal pride; "and it is not your misfortune that causes me to laugh, but the idea that crosses my mind on looking at you. States can, indeed, be of very little importance in God's eyes, since He is willing that a lame man should enjoy what he had given to a blind. See letter of Aurungzebe to Shah Jehan.

[22] The Green Palace at Samarcand, built by Timour, where rivals or relatives were killed, or the fire pencil applied to their eyes.

[23] Karmiz, the favourite drink of the Tartars, made of mares' milk.

[24] Cassos, little animals about the size of a barley-corn, which are seen upon the surface of the sea.

BOOK I. 1526.

[25] This feast is described in Timour's biography, quoted. Also by Ruy Gonzalez de Clavijo, a gentleman of the bed-chamber to King Henry III., King of Castille, who went on an embassy to Samarcand in 1403, and returned in 1408. His book was entitled—"Historia del Grand Tamerlan e dinarario y enanacion del viago y relacion de la Embasada que Ruy Gonzalez de Clavijo le hizo par mandedo del muy poderoso Senor Ruy don Enrique a Juana di Castilla-Sevilla, 1582.

[26] The Syeds maintain that the mantle of the Prophet fell on his nephew Ali, and was continued in a direct line through his descendants. Between them and the Sheahs, or worshippers of the race of the Kalifs, exists to this day a bitter feud.

	A.D.	
[27] Chizor, a Syed of the Punjaub, succeeded Mahmoud	1414.	Died naturally.
Mubarick, son of Chizor	1421.	Assassinated.
Mohammed V., grandson of Chizor	1433.	Died naturally.
Alla II., son of Mohammed V. . .	1447.	Abdicated in favour of Beloli, adopted son of Mohammed V., and died in peace.

CHAP. XIV.

A.D. 1347—1422.

HISTORY OF THE DECCAN.—THE MUSSULMAN DYNASTY FOUNDED IN 1347, BY ALLA BAHMINEE.—HE IS SUCCEEDED BY HIS SON MAHMOUD SHAH JEE.—THE REIGNS OF MUJAHID, DAROOD SHAH, MOHAMMED BAHMINEE, AND GHEAS.—FEROSE, SON OF DAROOD SHAH, ASCENDS THE THRONE IN 1397, AND REIGNS TWENTY-FIVE YEARS.

CHAP. XIV. 1347.

THUS far our attention has been chiefly confined to the north and north-western portions of India. Hindostan proper[1] has been the great battle-field, and Delhi, Agra, Canouje, and Lahore the prizes lost and won in the incessant contests of dynasties and religions. But before we enter on the golden age of Hindostan, we should cast a cursory glance over the southern, and scarcely less wealthy, portion of the peninsula, and consider the rise of those magnificent kingdoms south of the Nerbudda, that for 300 years defied all attempts at subjugation, and whose sovereigns vied in power and magnificence with those of Hindostan itself.

In the year 1309, Alla the Sanguinary invaded the country south of the Nerbudda, and established Mussulman supremacy in the Deccan. Thirty years later, this portion of the empire asserted its independence, and for upwards of 300 years was a constant source of danger and anxiety to the monarchs of Hindostan.

In the year 1345, during the reign of the abandoned Mohammed Toghlak, Guzerat rebelled, and many of the nobles fled to the Deccan, to escape the cruelty of their

BOOK I. 1347.

sovereign, and took service with his lieutenant, Kutullick Khan. Mohammed despatched his general, Ahmed Sacheen, with an army against the malcontents; but they defeated him with great slaughter, and being joined by the nobles of Berar, and some native rajas, they assembled at Dowletabad, and proceeded to the election of a sovereign.

Their first choice fell on an Affghan noble, named Ismael; but in consequence of a defeat he sustained from the generals of Mohammed, he abdicated the year following, assuming, in the place of the kingly title, that of Ameer-al-Omrah, or chief of the nobles.

Zuffier Khan, a general of Ismael's, was now unanimously elected to the throne of the Deccan, by the name of Sultan Alla Houssun Kangoh Bahminee, or Brahminee; the black umbrella, the colour of the Abasside Caliphs, was raised over his head, and the khutbah read, and coins struck in his name.

This happened in the year A.D. 1347, fifty-two years after Alla the Sanguinary first conquered Dowletabad. Houssun was originally an inhabitant of Delhi, and a dependant of Kangoh, the astrologer, a Brahmin high in the favour of Mohammed Toghluk; and in gratitude to his former master and benefactor he adopted his name, and thus by a strange contradiction Bahmine, or Brahminee, the distinctive name of the highest caste of Hindoos, was borne by the first Mussulman dynasty of the Deccan.

Kangoh, the Brahmin, was made treasurer of the new kingdom, and, as a rare distinction, his name, joined to that of the Sultan, was affixed to all edicts.

The introduction of a new religion amongst the rulers of Hindostan would naturally interfere considerably with the monopoly of the good things hitherto enjoyed by the Brahmins. They could no longer devote themselves, as a privileged class, enjoying superior advantages to the sovereign himself, in idleness and affluence, to religion, sensuality, and the sciences, but were often compelled to contest the battle of life with their baser-born brethren. Their superior education, however, opened to them fields of emolument closed to less intellectual orders.

Kangoh was the first Brahmin who took service with a Mussulman prince; but from that date Brahmins were engaged almost exclusively in the taxation and finance of the Mussulman kingdoms of the Deccan.

At the period of the foundation of this new monarchy, the whole southern portion of the peninsula, from Goa on the one side to Orissa on the other, down to Cape Comorin, owned the sway of the Rajas of Beejanuggur: their kingdom was populous, perfectly cultivated, and probably the richest in the world; their subjects were obedient and laborious, and the cyclopean remains of tanks and other works of public utility, that even now astonish the beholder, prove at once the enterprise of the people, and the beneficial nature of the government.

The Rajas of Malabar, Ceylon, and all the southern provinces, owned the supremacy of the Raja of Beejanuggur; and, for 700 years, this superb patrimony had descended lineally in the family of Kishna Raja.

The new Mussulman kingdom comprised the northern parts of the Deccan and Concan, and Koolburga, or Kalberga, near Hyderabad, was selected as the capital, and soon became the rallying point of all the Mussulmans of the Deccan.

Sultan Houssun Bahminee was a good sovereign, and presented a great contrast to Mohammed Toghlak, his contemporary on the throne of Hindostan. He was a prince of great learning, and carefully encouraged education throughout his dominions. One of his first principles of government was, that in all countries the pen ranked with the sword; and on one occasion being asked, how, without treasures or armies, he had acquired royalty in so short a space, he replied, by affability to friends and

BOOK I. enemies, and by showing liberality to all, to the utmost of his power.

1358. 1365. He was a man of peace; but towards the end of his reign he made one successful inroad into the Carnatic, and returned laden with the truly Eastern spoil of 200 elephants and 1000 female singers. He died in 1357, after a successful reign of eleven years.

Mohammed Shah Bahminee, his son, was a man of war. He made several hostile incursions into the neighbouring kingdoms of Goa and the Carnatic; and in the year A.D. 1365, in a drunken whim, lighted the flame of the fiercest contest between Mussulmans and Hindoos that had convulsed India since the days of Mahmoud of Ghizni. "One evening, when the spring of the garden of mirth had suffused his cheek with the rosy tinge of delight," or when, like King Ahasuerus, his heart was merry with wine, a band of musicians sang two verses in praise of kings, festivity, and music. The Sultan was delighted beyond measure, and commanded his minister to give to the musicians an order for a large sum on the treasury of his neighbour, the Raja of Beejanuggur, the most powerful of the independent princes of southern India.

The raja naturally treated the messenger with contempt, and marshalled his army to revenge the gross insult offered to his dignity. For a whole year a fierce religious war devastated these fair regions; the injunctions of their Prophet and the prospect of paradise, inspired the enthusiasm of one side, whilst the wanton slaughter of cows and the violation of temples and shrines, excited the fierce enmity of the other. No quarter was shown on either side, and even pregnant women and children at the breast did not escape the sword; we are told that 10,000 Brahmins and 200,000 Hindoos of inferior castes, were thus sacrificed to the whim of an Eastern king. The war ended in the total defeat of the Hindoos, the reduction of Beejanuggur, and the payment of the musicians by the defeated raja; when Mohammed heard of this termination of this gratuitous war, he merely exclaimed, "Praise be to God, that what I ordered has been performed; I would not let a light word be recorded of me in the pages of time." CHAP. XIV. 1365.

Owing to the atrocities committed in this war, an oath was sworn between the Hindoo and Mussulman princes, never to put to death a single prisoner after victory; well would it have been for this devoted land, if this holy compact had been faithfully observed. It was calculated that during his sanguinary wars, upwards of half a million Hindoos were slain, and so depopulated were portions of the Carnatic, that a century did not restore them to their former prosperity.

The Deccan was at this period, and has ever since been, famed for banditti. Mohammed tried hard to extirpate them, and during six or seven months, nearly 8000 heads were brought to Kalberga, and piled into a ghastly pyramid outside the gates; as a natural consequence the number of these offenders considerably diminished.

Mohammed's headlong career was thwarted by a haughty priest, whose independence of the sovereign power, reminds us considerably of our own proud churchman Thomas à Becket. In the third year of his reign the Sultan issued a proclamation, commanding all his subjects, of whatever degree, to repeat the oath of loyalty; all obeyed save a famous faqueer of Kalberga, called Shiekh Ein-ad-Dien, who refused, unless the Sultan should first give up drinking wine in public, discourage vice from his dominions, and avoid other errors repugnant to the divine law. When brought before Mohammed, and questioned regarding his refusal; he replied that once a scholar, a Syed, and a dancing girl were taken prisoners together by infidels, who promised to spare them if they would fall prostrate before their idols; threatening, if they refused, to put them to instant death. The scholar, agreeably to the casuistry of mental reservation, performed the ceremony, and the Syed also; but when it came to the turn

BOOK I. 1375.

of the poor dancing girl, she refused saying, "I have all my life been committing sins, and am neither a scholar nor a Syed, to atone for this crime by my other virtues." She therefore suffered. The Sheikh Ein-ad-Dien said, that his past life had not been sufficiently holy, to warrant his taking this liberty with his conscience; and that, like the dancing girl, he was resigned but firm in what he considered his duty. Mohammed excused him, and was so pleased with his courage and integrity, that he soon after promoted him to high dignity in the state.

Although only the second of his dynasty, Mohammed Khan was the richest sovereign of his race; he wrested from the Hindoo rajas and princes of southern India the accumulated wealth of centuries. He was possessed of the enormous number of 3000 elephants, and he sat on a throne made of ebony and inlaid with splendid jewels, that in value almost equalled the famed peacock throne of Agra.[2] Every year he was in the habit of making a tour of one quarter of his dominions, escorted by the governor and public officers; the time was employed in investigating the state of the provinces, redressing complaints, forming places of public utility, and in the pleasures of the chace.

Mohammed reigned seventeen years, and though terrible to his neighbours, his domestic policy contrasted most favourably with that of the contemporary sovereign of Hindostan. He was succeeded by his son Mujahid, A.D. 1375, the Rustum or Wallace of that age and country. Mujahid trod closely in the steps of his father, and from his youth up, his whole thoughts and vocabulary were of war and war's alarms. He was the strongest man in his dominions; and when quite a lad he slew a tiger of unwonted size and ferocity with a single arrow. When only fourteen years, one of the high officers of the court punished him at his father's request; he said nothing at the time, and even treated him with marked kindness; but some time afterward, during some public sports at the palace, he challenged him to wrestle, when he threw him and broke his neck. CHAP. XIV.

He renewed the war with the Raja of Beejanuggur, and penetrated as far as Seet Bundar Ramessa, on the Coromandel coast, opposite Ceylon; a spot sacred amongst Hindoos, as the scene of the exploits of their god Rama. Here he rebuilt the mosque erected by Alla the Sanguinary, about sixty years previous, which the Hindoo pilgrims had of course destroyed. 1378.

During this expedition he performed an exploit almost similar to that of Robert Bruce before the arrayed armies at Bannockburn. Having gone out to reconnoitre an opposing host of Hindoos with a single attendant, a raja of great valour and renown attempted to surprise and slay him. Mujahid seeing his intention sent back his attendant, and waiting for his assailant, with one blow of his sabre divided him from the shoulder to the navel. After a reign of three years during which the sword was seldom out of his hand, he was murdered by his uncle Daood Khan, who immediately mounted the throne. The death of Mujahid was the cause of great rejoicing amongst the Hindoos, who immediately turned their arms against the territories of his successor. After a reign of one month and five days Daood Khan was assassinated whilst prostrate at prayer, at the instigation of Rhuperwer Ageh, the "Refresher of the Soul," sister of the late Sultan. Rhuperwer Ageh now immediately raised Mohammed Bahminee, son of Alla, to the throne. He was humane, virtuous, and just; his empire remained at peace, and good government prevailed. He was the husband of one wife, and was a staunch supporter of his faith and its teachers. During his reign the poets of Arabia and Persia resorted to Deccan; and even Hafiz, the renowned bard of Shiraz, accepted an invitation to visit Kalberga; and had actually embarked for India when the roughness of the ocean deterred him; he returned to Shiraz, and contented himself with sending the following philosophical ode, for

BOOK I. 1397.

which the Sultan sent him the munificent sum of 1000 pieces of gold.

"The breeze of my garden is not to be purchased by the possession of gold.
My companion rebuked me, and said: Quit this spot? What whim hath possessed thee that thy cell is not to be valued?
Yonder royal crown, on which is set danger of life, is an heart-enticing ornament; but not worthy my loss of head.
From desire of pearls, the danger of the sea appeared easy to me; but I mistook; for one wave is not to be appeased by treasures of gold.
Is my heart dispirited in the assembly of friendship? All the gildings of art are not worth a cup of generous wine.
If Hafiz chooses to retire from the world contented with little, hundreds of pieces of gold are not worth one instant of vexation."

Mohammed was charitable as well as generous: he founded and endowed schools for orphans in all the great towns; he pensioned all the blind in his dominions, and during a severe famine he kept 10,000 bullocks, at his own expense, to carry grain to his suffering subjects. During his reign the kingdom had peace; and during a period of nearly twenty years there was only one slight disturbance throughout his dominions. Gheas succeeded his father, but almost immediately fell a victim to the ambition of Lallcheen, a Turkish noble.

The beautiful and accomplished daughter of Lallcheen had excited the passion of Gheas, who desired her in marriage. Lallcheen appeared honoured at the admiration of the young monarch, and invited him to his house, ostensibly for the purpose of giving him an opportunity of enjoying the society of his daughter, and of making arrangements for the marriage; but when the prince was overcome with love, or wine, or both, he attacked him with a dagger, and with the assistance of a eunuch, pierced out both his eyes: he then sent for the royal attendants one by one, as if by the king's order, and put them to death without difficulty, to the number of twenty-four.

Lallcheen, the king-maker of that age, placed Shumse, the brother of Gheas, on the throne, reserving to himself the real power, under the title of Mallek Naib, or Lord-Deputy; but after a few months both Lallcheen and his puppet king were overcome by Ferose Khan, and Ahmed Khan, sons of Daood Khan; and now was performed an act of retribution, that, as far as I am aware, is singular in the annals of revenge.

Lallcheen was delivered over to his sovereign Gheas, whom he had so treacherously blinded. Gheas had him placed before him, bound hand and foot, and killed him with one blow of his sabre. Shumse was blinded, and allowed to go to Mecca, where he lived many years; and Sultan Ferose, surnamed Al Ghazee, or the victorious, son of Daood, mounted the throne of Kalberga.

This was the golden age of the Bahminee empire, and Ferose the most splendid sovereign in India.

He was the patron and student of poetry, philosophy, and learning; three days in the week he gave lectures on botany, geometry, and logic; and it was said he excelled even Mohammed Toghlak himself in learning. He was never wearied of smiting the pagans of India; in twenty-four campaigns he was successful against the Hindoos; and everywhere he spread the faith, and raised the mosques of the worshippers of Islam.

Rigid in the theory of his faith, he relaxed somewhat in its practice; the use of music and wine, forbidden by the Prophet, he enjoyed under the excuse that as one elevated his thoughts, and the other did not affect his temper, he hoped to find mercy with a forgiving creator.

He was the most splendid polygamist of history; and the law of the Prophet, that limited the number of wives to four, he found a serious inconvenience to his happiness; to relieve his anxiety, and extend the bounds of his enjoyment, his courtiers told him he might marry as often as he chose, providing he divorced one wife before he took

BOOK I. 1398.

another; but this principle of weeding as he advanced, did not suit Ferose; he did not wish to pull up one beautiful flower from his garden because he had recently acquired another; he was a glutton of beauty, and desired to keep all. But his anxiety of mind was not of long duration; his vizier, as in duty bound, soon found a remedy for the affliction of his royal master; he observed that during the reign of the Prophet, the mutteah, or temporary marriage, was allowed and practised; and that it was still legal according to the tenets of the Sheahs or followers of Ali, although denied by the Sunis or followers of the Caliph. This solution of the difficulty was most agreeable to Ferose; he immediately adjured the Suni doctrine, as constrained and tyrannical, and embraced the more liberal and generous practice of the Sheahs.

He lost no time in taking advantage of his change of faith; he received into his harem in one day three hundred women, and despatched agents to all parts of the world to purchase slaves to replenish the vacancies caused by death or a change of taste.

He built a harem at Ferozabad on the banks of the Beemrah that was a city in itself. Here he secluded the most beautiful women of the known world, houris from Araby, Circassia, Georgia, Turkey, Russia, Europe and China vied in voluptuous charms with the high-caste races of India; with each he conversed in her own tongue; and so equal was he in the distribution of his favours, that each lady of the zenana believed herself the most beloved of the Sultan.

In the second year of his reign, Dewul Roy, Raja of Beejanuggur, with unexpected vigour, invaded his territories with an army of 30,000 horse and foot, and advanced as far as the Kistnah; but the sacred river being full, he camped on its banks in full security against the rage and indignation of the insulted Mussulmans.

Ferose marched in hot haste to avenge the insult to his creed and dignity, only halting en route, for a short period, to put to death a refractory zemindar, and 8000 of his subjects, who were foolish enough to be troublesome and refractory. CHAP. XIV.

When he arrived on the banks of the Kistnah, he found his Hindoo adversary apparently secured from all attack by the swollen torrent. This position, however, availed nothing against the daring enterprise of the warriors of Ferose's army; and the campaign was terminated by an act of gallantry that gives one a very favourable idea of the spirits and chivalry of that age and people. Whilst the Sultan was in doubt how to effect a passage in the face of the enemy, a cazi, or judge of the Koran attached to his court, volunteered to cross with a few men, and assassinate either Dewul Roy or his son. The offer was accepted, and some hundreds of hurdles were covered with leather for the passage of the troops in case the attempt succeeded. 1398.

In the mean time the cazi, attended by seven devoted friends, having crossed several miles lower down, entered the camp of Dewul Roy, in the guise of Hindoo mendicants. It would appear that morality was no more a necessary adjunct of mendicity in those days than at present; the cazi and his friends proceeded at once to the quarter of the camp inhabited by the dancing girls, and took up his abode with one of the most beautiful of that graceful though unfortunate class. The girl, it appears, was engaged to dance that night before the Roy's son; and the cazi, having exhibited to her his proficiency on the mundul, or stringed instrument played at the nautch, was permitted to accompany her as one of the band.

As is the custom in Deccan, many sets of dancing-girls were ordered to perform at the same time; and having finished their parts, the Roy's son called for the players and mummers. The dancing-girl now obtained leave for the cazi and one of his companions to show their feats. Having assumed the dress of women, they entered ogling and smiling, and so well imitated the mummers in playing, dancing, and mimicry, that the Roy's son was

BOOK I. 1398.

charmed with their performances. At length they each drew a dagger, and like the dancers of Deccan, continued to flourish them for some time, making a thousand antic postures in advancing, retreating, and turning round. At last, suddenly rushing upon the Roy's son, they plunged both the daggers into his heart, afterwards attacking his companions. Their remaining friends, who were watching without the tent, on hearing the alarm, ripped up the curtain and entered to assist them. Many of the company being much intoxicated, were easily put to death. The cazi and his friends extinguished all the lights, making their escape through the tent, mingled with the crowd. The outcry soon became general through the army, and great confusion ensued. In the mean time, 4000 of the Sultan's troops crossed the river on the rafts that had been prepared, and the Hindoo troops, seized with a panic, fled in confusion without waiting to be attacked. Next morning the Sultan crossed with his whole army, assaulted the Hindoo camp with complete success, gained immense spoil, and pursued the Raja to the vicinity of Beejanuggur.

The cazi was rewarded with the command of a division of the army, and was sent to lay waste the southern districts of Beejanuggur. During this campaign so many Brahmins fell into the hands of the Mussulmans, that their caste throughout the southern peninsula offered Dewul Roy large sums of money to purchase peace and their release. After much solicitation, Ferose consented to receive ten lacks of pagodas, about 400,000*l*., as the price of his prisoners and his retreat.

Two years later Ferose sent ambassadors with rich presents, and offers of assistance and attachment to the great Timour Beg, at that time conqueror of Hindostan; in return, Timour sent him a firman, granting him the empire of Deccan, Malwa, and Guzerat, with a right to the royal umbrella and all the insignia of office, accompanied by a sword from his own side, a dress of honour, a Turkish slave, and four horses, far exceeding in size and beauty the diminutive steeds of the Deccan.

The Sultan of Malwa and Guzerat did not approve of this recognition of superior empire in Ferose, and secretly entered into a league with the infidel Roy of Beejanuggur, to attack the kingdom of Kalberga.

The passions of mankind often hasten a climax that policy might be long in effecting; and again the beauty of woman was the cause of fierce and bloody war.

There resided in the village of Mudkul, within the territory of the Sultan of Kalberga, a Hindoo farmer, who was blessed with a daughter named Pertal, more graceful than the nine wives of Chrisna, and more lovely than the fabled houris of the Moslem paradise. What might have been her fate had she been left to mate amongst her own caste, and adorn the homestead of a young farmer in the peaceful village of Mudkul, is, of course, uncertain; but, unfortunately for the peace of the two kingdoms, the serpent, in the shape of a Brahmin, lately returned from a pilgrimage to the holy city of Benares, crept in, and instilled into the heart of the fair Pertal ideas of regal splendour and magnificence, and a sense of her own beauty, that caused her to heap scorn on the humble love of the surrounding rustics.

The recent pilgrimage of the holy man does not appear to have entirely erased from his heart all the pomps and vanities of a wicked world: he carefully instructed her in all the mysteries of music and dancing, and when these accomplishments were complete left her, with the promise of returning with a prince at least for a husband. In the character of a possessor of a jewel of great price, he proceeded to the court of Beejanuggur, where his account of the marvellous beauty of his accomplished pupil so inflamed the heart of the Raja of Beejanuggur that he immediately despatched the Brahmin with an offer of marriage, and the title of ranee, or princess, to the young lady; but, fickle as she was fair, she refused the

BOOK I. 1401. tempting offer, and expressed her conviction that she should become the wife of a Mahomedan prince. Irritated beyond measure at this avowed preference for a rival in faith as in arms, the Roy determined at once to attempt the invasion of Kalberga and the abduction of the lovely Pertal. Selecting for this delicate mission one of his most renowned generals, and giving him the command of 5000 of his best troops, he desired him to hasten to Mudkul, and bring by force the wayward beauty and her family. Unfortunately the Roy had omitted to inform the simple farmer of the honour intended for his fair daughter; and when the hostile troops appeared before his village, he and his family fled in company with the other inhabitants. Disappointed of their prize, the Hindoo troops vented their spleen on the surrounding villages and their innocent inhabitants, and returned laden with every species of spoil but that for which they had entered the enemy's country.

The magnificent polygamist, Ferose, the husband of a thousand wives, was not likely to pass unavenged so glaring an infringement of his rights to the first selection of beauty in his dominions. The order was at once given to boot and saddle; and breaking from the varied charms of the thousand houris of Ferozabad, he marched in haste to Beejanuggur. He assaulted the town, and actually obtained possession of some streets of the Hindoo capital, and at length only retired before overpowering numbers. He now attacked the Roy in the open field, and kept him in check four months; during which time his brother devastated the fairest portion of the Carnatic, and made 60,000 captives of both sexes. Peace was at length made, on condition that the Raja gave Ferose his own daughter in marriage, dowered with ten lacks of pagodas, immense quantities of the pearls of Ceylon, fifty choice elephants, together with two thousand men and women singers, dancers, and musicians.

Dewul Roy was a Brahmin, and the marriage of a daughter of that saintly caste with one of a different religion was an indelible disgrace; but necessity was his master, and no alternative remained. After the wedding, Ferose visited the Raja of Beejanuggur in his new character of son-in-law. The Eastern field of cloth of gold that celebrated this meeting was gorgeous and barbaric in its splendour. From the gate of the city to the palace, a distance of six miles, the road was spread with cloth of gold, velvet, satin, and other rich stuffs; and as the two princes rode side by side between masses of admiring subjects, crowds of beautiful boys and girls scattered gold and silver coin amongst the multitude. After a sojourn of three days in the Hindoo capital, Ferose and his bride returned to the Mussulman camp. This ostentatious friendship was only skin deep. A slight want of courtesy on the side of the Raja in declining to enter the camp of his son-in-law, entirely effaced all the good effects of the meeting; and they parted with mutual feelings of jealousy and secret thoughts of revenge.

On his return to his own capital, Ferose sent to fetch the fair Pertal, the unwitting cause of so much bloodshed, and of the degradation of the royal race of Beejanuggur.

When he beheld her, even his critical experience was astounded at her excellence. He swore by the beard of the Prophet, that all who had hitherto described her were in league with the father of lies to depreciate a beauty that far excelled anything he had ever conceived; but either the youthful princess of Beejanuggur had at length finally enthralled his wandering desires, or satiety had induced indifference; for he dismissed her with unwonted self-denial, saying he was too old for so much beauty, and gave her in marriage to his son Houssun, with whom her nuptials were celebrated amidst unequalled pomp and magnificence; and thus the promises of the Brahmin, and the matrimonial presentiments of the fair one of Mudkul, were agreeably fulfilled.

Shortly afterwards Ferose sought an excuse for invad-

BOOK I. 1401.

ing the territories of his father-in-law. He laid siege to the important fortress of Bilkondah; but his army was dispirited by an epidemic, which bears a strong resemblance to cholera, and being attacked by Dewul Roy with great vigour, was signally defeated. This was the first great victory obtained by the Hindoos over their unrelenting foes, the Mahomedans. Never was revenge more sweet to an oppressed and insulted race; and hard indeed did they strive, in this one victorious campaign, to wipe out the extortions and oppressions of the last one hundred years.

A general massacre of the Mussulmans took place; villages were burned and depopulated; mosques and holy places destroyed; and the haughty followers of Islam drank deep of the cup of humiliation they had for more than a century forced on the now triumphant worshippers of Brahma. There was a smell of death throughout the kingdom of Kalberga, and pyramids of heads were raised to mark the number of the slain.

This defeat was fatal to Ferose. Old and well stricken in years, the disgrace and humiliation was more than he was able to bear. He prepared his throne for his successor, and Houssun Khan was the object of his choice; but he was of fierce temper and debauched mind, and Khan Khanan, his uncle, determined to seize the throne. Anxious to secure the succession of the throne to his son, Ferose now sought to blind his brother; but he retired to Khan Khananpore, where he was shortly attacked by the troops of Ferose, to the number of 8000. Having only a small retinue of 1000 men, he was unable to meet them on the field with any chance of success; but a fortunate incident, somewhat resembling that which caused so signal a panic amongst the British troops on the battle-field of Bannockburn, now converted impending defeat into a decisive victory. There were close at hand a band of Brinjaris, or gipsies of Hindostan, with 2000 bullocks laden with corn from Berar, and 300 horses from Lahore. By the advice of one of his generals, Khan Khanan purchased them all, and mounted a man with a green and red flag on each ox. He placed some cavalry in front of this mock force, with orders to appear at a distance when the action should commence, and to proclaim that some principal omrahs had arrived from their jaghires to assist Khan Khanan. In the morning the engagement commenced; but no sooner did the generals of Ferose's army, who had all along been dreading the reinforcements that might join Khan Khanan, see this large force, preceded by a band of horsemen, advance with immense shouting and waving of flags, from behind a grove, than their hearts failed; and after a feeble resistance they retired from the field. Khan Khanan afterwards defeated Ferose in person, but refused to pursue him after the victory. At length Ferose, finding that public opinion was strongly against his son, and in favour of Khan Khanan, sent for Houssun, and told him, that such being the case, he had better resign in favour of his uncle; which he did. Khan Khanan then visited Ferose, who received him with pleasure. He declared him his successor, and charged him with the care of his son and kingdom. His worldly affairs thus settled, Ferose died after a reign of twenty-five years. He was a great monarch. He had more wives, and slew more Hindoos, than any former sovereign of India. He was just to his friends and terrible to his foes, and will compare favourably with most of the sovereigns of Hindostan.

CHAP. XIV. 1422.

NOTES TO CHAPTER XIV.

[1] Hindostan proper is generally applied to the regions north of the Nerbudda.

[2] It was called Firozeh, or cerulean, and was made of ebony covered with plates of pure gold, inlaid with pearls. Its value was 4,000,000*l.* sterling.

CHAP. XV.

A.D. 1422—1518.

HISTORY OF THE DECCAN CONTINUED. — THE REIGN OF AHMED SHAH; AND HIS DEFEAT OF THE HINDOO RAJA DEWUL ROY. — ALLA II. SUCCEEDS HIM IN 1434, AND REIGNS TWENTY-THREE YEARS. — THE REIGN OF HUMAIOON SHAH, SURNAMED "THE CRUEL." — THE DEATH OF HIS SON, NIZAM SHAH. — THE REIGN OF MOHAMMED SHAH. — THE RAPID DECLINE OF THE EMPIRE AT HIS DEATH.

BOOK I. 1422.

KHAN KHANAN ascended the throne in the year 1422, with the title of Ahmed Shah, surnamed Wullek, or the "Worker of Miracles." His first aim was to strengthen his army, and to avenge the late invasion of the Raja of Beejanuggur. He treated his nephew, Houssun, with great kindness, and allowed him to retire to Ferozabad, with ample means and retinue, and leave to hunt and divert himself within a limit of eight miles round his palace. This life suited him far better than the cares and anxieties of royalty, and during his uncle's reign he remained happy; but was afterwards blinded and imprisoned.

Ahmed also extended his generosity to the ministers of the late Sultan, and liberally rewarded them for their devotion to his brother's interest, although exerted against his own. Having somewhat settled the affairs of his kingdom, and stationed an army to watch his dangerous neighbours in Guzerat, he lost no time in marching with 40,000 horse to attack his old enemy, Dewul Roy. The warlike Hindoo was in no way loath to accept the gauge of battle; and, being joined by some powerful southern rajas, pitched his camp on the Jummedra, the boundary stream between the two kingdoms.

Ahmed soon arrived at the opposite bank, and, finding taunts and insults equally unavailing to induce the wary Hindoo to abandon his advantageous position, and attempt the passage, he decided upon adopting these daring tactics himself. Accordingly he despatched three of his most trustworthy officers with a body of troops to cross the river at some distant point during the night, and to advance stealthily up to the enemy's camp. By accident they surrounded a garden close to a plantation of sugar-canes, where the Raja was sleeping with only a few persons, and he had barely time to escape naked into the cane brake. He was soon caught by the soldiers of Ahmed, who, utterly ignorant of the value of their prize, and believing him to be only a common person, loaded him with cane, and obliged him to run with it before them. The Raja, rejoiced at being undiscovered, willingly took up the bundle, trusting to fortune for his subsequent escape. Ere long the Moslem plunderers found other booty more valuable than sugar-cane, and their prisoner, more precious than the kooh-i-noor itself, was suffered to escape.

Dewul Roy soon overtook his own troops, and, being recognised, was received with great joy. He retreated to Beejanuggur, whither Ahmed pursued him with all the ardour of unexpected success. Repudiating the humane treaty of his ancestor, Mahmoud, with a former raja of Beejanuggur, he destroyed men, women, and children with relentless fury; halting for three days to celebrate a festival, whenever the number amounted to 20,000. The temples and colleges of the Brahmins were, of course, de-

BOOK I. 1422. stroyed, and the defeat of Ferose most fully revenged. Marching straight to Beejanuggur, he reduced the city to great want and suffering; and at length only consented to make peace on condition of receiving a subsidy at the hands of the Raja's sons. The Hindoo prince entered the camp of Ahmed with thirty elephants, laden with the wealth of the golden realms of the Carnatic, and was received by the Sultan with great honour. He entertained him sumptuously for several days, when he sent him back with a retinue of twenty fine horses of Araby, a male elephant, dogs for the chase, and three trained hawks—birds till then unknown to the inhabitants of the Carnatic.

There is a superstition amongst the natives of India, that when rain fails it is a proof of the divine wrath against the sovereign. During this reign none fell for two years, and the suffering and distress was intense. Ahmed did all in his power to alleviate the misery of his subjects; and, at length, having taken counsel with the wise men, consented to pray for it. No sooner did he do so, than, wonderful to relate, rain fell in plenty, and he was immediately saluted with the title of Wullek, "the worker of miracles." After an attack on the Raja of Telinjana, the ally of Dewul Raja, in which he took his capital of Waroojol[1], killed Brahmins innumerable, destroyed their holy temples, and pillaged the hoarded treasures of ages, he returned to Kalberga, where he shortly afterwards marked his reign by a work more enduring than military success, by resuscitating, on the ruins of Bieder, the glories of the ancient capital of those Hindoo princes who, according to native tradition had, for 5000 years, possessed the magnificent kingdoms of the Carnatic.

The celerity with which cities rise and assume gigantic proportion under the absolute sway of oriental despotism has no parallel in the tamer progress of more constitutional kingdoms; and soon, some miles to the north of Kalberga, rose, as if by magic, one of the most splendid cities of

India, or of the world. The great mosque of Ahmedabad Bieder was, for centuries, unequalled for simple grandeur and solemnity; and the more delicate beauties of the Ivory mosque, inlaid with gems and mother-of-pearl, was long one of the favourite themes with which travellers delighted to illustrate the wealth and prodigality of the realms of the far East.

After some desultory wars with the King of Guzerat, in which he took Bombay, and one more pillaging expedition into Telinjana, the Sultan Ahmed died, after a most prosperous reign of twelve years.

Ahmed was brave, and occasionally cruel; but he was just, and remarkable for his regard to religion. In his reign there flourished a holy syed, called Mohammed Geesoo Derauz, whose sanctity was esteemed of so high an order by the Deccanee Mussulmans, that a learned man being asked to pronounce judgment between the comparative greatness of this saint and Mahomed, replied, with seeming wonder, that the Prophet was undoubtedly a great man, but that Syed Mohammed Geesoo Derauz was a very different kind of man from that!

Sultan Alla succeeded his father on the throne of Ahmedabad Bieder; but it was not till after a long campaign against his brother Mohammed, assisted by the Raja of Beejanuggur, that he obtained undisputed possession of the kingdom. He was soon involved in border wars with the Rajas of Concan, Sunjeer, and others; and in one protracted feud with the King of Khandeesh, his kingdom was only saved by the brilliant victories of his general, Mallek-al-Tigar, the Prince of Merchants.

During this campaign the Bahminee empire was more than once imperilled by the jealousies of the various mercenary chiefs and soldiers comprising the army. The Abyssinians at this period exercised considerable influence and control in military and state affairs in the Deccan; and their superior physique and independent spirit rendered them at all times subjects of great anxiety. Since the establish-

BOOK I. 1434. ment of the Mussulman kingdom in the Deccan, a large number of slaves were annually brought over by Abyssinian merchants, and sold throughout the country to the sultans and great chiefs; these, in their turn, purchased their own countrymen, and colonies and communities soon sprang up. These men having, as it were, an hereditary interest in the government and the military prestige, and united by long service to the Deccanee ameers, viewed with jealousy the increasing influence of the Moguls, Turks, and Persians, who were rapidly settling in the Deccan. So bitter did this feeling at length become, that the rival powers could not be employed in the same service; and when at length these foreigners, after the performance of some remarkable exploits, were ordered to take precedence of the Abyssinians and Deccanees, this jealousy was converted into the deepest hatred and revenge, and soon caused a catastrophe that again raised the drooping spirits of the Hindoo princes, and rang from one end of the peninsula to the other.

Soon after his successes in Khandeesh, Mallek-al-Tigar invaded the Concan with 7000 Deccan troops, and 3000 Abyssinian horse, in addition to his own Mogul and Persian troops, with the intention of reducing all the coast fortresses of Concan and Malabar. After considerable success he was persuaded by a treacherous Hindoo Raja named Sirkeh, to attack the Raja of Sunjeer, who owned the country around Kalich, a place often mentioned in the history of Aurungzebe's wars in the Deccan. Acquainted with the dangerous passes and poisonous climate of the western ghauts and jungles, Mallek-al-Tigar long refused to hazard so dangerous a campaign; but at length yielded to the assurances of the treacherous Sirkeh, that, "with a guide so skilled as himself, not a hair of their head's would suffer, and the rose of accomplishment would be gathered without trouble." At the outset Mallek was deserted by the Abyssinian and Deccanee troops, who

CHAP. XV. 1434.

refused to enter the forests; and he was obliged to trust for success to his own Mogul and Persian auxiliaries; true to his promise, Sirkeh for the first two days conducted the troops along a fair path; but on the third, he led them through "paths so horrible, that a male tiger through dread of the terrors of it would have become female; fuller of windings than the curly locks of the fair, and narrower than the paths of love; demons would have started at the precipices and ravines, and the ghoul have been panic-stricken at one view; the sun never enlivens the valleys, neither had Providence fixed bounds to its extent; the grass was tough as the teeth of serpents, and fœtid as the breath of dragons; death dwelt in the water and poison in the breeze; after winding, fatigued, weary and alarmed, through this dreadful path, they entered a dark forest, a passage through which was difficult even to the gale, bounded on three sides by mountains that seemed to have their heads in the clouds, and the other by an inlet of the ocean; there was no path to advance and none to retire except that by which they had entered."[2] Here Sirkeh deserted them, and hastening to the Raja of Sunjeer, informed him that he had lured the prey into his toils—the Raja, who had only been awaiting the signal, attacked them in the night, and slew nearly 7000 of them. The clashing of the trees, and the moaning of the monsoon, forming a fitting chorus for the groans of the wounded and the shrieks of the dying.

Mallek-al-Tigar, with many noble Syeds, and a few Abyssinian and Deccanee omrahs, fell victims to the treachery of the Hindoos, and a mere handful escaped to bear the sad tale of their comrades' fate. On their escape from this terrible jungle, the Moguls did not fail to taunt the Abyssinians and Deccanees with their cowardice, and threatened to inform the Sultan of their conduct. They retired to Jagneh to recruit, and in the mean time the Deccanees, alarmed at their threat of exposure, and anxious to secure the first hearing at court, sent

BOOK I. 1434. immediately to the Sultan, accusing the Moguls of having betrayed Mallek-al-Tigar, and of being in league with the Rajas of the Concan.

Enraged at their supposed treason, the Sultan immediately sent two Deccanee omrahs to execute vengeance on the Moguls. In vain they asserted their innocence, insisted that there was a mistake, and begged to communicate with their sovereign: they were now in the hands of their enemies, who, bent on their destruction, allowed no rumour of their innocence to reach the ear of the sovereign; every letter was intercepted, and every falsehood fabricated that could establish their treachery. Finding all hope of justice gone, the Moguls shut themselves up in the walled city of Jagneh, and with unequalled heroism, held it against the finest armies and generals of the Sultan.

At length provisions getting low, the Moguls determined on a sortie, with the desperate hope that some few would cut their way through the besieging force, and establish their innocence before the Sultan's throne. But treachery now completed the ruin their indomitable courage had deferred. A forged order from the Sultan, purporting to grant them a full pardon, on account of the number of Syeds amongst them, on condition that they quitted his territory, was concocted by the Deccanee omrahs, and sent to the besieged; and to put the seal of blasphemy on their infamous deceit, the omrahs swore by "the Almighty, by the Koran and the Prophet of God," that they should retire without injury to property or person.

Relying on the solemnity of an oath that to a Mussulman is the most sacred that can be made, these unfortunate men evacuated the fort with their wives and families, encamping outside whilst they were preparing for their march; for three days the Deccanee chiefs observed their oath; it took that time to enable these cowardly traitors to summon courage to perpetrate the treason they had devised. Although no longer protected by their walls, they durst not attack their noble foe, and again had recourse to treachery to supply the courage they wanted. On the fourth day they prevailed upon the Mogul chiefs to come to an entertainment; all the principal men attended, when at a given signal, armed men rushed in and put them all to the sword; whilst without, in their camp, 4000 Deccanees put every male, even the children at the breast, to death, reserving the women for their insults and their brutality; 2000 Moguls, of whom 1200 were Syeds of unmixed descent from Medina, Kerballa, and Nujeef, perished by this abominable treason. "Never," as the Moslem historian feelingly relates, "never since the days of Houssun were the Syeds so abused; but is it not astonishing that men who called themselves servants of the Prophet should so basely treat his descendants?"

Murder however will out, and such a murder as this had ten thousand tongues; "for every wound received by a descendant of the Prophet in this world," says the Koran, "a dozen witnesses will spring up in the day of accusation." Notwithstanding all their care, the truth did at length reach the ears of Alla, and terrible indeed was his wrath; condign punishment was executed at once upon the principal perpetrators of this foul deed; death and impalement rid the world of monsters who could so disgrace humanity; and providence struck with a loathsome leprosy the two omrahs under whose instruction the work of blood had been completed.

During this reign, Raja Deo of Beejanuggur, called a general council of his chief nobility and Brahmins, to inquire into the cause of the invariable superiority of the Mussulman arms; he proved to them that in extent, wealth and population, the territory of the Rajas of Beejanuggur far exceeded that of the Bahminee Sultans; but that still his army was always beat, and he desired to know the reason; some said that the Hindoo scriptures

BOOK I. 1434.

foretold the supremacy of the Mussulman for 30,000 years, and therefore their defeats were in accordance with the immutable decree of destiny; others with more reason attributed it to their inferiority in cavalry and bowmen. The Raja adopted the latter suggestion, and desired all his troops to be instructed in the use of the bow; he also encouraged the immigration of Mussulmans to his dominions, giving them villages and jaghires, and placed a Koran before his throne to which they might make obeisance; he soon had 2000 Mussulmans, and 60,000 Hindoos skilful with the bow, besides 80,000 horse, and 200,000 foot trained in the same way with spears and swords.

With this host he invaded the territory of Alla; three combats were fought, in one of which the Hindoos were victorious, and two of Alla's chief officers taken prisoners; nothing daunted, the Sultan sent word to Deo, that he had sworn an oath to destroy 100,000 Hindoos for every Mussulman who was slain; and he would not hold his hand, till the captivity of each of these chiefs was expiated by the death of 100,000 of his foes; the Raja feared the desperation of his enemy, although worsted, and consulting prudence, he made a treaty and retired from the Bahminee territory.

Like so many eastern potentates, Alla was a mixture of good and bad; he built and richly endowed an infirmary at Ahmedabad, and appointed to it Hindoo and Mussulman doctors; and he conferred a yet greater blessing on his subjects, by suppressing that curse of Indian cities, the marauding devotees or pilgrims, giving them the option of menial and laborious work, or of altogether quitting the country.

Like the wise king, he fell away from the paths of right and wisdom towards the end of his life; he gave himself up entirely to luxurious enjoyments, and relinquished all the task of government to his ministers; he drank wine in public, but poured molten lead down the throats of those who imitated him. One of the grandsons of the officer whose duty it was to examine weights and measures, to prevent the sale of intoxicating liquors, and to punish offences against morality, being captivated by the snares of a courtesan, and tempted by her to drink wine, became quarrelsome from the effects of it, and beating the woman cut off her side locks. The affair was complained of to the cutwul who confined both parties; but considering the rank of the officer, he considered it better to refer the decision of the case to the Sultan; who, being much enraged, ordered the offender to be carried into the most public square of the city, there to receive two hundred blows on the soles of his feet, and to take a solemn oath against drinking wine; the courtesan was led through the city dressed in an ass's skin, and afterwards banished the city. From a life of comparative celibacy, "he suddenly entertained 1800 beautiful women, and spent most of his time in drinking ruby-coloured wines, pressing the lips of silver-bodied damsels, or listening to the melody of sweet-toned musicians," and seldom appeared in public.

CHAP. XV. 1434.

He was eloquent, witty, and fond of learning; and on Fridays and holidays he would occasionally ascend the pulpit in which he read the Khutbah, describing himself in modest terms as "the monarch just, merciful, and patient, and liberal to the servants of God." But his right to these lofty titles did not always pass unchallenged; and on one occasion an Arab horse-dealer, to whom he owed money, being present at this enumeration of royal virtues, could not contain his indignation; and, alluding to the murder of the 1200 Syeds at Jagneh, called out in a loud voice, "Thou art neither the great, the patient, the merciful, nor the liberal, but the cruel and the false; who hast massacred the Prophet's descendants, yet dared to assume such vaunting titles in the pulpits of true believers."

Alla felt keenly the force of the rebuke; the merchant

BOOK I. 1457. was paid on the spot, and the Sultan retired in tears to his palace, where he soon after died of mortification of the foot, after a reign of twenty-three years.

Alla was occasionally unjust and severe; but well would it have been for his subjects had his life been prolonged. He was succeeded on the throne of Ahmedabad by his son Humaioon, commonly called Zelim or the Cruel. He was probably the greatest monster that ever disgraced humanity; the gods of India must, indeed, have been angry with their people, when they suffered such a demon to reign over them. Heliogabalus, Nero, Caligula, and the most abandoned monarchs of imperial Rome, were infants in atrocity and vice compared to this eastern monarch.

During his reign the main thoroughfares of the King's Market were adorned with stakes and cauldrons of scalding oil and boiling water, with which to boil and impale all who fell under his displeasure. The cutwul, or chief magistrate of his capital, was confined in an iron cage, and every day compelled to swallow some portion of his own flesh. Whilst irritated at some supposed or actual want of attention, he put to death 2000 of his troops by various tortures, the most cruel and lingering that could be devised.

From the balcony of his palace he witnessed his own brother cast to a voracious tiger; and foaming at the mouth with brutal passion, and biting his lips with rage till they dropped blood, he gloated over the agonised death of upwards of 7000 men, women and children, who were supposed to be involved in his revolt.

Accompanied by his brutal soldiery, he would often descend into the streets and snatch the bride from a wedding procession, and bear her away to his zenana; but the curse of Cain was on this man of blood: the curse of the fatherless and the widow haunted him by day, and scared him when at the height of his fiendish enjoyments. As his hand was against every man's, so did he feel every man's hand was against him. He lived a life of terror, which even drink, the last resource of the craven, could not banish. Out of pity to mankind, Providence did not long suffer such vice to go unpunished. After a reign of three years, he was, in a fit of intoxication, assassinated by his own servants; and has left a name unequalled in the annals of crime. CHAP. XV. 1460.

Nizam, his son, succeeded to the sovereignty of a crushed and terror-stricken nation. He was young, and unable successfully to resist the combined attacks of his powerful neighbours, the Rajas of Malwa and Orissa. He was defeated in a great action by Mahmoud, King of Malwa, who, after committing every imaginable atrocity throughout the Bahminee empire, established himself at Ahmedabad.

Mahmoud, like most Mussulman conquerors, was ruthless in war, but a strict observer of all the minute injunctions of his faith. Straining at forms and ceremonies, he disregarded the great truths of mercy and right. Seated on the throne of Nizam, he affected a policy of mercy and conciliation, and especially regarded the outward show of religion; he was very strict in the observance of the rules regarding things pure and impure, and particularly that one which enjoins the purchase of vegetables from the owner of the soil only. This hypocrisy was thus nobly rebuked by a celebrated sheikh, Molana Shumse: "You speak, O king, what can only excite ridicule and scorn. To invade the territories of true believers, lay waste their dwellings, and rob them of their property, and to pretend observance of the law in the trifling points of dress and diet, is folly and hypocrisy." The king acknowledged the truth of this bold censure; but said the empire could not be supported without such contradictory actions.

After keeping possession of Ahmedabad for nearly twelve months, Mahmoud was expelled by Mahmoud, the famous sovereign of Guzerat, who, with an army of 80,000

BOOK I. horse, marched to re-establish the power of the Bahminee dynasty.

1462. Mahmoud was at that time the greatest sovereign in India; he ruled over Guzerat for fifty-two years, and established a character for power and personal strength that reached the far distant capitals of Europe. He was represented by travellers as a prince of enormous stature, living on deadly poisons; and his breath was said to be so fœtid that even the flies that lighted on him died; and his usual mode of destroying his enemies was by breathing upon them.[3]

The reign of Nizam was an unfortunate one for his country, and he did not live long enough to redeem its tarnished honour. He died as he was just springing into manhood; and the flowery language of Persian history brings before us a tragedy somewhat resembling the charming pages of the Scotch novelist. It being the custom of the house of Bahminee for its princes to wed in tender years, the queen-mother sought in marriage for her son one of her own relations, and prepared the nuptial feast with royal pomp and magnificence. "On the night of the celebration, when the assembly of mirth was adorned, and the court full of pleasure and rejoicing, suddenly screams were heard from the royal apartments, and the voice of sorrow complained with loud sobs that Nizam Shah had departed this life, and left the world to other masters. The unblown rose of the royal tree suddenly perished by the destructive blast; the down of beauty had not yet grown on the flower, when death shed upon it the killing mildew."[4]

Nizam Shah reigned two years, and was succeeded by his brother, Mohammed Bahminee, who, at the age of fourteen, undertook the difficult task of managing a kingdom and a wife. Mohammed revenged the insults of Mahmoud of Malwa; and, invading his kingdom, extorted a favourable peace. His troops, under his powerful subject, Khajeh Gawan, afterwards subdued the independent Rajas of the Concan. He attacked Goa with one hundred and twenty vessels, and terminated a successful campaign by the conquest and annexation of that valuable seaport belonging to the Raja of Beejanuggur.

The Mahrattas, or inhabitants of the Concan, followed the same principle of life as their more inland brethren of the Deccan. Whilst the latter loved to hear "the lark sing and the mouse squeak" in the territories of their neighbours, they loved to hear the sea-bird scream on the wild ocean. They were pirates on a grand scale, and could send out a fleet of three hundred vessels to harass the trade and terrify the pilgrims of their Mussulman neighbours.

One cannot help contrasting the extent of this maritime enterprise, though turned to purposes so injurious, with the utter stagnation that now pervades the whole western coast of India. When three hundred vessels went out to rob, there must have been something to rob. Of the three hundred vessels that four hundred years ago frequented the ports of the Deccan and Malabar, but a few open trading boats now remain to enliven that splendid coast.[5]

If the last reign but one produced a sovereign, in comparison with whom the greatest demons of history appear angels, the present one could boast a subject worthy to contest the palm of rectitude and honour with Sully, Ximenes, or Sir Thomas Moore.

Henceforward the history of the Bahminee empire is the history of Khajeh Gawan, the great minister of Mohammed; and with his death its star of splendour set for ever.

Khajeh Gawan was one of the most noble characters we read of in any history; and the sketch of such a man, although imperfect, must be instructive. He belonged to the royal family of Persia; but, alarmed at the danger attending close consanguinity to the throne, he refused repeated offers of high office in the state, and betook him-

BOOK I. 1469. self to the wandering life of an eastern merchant. In his forty-third year he arrived at a port of the Deccan, en route to Hindostan, and was persuaded to enter the service of Alla II.; and during the reign of his son, Humaioon the Cruel, attained to the highest offices of the state. On the elevation of Mohammed Shaw he was made vizier; and from that period ruled the Bahminee empire with wisdom, justice, and benevolence. His generosity fully equalled his wealth, which exceeded anything of the kind before known in Deccan. Scarce a city of note throughout the Deccan but had some example to show of his generosity; and there was not a poor man in the country who had not daily cause to bless the name of Khajeh Gawan.

Gawan means cow; and the following amusing anecdote gives the cause of his adopting it. Sitting one day with the Sultan and his court on a terrace of the palace, a cow happened to low underneath, when one of the courtiers said, laughingly, "Oh, vizier, thou art a wise man, what saith the cow?" when Khajeh promptly answered, in the same strain, "She says I am one of her species, and should not sit amongst asses."

He was no less distinguished as a scholar than as a soldier. He greatly extended the bounds of the Bahminee empire; and his treatise on the science of arithmetic, and his garden of composition, were long esteemed by the literati of the Deccan.

On one occasion, when honoured by a visit from the Sultan, he presented him with wealth and curiosities that exceed even the credulity of the student of eastern history. Amongst other priceless articles are enumerated fifty dishes of pure gold, with covers set with jewels, each large enough to hold a roasted lamb; one hundred slaves of Circassia, Georgia, and Abyssinia, most of them accomplished singers and musicians; one hundred horses of Arabia, Syria, and Turkey; and one hundred pieces of superb china, never to be seen but in the palaces of great monarchs. He gave the king an inventory of all he possessed, to the last farthing, and delivered everything to him. But such generosity could not be tolerated by a generation of courtly vipers. A deep plot was laid for his life, and his very household servants were employed against him. Treasonable correspondence was forged, and his own seal put to it. In a fit of rage and intoxication, the Sultan gave ear to his enemies, sent for Khajeh Gawan, and, listening to no explanation, ordered an Abyssian slave to slay him on the spot. "The death of an old man like me," said this noble vizier, when he saw his doom was fixed, "is of little moment to myself; to you it will be the ruin of an empire and your own glory." When, kneeling down facing the kibleh, or point of prayer, he repeated the profession of faith, "There is no god but God, and Mahomed is the prophet of God;" and, thanking God for the blessing of martyrdom, he resigned his soul to the Divine mercy, at the venerable age of seventy-eight.

1469.

From that moment the kingdom of Mohammed began to slide from his grasp, and the house of Bahminee tottered to its fall. All the great nobles of Deccan fled in alarm, and refused to return to their allegiance; and the Sultan had to fill the important posts of the empire with men unfitted for them.

No sooner was Khajeh dead than remorse devoured the heart of his master, and destroyed his peace. In vain he punished all who had so cruelly deceived him, and heaped honours on the adopted son of his faithful servant. A thousand times an hour he regretted the act that had deprived him of the greatest subject of the age. His pleasure was gone from him; and, inwardly a prey to grief and sorrow, he passed a life of misery; till, at length, after a reign of twenty years, death seized him in a fit of drunkenness, exclaiming that Khajeh Gawan was tearing him to pieces.

From Goa to the mouths of the Kishna, and from the

BOOK I. 1482.

Nerbudda to the Beemrah, the whole country acknowledged the sway of Mohammed Shah of Ahmedabad. His capital was the most magnificent in India, his armies the most victorious; and, but for this one act of tyranny, and a dreadful famine that for two years decimated the Deccan, his reign would have been accounted one of the most glorious of the Bahminee dynasty.

Mohammed was the last actual sovereign of the line of Bahminee; for although during the succeeding forty years nominal sovereigns of Deccan ascended the throne of Ahmedabad, the great nobles, who had only been deterred from asserting their independence by the energy and power of Khajeh Gawan, almost immediately fell away, and divided the kingdom amongst themselves; and, in less than forty years, the four dynasties of Beejapore Golcondah, Ahmednuggur, and Berar, partitioned the magnificent territory of Ahmedabad.

The contests between the Abyssinians, Deccanees, and Moguls, were renewed in all their destructive bitterness, and anarchy and confusion harassed the land.

Thus this powerful monarchy, whose end strikingly foreshadowed that of the Mogul empire two centuries later, fell to pieces just seven years before the first Mogul emperor planted his victorious standard at Agra.

NOTES TO CHAPTER XV.

[1] North-east of Hyderabad.

[2] Ferishta's Deccan.

[3] Ramusis and Barbosa both give this description. Hence Butler:

> "The Prince of Cambay's daily food
> Is asp, and basilisk and toad,
> Which makes him bear so strong a breath,
> Each night he stinks a wife to death."

[4] Ferishta's Deccan.

[5] About ten years ago, a small steamer, of about five donkey power, was put on once a month from Bombay to Canaanore and Cochin and back; but it did not pay, and five years ago was taken off.

CHAP. XVI.

RECAPITULATORY.

CHAP. XVI.

BEFORE we proceed with the history of the great Mogul dynasty, the golden age of Hindostan, we will briefly reconsider the period that has already occupied our attention, and mark the effects of foreign rule upon the condition and institutions of the people.

For nearly four centuries the Mussulmans had been supreme in Hindostan. Thirty sovereigns, the great majority of whom were mountaineers of Affghan lineage, ruled in succession from the capitals of Delhi and Lahore. The wars of succession were incessant; but the great prizes of sovereignty were contested amongst the Moslems alone.

Pithowra of Delhi and Jeichund of Canouje (A.D. 1194) were the last native sovereigns of Hindostan, and with the fall of their capitals and the expatriation of the Rajpoots, the military spirit of the people appears to have ceased.

Nothing can more completely prove the utter prostration of the native powers, than the unopposed succession of thirty foreigners to the throne of Hindostan, many of them without even the claim of ordinary energy and vigour to defend their usurpations, without a sign from the great native princes.

The conquering element flowed uninterruptedly from the north: wave after wave of fierce and needy adventurers recruited the armies and monopolised the offices of state.

BOOK I.

But the fierce suns of Hindostan were ill suited to the mountaineers of Caubul or the natives of Bokhara and Samarcand. In the third generation the descendants of the northern conquerors offered a less vigorous obstacle to fresh invasion than did the original natives of the country. The slippered exotics in turban and flowing muslin robes, who thronged the courts and mosques at Delhi, did not offer a stronger contrast in habits and appearance to their stout ruddy grandsires who, in heavy leather boots, short tunics of thick cloth, and woollen caps, conquered for them, than they did in energy and warlike aptitude.

At this period, six Mussulman and two Hindoo sovereignties divided amongst them the great peninsula of India.

The Mussulman kingdoms were Delhi, Guzerat, the Deccan, Malwa, and Bengal; those still governed by Hindoo princes were, the Rajpoot principality of the west, and the great monarchy of Beejanuggur in the south.

The kingdom of Delhi reached from the Salt range and the mountains of Cashmere to Behar, and from Gwalior to the Himalaya, and was ever the supreme power in Hindostan. In the hand of a powerful monarch it exacted homage and tribute from its rivals, and even in its extremity of weakness and intestine ills was always safe from external aggression. The possessions of the kings of Delhi, though large and nominally under one king, did not possess the strength of unity: the monarchy was made up of many independent principalities, jaghires, and provinces, each ruled by an hereditary chief or zemindar, nearly all of whom were Affghans. When loved or feared by the great feudatory princes of Hindostan, the monarch of Delhi was supreme over an empire; but at the cry of "every man to his tent," synonymous with the retirement of every noble to his jaghire, was frequently left in one day with scarcely a single province.

Under Alla the Sanguinary (A.D. 1295) and Mohammed Tughlak (A.D. 1325), the empire comprised the greater portion of the peninsula of India, whilst under some of their successors it was restricted to half the capital itself.

Of the Mussulman sovereigns of Hindostan whose histories we have sketched, some few displayed benevolence and talents that would have adorned the annals of any empire; whilst many exulted in crimes that would disgrace the ordinary calendars of vice. On the whole, they were neither better nor worse than their contemporary sovereigns in Europe. Amongst the Stephens and Johns of England, the Pepins and Philips of France, the Popes that could sanction the extermination of the Albigenses and bless the Inquisition, it would be easier to find ten of the mould of Alla and Mohammed than one of the stamp of the good Ferose.

The rise of the Mussulman kingdom of the Deccan was as rapid as its career was brilliant and its dissolution sudden. In less than fifty years from the meeting of rebel nobles in the fortress of Dowletabad (A.D. 1325), the Bahminee monarchs almost equalled in wealth and power those of Hindostan. Whilst the armies of the latter found ample occupation in opposing the inroads of northern neighbours, or in barren contests with the warrior princes of Rajpootana, those of the former found a more congenial field for their prowess and cupidity in rifling the stored-up treasures of the Carnatic and the south.

Bengal, Guzerat and Malwa were small and insignificant as military powers by the side of their powerful neighbours of the Deccan and Hindostan. Guzerat, however, was the emporium of the then extensive maritime trade of the west coast; whilst Bengal, teeming with a redundant and laborious population, was then, as now, the wealthiest province of the peninsula.

The kingdom of Malwa had lately been on the decline, and had now fallen under the sway of Rana

BOOK I.

Sanga, the brave and able Rajpoot sovereign of Cheetore, who, taking advantage of the intestine commotion of his neighbours, had added to his hereditary dominions several neighbouring provinces, and was daily increasing in power.

The Hindoo kingdoms of Beejanuggur and Cheetore, equally famous in the history of the peninsula, shared very unequally the blessings of climate and soil.

Beejanuggur, extending from the Kishna to Cape Comorin, comprised the most fertile and populous regions of India, and its wealth was immense; whilst the Rajpoot principalities, composed of rugged mountains and impassable deserts, supported a population rich only in chivalry and manly enterprise.

Beejanuggur and Rajpootana represented respectively the empires of Peace and War. The aspects of nature as seen in their respective countries influenced the habits and pursuits of the inhabitants; whilst for 600 years the sovereigns of Beejanuggur devoted their wealth to increasing the fertility of an already prodigal nature, by those noble works of irrigation, that in their decay still constitute their glory and our shame, the warrior princes of Rajpootana, worshipping the sun, the sword, and the horse, and rejecting with scorn all pursuits of agriculture, raised, in emulation of nature's defences of mountains and deserts, the mighty fortresses of Gwalior, Rintimbor, and Calinga.

An intercourse of four hundred years and frequent intermarriages had indoctrinated the conquerors in many of the peculiar institutions of their subjects; the distinctions of caste, and the classification of things unclean, equally influenced their habits and their ordinary avocations. The distinctions of caste were fully recognised by the Mussulmans; and no Brahmin could treat with more withering contempt a chandalah or pariah than did a Syed or lineal descendant of the Prophet.

Whatever sinking of differences or observance of new

customs, caused any rapprochement between the rival races, was made entirely by the Mussulmans: the Hindoos remained unchanged in the slightest degree. "We want not," say the Brahmins, "that others should adopt our worship; let all men adhere to the religion of their fathers;" and, opposed to proselytism in every phase, they scorned all efforts to shake the faith of their conquerors, and resisted to the death any attempt against their own. In many instances, the governing class had cruelly persecuted the followers of Brahma; broken their idols, overthrown their temples, and massacred their priests; but these persecutions left no mark. The gentle pagan bent like a reed before the blast of Moslem intolerance, only to rise up the moment it was past. But indeed these persecutions had been the exception; toleration or indifference had been the rule of Mussulman domination, and it is doubtful whether the animosity between Hindoo and Mussulman, in the peninsula of India, ever attained the same vindictive spirit, and was attended with the same atrocious cruelty, as that displayed by Roman Catholics and Protestants in Christian lands.

The Mussulman faith was almost entirely confined to Hindostan, the Deccan, and Guzerat; and at the period we now write of, the name even of Mahomed was proscribed in the sacred city of Benares. The Mussulmans were still as the oil floating on the waters; and except at the various Mussulman courts, and amongst the mercenaries, the god of the Hindoos was still supreme in India. The mosques of Delhi and Agra attracted their thousands of turbaned worshippers; but millions of devout pilgrims still worked their weary way to the shrines of Juggernaut and Hurdwar, and the temples of Benares and Bithoor still overflowed with devotees from the furthest extremities of India.

During these four hundred years no perceptible change had taken place in the condition of the million. Under all despotisms, especially Asiatic, the prosperity of the masses depends entirely on the sovereign: under a beneficent monarch, like Ferose III., the arts flourished; cities sprang up as by the wand of a magician; commerce increased; aqueducts, bridges and roads enriched the land; irrigation received the attention which none but tyrants or fools deny it; and everywhere the barren land became a garden, and the deserts waved with corn; but on the other hand five years of dominion, such as that of Mohammed III., and all that we have described, disappeared to make way for misery and want. Flourishing cities were in a few weeks abandoned to owls and jackals; irrigation was neglected; the ground refused her increase; the scanty crops remained unhusbanded, "the ploughman overtook the reaper, and the treaders of grapes him that sowed the seed;" and the wretched inhabitants, flying to their jungles, sought, in the company of beasts of prey, a refuge from that fiercer animal, man.

The revolutions that convulsed capitals and supplanted kings in no way affected the native cultivator of the soil. Under all changes and chances he was still the hewer of wood and drawer of water, and continued toiling and moiling and fulfilling God's third curse on man. From time immemorial the land-tax was the chief source of revenue throughout the peninsula of India. This was the only earthly institution in whose stability the ryot had perfect and complete confidence, and the extent to which it was levied was the gauge by which he tested the nature of his government: when the land-tax was lightened, or the means of irrigation put within his reach, he considered his rulers were humane, and whether Affghan, Turk, or Mogul, deserving his obedience; when the land-tax was increased, and the means of irrigation were denied him; when the original tale of bricks was maintained, but he was deprived of the means of making them,—when the great and bitter cry went through the land, "there is no straw given unto thy servants, and they say to us, make bricks," he bowed to fate, and trusted patiently in his gods to restrain the avarice of his rulers. The contests and discords of the governing class did not affect him. He knew that no change of rulers would relieve him from the tax on his labour; he knew he must pay for it, and he cared not to whom; he viewed without interest and without hope the struggles of those who were contending for the fruits of his labour; he heeded not the disgrace of nobles or princes, and the most fearful vices of the sovereign were to him of far less importance than the condition of the tanks, or the ordinary irregularities of the seasons.

Foreign domination had made no change in the commercial organisation of the country. The trade of India still flowed through the old caravan routes to all parts of Europe and Asia; and the Persians and hardy nations north of the Indus still supplied the race of warrior merchants, who during weary marches of many thousands of miles, had to defend their merchandise from the flying Arabs of the desert, or the fierce pillagers of Central Asia.

They were the same race of picturesque traders who, unchanged in dress, language, or custom from the days of the patriarchs, may still be seen in eastern bazaars sitting cross-legged behind the piles of merchandise from the far country, their noble heads and romantic attire striking with wonder the trim-cut traveller of the West, who is reminded by their bronzed and perhaps scarred brows and bristling belts, of the vast difference that exists between the adventurous life of an Eastern merchant, and the peaceful routine of European trade.

Four centuries of foreign rule had in no degree modified the dislike of the natives of India to a maritime life. The Chinese, the Arabs, Persians, and Europeans who frequented the great harbours of Guzerat and Bengal, still monopolised the carrying trade; fleets of small native craft, it is true, flitted along the coasts of Malabar and the Concan, but they were content with the coasting trade, fishing or piracy; and with the exception of occasional

BOOK I. voyages to the Laccadives or Ceylon, scarcely ventured out of sight of land.

In considering the transactions of this period, the constant triumphs of the Mussulmans and the continued lethargy of the Hindoos, we must not forget whose accounts we study. There are no Hindoo historians; all our authorities are Mussulman; were it otherwise, we might have a different picture of the condition of the people, and of the course of events; we might learn that it was not so much the superior energy and warlike qualifications of the Mussulmans that established an empire, as the jealousies and dissensions of the Hindoo princes that lost one. As said the lion in the fable, when he saw a man represented killing a lion: "Humanâ hoc pictum manu, videres hominem dejectum si pingere leones scirent."

END OF BOOK I.

BOOK II.

CHAP. XVII.

THE EARLY FORTUNES OF ZEHYR-ED-DIN MOHAMMED, SURNAMED THE TIGER.

CHAP. XVII. 1500.

It was in the brilliant age of the Renaissance, that Zehyr-ed-din Mohammed, surnamed the Tiger, Khan of a small principality in Turkestan, founded the great Mogul Empire in Hindostan.

What a noble spirit of chivalry and adventure, of art and religion, was abroad in those self-same days of the sixteenth century; and how they blaze out with a splendour and renown, that cause all other ages before or since to appear dark and spiritless. During what other period of the world's history shall we find crowded into the short space of a hundred years, the chivalry, valour, learning, enterprise, the freedom of speech, the earnest devotion, the perfection of the arts, that distinguished that age of noble men?

The age that saw the chivalry of Scotland die gloriously on the field of Flodden, and the gallant Knights of St. John strive hopelessly with countless legions of Turks[1]; that with trembling pulse watched the cross pale before the crescent, and the city of Belgrade yield to the conquering sword of a victorious Sultan, saw also the burning of the Pope's bull before the awe-struck students of Wittengen, the rise and progress of the mysterious Society of Jesus, the adventurous voyages of Magellan, and the daring conquests of Cortez.

BOOK II. 1500.

It was this same bright spirit of chivalry, this devotion to the great and the good, that impelled the princely Francis to solicit knighthood at the hands of his subject Bayard, and prompted the mighty sovereign of Germany and Spain to pick up the paint brush of the great colourist of Venice.[2]

Then were the world's Olympic games, when each kingdom of the earth sent out a champion into the lists to bear aloft the pennon of his race: when Henry of England, Francis of France, Charles of Germany and Spain, Leo the Mæcenas of Popes, Barbarossa "the Pacha of the Seas,"[3] Solyman the Magnificent, each in turn contended for the sceptre of dominion, the palm of knighthood, and the right to direct and foster the arts and progress of the age. Theirs were the wars of giants[4], when armies fought with a pertinacity unnecessary in these days of scientific slaughters.

Uniting in his person the joint lineage of Genghis the great Khan, and Timour the mighty Beg, and combining in a remarkable degree the energy of those two conquerors, at whose nod the whole Eastern world had trembled, Zehyr-ed-din Mohammed was fitted both by nature and birth to take his place in the foremost rank of this gallant array of knights and sovereigns.

At the age of thirteen, when man has scarcely put aside childish things, he succeeded his father as Khan of Koukan, a small principality lying to the east of the great Mogul capital, Samarcand: and at once he found himself compelled to defend his birthright against the annexing propensities of his neighbours and relatives.

No sooner had he established his supremacy in his own dominions than his natural disposition for conquest displayed itself. Twice before he had attained the age of sixteen he crossed the river Sir and the mountains of Karabas, and seized and occupied Samarcand; in both instances he was speedily forced to return to quell the dissensions of his nobles, and to find his own kingdom and capital in the hands of his enemies. Twice he risked his kingdom for foreign conquests, and twice he lost it in the attempt. CHAP. XVII. 1494.

"It is good," says the Eastern sage, "to accustom the soul to grief and the stomach to hunger." Mohammed, or as we shall henceforth call him, Baber, illustrated this principle to the very letter. Like Timour, sorrow and hardship were his portion in youth, and adversity his teacher in middle age; but as the toad ugly and venomous bears yet a precious jewel in his head, so did untoward fate foster the precious qualities that ultimately guided him to conquest.

For years he was a wanderer and a fugitive in the mountains of his own kingdom, and it was unequalled energy and determination alone that saved him from enemies more numerous, as he himself expresses it, than "the hairs in his horse's mane." But a life of want and extremity amongst the mountains of Koukan was not destined for Mohammed the Tiger; the highland campaigns of petty chiefs did not satisfy the ambitious cravings of the descendant of Genghis and Timour. Although a beggar and a fugitive he was yet the son of Omar the lineal descendant of Timour. He was still by hereditary right acknowledged the chief of the wandering races and shepherd warriors of Central Asia, and, himself a wanderer and hardier than them all, who was so fitting a leader to conduct them to conquest?

The term Mogul is improperly used in nearly all histories and accounts of the East; in India, especially, all strangers, Persians, Tartars, all emigrants from the north and north-west, and indeed all Mussulmans with whitish faces, are called Moguls; but, in fact, the difference between a Tartar and a Turk is as great as between a Negro and a Moor, between a Chinaman and a Hindoo; the eyes, mouth, nose and ears of the Tartars are

BOOK II. 1501. remarkable and hideous, whilst the Turks are famed even by their rivals, the Persians, for their beauty. No epithet more insulting than Mogul can be applied to a Jaghatai Turk, and, except in their pastoral life, and a very remote resemblance in language, no similarity whatever exists between them.

Baber was connected with both Turks and Tartars: Turks from Timour, and Tartars from Genghis. All his affections, however, were with the Turks; and he always mentions the Moguls or Tartars with hatred and contempt. Jaghatai Turki was his native tongue, in which he wrote and spoke; it was the dialect of the great nomade races of Tartary, who still retained their aversion to the life of towns, and scorned the pursuit of agriculture as effeminate and base. Jaghatai Turki was spoken by the inhabitants of Cashgar, the Crimea, Samarcand, Bokhara, and the greater part of Turkey; the principal tribes of Persia, the Turkomans of Asia Minor, and of the Euxine; by the Uzbeks, the Kirghis, the Kaizaks, and numerous other tribes of Tartary; it was, in fact, the language of the deserts and the plains, in contradistinction to Persian, the language of cities and courts. The most corrupt dialect of Turki is that at present spoken by the Constantinopolitan Turks.

Baber had taken refuge in Dehkat, a mountain district, inhabited by Tajiks speaking Persian, and keeping large flocks and herds and brood mares, like wanderers of the Desert; it was in this inhospitable region that the conquest of the sunny regions of the south first suggested themselves to his mind. "I lived," says he, "in the house of one of the head men of the place. He was an aged man, seventy or eighty years old. His mother was still alive, and had attained an extreme old age, being at this time 111. One of this lady's relations had accompanied the army of Timour Beg when he invaded Hindostan. The circumstances remained fresh in her memory, and she often told us stories on that subject." These stories he never forgot; and from that date the conquest of Hindostan was never absent from his thoughts. CHAP. XVII. 1507.

The Moguls of Central Asia appear at this period to have taken mercenary service in the armies of Asia. The position of their young hereditary chief, beset on all sides by fierce foes, and turning upon each in succession like a baited tiger, was not without attraction to their adventurous spirits; by degrees he was joined in his mountain retreat by a few score of his countrymen, outlaws and fugitives like himself; and at the age of twenty-one he crossed the river Gihon, with 300 ill-armed followers and impedimenta reduced to two tents, and bent his steps westward, with the intention of invading the fertile province of Khorassan, the Region of the Sun.

At this period of his fortunes, his followers probably bore considerable resemblance in equipment and discipline to the motley following of the Highland chiefs of the same period, who with targe and claymore rushed fiercely on the English bowmen at Flodden. His ranks increased rapidly in number and quality as he advanced, and from all directions the Mogul mercenaries thronged to his standard, and hailed him as the great Khan of their race.

What might have been the fate of Asia had Khorassan and the shores of the Caspian and Persia been the field of conquest, it is needless to consider. At that time Caubul was in the crisis of one of its chronic revolutions; its capital was in the hands of an usurper, and divided interests offered a fair prospect of easy conquest. With the instinct of a conqueror, Baber saw his opportunity, and with the impetuosity of a Turk made himself master of the occasion.

The mountains of Affghanistan were crossed in safety, and the fortresses of Caubul and Ghizni occupied without

BOOK II. 1507.

a contest. Baber was now a professed marauder, a free lance on the grandest scale. He presented the remarkable spectacle of the hereditary sovereign of the most warlike people of the East, bereft of his own kingdom, and wandering abroad in search of any other he could pick up. It was completely a matter of indifference to him, and to his adventurous followers, to what direction they turned their arms—they had no right anywhere; the sword was their only claim, success their sole title; but the sword was Baber's "kingly stamp," and "where it did mark it took."

The empire of Timour, shaken and dismembered, and split into divers kingdoms, claimed and misgoverned by numberless usurpers, offered many tempting baits, from the frontiers of China to the shores of the Mediterranean. As the eagle soars round and round in his strong career, in search of prey, so did Baber, swooping from his eyrie amongst the mountains of Affghanistan, wheel in ambitious flight over the regions north of the Indus. He himself describes his dilemma with charming naïveté, and tells us in his memoirs, that at length, being unable to decide between the conflicting merits of the surrounding countries, he summoned all his most trusty comrades, and consulted them as to the next kingdom they should invade. As might be expected, this *embarras de richesses* gave rise to numerous and conflicting opinions—nearly every one of the surrounding countries had its special advocate in this council of braves. The particular merits of each individual province were cheerfully enumerated; and whilst some gave the preference to fertility of soil and salubrity of climate, others urged as inducements for conquest, the beauty of the dames, the excellence of the water, or the existence in perfection of some other quality that possessed peculiar claims of precedence in their eyes.[5] The most eloquent patriot could not probably have drawn more brilliant pictures of the climate, the fertility, and other blessings of their native land, to stimulate defence, than did these free lances to induce invasion. But the mind of Baber never wavered; the golden legends of his hostess in Dehkat had fully inflamed his imagination; and once established on the head waters of one of the chief branches of the Indus, he had little difficulty in inducing his followers to give the preference to Hindostan. It was not likely that a soul like that of Baber would rest satisfied till he had witnessed with his own eyes that teeming land whose priceless products had filled his earliest dreams, had beautified the palace of Genghis, adorned the jasper tomb of Timour, and filled with ravished wealth the magnificent ruins of his present capital, Ghizni.

It was rather more than a hundred years after his ancestor Timour, at the head of 100,000 Moguls, had crossed the Indus for the purpose of subduing Hindostan, that Baber, at the head of scarcely ten thousand horse, commenced a series of campaigns that were intended to terminate in the same result; but scarcely had he crossed the Rubicon, and planted his foot in the land of his desires, than unforeseen circumstances scattered his brilliant visions of conquest, and made him again a wanderer and an outcast.

It seemed to be the fate of this monarch constantly to lose one kingdom whilst seeking another, and for the third time in his life his absence in search of foreign conquest lost him his present possession. During an expedition to the banks of the Indus, the Mogul garrison mutinied in Caubul, and raised his cousin, Ryzak Khan, to the throne, and tempted by the gratuities of the usurper, the army of Baber deserted, and he was left with a few hundred followers; again was the star of his fortune obscured, but it was only to flash out with greater brilliancy when the ominous cloud was past.

The same circumstances that reduce ordinary men to the utmost extremity, will frequently afford to the great an opportunity of signalising themselves; such was the

BOOK II. 1507.

case with Baber. Here was a danger that delighted his chivalrous soul, an extremity before which the daring energy of his mind exalted itself. What pleasure is to a woman's cheek and passion to her eyes, that is danger to some men; then it is you see the mantling colour and the flashing eye that nought else can produce. Baber was such a man.

> "His was the soul
> That for itself could woo the approaching fight,
> And turn what some deemed danger to delight."

Danger was as the breath of his nostrils, the atmosphere on which he throve, and he loved it for its own sake, to the full as much as ever did Richard of the Lion Heart.

At once, without a moment's hesitation, he returned at the head of a few hundred men to Caubul, where he was met by his usurping rival with an army of 12,000 horse. Terrible in his wrath he dashed up to the very ranks of his revolted troops, reproached them for their perfidy, and upbraided their cowardice with bitter scorn. Never did pent-up lion glare more fiercely on the wretch that trembles under his insulting paw than did Baber, when, riding up and down the ranks, he defied his treacherous rival to mortal combat.[6] He who steals the lion's prey in his absence does not always care to hold it on his return, and Ryzak Khan, with baseness enough to usurp an empty throne, was wanting in the courage to retain it from its rightful lord; and he refused the combat.

But although their chief was a coward, the nobles of the Mogul race were not. Terrible as was Baber in his fury, and fearful as was the strength of one who swam the Ganges in thirty-three strokes[7], and who with a man under each arm could spring from one pinnacle to another of the pinnated ramparts seen in the East, five omrahs in succession advanced to meet him, and each in turn bit the dust before the invincible arm of this "demi-Atlas of the world, this burgonet of men."

Here was a feat of romantic daring that will bear comparison with any of the most brilliant deeds that illumine the pages of chivalry, and a knight worthy the sword or the friendly grasp of Bayard, or Gaston de Foix. Not the Cid Bivar, or the brave Roland on the plains of Roncesvalles, or the lion-hearted king himself, mowing down the Saracens like grass, before Acre or Askalon, ever performed a deed of greater heroism and might than this of Baber in the plains of Caubul.

It was not possible that a race like the Moguls, priding themselves on their valour and prowess, should long hesitate between the unequalled bravery of their hereditary chief and the cowardice of his usurping relative.

The army returned to its allegiance, and Baber was again sovereign of Caubul. The valour of Baber was equalled by his generosity; his cousin, Ryzak Khan, although despised, was forgiven, and it was not till after a second attempt of the same kind that Baber consented to his death.

For several years after this crisis in his fate, Baber with ever-watchful eye remained at Caubul, contenting himself with occasional attacks on the frontiers of India[8], varied by inroads into the neighbouring countries of Samarcand and Persia; and it was not till the year 1524, in the fortieth year of his age, that he heard from his spies that the golden apples of Hindostan were ripe for picking, and that trusting to the notorious dissensions that had weakened the imperial power at Delhi, he for the last time entered the Punjaub, and taking Lahore, pressed onward to the sunny regions of the south.

According to Abul Fazil, Baber was led by Divine inspiration to turn his mind to the conquest of Hindostan, but he himself would lead us to suppose that it was curiosity merely, and no Divine impulse, that induced him to visit that country. "He had never," he said, "seen the warm countries, and the land of Hindostan;" and we

BOOK II. 1524.

may safely conclude that the peculiar excellences he himself enumerates—"that it was a large country, and possessed abundance of gold and silver," added to the knowledge that the moment he should cross the Indus, he would be joined by Alim Khan, the Emperor's brother, with 40,000 men to assist him in his enterprise —were sufficient cause for action, without the additional incitement of supernatural inspiration.

Again, in the history of Hindostan, foreign invasion was prompted, and its success insured, by intestine brawls. Domestic treason is so universal in the Eastern courts, and the danger from the plots and jealousies of sons, brothers and nephews, so unceasing, that we can appreciate if not defend the political necessity that recognises the extermination of all male relatives as the first duty of the incoming sovereign. From time immemorial a peaceful death has been denied the Lord's anointed; in all countries and through all ages the happy demise of kings has been the exception. Violence, treachery, the fury of the fanatic, the impatience of expectant heirs, the revenge of disappointed ones, have hurried to their rest the great ones of the earth; few even of those who have died in their beds have escaped the conviction that those around them, who should be dearest to them, whose only thoughts should be to soothe their parting moments, were awaiting with impatience the sound of the passing bell to commence a fierce struggle for their crown. But it is in the East especially that this general principle has become a universal law; it is in the hollow crown of an Eastern king that the antic death delights to keep his court; it is there he sits "scoffing at state, and grinning at his pomp, till with the little pin he bores through his castle walls, and farewell king."

The law of right was at this period unknown in Hindostan; the man, whoever he might be, who had the courage to seize, and the strength to keep, the capital or the throne, was the acknowledged sovereign of the country; public opinion even encouraged this general spirit of usurpation. No disgrace attended failure; and whilst glory and imperial honour were the rewards of success, death alone was the penalty of defeat; and in the fierce contests of Eastern politics, where every man carried his life in his hand, death was often the least of evils. Alim Khan, the brother of the monarch of Delhi, was no exception to the usual run of the happy families of Eastern monarchs, and as we have before noticed, he only awaited the opportunity offered by Baber's presence to attempt his brother's overthrow.

The haughty manner and more than Eastern cruelty of Ibrahim Lodi had early fanned into flame the smouldering rebellion of his fierce Ameers. Like Mohammed III. he trampled alike upon prince and peasant, his relative and his slave; his maxim of government was that a king should have neither relative nor friend, needing only slaves. He was scarcely seated on his throne when a revolt broke out, headed by his brother, Jilal Khan, who proclaimed himself King of Juanpur and advocated the division of the empire. After several campaigns, Ibrahim defeated him, took him prisoner, and subjected him to a cruel death. The loss of their chief, however, did not smother the animosity of the great nobles of the empire; they had recourse to Alim Khan[9], the second brother of Ibrahim, and advanced his claim to the crown of Delhi.

Alim Khan, aware of Baber's intention to invade Hindostan, and anxious to secure his co-operation, at once sought his presence. It was formally agreed that in the event of success he was to be elevated to the throne of Delhi, and that Baber was to receive in consideration for his assistance the formal cession of Lahore. Baber furnished him with troops, and at once sent him back to commence the campaign, himself following more leisurely. Baber was by no means unwilling that the two brothers should waste their strength in contending for the

BOOK II. 1525. shadow, until he himself was prepared to grasp the substance; but the impetuosity of Alim Khan was nearly the cause of his ruin. No sooner did he find himself at the head of Baber's auxiliaries and his own armies, than he at once marched on the capital, where he encountered his brother Ibrahim and suffered a disastrous defeat.

Baber was at Sealkote when he heard of this inauspicious commencement of his enterprise. His intention had been to advance leisurely to an easy conquest in the wake of a successful ally; but his position was now changed, and he found himself compelled to fight for life against a victorious enemy with forces far superior to his own.

Here again was an emergency that roused the latent tiger, that fanned into flame the smouldering energies of his character; at once he sprang to his saddle, and, to use his own words, "placing his foot in the stirrup of resolution, and his hands on the reins of confidence in God," he crossed the Jumna at the head of 13,000 horsemen, and marched straight to the capital of Hindostan.

After the defeat of Alim Khan, Ibrahim lost no time in endeavouring to drive out the handful of Mogul invaders who had made so daring an inroad into his territories, and who now appeared completely at his mercy. He marched against Baber, and on the 21st day of March, 1525, the two armies met on the plains that surrounded the fortress of Paniput.

In all countries that have been subject to hostile invasion, certain districts have almost invariably become the great battle-fields on which their destiny has been frequently decided. The spread of plains, the flow and fords of rivers, and the passes of mountains will, in time, indicate the natural high road from one country to another, and keep the tide of conquest much in the same direction. As the fate of Italy has so often been decided on the plains of Lombardy, and as the fertile lands of Burgundy, and the lower lands of Chalons, have more than once been the great lists of Europe's chivalry, so, from the earliest ages of Indian history, the extensive plains lying between the Sutlej and the Jumna have been those on which the tide of invasion has dashed first and strongest. CHAP. XVII. 1525.

These plains, bounded by the deserts of Ajmere and Malwa on the one side, and the Jumna on the other, may be considered the great high road from the capital of Hindostan to the lands of their first Affghan and Tartar invaders. It was, then, on the plains between Kurnaul and Paniput, which had already seen more than one desperate struggle for the golden prize of the East, that Baber encountered the Affghan monarch of Hindostan.

The troops of Baber consisted entirely of cavalry[10], and did not number more than 13,000; whilst the army of Ibrahim consisted of 100,000 infantry and cavalry, supported by an imposing array of 1000 chain elephants; but the thousands of Ibrahim were composed chiefly of Mussulmans, whom a residence of many generations, in the sultry regions of Hindostan, had deprived of the warlike qualities of their Affghan and Gaurian ancestors; and of Hindoos, who, by centuries of misrule, had lost that fear of shame and love of glory without which numbers but add to the general weakness. The Khans of Timour's army who dreaded, in a continual residence in Hindostan, the rapid deterioration of their race, were correct in their anticipations: the enervating fountain of Salmacus[11] flowed also in the land of Hindostan; and the parching heats and relaxing rains of these sultry regions were as completely destructive to the mental and physical development of those northern races, as they have since been to the Portuguese, and would be to the British, in the third and fourth generation. The listless minds and languid frames of those composing the Mussulman army of Ibrahim offered but little similarity to the hardy warriors of Mahmoud and

BOOK II. 1525.

Alla; and the Moguls of Baber achieved as easy a conquest over them as their ancestors could have done, in years gone by, over the Hindoos themselves.

In every contest between the armies of India, and their hardier enemies from the north, the boldest and most daring tactics have always been the most successful; and the nation that designs to conquer or hold India, must rely on the superior energy and determination of its troops, and the dash and daring of its commanders, and on those alone for success. The warriors who have founded an individual, or a national reputation in Indian warfare, have done so apparently on the rashest principles of military tactics. The Mahmouds, the Babers, the Clives, the Wellesleys, the Napiers, of Indian fame, have universally disdained to make allowance for any disparity of numbers; they have depended upon the individual courage and superior breed of their troops; on the mutual reliance of discipline; and on the physical superiority of the northern over the eastern soldiers to carry them triumphantly to success against any odds.

India is the land where impossibilities in war have so often been successful, that they appear to have become the rule rather than the exception, of military action; and the moment the cautious head supersedes the daring heart, the tactics of delay those of immediate action, in fact, when a general seeks for his opportunity instead of making it, the incalculable advantage arising from the superior dash and daring of the northern over the eastern race is lost.[12]

Baber was well acquainted with Eastern warfare; he knew that whatever may be the result of delay elsewhere, in the East he who hesitates is always lost; and at once, in the face of apparent destruction, he made up his mind to attack the overwhelming forces of Ibrahim; and placing himself at the head of his steel-clad horsemen[13], he waved aloft the pennon of his race, and crashed like a thunder-bolt right through the crowded ranks of the king's army; and then wheeling, fell with irresistible fury on their rear. CHAP. XVII. 1525.

These daring tactics were crowned with instant success; the rout was complete; no less than 20,000 of Ibrahim's troops were left dead on the field; and on the spot where the battle had evidently raged the fiercest, surrounded by 6000 of the pick of the Affghan nobles, who had fought around their king, was found the body of the last Sultan of the Lodi race that reigned in Hindostan.[14]

The field of Paniput was a sad one for the Affghans: it was felt throughout India, that the Affghan dynasty had sustained a shock it would never recover, and that the conquerors of three centuries had succumbed to a fresher and fiercer race.

For many years the tomb of Ibrahim was a place of pilgrimage; the field of battle was believed to be haunted; sounds of wailing were long heard by night, and no good Mussulman would cross after dark without repeating the name of God.

The same year that heard the cry of mourning ring through the land of Scotland for the flowers of the forest cut down and withered with the chivalrous James on the field of Flodden, witnessed the not inglorious death of the proud and wicked Ibrahim, together with the chief nobles of his land, on the field of Paniput.

Baber immediately pushed on strong detachments to Agra and Delhi to secure the treasure and the throne; and again, after a lapse of 125 years, the dreaded Mogul stalked through the bazaar of the capital, and recalled, to the minds of the terrified inhabitants, the narrations of their ancestors of the fearful days of bloodshed that marked the presence of the relentless soldiery of Timour.

BOOK II. 1525.

When we compare this invasion of Baber, with any of a similar character of his predecessors, we are struck with admiration at the cool daring of the mind that designed, and of the hands that achieved it. Baber congratulates himself on his victory, and, in truth, neither before nor since has it been eclipsed in the rolls of Indian exploits. Only two Mussulman conquerors (Timour overran but did not conquer) had preceded him,—Mahmoud of Ghizni and Mohammed of Ghor,—but they were mighty sovereigns, monarchs of Khorassan and supreme in Charism and Samarcand, whilst their enemies were petty rajas, and Hindostan itself was dismembered; whilst Baber, although threatened by the Uzbeks in his rear, who could bring into the field 100,000 soldiers, had, with only 12,000 horsemen, attacked Sultan Ibrahim, who could bring into the field 500,000 men, and had actually 100,000 men and 1000 elephants.

On the third day he himself arrived at Delhi, and having sealed up the treasures, hastened on to Agra. On arriving at that city he found that the forts still held out, though Humaioon his son, who had been sent forward, had blockaded it so completely that, even had the treasures been broken open, nothing could have been carried off.

Bickermajit, the Raja of Gwalior, head of the most ancient family in Hindostan, had, after a long resistance, been compelled to surrender his property to Ibrahim, and to take service in his army; he had fallen in the late battle, and his wives and children, and some of his chief followers, took refuge in the fort of Agra. At the approach of Humaioon they tried to escape, but were intercepted and brought before him. Humaioon treated them with great courtesy, and preserved them from spoliation; in return for his generosity, they made him a present of jewels and precious stones, amongst them was the celebrated Kooh-i-noor, the Mountain of Light, valued by Tavernier at 880,000*l.*, that now graces the diadem of the first Empress of India. Humaioon presented it to his father who returned it to him.

The treasure discovered in Delhi and Agra was immense; but Baber of the Open Hand kept not a dinar for himself. The whole treasure was divided amongst his omrahs and their troops; and whilst they congratulated themselves on the acquisition of the gold that passeth away, Baber was satisfied with having earned a reputation for generosity, equal to that of the religious orders of Kalendar, whose rule it was to keep nothing for the morrow.

To Humaioon he gave seventy lacs, besides a palace with all it contained; to his ameers he presented sums of ten, eight and seven lacs, whilst he sent a present of tenpence or elevenpence to every citizen of Caubul.[15]

But although Baber had obtained the immediate object of his expedition, his position was as hazardous or more so than that of any former or succeeding conqueror of India. The capital certainly was occupied, but the country was not subdued. The defeated Affghans hated as much as they feared their Mogul conquerors; and, on the death of Ibrahim, numbers of the petty chiefs and rajas in all directions began to fortify their strongholds, and to harass to the utmost of their power the soldiers of Baber.

No wonder his troops were dismayed, and their hearts quailed. They were now two or three months distant from their homes, amongst a strange and hostile people, whose language they did not understand; who believed they were ogres[16], and who credited the most impossible stories of their cruelty and inhuman natures. Add to this, the country itself was unpopular amongst them, and many of his chiefs and omrahs, urged an immediate return.

BOOK II. 1525. Neither can we be surprised at it. Most of them were natives of Balkh, Bokhara[17], Samarcand, and Baber's own country of Koukan, and the affection of the natives of those regions for their own lands was proverbial. Balkh[18] especially, the mother of nations, the metropolis of Islam, the nursery of all that was great and good in the history of the Eastern world, was the peculiar object of the reverence and affection of all good Mussulmans. It was the paradise of the Jaghatai Turks; its language was the most elegant dialect of the Persian tongue, and its inhabitants believed that when God speaks mildly and gently to the cherubims surrounding his throne it is in the dialect of Balkh he addresses them. Here a thousand apricots the size of an apple could be bought for a shilling, whilst melons, the Mussulmans' delight, extolled by the Koran, as food and drink, acid and alkali, and which with women are styled the only two delicious things in nature[19], were too numerous to be sold.

Amid the parching heats of Delhi, they pined for the ice and baths, and the running streams of colder climes; they missed the mulberries and the figs, and the strawberries of Caubul, the grapes and apricots of Balkh, the goodly beeves and the fine horses of Samarcand; and they began to despise the wretched oxen and the pigmy steeds, the timid men and the dusky dames, the scentless roses and the tasteless melons of their recent conquests in Hindostan.

The discontents grew general and alarming; but Hindostan was rich and fruitful. It had fallen almost without a struggle, and Baber was not the man to sacrifice so glorious a conquest to the home-sick pinings of his nobles. Summoning all the chiefs, he explained to them his fixed determination of remaining in India, and urged those who were his friends to do likewise; but at the same time he disclaimed any desire whatever to retain in his army a single man who had "no stomach for the fight" that was impending; and gave all who desired it ample leave to depart; but, as with the English army before Harfleur, few availed themselves of the proffered passports and crowns for convoy.[20] CHAP. XVII. 1525.

Baber was a prince to ensure affection when he could not command success; and the same generous spirit that prompted him, on a former occasion, to spare his wretched cousin's life, induced him now with noble magnanimity to reward past services rather than punish present disaffection; and the only omrah of the whole army who quitted his chief in his extremity, was rewarded with the government of Caubul.

Established in the capital of Hindostan, Baber had nothing to dread from either Affghan or Hindoos singly; but his advent and conquest more or less dispossessed them both, and common interest in their territory and revenues induced them to make common cause against him. Singly, their opposition was of no importance, but united it became serious; all that was required, apparently, to ensure his destruction was a leader who should be able to unite the two great parties. Such a man was not long wanting. Rana Sanka, head of the Rajpoot principality of Cheetore, was the leader on whom the eyes of the inhabitants of Hindostan,—Hindoos and Mussulmans alike,—were turned in their extremity.

Born of the most ancient lineage of Hindostan, bred to battles and bloodshed, despising alike Affghans and Turks, and glorying in the chivalrous race who owned him as chief, and who looked forward to the time when he should regain the empire of his ancestors, and be seated on the throne of Nushirwan the Just, Rana Sanka was a warrior after Baber's own heart, a foeman in every respect worthy of his steel. His person bore unmistakeable signs of his valour and his delight in war. He was of middle stature, great muscular strength, and exhibited an unusual amount of wounds; he had lost an

BOOK II. 1525. eye and an arm, had a leg broken with a cannon ball and counted eighty wounds from lance and sword in various parts of his body: 80,000 horse, seven rajas of the highest rank, nine rajas of lesser rank, and 104 chieftains with 500 war elephants followed the standard of the Rajpoot prince.

For more than forty years he had been exercising his warrior subjects with predatory incursions into the neighbouring kingdom, of Malwa or Guzerat, or in more formidable warfare with the Affghan sovereigns of Hindostan. He had defeated in battle Sultan Mahmoud the great king of Malwa, and had annexed some of his most valuable provinces; twice he had made war on Ibrahim, and twice he had defeated him in pitched battle.

Constantly intent on restoring Rajpoot supremacy in Hindostan, Rana Sanka saw in the invasion of Baber an opportunity of destroying the Affghan dynasty; that once accomplished, he had little fear of disposing of the handful of strangers who hoped to rise on their ruin.

He opened communications with Baber at Sealkote, prior to the calamitous defeat of Alim Khan, in which it was arranged that whilst Baber attacked Ibrahim by marching on Delhi, the Rana was to attack him on the side of Agra; this latter part of the compact, however, he entirely neglected to perform, for, whilst Baber advanced and secured these two capitals, the Rana made no sign whatever.

The battle of Paniput, that fulfilled the first part of the programme by shattering the Affghan power, made it imperative on him at once to strike the blow that was to destroy the new race of invaders and establish himself in the ancient seats of Rajpoot supremacy.

In the mean time north, south, east and west, the flame of disturbance and discontent spread like wildfire amongst a host of discontented nobles and princes. Everywhere the Hindoos and Affghans united against the interlopers, till Rana Sanka found himself at the head of 100,000 of the picked warriors of Hindostan. CHAP. XVII. 1525.

This imposing array was at first successful, and the vanguard of Baber's army defeated with loss. But these moments of temporary disaster and waning confidence were those best suited to the genius of Baber. Like Marshal Massena[21], he was careless and heedless in all his preparations for a campaign; guiltless of forethought, but in the time of action unequalled in history for energy and startling deeds of daring. The tactics of Baber were rather those of a successful partisan than of a great conqueror; he would, at some particular crisis or emergency, rouse himself to extraordinary action, and probably for the time eclipse the greatest conqueror that had ever lived; but the success attained, or the crisis averted, he would sink again into indolence and indifference: his nature was that of the giant, confident in his strength, but unwilling to rouse himself until compelled to do so.

The energy of the conqueror never rests: it is always on full stretch, striving onward and allowing no circumstance to stay its progress. With him battles are merely the means towards the great end of conquest. Baber liked fighting for fighting's sake, and saw in a battle not so much the means of gratifying his ambition as the actual object of his delight. He would invariably rouse himself with fury for the fight that was unavoidable, and was always successful; but once victorious, he relaxed in his endeavours; and, like Hannibal and many great generals, was slow to take advantage of success.[22]

Finding his chiefs discouraged he called a council of war, but it was like that of Clive at Plassy, or of Nelson before the battle of the Nile, not to elicit from them an excuse for avoiding the contest, but to express to all his unflinching determination to conquer or die.

BOOK II. 1525.

The splendid chivalry of such a man as Baber could not fail to inspirit men so impulsive and warlike as the Moguls. He urged them as soldiers to prefer death to defeat, and as true believers to prefer a crown of martyrdom to a life of infamy. The inspiring fanaticism of the Moslem creed worked its effect; and when, watching his opportunity, he seized the Koran, and proposed that all in his camp, serf and noble, squire and knight, should swear on the Holy Book to die rather than desert the field, not one man of the whole army held back. The success of an army so animated could never be doubtful; the green standard of the Prophet unfurled to the "Alla il alla" of such a host, was sure to wave in victory. Baber could rely with the greatest confidence on his Mogul soldiery; but of his Hindoo levies he still entertained considerable mistrust. Like those of our own day they were apt to waver in their allegiance the moment any power entered the field strong enough to threaten the fall of their existing masters.

Although the forethought of Baber, in suffering so formidable an army to assemble without opposition, may be open to criticism, his dispositions in the field were those of a practised soldier; he was everywhere animating his troops and instructing his generals; and where-ever the contest raged the fiercest, and the war-cry of his chiefs waxed faintest, there was the calpac or lofty turban of Baber seen towering above the battle. But he was fighting against fearful odds, and for many hours, his army, completely outnumbered, was compressed into a circle, and hemmed in on every side by the superior forces of his assailants. Finding at length, however, that the enemy gained nothing, whilst his phalanx was as firm as at the first, Baber determined to change his tactics; and, placing himself at the head of the gallant tribes of Timour and Allum, he rushed with the fury of a baited lion on the foe. "Then," says Baber himself, in his memoirs, "that wonder of our age, Mustafa Rumi, charged with great slaughter, and made the heads of the Hindoos fall from their bodies like stars from the sky; and victory, whose countenance bedecked with waving tresses had been concealed beneath a veil, as the bride of futurity, came to greet the present;" the Heathens were scattered like teased wool and broken like bubbles of wine.

The army of the Hindoos and Affghans, exhausted with repeated onslaughts, and shaken by as many repulses, was soon completely broken. Baber, glorying in his might, charged through and through the now panic-stricken ranks, and in the evening not a cohort remained of the magnificent army that in the morning threatened his very existence.

In the golden age of superstition that prevailed between the reigns of Louis XI. and Charles IX. of France, when every prince or noble of any standing in Europe kept in his pay a private astrologer, a Ruggieri or Galleatti, to whom was entrusted the special care of his own particular horoscope; and divination by the stars, by mirrors, by numbers, by ghosts, and, in fact, by almost every natural and unnatural agent that existed, was distorted to the purpose of the black art; when the science of alchemy was credited by the learned, and the philosopher's stone was an object of actual search amongst the scientific, we cannot be surprised at any amount of credulity that prevailed amongst the nations of Asia; that great superstition was rife in the days of Timour we know from the implicit reliance that was attached to the words of those who predicted the success of his future career from the conjunction of the planets; and there is an anecdote connected with the last of Baber's many battles, that illustrates at once the superstition of this Eastern warrior, and his magnanimous and forgiving nature. An evil-minded astrologer called Scheriff, who, like the son of Imlah, delighted in predicting evil against the king con-

BOOK II. 1527.

tinually, had noised it far and wide through the army, that Mars was in the west, and that, consequently, those coming from that quarter would be victorious; as this had direct allusion to the army under Rana Sanka, it implied the defeat of Baber.

Whether Baber was credulous enough to attach much weight to the fact of any particular planet being in its appointed place in the heavens at any particular moment, or whether like the great Roman emperor[23], on a similar occasion, he treated the whole subject with derision, does not much signify; but the many-headed are always credulous, and greedily swallow anything that at all savours of the supernatural. These sinister reports accordingly had the usual effect of confirming the cowards in their fear, and of giving a plausible excuse to the discontented to hang back from the contest. Baber, being annoyed with this evil prophet, had him arrested, but whether, like him of Samaria, he was nourished on "the bread of affliction, and the water of affliction," till the termination of the contest, we are not told. As the King of Israel never did return in peace, we are ignorant of the fate of Micaiah; but when the Sultan Baber returned, flushed with his splendid victory, he sent for the soothsayer, and instead of quartering him with wild horses, or putting out his eyes, or cutting out his false tongue, which would have been quite in accordance with the practice of the age, he gave him a lac of rupees, with a mild exhortation to go and prophesy no more.

Mohammed Baber was forty-four years of age, when, by the overthrow of the allied Affghan and Hindoo forces, he seated himself on the throne of Delhi, and finally established the Mogul dynasty in Hindostan.

After his last great victory over the Rajpoot chief, Sanka, his life was one of uninterrupted peace; his wars were now ended, his sword was turned into a ploughshare, and his superabundant energy found employment in the cultivation of the arts of peace, and in the pursuits of literature. He spent his time in restoring aqueducts, relieving taxation, planting delicious gardens, and raising the exotics of his native land; in cultivating the sister arts of poetry and music, in both of which he was a proficient, and in recording in plain unvarnished language the history of his own life, which, interspersed with genial anecdotes of his mother and sisters, his fellow-soldiers and his animals, constitutes one of the most charming and interesting autobiographies in any language. CHAP. XVII. 1527.

But "nihil est ab omni parte beatum," and Baber with his many exceeding great virtues, had one damning vice, common, indeed, to many great minds, and especially common to his own race and lineage, but none the less fatal on that account. From the earliest ages the Scythians and other nations of Central Asia had been renowned for their mighty powers of drink, and before the sobering injunctions of Mahomed had reached their country, Bacchus was their household god, and the presiding deity of their future paradise, which, like that of the early Germans, was one of immortal drunkenness.[24] Drinking has always been the vice of the Turki race, and so universal was the evil, at the advent of Mahomed, that he found it necessary, gravely to enjoin his disciples not to come to prayers till they were sober enough to know what they were saying.

Many of the greatest conquerors and warriors of the ancient world were renowned for their noble thirst and powers of absorption. The drinking-bouts of Cyrus, and Darius first king of Persia[25], are all famous in story; and whilst Alcibiades played practical jokes and insulted his hosts when drunk, and Alexander burnt cities and killed his best friends when maddened with wine, neither the philippics of Demosthenes nor the sharp irony of Cicero could limit the potations of Philip of Macedon or restrain the more than imperial excesses of Antony.[26]

But even the debasing effects of intoxication could not change the splendid nature of the noble Baber; and as he

BOOK II. 1527.

approached his end, generosity, his distinguishing quality, blazed out in a bright flame, that history can scarcely parallel. He had only occupied the throne of Delhi four years, when the life of his favourite son Humaioon was despaired of, and he was brought to Agra in a dying state. Every means was taken to drive away the disease; but in vain. As the Persian philosopher shrewdly observes: "If gods, destiny, and the blunders of the medical class did not sometimes agree, we should never die." The physicians pronounced their skill at fault; the garden of their art supplied no herb that could charm death's fatal power; and the wise men agreed that there remained but one chance by which the Sultan could preserve his son's life,—and that was a propitiatory offering to the Almighty of what he loved most on earth. The noble nature of Baber at once perceived an opportunity of indulging its generosity. His son's life was what he loved most on earth, and next to that he valued his own—he would give one for the other; he would devote his life to heaven as a propitiatory offering for his son: he turned a deaf ear to those counsellors who insisted that it was only the most cherished of our earthly goods the gods required; and refused to listen to those who tried to persuade him to devote the Mountain of Light[27] to this purpose; his generous soul allowed of no escape from the act of devotion he meditated. Life was what the angel of death required, and life he should have—the life of the father for that of the son. Walking three times round the body of the insensible Humaioon, and performing certain Mahomedan rites and incantations, he is supposed to have borne away the evil spirit that was vexing his son, and from that hour Humaioon began to flourish and the health of Baber to decay.

We of course know that unless the disease of Humaioon was infectious, Baber could not have contracted it, and even then his suffering could not have relieved his son; but that knowledge in our own age, does not in any way lessen the devotion of the act in those days of darkness and superstition. CHAP. XVII. 1527.

Baber, as well as his chiefs, fully believed that he was sacrificing himself for his son, and contracting a disease that must cause his death; and he has a right to the full glory of an actual self-sacrifice.[28]

Tenderness and devotion, the especial virtues of woman, constitute the brightest jewels in the female crown; unlike earthly gems their value does not consist in their rarity, and if temples of piety, as in the case of that noble daughter of Rome who nourished her mother at the risk of her life, were raised at every fresh instance of the display of these qualities in woman, doubtless, the world would soon be covered with structures to commemorate the devotion of thousands who have died for their children, or their husbands, or have shared with either the fate it was not in their power to avert.[29] But amongst men self-sacrifice is not so common a complaint, and their history furnishes many more instances of remarkable attachment to self, than of sublime devotion to others.

The histories of Constantine the Great, of Peter of Russia, and Philip of Spain[30], furnish us with sufficient instances of paternal cruelty, but we must search closely before we find as many of paternal devotion.

The history of the world does not, as far as I am aware, furnish another instance of a renowned warrior, in the prime of life, and the pride of successful dominion, devoting himself to certain death for the sake of a sickly son, not amidst the fury and shock of battle, or the excitement of mortal strife, but calmly and deliberately, in the depressing influences of the sick room, and in the face of the horrors and agonies of unknown disease.

For a parallel to this supreme act of devotion, we must go back to the days of fable and the mythological tales of the Argonauts; when Alceste, being informed by the physicians that her husband would not recover

BOOK II. 1527.

until human life had been sacrificed, at once devoted herself to death. Baber survived the recovery of his son but a very few weeks. With the last words of the Mahomedan formula, "There is no god but God," on his lips, and a tear drop, the only symptom of approaching death, in his eye, the soul of the great Zehyr-ed-din, Mohammed the Tiger surnamed the Victorious, passed into the hands of his Creator.

In tastes and habits Baber was essentially a mountaineer, and though the excitement of conquest and wheels of empire kept him in Hindostan, his heart was with the glorious mountains and rushing streams of his early conquests.

From the lofty minarets and gorgeous halls of the Charbagh Palace near Agra, his thoughts wandered back to the orchards and gardens of his loved Caubul. During his last sickness he remembered with yearning affection the scenes of his youth, and wished finally to rest amongst them. By his dying request his remains were taken to Caubul[31]; and to this day a humble mosque, surrounded by large beds of flowers, on the summit of the Baber Baghshah, a picturesque hill outside the city, commanding a noble prospect of mountains and plains, attests the respect that was paid to the last will of Baber.

We may search history in vain for a parallel to this great monarch. Eastern story especially affords but few of his metal. Learned in all the learning of the East, he combined the fanciful theology of Mahomed and the abstruse studies of the Moorish doctors, with a thorough knowledge of the Parsee literature, and flowery poetry of his native land of Turkestan. He wrote a learned treatise on prosody, and his collection of Turki poems entitle him to a high rank amongst the scholars and poets of his own country.

Merciful for a Mogul, tolerant for a Mussulman, affectionate as a son, devoted as a father, successful as a ruler, and unequalled as a partisan; generous as Hakim, chivalrous as Bayard or Roland, courting danger with the fierce delight of Richard of England, and sharing his love of battles without his stain of cruelty; genial and hearty to his friends, and forgiving to his foes; one who could weep for the playmate of his youth, and forgive the treason of his later years; a botanist, a historian, and a genial student of natural history; who could recount with equal simplicity and pleasure the growth of a new plant[32], an anecdote of a favourite animal, or the success of his greatest victory, we find united in him the noblest qualities of East and West, the refinement of civilisation with the perfection of native chivalry; and to him might be applied the panegyric of the great French philosopher on the amiable Sybarite of Rome, "that the only thing that could be laid to his charge was that he did not know how to be vicious."[33]

The life of the Sultan Baber, written by himself, and translated by Erskine, is one of the most charming and instructive volumes of Eastern literature. The evident truth and earnestness of his narration, the magnitude of his deeds, equalled only by the simplicity with which he describes them, are unrivalled in any autobiography extant.

As he fought so he wrote, going straight to the point; and to few does the praise awarded to Cæsar, "Eodem animo scripsit quo bellavit," apply with greater force than to Baber, the great founder of the Mogul dynasty.

His gossiping narrations of his lumbago, his drinking-bouts, his friends famous for leap-frog, his first razor, his shyness in carving a roast goose, and the consequent loss of his dinner, furnish very quaint and amusing pictures of the domestic life of the Moguls during that period.

His criticisms on his friends are redolent of strong sense and harmless satire. Of one lady who was a great talker, he said, "There can be no doubt that a great

BOOK II. 1527. talker must often talk very foolishly;" of another, he remarks, "his poetry is flat and insipid;" and then naïvely adds, "and it is surely better not to write at all than to write in that style." And a letter written to his son Humaioon when just entering manhood, appears more suited to Lord Chesterfield than to the great warrior of the Moguls. "In compliance with my wishes, you have indeed written two letters, but you certainly never read them over; for had you attempted to read them, you must have found it absolutely impossible, and would then have undoubtedly put them by. I contrived, however, to decipher and comprehend the meaning of your last letter, but with much difficulty. It is excessively crabbed and confused. Whoever saw a Moamma or charade in prose? Your spelling is not bad, but yet not quite correct. Your letter may indeed be read, but in consequence of the far-fetched words you have employed, the meaning is by no means intelligible. You certainly do not excel in letter-writing, chiefly because you have too great a desire to show your acquirements. For the future you should write unaffectedly, with clearness, using plain language, which would cost less trouble both to the writer and the reader."[34]

Of the state of society, or of the intellectual enlightenment of the Moguls and the other races of India at this period, we know little but what we gather from Baber's biography; but as it is the property of intellect to attract kindred spirits, and as the love of letters scatters its influence far and wide, it is probable that the Sultan was not the only accomplished man of his court. The fashions, whether good or evil, set by the monarch, are quite certain to be followed at no distant period by those who live on his smiles; and when it became evident that the study of the arts, and the pursuit of literature, were the surest road to the good graces of Baber, we may rest assured his courtiers used their best efforts to attain proficiency in both. It was the strong intellect and polished mind of Baber that formed the nucleus of that brilliant society of genius and learning that illumined the court of Hindostan, under the reign of his grandson Akbar. CHAP. XVII. 1527.

The gradual progress of the Europeans in the land they were finally destined to rule, is a subject of great interest; the Portuguese obtained the first considerable grant of land in that country in the year 1520. About forty years after the first expedition of the gallant Vasco de Gama reached the coast of Malabar, they gained possession, by treaty, of Bom Bahia, or the good harbour, the present Island of Bombay, and firmly established themselves both at Goa and in Bengal; but it was not only the increasing possessions of the "idolaters of the West,"[35] that mark this period of Indian history; there arose also about this time a small cloud in the north, that, insignificant at first and unnoticed by Baber, gradually attained sufficient magnitude to endanger the empire of his successors, and later still, to re-establish the tottering empire of their conquerors.[36]

Nannuk, a young Hindoo of good caste, who had been educated by a Mussulman of great learning, and initiated in all the observances of the Moslem faith, was seized with the laudable desire of uniting the rival creeds of Brahma and Mahomed. Considerable success attended his efforts; and under the name of Sikhs, there arose a sect who wore the peculiar garb, and lived the life of faqueers, and whose lives were marked by great devotion and toleration. Contrary to the unvarying practice of the Hindoos, all converts were freely admitted; but those of the Mussulman faith were the least esteemed.

Religious enthusiasm will always attract followers; and whether in the case of Nannuk, or of the Anabaptists in the sixteenth, or of Joe Smith in the nineteenth century, we see that novelty in religion, as in all other matters, offers an irresistible claim to the multitude; and too often we are forced to acknowledge that the success of

BOOK II. 1527.

the preacher who exalts the blessings of a future state, will be in proportion to the latitude he allows in the enjoyments of the present.

The new faith of Nannuk soon became the refuge for those whom the pride or persecution of more ancient creeds had banished from their communities. Their power increased with their numbers, and they soon found it quite as easy to seize as to beg, and having given their neighbours every opportunity of exercising their charity, by exacting all they had to give, they did their best to compel them to exemplify their other quality of longsuffering, by seizing everything they desired: they banded themselves together, and having obtained a tract of territory near Lahore, they gradually extended their tenets till they became one of the most powerful states of the North-west.

NOTES TO CHAPTER XVII.

[1] Solyman attacked Rhodes with 140,000 men and 400 ships.

[2] Francis I. was knighted by Bayard after the battle of Marignano. On the occasion of Charles V.'s visit to Titian, then an old man, he picked up the paint brush that had fallen from the great master's hands.

[3] Barbarossa was appointed by Solyman the Magnificent "Pacha of the Seas."

[4] The Spanish and French troops fought two whole days on the banks of the Sesia, where Bayard fell. The battle of Marignano lasted the same time, and Trivulzio, the French commander, who had seen eighteen battles, exclaimed, "All other battles compared with this were but children's sports. This is the war of giants!"

[5] See Erskine's Baber.

[6] The description of this scene bears a striking resemblance to that of Richard at Templestowe. "Your maidens are but sun-burned, if they are not worth the shiver of a broken lance," was the taunt of the Lion-hearted king.

[7] He boasts of having swam every river he ever crossed. But where?

[8] He made five inroads into India in seven years.

[9] Historians differ considerably as to who this Alim Khan, or Ala-ed-din, really was; he is variously represented as the uncle, brother, and son of Sultan Ibrahim.

[10] All Eastern campaigns have been conducted with immense bodies of cavalry; it has invariably been the arm of invasion, but has succumbed to disciplined armies of foot soldiers. It was the Macedonian phalanx that overthrew the legions of Persia, the Roman legions that conquered the world, and the French infantry that destroyed the fierce Mameluke cavalry at the battle of the Pyramids. Alexander never had much cavalry, and Cæsar had only 4000 horse with him at the battle of Pharsalia. The Egyptians are supposed to have had no cavalry at all. It is curious to look back and consider the various modes of warfare that have existed in the world, and in turn died out before others. The Trojans and Greeks fought in two-horse chariots. The Chinese, according to Confucius, in four-horse chariots. The Jews, we know, used donkeys almost entirely. The thirty sons of Jair, Princes of thirty cities, each rode on an ass—Judges x. 4. Saul had nothing but she asses. When Absalom killed Ammon, his brothers cleared out on the mules, and he himself was riding a mule when he was killed.

[11] Salmacus, a fountain of Halicarnassus, that rendered all who bathed in it effeminate.

[12] At Plassy 900 Europeans, 2100 Sepoys, and a few 6-pounders, defeated and pursued 18,000 horse and 50,000 foot. At Assaye 4500 British attacked and defeated 30,000 Mahratta cavalry and 20,000 regular infantry.

[13] The Moguls wore complete armour.

[14] To use Baber's own curt but forcible description, "in the battle of Paniput Ibrahim was sent to hell."

[15] Generosity was much admired by all Mussulmans, and the severest satire ever uttered by the Persian poet, Ebn-al-Hobaigah, against his countryman was, that "their men had not the heart to give or their women to deny."

[16] The ogre of fables and fairy tales was so called from the Oighurs, a tribe who composed the van of the Mogul army, and to whom cannibalism and other atrocities was generally attributed.

[17] In Mogul language *Bokhar* is the common appellation for learned men.

[18] So greatly was Balkh distinguished during the reigns of the immediate successors of Genghis Khan, that it was denominated Koblah-al-Islam, the metropolis of Islamism.

[19] Eastern proverbs say there are only two beautiful things in nature, "women and roses," and only two delicious ones, "women and melons." The seven wise men consulted by Periander, tyrant of Corinth, at once agreed that they saw but two beautiful things in the world, "roses and women," and only two good ones, "women and wine."

[20] "But he that hath no stomach for this fight, let him depart; his passport shall be made, and crowns for convoy put into his purse: I would not die in that man's fellowship, who fears his fellowship to die with us." Henry V. to his soldiers before Harfleur.

[21] There was this great difference between Soult and Massena: Soult was most far-seeing and elaborate in all his preparations for battle, but rather failed at the moment of action; Massena was weak and indolent in his preparations, but when the time came his vigour and energy generally insured success.

[22] "Non omnia nimirum eidem Dii dederunt," as Maherbal sorrowfully

BOOK II. 1527.

exclaimed to Annibal after the battle of Cannæ, when he refused to advance on Rome, that moment within his grasp,—"Vincere scis Annibal, victoria uti nescis."—*Livy.*

[23] An astrologer wanted to frighten the Emperor Vespasian from going to war on account of the sudden appearance of a comet. The emperor paid no attention whatever to the warning; but when at length they bored him with their lamentations, he said, "for my part, my friends, I think it must relate to the King of Parthia; for, see it has long red hair just like his, whilst I am bald."

[24] A story is told of an old Turk who left his wife in pledge to a wine merchant, having expended all he had in liquor.—Maximinus, a Roman emperor, could drink in a day seven gallons of wine, and eat thirty or forty pounds of meat.—Cambles, King of Lydia, was an uncommon hard drinker. He ate his wife when drunk, and did not know it till he found her hand in his mouth on awaking! He ought to have been translated to the Fiji Islands.

[25] Darius, first King of Persia, wrote his own epitaph; in it are these words: "'Ηδυνάμην καὶ οἶνον πίνειν πολὺν καὶ τοῦτον φέρειν κάλως"—I could drink much and carry it well.

[26] When the courtiers of Philip boasted before Demosthenes of the quantity their master could carry, he said it was the quality of a sponge rather than of a sovereign. Alexander's herculean goblet of two choæ held seven pints; he frequently drank it off by way of bravado. There was no tobacco in those days, and probably no coffee. The hookah and the coffee cup did not therefore supply the same solace to Eastern domestic life. Having nothing to do, Baber drank.

[27] The Agra diamond weighed eight miskals; its history was very ancient. A miskal is four drachms.

[28] Robert, son of William the Conqueror, was dying from a wound, by a poisoned arrow, the doctors said could only be cured by some one sucking the wound. Robert swore he would never be cruel and unjust enough to let another die for him; his wife, however, seized the moment when he dosed and died in his place.

[29] Paulina, wife of Seneca, opened her own veins when her husband was bleeding to death, and could scarcely be saved. Evadne, wife of Ceparius, one of the Septem contra Thebas, threw herself into her husband's funeral pile and perished.

[30] It will repay the student of history, to compare the haughty contempt of public opinion exhibited by Constantine, who executed his son Crispus, without deigning to give any reason whatever for it, with the conduct of Peter, who submitted to the judgment of Russia, of Europe, and of posterity, the reason that compelled him to kill his only son; and with the diligent excuses of Philip, who, never for one moment allowing that he caused the death of Don Carlos, made all sorts of apologies for his ill treatment.

[31] When Anaxagoras was asked if he would have his body taken to his birth-place at Clazomene, he said—"What signifies it? The road to the infernal regions is as short from one place as from another."

[32] The pine-apple was introduced by Baber, from the Portuguese. The Gulafshaun, or Garden of Delight, at Agra, produced as many as 100,000

in one year, together with roses, jessamines, sandal-wood trees, and all the fruits of Caubul.

[33] The remark of the Abbé St. Real on Lucullus.

[34] Erskine's Baber.

[35] The first European conquerors were supposed to be idolaters, from their frequent prostrations before shrines and images.

[36] The Sikhs seriously menaced the empire of Aurungzebe, and most materially assisted in repressing the rebellion in 1858-9.

CHAP. XVIII.

A.D. 1530—1555.

THE DISSENSIONS THAT ARISE AT THE DEATH OF BABER.—THE REVERSES OF HIS SON HUMAIOON.—THE BIRTH OF MOHAMMED AKBAR.—THE DEATH OF HUMAIOON BY ACCIDENT AFTER A NOMINAL REIGN OF TWENTY-FIVE YEARS.

BOOK II. 1530.

THE battle of Kanwa had broken the last hopes of Affghans and Rajpoots alike: under any circumstances their alliance could only have been temporary, and no sooner was it felt that the die was really cast, that Baber had the strength and will to remain in Hindostan, and that the rule of a new and more vigorous race was fairly inaugurated, than from all sides the rebel chiefs sent in their adherence to the new order of things. The generous policy, manly deportment, and conspicuous valour of the new conqueror, inspired his friends with confidence and struck terror into his foes. Within twelve months of his advance into Hindostan and eight after the defeat of Ibrahim, his sway extended from Attock to Bahar and from Kalpi and Gwalior to the mountains of Minala. Had his overruling influence been prolonged for a longer period, there is little doubt that the Mogul dynasty would have been at once firmly established; but his reign only lasted five years in Hindostan, too short a period to establish on a sure footing the succession of his much loved son Humaioon; and no sooner was he dead than the splendid empire raised by his own individual vigour began to totter for want of the same quality in his son. With his last breath he enjoined peace and good-will amongst his children; and Humaioon, with benevolence rare in an eastern prince, sought by all means in his power to obey these last injunctions. He behaved with the greatest generosity towards his brothers, but unfortunately without securing their hearty support. He assigned to Kamran the kingdom of Caubul and Candahar, and afterwards added the Punjaub and the countries on the Indus; whilst to Askeri he allotted Mewab; and to Hindul, Sambal. But this magnificent generosity failed to secure their hearty support, and from the commencement of his reign the usual domestic feuds, cruel as the grave, were his lot.

The wars of Baber had been chiefly with the Affghan race, who since the conquest of Mohammed of Ghor, had more or less supplied sovereigns to the throne of Hindostan, and it was from this haughty race that the first murmurings of the impending storm were heard.

Shere Khan, an Affghan chief of great talent, valour and influence, was the fomenter and leader of this discontent. He was without doubt the foremost man in India after the death of Baber: he was a warrior of great ambition, and possessed in an extraordinary degree that first requirement in an eastern conqueror, immense physical strength: he had in his youth killed a tiger with one blow of his scimitar, and through a life of battles remained unconquered. He had held a jagheer under Baber, who frequently remarked him as a man of energy and likely to become great, and between these two kindred spirits a friendly admiration appears to have existed. Whilst in attendance at Baber's court, Shere had many opportunities of remarking the power and wisdom of the new comer: he did not appear to have been much struck with either, and he frequently observed that, "if he could only unite the Patan forces, he would soon drive them out." From his youth he was impressed with, and stimulated by, a conviction that he

BOOK II. 1531. should eventually attain supreme power in Hindostan. This aim was never absent from his mind; and his favourite saying that, "two swords could never rest in one scabbard," showed his determination to stand no rival in Hindostan. Immediately on the death of Baber, Shere threw off the mask of dependence, and established himself in Bahar; and shortly after marrying a rich widow, he became master of Chinar, a strong fortress in the province of Oude, and its dependencies, together with a large treasure. Shortly after he conquered Bengal and being supported in his rebellion by Bahadoor Shah, another powerful noble, who at the death of Baber had seized the kingdom of Guzerat, he was able to assume a threatening attitude towards his sovereign.

In 1531, the year after his succession, Humaioon demanded the fortress of Chinar of Shere, and being refused he marched to occupy it; but in the mean time Bahadoor took the field with a large army, and threatened the Rajpoot capital of Cheetore. Humaioon immediately patched up a peace with Shere, and turned the point of his spears to Guzerat; but for some unknown reason did not proceed further than Gwalior; the Rana of Cheetore, disappointed of the promised protection of Humaioon, made his own terms with Bahadoor, and purchased peace by the payment of a large treasure. Bahadoor now ventured to enter Hindostan, and threatened Agra; he was, however, defeated by Hindul, the brother of Humaioon, and forced to retire. In the following year he again attacked Cheetore; but this time the gallantry of Humaioon was enlisted, and chivalry inspired a display of energy that duty had been unable to exact. From time immemorial there has existed amongst the Rajpoot races a chivalrous institution known by the name of the "Festival of the Bracelet." It was celebrated in the spring, and whatever its origin, it is one of the few occasions, when an intercourse of gallantry of the most delicate nature is established between the fair sex and the cavaliers of Rajasthan. On these occasions the Rajpoot dame sends to the object of her choice a bracelet with the title "of adopted brother." If he accept the pledge and send in return a corset or simple vest of silk or satin, worn by Rajpoot women of rank, he binds himself to hazard his life on all occasions for the safety of his fair lady, or even to gratify her whim by any act of devotion she may require. The bracelet may be sent by maidens; but only on occasions of urgent necessity and danger. Whole provinces of Rajasthan have at times been lost and won by the enthusiastic valour of "the bracelet-bound brother" of some distressed or ambitious princess. At the second invasion of Bahadoor, Kurnarath, the Queen of Cheetore, sent the bracelet to Humaioon, who, although at that time carrying on a war in Bengal against Shere, felt bound to obey it. So flattered was he at being chosen as the champion of the Queen of Rajasthan, that he pledged himself to obey her behests, "even if the demand were the castle of Rinthambar," the most cherished stronghold of the emperors of Hindostan. He set out immediately for Cheetore, but arrived too late to save the fair queen, although he amply avenged her death. Bahadoor had already taken Cheetore, after a determined resistance; victory being crowned by the death of 10,000 warriors and the self-sacrifice of all the women. Humaioon shortly after fell upon the forces of Bahadoor and utterly defeated him; he pursued him closely to the sea-coast, and arrived at Cambay only a few hours after he had taken ship to the small island of Diu.

On the occasion of Humaioon's first march to relieve Cheetore and his sudden halt at Agra, Bahadoor entered into a treaty with the Portuguese of Surat, and having by their assistance raised a force of 6000 Abyssinians or Negroes, marched to Ahmedabad; and doubtless the dread of falling into the hands of these fierce strangers was an additional cause for the unfortunate queen and her devoted subjects performing the supreme sacrifice of the johur.

In the meantime the rebellion of Shere gained head.

BOOK II. 1531. And he had signalised himself by the capture of Rhotas, one of the most remarkable feats of Indian warfare. The fortress was situated upon the top of a lofty and almost inaccessible hill, the only entrance to which was a very narrow road, through a steep ascent of two miles: this important pass was protected by a gateway of amazing strength, that laughed to scorn all assaults from without; whilst within the walls a large space of very fertile land furnished the garrison with grain and fruit, and a plentiful supply of very excellent water found everywhere a few feet from the surface, sufficiently secured the garrison from the terrors of famine or drought. Seeing no chance of taking the place by force, Shere had recourse to a ruse, as successful as it was bold. He sent to the governor Hurry Krishna Raja, who though a Rajpoot of courage and conduct, was also credulous and fond of money, to say that he purposed trying to reconquer Bengal, and wished him to take charge of his women and treasure till his return. Krishna Raja at first refused, but soon after relented. As soon as his consent to the proposal was obtained, Shere provided a number of dhoolies or litters, employed by Mahomedans of rank for the removal of their females from one place to another, within these he placed armed men, disguised in female attire, excepting only the first three, which really contained women; having also filled 500 money-bags with leaden bullets, he disguised some of his best soldiers as peasants, and entrusted to them the pretended treasure: they followed the dhoolies on foot and were provided with sticks to assist their progress up the hill with their ponderous load. Krishna was not directly duped; for remembering the fall of Asseer, a fort in Deccan, which was surprised in like manner by Nuseer Khan Farooky, ruler of Candeish, he had the three first dhoolies carefully examined, but finding only women, he was satisfied; and, with Rajpoot delicacy towards the fair sex, he allowed the others to pass unexamined. An entrance once secured, the conquest was easy, and Krishna barely escaped with life. Shere had now secured an impregnable retreat, and felt the courage that arises from the possession of a *point d'appui*, whence he could at all times threaten his enemies and at the same time defy their powers.

CHAP. XVIII. 1531.

Hearing of Shere's treachery and success, Humaioon sent Hussein[1], a Turcoman noble, to desire him immediately to send the umbrella, the throne, and the treasure of his new conquest of Bengal; to evacuate Rhotas and to restore the treasure and territory he had seized. Shere received the ambassador civilly enough; but replied that as it had cost him five or six years' toil, and the loss of a great number of his soldiers to subdue Bengal, it was impossible he could resign that conquest. Shortly after, Shere, in his turn, sent a famous Affghan dervish to treat of a peace with the emperor. The accounts of Shere's power and resources were unanswerable, and Humaioon was feign to accept the humiliating conditions of surrendering Bengal and Bahar, on the payment of a voluntary subsidy. But this display of weakness only strengthened the ambition of Shere: he immediately adopted means to make himself sole master of Hindostan. The day after the ratification of the treaty, he treacherously attacked the army of Humaioon, encamped on the banks of the Jossa, drove thousands into the river; and it was only by the assistance of a waterman that Humaioon escaped, and fled to Agra. Arrived at his capital, he made one short stand for the maintenance of his crown; his nobles crowded round him; and Cuttub the son of Shere, having rashly advanced too far, was defeated and slain, and his head sent in triumph to Agra. Taking heart of grace, Humaioon now advanced against Shere; but destiny had decreed the temporary fall of the Mogul dynasty. Again his army was dispersed, and hard pressed by the conqueror in Agra, he was forced to fly almost unattended to Lahore, from whence he returned to the Indus. Humaioon scarcely escaped with his life; and it

BOOK II. 1542. was only by a most hazardous and harassing march, in which nearly all his companions perished of madness or thirst, in those very deserts that had so nearly proved fatal to the army of Mahmoud of Ghizni, and after enduring patiently every insult that could embitter the cup of fallen majesty, that he reached a secure refuge in the territories of the friendly Rajpoot sovereign of Ajmere.

Here in the fortress of Ammercote, built on an oasis in the centre of the famed Marwar, the region of death, a desert as parched and fatal to vegetation and animal life as the great Sahara itself separated from the busy world without by a belt of several hundred miles of burning sand, navigable only by the sun-proof native and the enduring ship of the desert, was born of the sultana Hamida Banee, daughter of one of the most distinguished of Baber's Rajpoot allies, Jelal-ud-din Mohammed Akbar, destined to be the most enlightened legislator of his age, and the greatest monarch that ever mounted an eastern throne.

Although, Humaioon in his desert fortress was safe from all the hostile designs of his enemies, it was not so with his generous protector, whose border provinces were at the mercy of Shere Khan. After a short and anxious respite, finding all hope of a successful defence for the present denied him, Humaioon despatched his wife and her newborn infant to Caubul, and himself sought a more secure refuge with Shah Tahmash, the powerful monarch of Persia.[2]

Shere Khan was a magnificent monarch, combining many of the enlightened notions of his great master, Baber, with much of that picturesque[3] and ostentatious chivalry that has in all ages distinguished his people. But he was tainted with the cruelty and want of faith that has always tarnished the reputation of even the most brilliant sovereigns of the Affghan race.

The Affghans had now for many centuries been the

merchant princes of Hindostan. From their commanding position on the frontiers, and their long possession of the great mercantile cities of Peshawur and Lahore, they managed to engross the greater part of the overland trade to the kingdoms of Central Asia, and the northern districts of China. It is probable, therefore, that it was as much the interests of his own country and people, as the advantages to be derived by his new subjects in Hindostan, that prompted Shere Khan to exert himself so energetically to improve the trade, and the means of transit throughout his dominions; whatever may have been the cause, the effects were equally beneficial. From one extremity of his considerable empire to another he established horse posts, and planted the high roads with fruit trees to refresh and protect the weary traveller; and from Bengal to the Nilab, a branch of the Indus, for a distance of 1500 miles, he built a caravansary at every stage, and dug a well at every two miles. Although he built and endowed many magnificent mosques, he observed the most perfect toleration in all religious matters; and during his reign, the Brahmin in his temple enjoyed as perfect security in the exercise of his childish worship, as the Syed himself did in the most sacred mosque of Hindostan. In 1543 Shere marched to Rajpootana, for the laudable purpose of chastising Paran Mull, the Raja of Rasim, for keeping the regal allowance of 2000 concubines and dancing girls in his harem. This extravagant indulgence in female charms was too great an encroachment on the privileges of royalty to be borne in patience. After a gallant defence Paran Mull capitulated, on the terms of reducing the complement of his women, but marching out with all his arms, treasure, and garrison. Shere, however, who never kept a treaty that he did not like, surrounded the small band of Rajpoots, consisting of 4000 men, and massacred them to a man; but not until double the number of his own troops had paid the penalty of his treachery.

BOOK II. 1544. In the year following, Shere again invaded Marwar, and made war with Maldeo, the most powerful of the Rajpoot chiefs. Shere had an army of at least 80,000 men, whilst, by treachery and distrust, that of the Rajpoots was reduced to 12,000. Maldeo, however, repulsed him several times and would have defeated him, but for the arrival of reinforcements. The sandy country of Marwar produced only scanty supplies of barley; and when Shere, after his hard-earned victory, saw how much he had risked for so small advantage, he exclaimed bitterly, "that for a handful of barley he had almost given the empire of India to the winds." He then besieged and took Cheetore, and in the year following laid siege to Cullinder, a fortress only second in strength to Rhotas. In consequence of Shere's treacherous conduct to Paran Mull, the Prince of Cullinger would make no submission, and resisted to the death. Advances in regular form were made, trenches were dug, mounds raised for artillery, and mines sunk under the rocks. After some weeks' bombardment, Shere with several of his omrahs was severely wounded by the bursting of a shell; although cruelly hurt, and breathing with great pain, he encouraged the prosecution of the attack and continued to give his orders. In the evening news were brought to him that the place was taken: he had strength to exclaim, "Thanks be to Almighty God!" and immediately expired.

Shere Khan was a great sovereign: he spent fifteen years in a military career, and sat on the musnud of Humaioon five years. In obedience to Heaven's first law, and sensible that without order labour is but sorrow, he adopted the principle of the great Saxon sovereign, of dividing the day into four equal parts, allotting each with constant regularity to the same purposes: the first was devoted to the administration of justice; the second to the regulation of the army; the third to worship; and the fourth to rest and recreation. But the day was far spent when Shere Khan mounted the throne; the evening of his life was at hand; and he had only occupied the throne of Hindostan for five years when his crown descended to his son. CHAP. XVIII. 1545.

No sooner was Shere dead, than Humaioon left Persia and marched to Candahar, whence he steadily advanced to Caubul: here he was reunited to his son Akbar and his Rajpoot mother. Akbar was then four years old. Humaioon was overcome at seeing him, and taking him in his arms, exclaimed, "Joseph by his envious brethren was cast into a well; but he was eventually exalted by Providence, as thou shalt be, to the summit of glory." But the Affghan power was still too powerful, and Humaioon was again compelled to leave his country.

It was in the rocky capital of Caubul, amidst the fierce warriors of the mountains, that the young Akbar increased in wisdom and in stature, and learnt that simple and manly canon of the soldier's life, "to ride, draw the bow, and tell the truth," that from the earliest time has, by word at least, been enjoined the youthful chivalry of the East. And it was amongst the society of the warrior scholars of the school of Baber, that he acquired that love of learning and admiration of science that made him the most profound and liberal sovereign of his age. He imbibed amid the institutions and religions of a foreign land, that noble and enlightened toleration and love of progress that has associated with the name of Akbar the acts and virtues of one of the greatest legislators of the human race.

Shere Khan was succeeded by his son Selim, who, during a prosperous reign of nine years, walked in the steps of his father, and did more to develope the resources of the rich provinces that acknowledged his rule, than any sovereign had accomplished since the good Ferose. Had any number, however small, of the twenty-nine sovereigns composing the dynasties of the Affghans and Syeds, who in succession occupied the throne of Delhi, been gifted with the same liberal spirit of progress and toleration

BOOK II. 1554.

as Selim and his father Shere Khan, the biography of Baber would have contained a very different account of the wealth and prosperity of Hindostan, to that which he describes as existing at the time of his invasion. During the two centuries preceding the conquest of Baber, scarcely twelve years had ever elapsed without some successful revolution. Under these circumstances any permanent progress was hopeless. Although prosperity might occasionally interfere during those rare periods, when an enlightened sovereign happened to be at the helm, it was merely a temporary season of amelioration, which the next commotion was almost sure to sweep away.

During the two years that succeeded the death of Selim in 1552, no less than four princes of the race of Shere Khan, ascended the throne of Delhi. This rapid and sanguinary substitution of princes of the same race, was too much even for the restless nobles of Delhi: and in 1554 Humaioon was recalled by the unanimous voice of the small, but omnipotent oligarchy, who always surround an eastern throne.

After a banishment of twelve years, Humaioon now marched on to Agra and Delhi, in company with his son Akbar. He defeated Secunder, nephew of Shere, under the walls of Sirhind; and the sceptre of empire passed for ever from the Affghans. Although restored to his throne, Humaioon did not live to regain his original possessions. By an extraordinary coincidence, six months after his return, he was killed by an accident, almost similar to the one which deprived him of his grandfather thirty years before.

He was descending from the terrace of his palace of Delhi, when the mueddin of the royal mosque called to prayer; the emperor immediately paused, and having, according to custom, repeated the creed of Islam, he seated himself on one of the steps until the functionary had ceased his summons. As he rose, he slipped on the

ble steps, and being taken up insensible died, at the age of fifty-one, after a nominal reign of twenty-five years in India and Persia. Exactly thirty years before Amer, the father of Baber, fell by accident from the roof of his pigeon-house and was killed.

CHAP. XVIII. 1554.

Humaioon was buried on the banks of the Jumna, where Akbar raised over him one of the finest mausoleums that even the sunny land of India can boast; composed entirely of marble, and remarkable more for perfect symmetry and simplicity than for elaborate excellence; it strikes all beholders with admiration; and in many minds will contest the palm of perfection with the more elaborate Taje. The tomb of the emperor is surrounded by those of the several omrahs who had continued faithful to him in his many reverses. In this tomb of the first hereditary monarch of the Mogul race, the last Mogul emperor of Delhi was taken prisoner, and his sons shot, by Captain Hodson, in 1858.

NOTES TO CHAPTER XVIII.

[1] A curious story is related of this Hussein. During Humaioon's flight to Persia, he was cruelly robbed and insulted by his suite; amongst the culprits he suspected Hussein of stealing a box of trinkets, and desired Kafur, one of the eunuchs, to cut off part of his ear. Kafur mistook the order, and cut it off altogether. On this the emperor, being angry, sent for a surgeon and had the ear sewn on again; assisting in the operation, and apologising for the mistake.

[2] Persians have in all ages boasted of their hospitality.

[3] Dirt is said to be one of the elements of the picturesque; and if Baber's account of the Affghans, "that they never changed their clothes till they were worn out," was correct, their claim to this characteristic is undeniable.

CHAP. XIX.

A.D. 1554—1578.

AKBAR ASCENDS THE THRONE IN 1554.—HE RE-ESTABLISHES THE MOGUL POWER IN HINDOSTAN.—THE HEROIC DEFENCE OF THE HINDOO QUEEN DURGETTI AGAINST HIS GENERAL ASIPH JAH.—THE THIRD SACK OF CHEETORE.—THE CHIVALROUS DEFENCE OF PERTAP.

BOOK II. 1554. THE life of Charles V. is the history of Europe during a period of almost fifty years; that of Akbar embraces the history of Hindostan for almost the same period. In the same year that the great Emperor of the West resigned his crown in favour of his son Philip, Akbar "the victorious," "the glory of the House of Baber," "the example of renown to the Kings of the Earth," succeeded his father on the throne of Delhi. He was only fourteen years of age; his kingdom was rent by innumerable fierce and powerful foes; and he mounted the throne amidst a sea of troubles and reverses; his enemies soon made themselves masters of Agra and Delhi; and in less than a year the provinces west of the Indus were all that remained to him of his Indian dominions.

It is only natural to suppose that, at so youthful an age, his immediate attendants would exercise considerable control over his actions; accordingly, we find that for the first four years of his reign, his uncle Behram Shah, called Khan Baba or King's Father, a Turkoman noble of great power and talent, kept him in the most complete subjection: punishing and pardoning, and disposing of the great offices of the state, and even of the person of the king himself, with a magnificent independence, that reminds one of the haughty control exercised by the great Earl of Angus over his youthful sovereign James V. During this period Behram slowly and laboriously recovered the lost conquests of Baber and Humaioon; and reestablished the Mogul power, that had again succumbed to the Affghans and their adherents. It is probable that this task would never have been accomplished but for the bitter and unceasing enmity that existed between the Hindoo and Affghan princes, and rendered unity of action, even against the common foe, almost impossible.

CHAP. XIX.

1554.

Akbar's most formidable enemy was a Rajpoot chief, named Himu, who had been vizier at the court of the Patan emperor Mahommed: at the death of Humaioon, he had succeeded in making himself master of Delhi and Agra, and openly proclaimed himself sovereign of Hindostan. When Akbar marched to regain his capital, Himu met him with 100,000 horses and 50,000 camels, and mounted musketeers, and 3000 elephants, trained to the field. His confidence equalled his power; and the night before the action he sent a message to Akbar, that he was young, and must not imagine he was able to sustain a contest with a monarch of his superior might. "Come not," said he, "within the reach of my numerous and resistless troops and elephants, lest in the collision thou come to harm. I resign to thee all the territories eastward from the Jumna to the uttermost limits of Bengal—be mine the remainder of Hindostan."

Akbar in reply reminded him there was little cause for boasting of success over his former Affghan rivals. "Where," said he, "is the glory of throwing a chain over a slave? Without experience of a battle, or having known aught of a shock with the warriors of my race, what canst thou conceive of the horrors of an equal conflict? The shadows of night disappear at the approach of day, when the lord of light unsheathes the sword of splendour: at to-morrow's dawn come to the field in thy strongest

BOOK II. 1554.

array—we shall then see whom God is disposed to favour." This battle was fought at Paniput, a field always propitious to the House of Timour.[1] Himu, after showing desperate valour, was slain, and his dead body brought to Akbar. Behram urged him to insult the corpse, and cut off the head with his own hands: he answered, that some time back, whilst amusing himself in his father's library, and looking at some pictures, a portrait was placed in his hands, which he was told was Himu. "Instantly," said he, "I tore the thing to tatters, and threw it away from me; let it suffice now that the man has met with his deserts; I considered that I had then achieved my victory over him."

Ferishta relates the story in another form, that illustrates more distinctly the sanguinary code of justice under which Akbar passed his kingly apprenticeship, and the nature of the power usurped by the haughty Behram. According to that, the unfortunate Himu, after losing an eye, and showing the most devoted courage, was brought a prisoner to Akbar. Behram told him it would be a meritorious action to kill the brave infidel with his own hand. Akbar, in compliance with the advice of his tutor, drew his sword; but only gently touched the head of his captive, at the same time bursting into tears of compassion. Behram, looking sternly upon him, intimated that the ill-timed clemency of his family was the source of all his misfortune, and with one stroke of the sabre severed Himu's head from his body.

The cruel and imperious rule of Behram was soon distasteful to the young prince; and at the age of eighteen he seized the opportunity of a hunting-party to return suddenly to Delhi, in the absence of his minister, and there to proclaim himself sole and irresponsible manager of his kingdom.[2]

Behram followed his young master to Delhi, but finding his influence destroyed he withdrew from the court, and maintained a haughty reserve. An accident, however, soon fanned his smouldering wrath into a fierce flame. Akbar was fond of elephant-fights, and during one of these displays an infuriated monster broke from his keeper and ran over Behram's tent. Roused thus unceremoniously from his sullen reserve, the rage of Behram knew no bounds: he would receive no explanation, and treated it as a premeditated insult; he withdrew altogether from the capital, and collecting around him some discontented omrahs, actually ventured to enter the field against his sovereign.

When the young monarch of Hindostan found it necessary to teach the lesson of humility to his too-magnificent subject, this Wolsey of the East, he did not, like the fickle sovereign of England, despoil and hunt to death the man to whom he owed so much of his power and success; and when, after two years of unsuccessful rebellion, Behram came in the greatest distress, with his turban round his neck, to humble himself at his master's feet, Akbar raised him with his own hand, gave him a dress of honour, and placed him in his former station at the head of his omrahs. He freely forgave one whose best years had been devoted to his and his father's service; and offered him the choice of three roads to advancement—the command of the frontier, then the seat of war; a residence at court; or a royal retinue and income, to enable him to make a becoming pilgrimage to the tomb of the Prophet. Behram chose the latter; and in the language of the East, "having contracted his skirts from the business of the world, and his heart from the pursuits of vanity and ambition, he turned his face from this world to another, and pursued his pilgrimage to Mecca."

Once freed from the influence of Behram, the natural disposition of Akbar showed itself in even brighter colours than before: the generosity; the love of justice; and the hatred of tyranny; so conspicuous in the character of this prince, distinguished him far above all others of his race,

BOOK II. 1565. and are more remarkable when we remember the hard merciless school in which he was educated.

The restoration of the Mogul power was in no degree arrested by the disgrace and dismissal of Behram. Akbar at once proved his ability to regain and to govern the lost provinces of his empire: by turns he recovered Ajmir; and Gwalior, the Vincennes of an Eastern Versailles; and after a fierce contest drove the Affghans, with loss, from the fertile province of Oude. At the age of twenty-five, after nine years of incessant warfare, spent in repressing sedition and punishing open rebellion in almost every part of his dominions, Akbar had firmly established his rule over all the provinces conquered by his grandfather Baber; and he began to turn his longing eyes to fresh conquest in the Deccan, the golden regions that have always engrossed the superfluous energy and wealth of the sovereigns of Hindostan.

The march of Akbar lay through the forests of Khandeish, at that time tenanted by large herds of elephants, now unknown north of the Neilgherry Hills. The young monarch had been educated in the Persian school of chivalry and adventure. "Train up thy son in the exertions of the chace," say the precepts of that warlike race, "and when the day of battle arrives he will subdue his fears." He was the mightiest hunter since the days of Nimrod; and on grand occasions he would turn out whole armies for a campaign against the wild denizens of the forest and the plain. So keen was he in all that related to sport, that he kept a clerk of the chace to note down every head of game that he killed, and what gun he had used on each occasion. In this paradise of sportsmen, Akbar spent several months; and whilst he judiciously combined business with pleasure; by alternately hunting the monarch of the Indian forests; espousing a king's daughter; or chastising a rebel prince; his general Asiph Jah was engaged in a campaign, which has left an enduring stain of cruelty on his own name, while it has gilded with unfading glory that of the heroic queen who was his antagonist. CHAP. XIX.

The small territory of Gurrah, in Gundwana, a district of Bundelcund and Orissa, 300 miles long and 100 broad, and fertile and prosperous to an unparalleled degree, was ruled by a Hindoo queen, named Durgetti, famed throughout the Deccan for her beauty and her accomplishments. 1565.

In this favoured district, safe from foreign invasion, ten sovereigns of her race had reigned in perfect peace, bent only on securing the happiness and prosperity of their subjects, and in laudable efforts for increasing their own treasure. In the case of Durgetti, however, prosperity had not induced the loss of energy and resolution that so often accompanies it; and history does not contain an example of courage more admirable, and constancy more heroic, than that displayed by the unfortunate Queen of Gurrah.

Indignant rather than alarmed at the approach of the Moguls under Asiph Jah, she summoned her peaceful yet devoted subjects, and, mounted on a swift elephant, a helmet on her head, a quiver by her side, and a burnished lance in her hand, she advanced at the head of 1500 elephants, 8000 horse, and some foot, to drive the invaders from her soil. Whilst thus displaying the daring of Thomyris or Boadicea, she was not wanting in the consummate generalship of Artemisia.[3] Finding that her troops, unused to warfare, were getting into disorder by advancing too rapidly on the enemy, she halted, and reforming them, gave orders that none were to advance till the signal was given from the royal elephant. The unexpected energy of the men of Gurrah took the Moguls by surprise; they were driven back almost without resistance, and 600 left dead on the field.

Could the victorious queen have enforced her tactics, and persuaded her nobles to support her in a night-attack on the discomfited Moguls, her kingdom and her throne

BOOK II. 1565.

would have been saved. But her subjects were not a warlike people; they had never liked fighting for fighting's sake; and with the majority of the world they found greater delight in enlarging on the glory of past encounters, than in hazarding fresh ones.

They refused to second the queen's energetic designs; and the next day, when Asiph Jah attacked them with fresh troops, they were seized with a panic, and, flying before the guns and lances of the Moguls, left their heroic queen, supported by only four chiefs, to bear the brunt of the battle. Deserted by her troops, agonised at the loss of her son—who, after fighting with great valour, was slain by her side, pierced through the eye with an arrow—and struggling against the faintness that oppressed her, she refused the most urgent solicitations of those who yet remained with her to fly for safety. "It is true," said she, addressing Adhar, the chief officer of her household, "we are overcome in war, but shall we also be vanquished in honour? Shall we, for the sake of a lingering ignominious life, lose the reputation and virtue we have been so solicitous to acquire? No! let your gratitude now repay that service, for which I lifted up your head, and which I now require at your hands. Haste—let your dagger save me from the crime of putting an end to my own existence!" Adhar still refusing to fulfil the "immortal longings of her soul," she snatched the dagger from his side, and plunged it into her own bosom. Where in the history of ancient or modern days can we find an example of heroism more noble, or constancy more illustrious, than that which irradiates the last moments of this royal princess of Hindostan?

But the leisure of Akbar was not of long duration: he had overcome the open enmity of his hereditary foes; but he had now to encounter the hidden discontent of his own religion and kindred. He was the first sovereign of India who made no distinction between Hindoos and Mussulmans, in those he raised to power; he aimed at being sovereign of a united people; and maintained that each class and creed had an equal claim to his countenance and support. He treated with undisguised contempt many of the most revered forms and superstitions of the Mussulmans; and amongst other things had the strongest objection to a beard, the Mussulman's most cherished ornament, which he would hardly admit into his presence. CHAP. XIX. 1565.

These causes of discontent were increased by his marriage with two Rajpoot princesses of the Houses of Jeipur and Mewar; and he was openly accused by the Uzbeks, his own tribe, of being too partial to the Hindoos. Many leaders revolted, and, being joined by Khan Zeman and Bahadoor Khan, two powerful omrahs, they seized the soubahs of Oude and Allahabad.

This rebellion was put down by an act of daring, worthy the grandson of Baber the Tiger. The enemy was encamped in absolute security thirty miles from the Ganges, then rolling down its turbid waters at the very height of the periodical rains. It was night when Akbar reached the opposite bank: no boats were procurable, and his officers tried in vain to stay his impetuous advance. But nothing daunted him: without hesitation he forced his elephant into the stream, and, followed by about 1000 of his bodyguard, reached the opposite shore. Without waiting for the remainder of his troops, he made a forced march; and in the morning the enemy were startled from their security by hearing in their very front the deep ominous sound of the royal Nakarah,[4] that announced the presence of the dreaded Mogul! No efforts of the leaders could arrest the panic that seized the rebel camp: Khan Zeman and Bahadoor Khan both fell into the hands of Akbar, and when the sun rose their army had vanished like the morning mist.

The pages of Indian history are rich in numerous instances of the heroism and devotion of the gentle sex, in defence of their honour, or in blind obedience to the

BOOK II. 1566. cruel tenets of their faith. The history of the heroic Queen of Gurrah is by no means a solitary one; and an anecdote connected with this exploit of Akbar, exhibits devotion as complete, if not as conspicuous. Bahadoor Khan[5] possessed a Hindoo mistress, who is said to have been one of the most beautiful women ever seen in India. She was accomplished as she was fair; and her verses were esteemed the most beautiful in the Hindoo language. During this sudden swoop of Akbar on her rebel lord's camp, she fell into the hands of a Mogul chief famed for his fierce and cruel nature: finding herself unable to resist his importunities and threatened violence, she appointed an hour to meet him. Arrayed in her most splendid attire, on which she sprinkled the richest perfumes, she lay down on a couch with a mantle drawn over her face; her attendants thought she had fallen asleep, and endeavoured to awake her on the approach of her enemy, when to their horror they found she had taken poison, and was already dead!

In the year 1566 Oody Singh, monarch of Rajpootana, grandson of the brave Sanka Rana, who contested with Baber the empire of Hindostan, took advantage of these disturbances to harass the border provinces of Hindostan; and in the spring of 1567 Akbar marched from Agra, at the head of a powerful army, to effect the conquest of Rajpootana and lay siege to Cheetore. There is an anecdote connected with Oody Singh, or, as he is more commonly called, Oody the Fat, that illustrates the marvellous devotion to the royal line that distinguishes the chivalrous race of Rajpoots. Shortly after the death of Sanka, the nobles, disgusted with the insolence and cowardice of his son Bikramajeet, conspired against him, and elected Bunbeer, the natural son of Pirthiraj, a famous warrior of their race, to the throne. Bunbeer, assisted by the confederate nobles, immediately slew Bikramajeet; intending at his leisure to destroy Oody his son, then six years of age. The story is thus told: the child was asleep "after his rice and milk," when his nurse heard the screams from the women's quarter; and the barber, coming in directly after, to take away the remains of the dinner, told her of the cause—the assassination of the Rana. Aware that the murder of the father was but the precursor to that of the son, the faithful nurse put her charge into a fruit-basket, and covering it with leaves gave it to the barber to take to the fort. She had scarcely time to substitute her own infant for her prince, when Bunbeer entering inquired for him; she dared not speak, but pointed to the cradle, and unmoved beheld her child die!"

CHAP. XIX. 1567.

Cheetore, the capital of Rajpootana, is situated on a hill flat at the top, and walled in to the extent of ten English miles; there was only one ascent to it, cut out of the solid rock, and defended by four magnificent gates. The first attack of Akbar on this renowned fortress was unsuccessful; he was repulsed by the concubine queen of Oody, who, fully armed, drove back the besieging forces, and penetrated to the royal tent. Oody praised her before his nobles, and said he was indebted to her for the safety of his capital,—a fancied imputation on their courage which so enraged them that her life was sacrificed to their fury.

After the death of this valiant lady, the honour of the defence was shared by Jeimal of Bednore and Pulta of Kailwa, a noble young chief only sixteen years of age. After several months spent in the close investment of the fortress, during which his troops were constantly repulsed, the personal skill of the Emperor was the means of terminating a siege that was seriously taxing the resources and constancy of his army.

Akbar was the best shot in his dominions, and, being one night in the advanced trench, he saw Jeimal, the brave leader of the defence, busily engaged in the ramparts, encouraging his men in repairing the breach. Akbar sent for his favourite gun, called "Droostandauz"

BOOK II. 1567.

(straightforward) with which he had slain several thousand head of birds and beasts, and, watching his opportunity, shot his enemy in the forehead, dropping him in his tracks. The besieged, losing courage with the fall of their chief, determined to court the death they could not escape; and, according to their cruel custom, slew their women and children, and clothing themselves in yellow, the colour of mourning, rushed out and died to a man amongst the horsemen and elephants of Akbar.

The death of the young chief Pulta of Kailwa is one of those romantic incidents that add such conspicuous brilliancy to the pages of Rajpoot history. His father had fallen at the beginning of the siege; and after the death of Jeimal, when all hope of saving the city was gone, his mother desired him to put on the saffron robe and join his father in Paradise. With alacrity he prepared to obey her commands; and in order that he might have nothing to regret in this life, she armed herself and his young bride, and, descending the rock, fell in the sight of both armies, in an onslaught on her foes.

This was the third sack of Cheetore, the two former being that of Allah the Sanguinary, A.D. 1295; and of Bahadur sultan of Guzerat, with his Abyssinians, in 1533. On the first occasion twelve royal princes defended the "crimson banner"[6] to the death, and several thousands of both sexes performed the Johur; at the second sack under Bahadur, 13,000 women, headed by Karnaveti, the bracelet-bound sister of Humaioon, performed the Johur; whilst on this, the third occasion, 8000 Rajpoots, with all their wives and families, gloried in the same dreadful rite. The Rajpoots may indeed be proud of the heroism of their women; and the third defence of Cheetore especially stands conspicuous for noble examples of female devotion.

Akbar utterly destroyed Cheetore, and it never reassumed the distinction of the queen-fortress of Rajasthan: he slew most of the chief inhabitants, and displayed a severity quite at variance with his accustomed humanity and particularly strange when we remember his Rajpootni origin; his double marriage with princesses of Jeipur and Mewar, and the numerous princes of that race who served in his army.[7] Many of Akbar's most successful and most favoured generals were Rajpoots. At court the highest place of honour amongst the assembled princes was always allotted to the Rana of that race; in the magnificent hall of audience at Agra he stood at the right hand of the forty-seven princes, who, each by his silver pillar, daily attended at the divan of the Mogul. After the Battle of Cannæ, Hannibal collected three-and-a-half bushels of knights' rings; after the last sack of Cheetore, seventy-four-and-a-half maunds of cords of distinction, from the necks of knightly Rajpoots, were brought to the tent of Akbar.

CHAP. XIX. 1570.

The famous fortress of Rhintamboor, whose strength had become a proverb among the Moguls, was the next object of Akbar's ambition; and in the spring succeeding the fall of Cheetore he besieged it in person; he had been some time before its impregnable walls without the hope of surrender; when a Rajpoot chief, Bhogwandas of Ambir, and the celebrated Raja Maun, also a Rajpoot, and Akbar's most trusted general, determined if possible to corrupt the integrity of Soorjun Hara, who held the castle for the Raja of Mewar.

The courtesy of immemorial custom permits to belligerent Rajpoots free intercourse during any truce or suspension of hostilities: warriors who had been fighting to the death all day would constantly meet at night for friendly gossip. During the protracted siege of Rhintamboor, Raja Maun obtained frequent access to the castle for a friendly chat with his opposing countrymen; on one of these occasions the Emperor Akbar accompanied him, in the guise of a mace-bearer. Whilst conversing, an uncle of Soorjun recognised the Emperor; and with the

BOOK II. 1570.

sudden impulse that arises from respect, took the mace from his hands, and placed Akbar on the cushion of the governor of the castle. The Emperor's presence of mind did not forsake him: "Well, Raja Soorjun," said he, smiling, "what is to be done?" To which Raja Maun, without giving time to the astonished governor to reply, answered, "Leave the Rana of Mewar, give up Rhintamboor, and become the servant of the Emperor with high honour and office." The proffered bribe was magnificent; including the government of fifty-two districts, whose revenues were to be allotted to him, on furnishing the customary contingent of troops; with liberty to name any other terms, which should be solemnly guaranteed by the Emperor. The bribe was too tempting, and Akbar returned to his camp, carrying back with him the keys of Rhintamboor.

The Rajpoots were divided into numerous tribes, whose rivalry was not unfrequently settled in a manner that reminds one of the fierce contest of the clan Chattan and clan Quhele before Robert III. of Scotland, on the North Inch at Perth.

Colonel Tod, the Froissart of Rajpootana, has preserved the following narrative, that illustrates conspicuously the fierce devotion of that race of warriors, whose god was the God of Battles, and who were never known to turn their backs on a foe.

Shortly after Akbar had retired from Cheetore, the Rana Pertap, who had succeeded his father, Oody the Fat, determined to try and recover some of the frontier fortresses that had fallen into the hands of the Moguls; and he assembled all his chiefs for the attack on Ontala, a frontier fortress in the plains, about eighteen miles from Cheetore.

When the chiefs assembled in council, and the plan of attack was decided upon, a fierce dispute arose between the chiefs of the two powerful clans of the Chondawuts and the Suktawuts, as to which had the right to lead the assault. The former claimed precedence as an hereditary privilege; whilst the Suktawuts urged their superior valour as an unanswerable claim for the vanguard. The dispute would probably have terminated in a combat on the spot, had not the Rana assigned the van to the clan that first entered Ontala, and thus turned to the best advantage the fierce rivalry of his chiefs.

Ontala was situated on rising ground, surrounded by a wall of solid masonry, a stream flowing at its base; the walls were strengthened by round towers at short intervals, and one gate alone gave admission to the castle. The rival clans moved off to the attack a few hours before daybreak: the chief of the Suktawuts made directly to the gateway, trusting to the elephant he rode to force the gate; whilst the Chondawuts, furnished with ladders, and guided by a shepherd of Ontala, attempted to scale the walls. Both parties received a check; the chief of the Chondawuts was shot dead as his foot pressed the topmost step of the ladder; and projecting spikes deterred the elephant of the Suktawut chief from applying his strength to the gate. The shout that accompanied the fall of the Chondawut chief was mistaken by the rival clan for a signal of success; their leader could stand it no longer—with desperate devotion he placed his body on the spikes of the gate, and commanded the mahout, on pain of instant death, to drive the elephant against him. His terrible command was obeyed: the human cushion protected the head of the elephant, and the gates gave way. But even this devotion failed to purchase the honour for his clan; for as his men rushed into the city, over the dead body of their chief, they heard the triumphant shout that announced the success of their rivals; the dead body of the Chondawut chief was already in Ontala! As he fell dead from the ladder, his body was seized by his kinsman, a warrior known through Mewar as the Mad Chief of Deoghur, who rolled it in his scarf, and tying it on his back, mounted the ladder, and driving back the defenders

BOOK II. 1570. with his lance, threw it over the parapet of the fortress, shouting, "The vanguard to the Chondawuts—we are first in!"

The Rajpoots never recovered the invasion and severity of Akbar. Their princes and chiefs, it is true, still struggled on, with their wonted chivalry and devotion, in attempts to regain their lost position, but in vain; from that date their existence as a strong independent monarchy or principality ceases. They were still the most daring and successful warriors in India; no army could take the field with any chance of success without a Rajpoot contingent; but as a nation they were ever after subject to the Moguls, and later still were cruelly oppressed by the Mahrattas. The annals of Rajpootana are replete with the most charming and inspiriting relations of chivalry and devotion. In these their latter days, the position of their sovereign and princes was almost identical with that of Robert the Bruce and the early warriors of Scotland, when struggling for existence against foreign invasion and domestic treason. The nature of the country, composed of mountains and streams, and castellated strongholds, increases the similarity between the translations of Colonel Tod and the charming compilations of Sir Walter Scott.

Pertap was a high-spirited prince, who displayed to perfection the brilliant qualities of Rajpoot chivalry. Alone amongst the Rajpoot royal families, he scorned all matrimonial alliance with the monarchs of Hindostan; and when in poverty, and flying from his enemies, he refused to eat with Raja Maun, the favourite Rajpoot general and brother-in-law of Akbar, saying "He could not eat with a Rajpoot who gave his sister to a Turk, and who probably ate with him."

Hopeless as was the Rajpoot cause, Pertap would not allow that his country was conquered, and determined to strike one more blow for its independence. Nine years after the fall of Cheetore he assembled a force of

22,000 men in the Aravulli hills, and attacked the Mogul army of occupation, encamped on the plains of Haldighat, under Prince Selim, afterwards the Emperor Jehangire, with great vigour and determination; the battle was fiercely contested, but the defeat of the Rajpoots was complete; of the 22,000 warriors who descended into the plains to attack the Mogul army scarce 1000 regained their fortresses.[8] CHAP. XIX. 1570.

The escape of Pertap is a charming romance that somewhat reminds one of the friendly recognition occasionally interchanged between the Greek and Trojan warriors before the walls of Troy.

He had borne himself nobly in the fight; and mounted on a dark grey charger, famous throughout the country for its beauty and courage, he had forced his way to the royal elephant and slain the driver, although unable to reach the Prince Selim; but valour was unavailing against unequal odds, and at length, covered with wounds, he was forced to fly unattended on the gallant steed that had borne him through the terrible day; his flight was perceived by two Mogul leaders of Selim's army, the chiefs of Moultan and Khorassan, who pursued him across the plain, closely followed by an unknown warrior who dashed unexpectedly from the ranks: the race was a close one and watched with eager interest by the warriors of the Mogul host: already the gallant horse of Pertap was beginning to flag, and his escape to the mountains appeared impossible, when an intervening gully hid both pursued and pursuers from view; his death or capture appeared certain; what then was the astonishment of the Mogul army to see him emerge unpursued, whilst the unknown warrior returned alone towards the army. He was immediately led before Selim and questioned as to the disappearance of the two chiefs and the escape of Pertap: his answer was that Pertap had slain them and then escaped. Selim, however, doubted this story, and pledged his word to forgive him if he would confess the truth;

BOOK II. 1575. thus assured, he confessed that he was Sukta the brother of Pertap, and that the two chiefs had fallen by his hand. In early youth Pertap and his brother Sukta had quarrelled, and the latter had left Mewar and served under Akbar. He was in attendance upon Prince Selim at the battle of Haldighat and his heart was hardened towards his brother, but when he saw the blue horse flying unattended, resentment ceased and affection urged him to follow. "The burden of a kingdom," said he, "was on my brother's shoulders, nor could I see his danger without defending him from it."

Selim kept his word and dismissed him to his brother, with whom he afterwards did good service for Mewar.

For many years after the defeat of Haldighat, Pertap led the life of a hunted animal; so closely was he followed, that four times the food actually prepared for him was abandoned for want of opportunity to eat it. In his greatest misery his fortitude remained unshaken, and the admiration of Akbar was extorted by the account of a spy who found the Rajpoot monarch and his chiefs seated at a scanty meal, maintaining all the etiquette observed in prosperity; the Rana bestowing the dish of honour on the most deserving, which, although in this instance consisting only of the wild fruits of the country, was received with all the reverence of better days.

The constancy of Pertap met its reward at the hands of the chivalrous monarch of Hindostan. He restored to him a portion of his territory, and allowed him to found the new city of Oodipur. The last few years of his life were spent in peace; but till the time of his death he would never enter a palace, fearing the love of ease would induce him to forget his duty to his country.

He died enjoining a continuance of war to his son; and thus does the able chronicler of Rajpoot heroism describe his last moments. "Pertap was lying on a wretched pallet in a lowly dwelling surrounded by his chiefs, when a groan escaped him: his uncle enquired 'what afflicted his soul that it would not depart in peace?' 'It lingered,' he said, 'for some consolatory pledge, that his country should not be abandoned to the Turks,' but when his brave companions pledged themselves to guarantee the honour of his son, and swore by the throne of Cheetore that they would not permit mansions to be raised till Mewar had regained her independence, the soul of Pertap was satisfied, and with joy he expired."

CHAP. XIX. 1575.

NOTES TO CHAPTER XIX.

[1] Baber gained the empire of Hindostan at Paniput. Akbar two victories. Humaioon one over Lodi the Affghan.

[2] His escape from the trammels of his powerful subjects bears a marked resemblance to that of James V., when he fled by stealth from the control of Angus, the head of the family of the Red Douglasses, and rode by night from Falkland to Stirling, where he proclaimed himself king.

[3] *Thomyris*, queen of the Massagetæ. She attacked Cyrus at the head of her army, killed him and cut off his head, and flung it into a vessel full of human blood, exclaiming, "Satia te sanguine quem sitisti."

Artemisia assisted Xerxes with her fleet in his expedition against Greece. It was in reference to her that Xerxes remarked that, "his women fought like men and his men like women." The Athenians being ashamed to fight with a woman, tried to compass her assassination, and offered 10,000 drachms something under 5000*l*., for her head.

[4] The nakarah was the imperial kettledrum.

[5] See Elphinstone's *India*.

[6] The Rajpoot banner.

[7] Humaioon married one daughter of Hassan, Khan of Mervat, Behram another.

[8] Tod's *Rajasthan*.

CHAP. XX.

AKBAR OBTAINS THE FORTRESS OF RHINTAMBOOR BY STRATAGEM.—THE BIRTH OF HIS SON JEHANGIRE.—THE MAGNIFICENCE OF THE COURT OF AKBAR.—HE REMOVES THE SEAT OF GOVERNMENT FROM DELHI TO AGRA.—HIS ENLIGHTENED POLICY.—HIS REVENUE SYSTEM.

BOOK II.

A.D. 1576–9.

DURING the years 1576-7-8, and 9, Akbar was chiefly employed in the conquest of Bengal, styled also the Paradise of Regions, an undertaking of no mean importance when we consider that its ruler Rajah Maun Sing had 280 sons, all of whom had erected hill forts, and were united in their support of their father. But Bengal was not singular in its number of strongholds, for it appears that during Akbar's reign the number of fortified places was very large; there being in Hindostan alone not less than 2400 fortresses of competent strength.

It was not only in the Deccan, Rajpootana, and Bengal, that the armies of Akbar spread the glory of his name and the renown of his victorious rule. Cashmere, the garden of the world, was annexed during his reign, and Cabul, Lahore, and Moultan, were numbered amongst his twenty-two provinces. The power and dominion of Akbar were far greater than those of any sovereign who had preceded him on the throne of Delhi. From the Hindoo Khoosh to the table land of the Deccan, and between the mouths of the Ganges and the Indus, his power was felt and acknowledged.

There is nothing in the East now at all resembling the magnificence of Akbar's court, and well may a patriotic native sigh over the fallen grandeur of his country. In gold and jewels he was doubtless the richest monarch of the world, and his state far exceeded that of any former sovereign of Hindostan. Although Akbar abstained from meat on Fridays and Sundays, and on other days was content with milk, curds, rice and turmeric, one hundred dishes were always ready to be served at a moment's notice.

Thirty millions sterling composed the magnificent revenues of this mighty prince; and the jagheers and soubahs bestowed, and resumed at will, amounted to twenty millions more. Three hundred thousand cavalry, the same number of infantry, and a thousand elephants, constituted the standing army that curbed the dangerous ambition of his powerful nobles, and enforced the friendship of foreign princes.

The court of Akbar was the most splendid, as well as the most polished, of the day; the love of pomp and display distinguishes the Moguls above every people of the East; and the priceless jewels and the tissues of gold and silver that graced the persons of the nobles, and their more than regal followings, often amounting to many thousands of armed retainers, caused Delhi and Agra to resemble rather the resort of many friendly independent princes than the capitals of one mighty monarch.[1] Under the enlightened patronage of Akbar himself, and the emulation of his princely subjects, genius received that support and encouragement without which both arts and science die; and the presence of men of letters and learning, attracted from all the regions of the East, added the crowning jewel of wisdom to the court of Akbar, and combined to render his capital the glory of the world and the wonder of mankind.

Unlike Baber, who was an adventurer from his youth, Akbar was the hereditary sovereign of a great kingdom, and he sought his own renown, and the wealth and prosperity of his people, not so much in those fierce wars of annexation by which his ancestors had gained foreign

BOOK II.

A.D. 1576–9.

subjects at the cost of the blood and lives of their own, as by the steady, though gradual, amelioration that arises from the cultivation of the arts of peace and civilization. The secret of Akbar's great success, as the ruler of a divided and tempest-torn empire, lies in the broad noble paths of policy which he laid down for himself, and which he suffered no personal fancy or family interest to overthrow. Strange as it may appear to us, the chief objects he kept in view, in the selection of the governors of his numerous provinces, were, first, the welfare of the kingdom and people to be governed, and next his own glory and renown. The advantage of the individual, whoever he might be, never for a moment weighed against the good of the million; nor were private fortunes realised at the expense of the federal glory of the state. His treatment of the soubahs and governors of provinces, after their appointment, will strike us as even more remarkable than the mode of their selection. From the moment of their appointment they were subject to the closest supervision, and a very correct account required of their stewardship; indifference or inefficiency did not, as now, boldly soar far above all criticism; nor was negligence then encouraged by the confidence that the same interest employed to obtain an appointment would be all-sufficient to suppress any subsequent censure or inquiry.

Akbar removed the seat of government from Delhi to Agra, on account of the difficulty of navigating the Jumna in dry weather; the river was navigable all through the year up to Agra; but during the dry season a portion of its bed, to the extent of 150 acres, was cultivated annually, and yielded superior garden crops.

Agra had been a city of importance before the Mahommedan conquest, and was spoken of in terms of admiration by the poets of Ghuznee; and we have the authority of Jehangire for believing that at this period it was the finest city in India. The citadel built by Akbar was magnificent; it was commenced in 1563, and finished in four years; its circuit was a mile, and in the size and immensity of its stones it was truly Egyptian; whilst the delight of the Gulafshawn, or rose-diffusing garden, erected by Baber, and adorned with the wild pine, the plane and the betel, was long the boast of Hindostan. The magnificence of Akbar in adorning the city was imitated by his lords; they vied with each other in gorgeous erections, and it was ranked with Gwalior and Muttra, then esteemed as surpassing all the cities in the known world. The trade of Agra was immense: Jehangire tells us that "for nearly eight months in the year, which is the dry season, not less than five or six thousand horses daily entered the city from Cabul and countries in that direction; and such was the rapidity of their sale, that not one could be bought the following day."

Here, overlooking the Jumna, and protected from intrusive glances by a most elaborate marble screen-work, was the harem, where the great Akbar secluded from the vulgar gaze the choicest beauties of the eastern world. Akbar's harem numbered 7000 souls, 5000 of whom were women; each had a separate room, and they received regular pay, varying, according to their beauty or other merit, from 600 to 1000 rupees per month.

About twenty-four miles from Agra, in the direction of Delhi, Akbar built a magnificent palace on the summit of the sandstone hills of Futtehpore Sikri. The walls enclosing the royal palace, its offices and courts, were six miles in circumference, and had within their limits some of the highest points of the Bhurtpore or Biana range of hills. Here Akbar kept his enormous hunting establishment and witnessed the fights of wild animals, then a popular spectacle in the East. All that now remain to tell of the magnificence of the pleasaunce-house of the Mogul are scattered ruins and embankments, and the remains of a tank upwards of twenty miles in circumference.

Till Akbar was twenty-eight years of age he had no

BOOK II. A.D. 1576–9.

male child that survived above an hour, and in order to propitiate Lucina, the goddess of babes, he made a pilgrimage on foot, attended by all his court, from Agra to Ajmere, a distance of upwards of 200 miles, at the rate of ten miles a day, to offer up his vows at the tomb of a famous Dervish.

It would appear the holy man did not possess the charm desired by Akbar; and the year following he took his favourite mistress to the house of another famous saint, Sheikh Selim at Sikri, and left her that she might derive the necessary benefit from the prayers of that holy man; here she remained several years, till at length her faith or the importunity of the Sheikh was rewarded, and she bore a son, who in honour of his spiritual father took the name of Selim, and afterwards ascended the throne under the title of Jehangire. Jehangire always styled himself Sheikh Selim's slave, and in his honour had his ears bored, and wore earrings, the badge of servitude.

This was not the only occasion on which the piety of Akbar was rewarded in the miraculous production of progeny; a short time before, his favourite son Daniel was born in like manner in the house of another holy Sheikh of the same name.

Akbar was the exact contemporary of Queen Elizabeth of England; raised to the throne three years sooner, he was gathered to his fathers two years later than that Virgin Queen. During two centuries the natives of Britain, amidst a rapidly progressing civilization, looked back with pleasure to the days of good Queen Bess; and amid the utter stagnation of everything that can ameliorate the lot of humanity, the native of India has to this day but too good cause to recall with bitterness the days of plenty and prosperity enjoyed by his ancestors under the great Emperor Akbar.

Queen Elizabeth owed a great proportion of the remarkable success of her reign to the administrative talents of the great men who served her crown; whilst Akbar was no less worthily seconded in his noble endeavours to ameliorate the condition of his subjects by the devoted talents of two of the most enlightened men that ever adorned an eastern court. What Burleigh and Bacon were to Queen Bess, what Sully was to Henry Fourth, that Abu-l-Fazl and his brother Feize were to Akbar, at once the ministers and confidants of the sovereign, the favourites of his hours of relaxation, the councillors of his kingly duties, and the truthful historians of his reign: the first was the most enlightened statesman, and the second the most profound scholar of the day; and during a quarter of a century these admirable men devoted their energies to fostering and giving life to the noble designs of their great master. In the works called the Ayeen Akbary, and the Akbar Nameh, the joint composition of these two brothers, we have the most exact records of the population and religion, the arts and sciences, revenue and produce of the country, together with the minutest incidents connected with the acts and sayings of that great king of the East.

Abu-l-Fazl and Feize were the sons of a learned Mussulman, who from a Sunnee, or follower of the Caliphs, became a Shia or disciple of Ali; nothing could be more bitter than the animosity existing between these two sects, and he was consequently exposed to the most galling persecution; Feize was the first Mussulman who applied himself to a diligent study of Hindoo literature and science; he pursued his studies under a learned Brahmin at the holy city of Benares. This Brahmin believed him to be a neophyte of his own caste, and initiated him carefully into all the learning of the Brahmins; when, at length, he discovered his error, his despair was intense; he prepared the funeral pile to destroy himself, having violated his most sacred oath in imparting the secrets of his caste to a stranger; it was only on Feize's solemn promise never to divulge his lore

BOOK. II. A.D. 1576–9.

that he consented to live. From the twelfth year of his reign, to the year before his death, these two brothers were the inseparable friends, advisers, and companions of Akbar. The power of the pen was great in the days of the Mogul, and it was a common saying in Asia that the pen of Abu-l-Fazl was even more fatal than the sword of Akbar.

The famous revenue system of Akbar, designed by the Hindoo Rajah Todah-Mul, and fully described by Abu-l-Fazl, was founded on the most minutely laborious survey ever undertaken. It was intended to effect three objects; first, to obtain a correct measurement of the land; secondly, to ascertain the amount of the produce of each measure, and to fix the proportion that each ought to pay to the government; and thirdly, to settle an equivalent in money for the proportion so fixed. To effect this a new and most careful measurement of the lands was made, and the fairest possible average of value struck; every peculiarity of the district was taken into consideration; the exact nature of every kind of soil, the command of water, the security of the village, were all carefully calculated; and, that not even a shadow of complaint should exist, the leather rope with which the surveys were ordinarily made, and which was apt to stretch with the dews of morning, and shrink with the midday sun, was changed for a rod which was unaffected by like causes.

The assessment was one third of the produce of the soil, and the commutation was fixed at an average of produce for nineteen years; but every man, who thought the assessment claimed too high, could insist on an actual measurement and division of the crop, and might pay in kind if he considered the commutation unfair.

The settlements were at first annual, but were afterwards changed to ten years, and at the same time all vexatious fees and taxes to officers were abolished.

Akbar destroyed the whole system of middle-men, and with one stroke of his pen swept away the payment of many taxes on the necessaries of life. In the seventeenth year of his reign the taxes on oil, salt, sugar, and perfumes, on copper utensils, on linen and woollen cloths, on fuel and grass, in fact everything the ryot most used for food and raiment, were repealed; only those articles the rich used, and could pay for, were still taxed; elephants, camels, horses, silken stuffs, warlike weapons, sheep and goats, all paid 1 per cent. There was neither salt-tax nor spirit-tax, and the tax on opium, which is now considered a pillar of wealth, but which is in reality a monument of shame, was unknown to him.

Under the old Hindoo regime, the land-tax, as we have before seen, was $\frac{1}{6}$th or 16 per cent. Shere, the Affghan, raised it to $\frac{1}{4}$th or 25 per cent.; whilst Akbar increased it to $\frac{1}{3}$rd or 33 per cent.; but Abu-l-Fazl asserts that owing to superior manangement, Akbar's taxation was in reality the least oppressive.[2] The abolition of so many indirect taxes naturally diminished the nominal revenue of the country; but it also diminished the defalcations in realising it; so that, whilst the profit of the state remained nearly the same, the pressure on individuals was much lessened.

From time immemorial, the Hindoo land-tenure has been between the ryot and zemindar; the ryot got enough profit to keep him till next harvest, whilst the remainder was stored up in the granaries of the zemindar. The Mogul Tartars, when they conquered India, extended this system of necessary policy throughout the country; instead of seizing the lands of the vanquished, they confirmed them in their possession; the numbers of the conquerors bearing no proportion to the conquered, self-preservation obliged them to reside together, and to hold the sword in their hands: had they scattered apart, and attempted to settle in different provinces, they would soon have ceased to be a people, and their power would have been broken piecemeal. They retained therefore their military as distinct from their proprietary character;

BOOK II. A.D.1579.

when they reduced a province, they made the taxes paid to former princes the invariable rule of their imposts; the people almost unwittingly changed their government; but the change was a beneficial one; it was the substitution of a mild despotism for a fierce exacting tyranny The territory of Akbar did not nearly equal in extent our own, for we cannot allow that his possessions of Cabul, Oude, and Lahore, were at all equivalent in value to the Deccan, and the whole of the Madras presidency; but there is ample cause to believe that his revenues were much larger, and his taxation less grinding.

Whatever may have been the faults of Akbar's revenue system, there is little doubt that the country increased as much in value and prosperity during his reign of fifty years, as it has decreased during our domination of one hundred. The land-tax of Akbar amounted to twenty-five millions, ours to twenty-one; his assessment never exceeded 33 per cent., ours frequently exceeds 60; the whole twenty-five millions that swelled his revenues were sooner or later distributed over the country; of the twenty-one millions that form our Indian revenue, an annual sum of five millions comes to this country never to return.

The returns procured by Akbar and Abu-l-Fazl were actually intended to illustrate the true condition of the country; to exhibit the actual wants and requirements of his subjects, and to ascertain the most practical plan for their amelioration; they were designed to remedy abuses, and to expose misrule; and where these did exist they were laid bare without favour or affection. The Ayeen Akbary and the Institutes of Akbar, were written by Feize in the fortieth year of Akbar's reign, and the power, terseness, and simplicity of those annals founded on facts, cemented by honesty and surmounted by truth, will indeed appear marvellous to those accustomed to seek for truth through the maze of circumlocution and detail that mystifies the official publications of our day.

Whilst the enlightened Feize chronicled the important events, catalogued the resources and productions of the country and the people, and drew up those truthful reports in accordance with which oppressive taxes were lowered or abolished, religious toleration enjoined and enforced, and justice and security ensured alike to the prince and the peasant, the innocent and the guilty; his brother, Abu-l-Fazl, established schools all over the country, in which the natives were taught the arts, literature and history of other nations, in books translated into their own language by the express command of the Emperor.

In the schools Akbar founded, everyone was educated according to his circumstances and distinct views of life: he did not foolishly presume to insist upon the superiority of his own language over all others spoken in his dominions; he did not require the thousands to learn the language of one before they could profit by his knowledge; but he required that one should learn the language of the thousands that he might instruct them. He did not shut the door of knowledge to all who could not enter in by the narrow gate of his own vernacular; it was not the learning of the parrot, the repetition of mere words, that he wished to impart to his subjects; he knew that if he wished to civilize and ameliorate the masses it must be by information and education, imparted in their own language; not in that of the conquerors.

It was not then, as now, necessary for the student to devote long years to the study of the strange and difficult language of his rulers before he could profit by their literature. The poetry of Persia, the learning of Arabia, together with the theology and science of the wise men of the West, were translated into the numerous languages spoken by the several nations of his subjects; and in that form the page of civilization was not, as now, legible to the few, but one which all who ran might read.

Noble as were the political principles and conduct of Akbar, the quality which, in a Mussulman, strikes us with

BOOK II. A.D.1579.

the greatest admiration is the remarkable display of religious toleration that obtained for him the proudest title a sovereign can earn from subjects of a divided faith, that of "the guardian of mankind." Although Timour the Tartar was a famous Shia, or worshipper of Ali, his descendants very soon became Sunnees, or believers in the Caliphs. These rival sects hated each other with bitter hatred, and many have been the bloody contests between them.

Akbar himself was a Deist, and had no sympathy with the intolerance of his countrymen about matters of no material importance. He was excessively liberal in religious matters, professing openly that, in his opinion, God could only be worshipped by following reason, and not by yielding implicit faith to any revelation. He was the first sovereign of India who made no distinction between Hindoos and Mussulmans in those he raised to honour: he aimed at being the sovereign of a united people; and to reconcile the antagonistic creed of his subjects, and to make both religions less tyrannical and less oppressive, he constituted himself head of the church and promulgated the creed, "there is no God but God and Akbar is his Khalif."

As regarded the Mahommedan religion, he commanded that prayers, fasts, pilgrimages, public worship, should be optional; he removed the penalties on the use of unclean animals, the moderate use of wine, and on gaming and dice, and circumcision was not allowed till the age of twelve, when the person was old enough to judge of its use.

As regarded the Hindoos, he forbade the slaughter of all animals for sacrifice, trial by ordeal, marriage before the age of puberty, and the burning of widows against their will; he also permitted widows to marry a second time contrary to Hindoo laws.

Akbar took a glorious pride in allowing every sect and creed to worship God in whatever form their reason or their imperfect lights enabled them to see him. He did not, as many of the great and mighty in the world have done, and been canonized for it too, enter a dark room with the dazzling light of religious intolerance in one hand and the sharp sword of persecution in the other, and smite and revile all who did not at once see as he did. CHAP. XX. A.D. 1579.

Sending one day for the Mullah Gheas-al-Dien, a very celebrated divine of Persia, much respected for his abilities and purity of life, he asked him, "which was the best of all the various sects of Islam?" He replied, "suppose a great monarch to be seated in a palace with many gates all leading to it, and through whichever you enter, you see the Sultan and can obtain admission to his presence: your business is with the Prince and not with those at his gate;" signifying that it was a matter of utter indifference who kept the door, whether Mullah, Brahmin, or Priest, or by which door you entered, so long as it led to the throne. Akbar wishing to elicit another argument in support of liberal doctrine, asked him "which in his opinion was the best of all faith?" He replied that, "the best man of every faith, in his idea, followed the best faith."

The progress of Mohammedanism in some parts of India was very slow, and at this period the name even of Islam was proscribed in Benares. The great mass of Akbar's subjects were Hindoos; their supple creed might bend before the whirlwind of Moslem fanaticism, but it always sprang erect again when the storm was past; they never attempted to increase the number of their own religion, or to interfere with that of their fellow subjects; and except in cases of extreme oppression and exasperation, they seldom supported their belief with the sword, or turned on the heel that crushed them. A people so numerous and so completely swayed by a hereditary priesthood could only be happily governed by conciliating the good-will of the priestly caste, and by securing to them the free exercise of the rites and ceremonies of their faith.

BOOK II. A.D. 1579. Under the weak and injudicious predecessors of Baber, Moslem intolerance had gained head, and the influence and wealth of the Hindoo faith proportionately decreased; but the beneficent reign of Akbar immediately re-established the rightful equality; and whilst all vexatious imposts, that impoverished the shrines, irritated the priesthood, or interfered with the enjoined pilgrimages of the worshippers of the Hindoo Trinity, were abolished, the contentment of the great mass of his people was insured, and the faith by which alone more than one hundred millions looked for salvation, was permitted to flourish, free from the taunts and indignities of the hitherto triumphant creed.

But it must not be supposed that his liberal policy was inaugurated without much bitter animosity amongst the bigoted omrahs of Akbar's court. The following letter to his son Prince Selim, afterwards the Emperor Jehangire, who urged him to persecute the Hindoos and destroy their temples, remains as a noble testimony of his liberality, and of the bitter spirit of persecution he had to curb.

"My dear child.—I find myself an omnipotent sovereign, the shadow of God upon earth. I have seen that he bestows the blessings of his gracious providence upon all his creatures without distinction. Ill should I discharge the duties of my exalted station, were I to withhold my compassion and indulgence from any of those entrusted to my charge; with all the human race, with all of God's creatures, I am at peace; why then should I permit myself under any consideration to be the cause of molestation and aggression to any one? or besides, are not five parts in six of mankind either Hindoos or aliens to the faith? and were I governed by motives of the kind suggested in your enquiry, what alternative can I have but to put them all to death? I have thought it therefore my wisest plan to let these men alone; neither is it to be forgotten, that the class of men of whom we are speaking, in common with the inhabitants of Agra, are usefully engaged either in the pursuits of science, or the arts, or of improvements for the benefit of mankind, and have in numerous cases aimed at the highest distinction in the state; there being to be found in this city men of every description and of every religion on the face of the earth."

In accordance with his principles of perfect toleration, Akbar allowed the Jesuits to build churches in Agra and Lahore, and even endowed colleges. Not content with extending perfect toleration in religious matters to all classes of his subjects, his strong intellect took considerable interest in the doctrines and disputes of the several Moslem, Christian, and Hindoo schools of theology; and he found especial delight in encouraging, and listening to the learned discussions carried on, between astute Brahmins and keen Jesuits, and the scornful Moslems of his own intolerant faith, who by his express command, frequently assembled to discuss their several articles of faith in his presence. He took a secret pleasure in exposing and laughing at the violence and intemperance that on all sides marked these verbal exercitations.

On one occasion, when three Jesuit missionaries from Goa arrived at Agra, to discuss certain doctrinal difficulties, with the Mullahs, before the Emperor in person, he appears to have pitted them against each other much in the same manner as he would his elephants, in whose ponderous combats he took so much delight. He began by informing the startled missionaries, that an eminent Mullah had undertaken to leap into a burning fiery furnace, without any other defence than the Koran he carried in his hand, and expressed a hope, that in order that the discussion might commence on equal terms, one of their number would display a similar amount of confidence in the Bible. At first the missionaries shrank from this unexpected proof of confidence, and modestly but firmly declined the unwonted "*auto-da-fé.*" It was only

BOOK II. A.D. 1600–3.

when irritated beyond endurance by the taunts heaped upon them by the triumphant Mullahs, and beginning to suspect that the very common game of "brag" had been studied in the schools of Agra, to the full as much as in the other parts of the world, that they agreed to the terms: with this difference; that instead of rashly leaping into the furnace, they should deliberately walk in, in company with the Mullahs, each bearing aloft the emblem of his faith. The Mullahs, who with all their unmeasured virulence, do not appear to have possessed the complete confidence in their creed, exhibited by the 450 prophets of Baal on a similar occasion, now in their turn declined the ordeal, replying only by a torrent of abuse, which the Emperor found it necessary to check.

Although Akbar gave his full support to the general faith of the Hindoos, there were some observances of their religion, the injustice and inhumanity of which roused his strong opposition. By the most active personal exertions he suppressed all involuntary Suttee; and on one occasion, hearing that a Hindoo Rajah of great power intended forcing his son's widow to mount the funeral pyre, he rode in hot haste a long distance, in order by his presence to stay the intended sacrifice. "Immemorial custom," says the Institutes of Menu, "is transcendant law, approved in the sacred scriptures, and in the code of divine legislators; let every one therefore of the three principal classes, who has a due reverence for the supreme spirit which dwells in him, diligently and constantly observe immemorial custom."[3] Suttee has this unanswerable recommendation of immemorial custom; and nothing but force will ever completely suppress an observance sanctified by such antiquity, and so plainly enjoined by their religion, as the immolation of high caste Hindoo women on the funeral pyre of their husbands: and indeed Hindoo widows have not much choice in the matter: their future is so utterly miserable and hopeless if they neglect this barbarous observance, and so blessed if they respect it, that there are few who hesitate long on the subject. According to the Gentoo laws, every woman who thus burns shall remain in paradise with her husband three crore and fifty lacs of years; whilst those who neglect it are ordered to cut off their hair, cast away their ornaments, preserve inviolable chastity, and to labour in the service of their children; and even then their future is not secured.[4] A woman who becomes Suttee after the death of her husband obtains pardon both for her own and her husband's sins, so that they may both remain long in paradise; and even if the husband should have gone to hell, "just as a snake charmer draws out a snake from his hole, so would the woman draw her husband out of hell, and place him in paradise." As a devout follower of the amorous prophet of Mecca, who out of his seventeen wives made choice of sixteen widows, Akbar abolished all legal difficulties about the marriage of widows amongst the Hindoos, and tried to ensure to them the same matrimonial chances as their spinster fellows; but against the prejudice of 3000 years even he could effect little: neither arguments nor force could ever make the Hindoos recognise as admissible a union forbidden by all the most revered articles of their faith, or to abandon a custom sanctified to them by immemorial custom.

CHAP. XX.

A.D. 1600–3.

The last few years of Akbar's reign were embittered by domestic calamities: the death of his eldest and favourite son Daniel by drink; the rebellion of his second son Selim; the death of Feize; and the cruel murder of his dear friend Abu-l-Fazl.

The death of Prince Daniel of drink, at the age of thirty, offers a remarkable illustration of the ruling passion strong in death. Daniel, like his father, was a famous shot, and had a favourite gun called "Jennauzah, the bier," because he never missed with it. Like his brother Selim, and indeed most of his race, he was a desperate drunkard, and being seized with an attack of delirium tremens at Burhampore, he was closely watched, and instant death

BOOK II. A.D. 1600–3.

threatened against whoever should give him the poison he craved; after trying every means to elude the watchfulness of his friends, he at length tempted one of his guards by a large bribe to conceal some spirit in the barrel of Jennauzah and bring it to him; this last debauch caused his death, and his favourite gun thus literally became his bier.

The grief of Akbar at the death of the faithful and accomplished Feize is thus touchingly described: "It was midnight when the news reached him that Feize was dying; he hastened to his apartments, but found him already insensible; he raised his head and called out to him with a familiar term of endearment, 'Shekhji, I have brought Ali the Physician to you, why do you not speak?' Finding he received no answer, he threw his turban on the ground, and burst into the strongest expressions of sorrow. When he had recovered his composure, he went to Abu-l-Fazl, who had withdrawn from the scene of death, and remained for some time endeavouring to console him before he returned to his palace." [5]

But it was the death of Abu-l-Fazl that put the finishing stroke to the domestic calamities of Akbar. A report was industriously circulated by the enemies of this great man that he was poisoning the pure fountain of Islamism in the heart of Akbar. This was an excuse for a revenge on a stern and troublesome mentor that was too tempting for the honour or duty of Prince Selim: he employed Madhucar Jah, a Rajpoot adventurer, to slay the aged Minister, and bring his head to Court. The murder of a powerful Vizier is no unfrequent occurrence in Eastern courts, but it is not often we find a son glorying in being the assassin of his father's most beloved friend; yet that such was the conduct of Selim is known from his own cruel boast. In his autobiography we find these words: "Actuated by these reasons," (viz. a fear that Abu-l-Fazl was weakening Akbar's Moslem intolerance,) "it was that I employed the man who killed Abu-l-Fazl and brought his head to me."

Akbar was much distressed, and for two days and two nights took neither rest nor food; he was ignorant of his son's guilt, and even made the sad occasion an opportunity for seeking to renew the affectionate relations that for some time had ceased between them.

Four years before the death of Akbar, Queen Elizabeth despatched the English consul at Constantinople overland to India with an autograph letter to the Great Mogul, soliciting certain trading privileges: but the Jesuits, already firmly fixed in India, and jealous of any European interference, frustrated all his efforts, and made his journey of no avail. A few years afterwards, however, the English by special invitation of the native princes, formed an establishment on the coast of the Carnatic, about sixty miles from Madras, and in 1653 a further grant was obtained and Fort St. George erected.

It has been observed that the happiest reigns furnish the fewest events for the pen of the historian; and the last twenty years of the reign of the great Emperor illustrates the truth of this remark. During that period the country enjoyed a profound peace that was hitherto a stranger to Hindostan; the sovereign himself had exchanged the pursuits of war for those of peace and goodwill; and in the seclusion of his royal palace on the banks of the Jumna at Agra, or wandering amongst the jujube and the peepul trees in the splendid gardens laid out by Humaioon his father, he devised those wise counsels and benevolent edicts that revived the fertility of an impoverished land and roused the energy of a crushed race. The energetic efforts of an enlightened monarch like Akbar, enjoying the revenues of upwards of twenty provinces, and delighting in the progress and prosperity of his subjects, extended over a lengthened period of fifty years, could not fail to effect a wondrous and lasting improvement in the condition of the country and people of Hindostan.

Golden indeed will that age always be considered, in

BOOK II. A.D. 1605.

which peace and security, plenty and improvement, succeed to the blasting contention of many dynasties of restless and usurping tyrants. No wonder that to this day the glory of the great Shah Jumga Mahommed Akbar, the Victorious, is sung as more than mortal, and his wealth and power exaggerated by the traditions of those to whom his power and justice had ensured the hitherto unknown blessings of peace and security.

But whoever comes to the feast of life must drink the cup of death; dread Atropos with her sharp scissors divides the thread of life, that her sisters have so carefully spun, with the same indifference, whether it is that of the greatest monarch or the meanest slave; the benefactor or the curse of the human race.

Akbar was now getting old, his course was nearly run, and finding his dissolution at hand, he devoted his remaining hours to words and works of benevolence and magnanimity. Sending for his son Selim, he desired him to dispatch a messenger to summon every Ameer without exception to his presence; "for I cannot endure," said he, "that any misunderstanding should exist between you and those who for so many years have shared in my toil, and been the associates of my glory." After wistfully regarding them all around, he entreated them that they would bury in oblivion all the errors of which he could be justly accused; then desiring Selim to draw near, he threw his arms about his neck and addressed him in the following terms: "My dear boy, take this my last farewell, for here we never meet again: beware thou dost not withdraw thy protecting regard from the secluded in my harem; that thou continue the same allowance of subsistence as was allotted by myself; although my departure must cast a heavy gloom upon thy mind, let not the words that are past be at once forgotten. Many a vow and many a covenant have been exchanged between us; break not the pledge which thou hast given me; forget it not. Beware! many are the claims I have upon thy soul. Be they great or be they small, do not thou forget them. Call to thy remembrance my deeds of martial glory: forget not the exertions of that bounty that distributed so many a jewel; my servants and dependants when I am gone do not thou forget, nor the afflicted in the hour of need: ponder word for word on all that I have said. Do thou bear all in mind, and again, forget me not." On the night of Wednesday 10th of October, 1605, when one watch and four sections of the night were past, in the sixty-fourth year of his age and the fiftieth of his reign, the soul of Akbar Shah, the Ornament of the World, the Asylum of Nations, King of Kings, the Great, Fortunate, and Victorious, took flight to the realms above. Honour is his escutcheon, and the love of succeeding generations has embalmed his name.

The funeral of Akbar was worthy the magnificence of his Empire and the glory of his titles. Selim and his three sons bore the coffin out of the gates of the castle; here Selim left it, and his sons and the powerful officers of his household, relieving each other, bore it to Secundra on the banks of the Jumna, a distance of four miles; where to this day, under a gorgeous tomb, erected at an expense of 1,800,000*l.*, the remains of the great monarch rest.

Akbar was the glory of the Mogul race, and stands without a rival in the history of Hindostan: the length of his reign, the wondrous splendour of his court, the purity of his domestic administration, and the dignity of his foreign policy, renewed to the dusky people of Hindostan a golden period of peace and prosperity similar to that enjoyed by the citizens of Rome under the beneficent rule of the Antonines. He was the noblest sovereign that ever mounted a throne, whether in East or West; his humanity, justice, energy, temperance, generosity, and splendid courage present us with a type rare indeed in the kingly caste; his justice knew no distinction of persons; his generosity no bounds; his

BOOK II. A.D. 1605.

integrity had no reserve: "he never," he said, "knew a man to lose himself in a straight road." So unremitting were his labours for the good of his subjects, that taking day and night together, he seldom slept more than four hours: his consideration for all about him was extreme, and we read that at one of his most important councils, Beilig Begum, his old nurse, was present by his express desire. His personal courage was of that daring nature that distinguished his grandfather Baber: he took delight in dangers that were too great for ordinary mortals: his sports and his exercises were marked by the same exuberant vigour: he would ride from Agra to Ajmir, a distance of 220 miles, in two days for pleasure: in the combats and taming of wild elephants he took especial delight, and he would frequently spring from the back of a tame elephant to that of the most furious and refractory, known to have killed many a keeper; and on some occasions, when the animal was too furious to admit of any approach, he has dropped from a wall or tree on the neck of the enraged beast: courting the rage of the forest king, he was equally daring with the lord of the jungle; on several occasions he attacked and slew a royal tiger unassisted, and once seeing a tigress with five young ones on the road before him, he spurred on his horse, and before she could spring upon him, stretched her dead with one blow across the loins.

Daring and rash in action, successful as a partizan, and exposing his life on all occasions with the reckless chivalry of his grandfather Baber, he possessed in a far higher degree the *ars imperatoria*, the qualifications of a great commander, and the genius of a wise king. The most brilliant annals of chivalry can offer nothing more conspicuous than the following anecdote: on one occasion he had given the order for the assault of a strong fortress, and was himself leading the attack, when a haughty young Rajpoot, indignant at some fancied slight of the Emperor, tore off his armour and declared he would go into action without any. Without a moment's hesitation, Akbar divested himself of his own defensive armour, saying he could not allow his chiefs to be more exposed than himself.

On another occasion, when besieging the citadel of Daood, a rebellious Rajah, he became impatient of delay and challenged him to single combat; saying, "Though I have a thousand in my army as good men as you, rather than fatigue my troops with a siege, I will put the whole upon the issue of a single combat between you and me; and let him take the fort who shall best deserve it."

His exploits in war eclipsed those of any former hero of Hindostan. Clad in complete armour, with lance in hand, and his smiting scimitar, "the conquest of empires," by his side, mounted on his noble steed Koparah, that did not quail before the charge of an infuriated elephant, his was indeed the aspect of a demi-god; and the ringing war-cry of "Alla hu Akbar," with which his princely Emirs followed him to a charge, that scattered his foes like a thunderbolt from heaven, was enough to rouse the heroes of the Walhalla from their cups.

The person of Akbar is thus described by his son Selim: He was tall in stature, of a ruddy nut-brown complexion; his eyes and eyebrows dark, the latter running across into each other; handsome in his exterior, he had the strength of a lion, which was indicated by the extraordinary breadth of his chest and length of his arms: on the whole his exterior was most captivating.[6] A black mole which he had on his nose, was declared by those skilled in the science of physiognomy to prognosticate an extraordinary career of good fortune; neither indeed could he be considered very unfortunate, who sounded the great drum of sovereign power for a period of fifty years over the whole of Hindostan, and that without a rival or an opponent."[7]

NOTES TO CHAPTER XX.

BOOK II. A.D. 1605.

[1] Some idea may be formed of the power of the subjects of Akbar, from the fact that at his death one noble, Riza Maun Sing, had twenty thousand armed retainers, of the Rajpoot tribes, in and about the city, ready at a moment's notice to execute his slightest wish.

[2] It remained for British conquerors, with the bayonet in one hand and the Bible in the other, to double and quadruple the exactions of their Hindoo or Mogul predecessors, and within fifty years to raise the direct tax on land to the unheard-of amount of 66 per cent., in addition to a most oppressive system of indirect taxation.

[3] See *Institutes of Menu*, chap. i. sect. 108.

[4] In the oriental collection, there is a painting from the life of an Indian fakiress: in expiation of her pusillanimity, in not daring to burn with her husband, she resolved to consume life by slow degrees, her body being suspended from a tree by a rope passing under her arms, and wasted by the smoke of a fire burning just beneath her; she is standing on one foot, the other being tied up.

The Suttee was observed amongst the northern nations; Nanna was consumed in the same fire with the body of her husband, "Balder the Beautiful," one of Odin's companions.

Diodorus gives an account of an Indian woman who burned herself with the body of her husband, in the army of Eumenes. She distributed all her bangles and jewels to her friends; the whole account reads as if it occurred yesterday.

There are two ways of performing Suttee in India. In the South they used to dig a pit about ten feet long and six broad, and fill it with logs of wood; one great piece is set at the brim of the pit ready to fall in at the pulling of a string; the wood is saturated with butter, oil, &c., and then the husband's corpse is placed upon it, and it is set on fire; it blazes instantly. The widow takes leave of her friends and relations, walks three or four times round the grave to the sound of trumpets and hautboys, then jumps into the flame, when a Brahmin pulls the string, down falls the beam of wood, and all is consumed together.

In the other case, a pit is made, the widow mounts the pile, and seats herself with her husband's head in her lap, when the pile is lighted, and she is consumed very slowly.

The word *suttee* in Sanscrit means *saint*.

Every woman too who becomes a Suttee, should she again assume corporeal form, would have that of a man not that of a woman; but if she did not become a Suttee, she would never in the realms of Metempsychosis have any other body but that of a woman. It is considered the duty of a woman to enter the fire in which her husband is burning, unless she be pregnant. A Brahmin's wife must burn with her husband in the same fire, and so become Suttee; others may burn elsewhere. It is not considered right, however, to force a woman into the fire; and in like manner, a woman desiring to become a Suttee is not to be kept back from her purpose.

The doctors have said that the original intention of the rights of Suttee was, "that the woman should, after the death of her husband, consume all her desires, and thus die to the world, before her natural death; for in the language of mysticism woman means *desire*, and the intention is that she should cast away her desire, not that she should throw herself as a dead carcass into the fire, which is abominable."

CHAP XX. A.D. 1605.

The famous Job Channock, Company's agent in Bengal in 1690, rode out one day to witness a Suttee. The young widow was fair to look upon and unwilling to quit this wicked world; and Job was so smitten with this beauty in distress, that he sent his guards to take her by force and conduct her to his own house. They lived lovingly together many years and had several children. Unfortunately for the success of the experiment, she made him a pagan, instead of herself becoming a Christian; he buried her decently, and ever after annually sacrificed a cock on her tomb in the manner of the ancients.

See a Persian book called *Dalistan*, translated by Rev. Samuel Lee.

[5] Elphinstone.

[6] Moles are much appreciated in the East.

> "Their musky locks have each a spell;
> Each hair itself ensnares the heart;
> Their moles are irresistible,
> And rapture to the soul impart."—*Firdausi.*

And in one of the Odes of Hafiz :—

> "I would give for the moles on her cheek
> The cities of Samarcand and Bokhara."

[7] *Autobiography of Jehangire.*

CHAP. XXI.

JEHANGIRE ASCENDS THE THRONE OF HINDOSTAN IN A.D. 1605—THE REBELLION OF HIS SON CHUSERO.—THE ROMANTIC HISTORY OF NOOR MAHAL, "THE LIGHT OF THE HAREM."

BOOK II. 1605.

SELIM was thirty-eight when he seated himself on the throne of his expectations and wishes, and assumed the high-sounding title of Jehangire or "conqueror of the world." He placed the crown on his brows at the instant the sun rose above the horizon, in order that he might have a favourable omen; he tells us with childish delight, in his autobiography, that his crown was made on the model of that worn by the kings of Persia, having twelve points, each of which was surmounted by a diamond which was worth 150,000*l*.

For forty days and nights Jehangire kept high festival at Agra, and offered to the world scenes of festivity and splendour seldom paralleled even in the annals of oriental magnificence.

With the exception of a small cloud that darkened the horizon of the Deccan, his empire was at peace; for a time the spirit of the great Akbar continued still to awe the hot heads and ready arms of the fierce nobles of the kingdom; but this state of repose did not last long, and ere four little months had passed over the grave of the mighty dead, plots and counterplots again agitated the kingdom and threatened the throne itself.

At this period the feudal system of Hindostan was at its

height; the power of the great lords was immense, and the armies of retainers that accompanied them to the capital rendered their presence a source of greater danger than of security to the Emperor. One of the chieftains, Raja Maun Singa, kept court at Agra during the latter part of the reign of Akbar and the commencement of that of Jehangire with 20,000 armed followers and Rajpoots of his own tribe.

The discontent and restless spirit of the great omrahs soon assumed a consistent form, and a leader was found in Prince Chusero, the eldest son of Jehangire, then seventeen years of age.

From boyhood Jehangire and his son Chusero had been on bad terms, and Akbar had frequently to interfere to soothe the unnatural severity of his son.

This estrangement increased after the death of Akbar, and it wanted but the intrigues of Chan Azim, a leading omrah of the court, to bring about an open rupture. Having secured the support of several omrahs, he induced Chusero to escape from Agra and to put himself at the head of the discontents. Chusero marched to Delhi, where he was joined by 10,000 men: for some time his fortunes almost outweighed those of his father, but the decision of Asiph, the son of Dias, the favourite minister of Akbar, and of Mohabit Khan, a renegade Rajpoot of great talent and influence, soon marshalled against him an irresistible force. He retired to the Punjaub, where he was overtaken by Mohabit Khan, and being defeated before Lahore, was after a long pursuit taken prisoner.

Defeated and brought before Jehangire with a golden chain from his left hand to his left foot, according to the custom of the race of Genghis and Timour, he received his sentence of perpetual imprisonment.

His two leading advisers were sewn up in raw oxhides and thrown into the streets of Agra: the sun contracting the skin soon caused the death of one, when by the Emperor's orders the other was kept softened by

BOOK II. water night and day, till worms devoured the wretched victim.

A.D. 1606. Three hundred of his followers were impaled alive, on each side of the main thoroughfare of the city, and Chusero was daily taken on his elephant to witness the ghastly spectacle as long as one remained alive.

Chusero was very popular with the people, and his unfortunate fate was much commiserated. He was handsome and generous, and especially skilled in warlike pursuits; with much thoughtlessness, he retained a considerable portion of the fine nature that appears to have distinguished so many of the race of Baber.

When urged to sanction his father's assassination, which would at once have secured him the throne, he refused; saying, he desired only his confinement. "My father," he said, "can live without a throne; I cannot enjoy life stained with a father's blood."

Chusero was never forgiven; he was kept a prisoner, and kept in total ignorance of all affairs of state. Sir Thomas Roe once met him surrounded by his guards; he was profoundly ignorant of all events of the day, and had never even heard of the English or their ambassador.

He died in 1621, after an imprisonment of fifteen years, not without suspicion of foul play.

Jehangire had three other sons, Prince Parvez the eldest; Prince Khurrum, soon after called Shah Jehan, the second; and Prince Shehriar the third; Shah Jehan was his favourite, and in 1616 he conferred upon him the title of King, signifying his election as heir apparent to the throne.

The small cloud that had appeared in the Deccan had increased till it darkened the frontiers of Hindostan, and compelled the active interference of Jehangire.

The power of the Deccane monarchy was never greater than at this period. Malek Amber, an Abyssinian, a warrior and statesman of great genius and enterprise, had ruled the country for nearly forty years, during which period he had, on a smaller stage, played the part of the wise and beneficent Akbar. He had closely copied Akbar's revenue system, and had restored health and confidence to the oppressed inhabitants of his country. To this day the name and benevolent rule of this noble African are recalled with respect by the inhabitants of that impoverished region. He had built a magnificent capital at Aurungabad, and possessing all the sea-board of the Concan and the Deccan, he had strengthened his military power with European ordnance, and numbered many European adventurers amongst his superior officers.

Encouraged by the defection of Chusero, Malek Amber seized a favourable opportunity for occupying the city and fortress of Ahmednuggur. Jehangire sent against him his favourite general, Abdullah Khan, but the artillery and European energy of the troops of Malek Amber were too powerful for the essentially Asiatic tactics and equipments of Abdullah's army. He was defeated with great slaughter and obliged to retire to Agra. A few years later Malek Amber again invaded Hindostan, but was defeated by Shah Jehan, and forced to make overtures which included the cession of a considerable territory and the payment of a large sum of money. This campaign, however, established a mutual friendship between Shah Jehan and Malek Amber, that some years later nearly overthrew the throne of Jehangire.

It is now time to turn from the monotony of the incessant frontier wars, that form so prominent a part of the History of the Princes of India, to an event that far more than the rebellions of his sons, or the conquests of his generals, influenced the conduct of Jehangire for a period of nearly twenty years. In all ages of the world women have attracted and repelled, been adored and oppressed; men have by turns been their tyrants and their slaves; ennobled or debased by their influence. If we examine the histories of the greatest men, or seek the

BOOK II. A.D. 1606–12.

real causes of many of the most startling changes that have taken place in the conduct of the world's affairs, we shall find that the influence of woman has been the most powerful agency, incessantly at work, often invisibly, and giving only occasional evidence of its existence, by some striking eccentricity in the revolving orbit of human events. The history of the two sexes shows that their power and influence have been fairly balanced, and that whatever humiliation women may, as a race, have occasionally suffered from man, has been more than counterbalanced by the supremacy they have individually exercised.

This was the case when Mher-al-Nissa "the sun of women," called also Noor-Mahal, "the light of the harem," ruled during twenty years the Sultan Jehangire, and his mighty empire of Hindostan, with power as absolute as was ever exercised by Semiramis or Cleopatra over the kingdoms of Assyria or Egypt.

Like one of those diamonds of great price that once in every five or six hundred years Plutus drops into the world to excite the cupidity and rouse the jealousy of the human race, she was a miracle of beauty, wit, tact, and talent, sent astray by some mischief-loving god, to dazzle, attract, and confuse the judgment of the weaker animal man.

In Christian and pagan countries, where the rights and equality of women are recognised facts, we are accustomed to see them exercise supreme rule openly and before the world; but amongst Muslims, who cherish the inferiority of the female sex as an article of faith; whose gospel teaches that women are deficient in everything but cunning; that pride, envy, anger, violence, deceit, falsehood, infidelity, and baseness are their ruling passions; and whose social law excludes them from the perusal of holy books; from any share in the paternal property, and from even eating with their husbands; the circumstance of a woman grasping and retaining supreme power for so long a period; throwing aside the enjoined seclusion of her sex, and openly taking part in the councils and strifes of the kingdom, without losing caste or being denied the respect of her subjects, goes far to establish the proof of the old proverb, "ce que femme veut, Dieu veut!" and is a remarkable example, perhaps unparalleled in the world, of the power of beauty, talent, and strong will over the combined prejudice of faith, tradition, and immemorial custom.

Her father, Chaja Aiass, was a Tartar of noble blood but indifferent circumstances, whom present poverty and the reports of distant wealth, had induced to leave his native wilds for the sunny land of Hindostan.

To add to the great hardships inseparable from an emigration of many thousand miles, his wife brought forth a daughter in the midst of the great solitudes that separate Western Tartary from the frontiers of India.

Starving and exhausted, all hope of carrying the new-born infant with them quickly vanished; and the only chance of saving their own lives was to leave it to its fate and press onwards to the habitations of men. Dire indeed must have been the contest between the yearnings of nature and the stern dictates of necessity; and when at last the moment arrived when it was absolutely necessary to abandon the child, the agonized mother laid it under a tree, and covering it with leaves, retired to a distance, that, like the Egyptian woman of old, "she might not see the death of the child."

The "well" in this instance was vouchsafed, in the welcome appearance of some travellers, who succoured the melancholy trio, and enabled them to reach the court of Akbar at Lahore. Little did the wife of Aiass imagine that the puling desert-born babe, so unexpectedly restored to her arms, was destined to be a fountain of marvellous light, before whose glory the whole Eastern world would stand entranced as one man.

Poverty is not the accustomed road to power; for "the

BOOK II. A.D. 1612.

poor man's wisdom is despised," says Solomon, "and his words not heeded;" but Aiass had friends at court, and his feet once planted on the ladder of promotion, their aid soon enabled him to step over the heads of his less favoured rivals. His diligence and ability attracted the attention of Akbar, and before many years had elapsed, he was appointed High Treasurer of the Empire, the highest office of the state.

Carefully nurtured, and educated in all the arts and accomplishments of the most luxurious capital of the world, his daughter Mher-al-Nissa, rapidly attained that perfection of beauty and wit which was to lay Hindostan at her feet. So brilliant a jewel, even in the homely setting of poverty, could never have escaped attention; but assisted by all the costly splendour belonging to the daughter of the first subject in the kingdom, it was irresistible.

Sensible that empire was her destiny, and confident in her absolute power to mould mankind to her will, this "sun of women"[2] felt that the young heir to the throne had but to see her to yield instant homage to the majesty of her charms; and she waited with perfect confidence for the moment when fortune should present her to Prince Selim, heir to the throne and power of the mighty Akbar.

The opportunity was not long wanting: she frequently accompanied her mother to the harem of Akbar, and on one occasion met the young prince.

Feeble as the sex are always described to be, the very weakest among them is far too powerful for the strongest man that ever breathed: what chance then had the young and impulsive Selim with the loveliest woman of her day?

> "Not Esther's self, whose charms the Hebrews sing,
> E'er looked so lovely on the Eastern king"

as did Mher-al-Nissa, when apparelled in the graceful zara, worn by the Mussulmani women of Hindostan; her face and shoulders shaded by a veil of the transparent tissues of Seronge, which enhanced the beauty it scarcely pretended to conceal, she shone on the troubled gaze of Prince Selim in all the dazzling splendour of her voluptuous charms. CHAP. XXI. A.D. 1612.

When, in defiance of the injunctions of the Prophet, she sung the wild airs of her native country, it was more pleasing to his ears than rain in a parched land; and when she danced before him, the Tetrarch himself could not have been more completely enslaved.

One more interview completed the conquest, which the first glance had placed beyond a doubt, and Selim demanded the hand of Mher-al-Nissa, or as we shall now call her, Noor-Mahal, "the Light of the Harem," in marriage. But here an unforeseen difficulty arose to check his headlong passion and her deliberate designs. Her father Aiass did not share the ambition or discernment of his daughter. He had formed no designs of entrapping the heir apparent; and satisfied with a less splendid alliance, had betrothed his daughter to Shere Afkun, "the overthrower of the lion," a young Persian, lord of a vast Jaghir in Bengal, and the most powerful and accomplished noble of the court of Akbar. It was in vain that Selim petitioned his father to annul the engagement, or attempted to terrify the gallant Shere into renouncing his right to the possession of the most beautiful woman in the world.

The Emperor was incapable of injustice, even in favour of his own son; and Shere Afkun was indifferent to danger, although it was threatened by the heir to a throne.

Noor-Mahal was evidently "une femme à tout faire," and although still desirous of sharing the throne of the future Emperor of the Moguls, ambition did not blind her reason; she recognised the possible danger of falling between two stools, and with an amount of caution worthy of all admiration, she preferred present nobility with the high-born and magnificent Shere Afkun to possible sovereignty as the wife of Prince Selim.

Here of course the affair should have terminated, and Selim waited till time had healed the scar of his wounded

BOOK II. A.D.1612.

affections, or death had removed his successful rival; but, alas! love and honour, those two great tyrants of the human race, do not always pull together. Stolen waters always will be sweet, and bread eaten in secret retains its charm to the end. In the court of love every prize is considered lawful gain, and in these matters "non hospes ab hospite tutus," no man is secure, and he is wrong who confides too implicitly even in his friend. Passion will urge a man of the greatest honour, generosity, and chivalry, to the commission of crimes which no other motive in the world could induce.

Selim possessed none of these saving qualities; disappointment sharpened the barb of revenge and the fiery dart of passion; and numberless were the plans he formed to circumvent the death of his successful rival, and fabulous the deeds of strength and valour by which this Samson of Hindostan freed himself from the Prince's cowardly schemes.

Whether his enemies had "ploughed with his heifer,"[3] and Noor-Mahal was privy to the the numerous plots against her lord's life, by which she was to be raised to the Imperial throne, does not appear; but when Akbar died, and Selim mounted the Nusmud of the Moguls, he was able to do openly what before he had contrived in secret. The death of Shere Afkun was immediately achieved; he was slain in open day after a desperate defence that was long remembered in Bengal: his widow did not display any very inconsolable distress; and whatever might have been her devotion to the man she loved, during his life, she showed no kind of reluctance to become his murderer's empress at his death. She enacted the part of the wife of Uriah, in a similar tragedy, with like equanimity.

We do not know how long the widowhood of the frail Bathsheba lasted; but the four months and ten days, the time appointed by the Koran as the term of widowhood, was all too long for Noor-Mahal, and within a month, a little month, she announced her readiness to add her matchless charms to the varied attractions of the zenana of the "Lord of the world."

For some inexplicable reason, it appears that, when brought to court, she was treated with considerable harshness and neglect; confined to the worst apartments, and restricted to the smallest yearly allowance permitted by the laws of the zenana. Once in possession of what he so much coveted, the object itself seems to have lost all value in the eyes of Jehangire; and for nearly six years he never visited the object of his former love; but at length attracted by the hourly repeated tales of her beauty, accomplishments, and wit, and his curiosity awakened by the descriptions of the elegance and luxury of those apartments which he intended to make the very reverse, he determined to see with his own eyes the divinity that so completely engrossed all hearts at his court. A strange custom of the Mogul court, subversive of all the eastern rules of female seclusion, gave Noor-Mahal an opportunity of attracting the Emperor's attention. On the Noroze, or festival held on the ninth day of the new year, was celebrated a kind of carnival in the king's seraglio in the palace of the Mogul: at this fancy fair the ladies kept the stalls and sold whatever they chose, such as fine purple and gold, rich embroideries of the new fashion, ribbons, and cloth of gold, cloth worn by fine ladies, and all other merchandize. By this means the budding beauties of the court were brought under the king's notice. The great feature of the fair was the marketing of the king, who came in person to bargain, and haggled with the she-merchants of his court; driving them down; asserting that things were too dear; that he would not be imposed upon; that the merchandize of others was much better, &c. &c. The women, on the other hand, ignored the kingly rank, and ran up the value of their goods, insisting upon a high price; often coming to high words; and telling him to go about his business;

BOOK II. A.D. 1612.

that they would have nothing to do with such skin flints as he; that he knew nothing about it, &c. &c. The Begums likewise did the same, and in no real fair was such loud wrangling and railing, or such cries and noises heard. As might be expected, much mischief originated at these fairs, where maidens and wives were alike submitted to the admiring gaze of the Mogul; and all alike sold their wares, some their work, and some their beauty, to the highest bidder. It was not often that the Mogul solicited in vain; and many a bitter hatred and rebellion originated in the fancy fair of the Noroze. "Your wife returns to her abode, tramping to the tinkling sound of ornaments of gold, and gems on her person," writes one Rajpoot chief to his friend, "but where, my brother, is the moustache on your lip?" meaning his honour.

At one of these fairs Akbar was once in peril of his life from a spirited woman, who, instead of listening to his tale of love, presented a dagger to his breast. Jehangire had multiplied these fancy fairs, and they were now held on all feast days. At this period nothing was fashionable amongst the ladies of the court but the work of Noor-Mahal; by this means she accumulated much money, with which she repaired and beautified her apartments and clothed her slaves in the richest tissues and brocades, while she herself affected plain and simple attire.

The Emperor, who was a constant buyer, found that on all occasions the articles most sought after were those of her needle-work:[4] every room in his seraglio was adorned with it; and at length curiosity vanquished his determination, and he resolved to be himself an eye-witness of all the marvels he had heard of the "Light of the Harem."

He resolved to surprise her, and communicating his intention to no one, he suddenly entered her apartments, where he found everything so elegant and magnificent, that he was struck with amazement; but the greatest ornament of all was Noor-Mahal herself; she was half reclined on an embroidered sofa, in a plain muslin dress,[5] which exhibited her matchless shape to the best advantage, and became her better than all the richest brocades of Bagdad or the finest embroideries of Cashmere. Her slaves sat in a circle round her, at work, attired in rich brocade; she slowly rose, in evident confusion, and received the Emperor with the ceremony of touching first the ground and then the forehead with her right hand; she maintained silence, an eloquence that, backed by beauty, is often more effective than words, and stood with eyes fixed on the ground. Jehangire overcome by her beauty, did not for some time recover from his confusion; he admired her shape, her stature, her complexion, her grace, and that inexplicable voluptuousness of mien, to cultivate which is the first lesson of the zenana.

At length he sat down on the sofa, and required Noor-Mahal to be seated by him; the first question he asked was, "why this difference between the appearance of Noor-Mahal and her slaves?" She shrewdly answered, "those born to servitude must dress as it shall please those they serve; these are my servants, and I alleviate their burden of bondage by every indulgence in my power; but I that am your slave, O Emperor of the World, must dress according to your pleasure and not my own." "*Cosi si pigliano gli volpi*," by such means are foxes taken.

Noor-Mahal had in her retirement cultivated that modesty that is more valuable than fine gold, and that charm of tender melancholy that supplies the keenest arrows in Cupid's quiver. One interview was sufficient to establish with greater power than ever her influence over Jehangire. Clasping her in his arms, he begged forgiveness for his long harshness; and throwing round her neck a necklace containing forty pearls, each worth 4000*l.*, he ordered her to be proclaimed Empress of the World.

From the humblest apartments of the zenana she was removed to those of the Sultana. As an especial mark

BOOK II. A.D. 1612.

of favour, she was allowed to take the title of Shahi, or Empress, and her name changed from Noor-Mahal, "Light of the Harem," to Noor-Jehan, "Light of the World;" whilst the gold coin of the realm was stamped with this inscription by order of Jehangire: "gold has acquired a hundred degrees of excellence in receiving the name of Noor-Jehan." This occurred in the sixth year of his reign and the forty-fourth of his age. "Age could not wither her, nor custom stale her infinite variety." For nearly twenty years this remarkable woman, the especial heroine of Eastern romance, ruled without a rival throughout the length and breadth of Hindostan.

Her magnificence was beyond all bounds. "In the whole empire," says Jehangire in his memoirs, "there is scarcely a city in which the Princess has not left some lofty structure, some spacious garden, as a splendid monument of her taste and magnificence."

No appointment of the most trifling nature was made in the state without her interest, and no treaty concluded without her consent. As a natural consequence of her unbounded influence, and the rapid elevation of her northern relatives, Tartary came into fashion; and whilst under James I. of England the canny Scots were monopolizing the fat things of the sister kingdom, the no less needy young nobles from Western Tartary, with threadbare garments and sharp swords, crowded in numbers from their native solitudes, to seek their fortunes under the friendly shade of the great Empress of Hindostan.

Noor-Jehan's power was cemented and established by the rise of her father and brother, and by the intermarriages of her family with that of Jehangire. Her father was Prime Vizier, whilst her brother, Asiph Khan, was advanced to the position of first omrah at court. Shah Jehan, the Emperor's favourite son, married her niece, the daughter of Asiph Khan; whilst Prince Shehriar married her own daughter by Shere Afkun.

NOTES TO CHAPTER XXI.

[1] The whole crown would be worth 2,070,000*l.*

[2] Mher-al-Nissa signifies "sun of women."

[3] See Judges xiv. 18.

[4] Indian women have the finest touch in the world. They wind off the raw silk from the pod; each pod is divided into twenty degrees of fineness; and so exquisite is the touch of these women, that whilst the thread is running through their fingers so swiftly that the eye can be of no assistance, they will break it off at each change from the first to the twentieth, and from the nineteenth to the second.

[5] "When ladies smile in virgin robes of white,
The thin undress of superficial light."

CHAP. XXII.

THE REBELLION OF SHAH JEHAN.—HIS DEFEAT.—THE DEATH OF THE GOOD VIZIER AIASS, THE FATHER OF NOOR-MAHAL.—THE CONCLUSION OF THE REIGN OF JEHANGIRE.—HIS DEATH IN 1628 A.D.

BOOK II. A.D. 1612–21.

THE death of Chusero, whether natural or caused by his relatives, appeared to secure Shah Jehan's position as heir to his father's throne; but in reality it had the very opposite effect. Noor-Mahal, who for many years had strenuously supported Shah Jehan in his father's favour, now suddenly transferred her affection and influence to the youngest son, Prince Shehriar, who had lately married her own daughter by Shere Afkun: she feared the military genius and determined character of Shah Jehan, and felt that with such a sovereign her power would entirely vanish. Prince Shehriar was the very reverse; he was pliant and indolent, and completely under her influence; and it was evident that if she could secure the succession to him, her power would outlive her husband's death. Asiph Khan supported the ambitious designs of his sister, and favoured her advocacy of Prince Shehriar to the exclusion of his own son-in-law Shah Jehan.

Shah Jehan did not long bear with the intrigues and plots of those who wished to deprive him of his birthright. He suddenly withdrew from court, and being joined by the discontented nobles, who were always ready to take up arms if a prince of the blood would join them, he managed to collect a considerable army, and marched against his father at Delhi; he was however repulsed and forced to retire to Agra, where he was again defeated.

Jehangire attempted a reconciliation with his son; but the demands of the latter were so exorbitant, that indignation overpowered whatever paternal affection remained; and he determined to take the field against him in person, having previously sent Prince Shehriar to arrest his progress.

Shah Jehan, conscious of his strength, and trusting to the jealousy that he knew very generally existed amongst the omrahs towards Noor-Mahal and her brother, was undaunted by his father's threats or commands, and waited his opportunity to attack him with advantage: the armies were encamped close to one another, and the danger of Jehangire was imminent, when Mohabit Khan, with the troops of the Punjaub under his command, providentially arrived to his relief.

The next day Shah Jehan was defeated with great slaughter, and with a remnant of his army he barely escaped to Orissa, and finally to Bengal. In this latter province he again gained head, and defeating the hereditary Rajah, possessed himself of the country; thence he marched to Bahar and very nearly seized the city of Allahabad. The year following he united his forces to those of his former enemy Malek Amber; and after several successful campaigns, he again turned the point of his spears to the capital; there, after displaying great gallantry, he was a second time defeated by Mohabit Khan and forced to fly to the Deccan. Here he remained until, the case becoming hopeless, he prayed for forgiveness. Jehangire immediately granted it and sent for him to Court; but Shah Jehan, afraid of the influence of Noor-Mahal, contented himself with sending his women and children as hostages for his good behaviour, while he travelled about the kingdom with an escort of 500 men.

Mohabit Khan, to whom Jehangire was thus for the third

BOOK II. A.D. 1612–21.

time indebted for the safety of his kingdom, was an apostate Rajpoot; he was the son of Sugra, who had been appointed by Akbar king of Cheetore, in place of Umra the son of Pertap, who refused to acknowledge the Mogul power. He was the most successful general of the day, and had only to raise his standard, whether for the defence of the throne, or to further his own ambitious views, to collect at once an army of tried warriors around him.

The magnificent homage of this powerful subject was naturally alarming to Jehangire; and he dreaded a repetition of the tyranny exercised by the great Behram Shah over his father Akbar. In these suspicions he was secretly encouraged by Noor-Mahal, who could ill brook so formidable a rival; and a trifling difficulty with her brother Asiph, was scarcely required to make her his declared enemy.

Mohabit and Asiph, having disputed about a question of precedence, they referred it to the Emperor; he decided in favour of the latter, giving as his reason, that "the pen always took precedence of the sword."

Shortly afterwards, Mohabit by the machinations of the Empress was accused of treason, and commanded to appear before the Emperor: he agreed to attend at court if his safety were guaranteed, and marched with 5000 faithful Rajpoots to Lahore, where Jehangire then resided. When within a short distance of the camp, he received the commands of the Emperor to halt, until he had accounted for the treasure of Bengal. Mohabit dispatched his son-in-law to explain the disputed matter; but he was stript and bastinadoed, and sent back to him disgraced. Mohabit displayed no outward signs of anger; but his was not a nature to suffer this insult to pass unrevenged.

The Emperor was at this time encamped on the Ghelum, on his march to Caubul; and the carelessness of his officers soon gave Mohabit an opportunity of carrying his plans into effect. The morning of Jehangire's arrival the main body of his army crossed the river for the next camping ground, leaving the Imperial camp to follow later in the day.

No sooner did Mohabit perceive the separation of the Emperor from the main body of his troops, than he advanced at once to the bridge, and setting it on fire, effectually prevented the return of the Imperial guards. Leaving 2000 men to guard the flames, he pressed on to the Imperial tent, and entering the Emperor's presence, explained to him that his act was one of necessity, to save himself from the snares of the Empress: he then placed him on an elephant, and took him to his own camp, assuring him of his safety, and adding significantly, "and I also am determined to be safe."

During the confusion Noor-Mahal had escaped in disguise across the river, and joining the Imperial army, had informed her brother Asiph of his master's misfortune. She urged his immediate rescue, and upbraided the omrahs with their want of daring, in leaving the Emperor in the hands of a traitor.

The next day this daring woman mounted on an elephant, and accompanied by her daughter, headed the troops, who attempted to ford the Ghelum in order to rescue their monarch: three elephant drivers in succession were killed before her howdah; and three times the ponderous animal itself was hurt in the trunk. Her daughter was wounded in the arm and sank fainting at her side; but Noor-Mahal never wavered; she encouraged her panic-stricken troops, and with killing effect poured the contents of four quivers of arrows upon her foes.

The Rajpoots pressed into the stream to seize her, but she refused to fly; and until the master of her household, mounting her elephant, turned it away in spite of her threats and commands, she did not relinquish the hopeless contest.

The defeat of the Imperialists was complete; but the chief object of Mohabit was to destroy the power of the Empress, who had escaped to Lahore.

BOOK II. A.D.1626.

Through his influence, she received letters, on her arrival there from the Emperor, saying that matters were now amicably arranged, and urging her to join him.

She immediately set out for this purpose, and when within a short distance of the camp was met by a strong body of Rajpoots, who although sent ostensibly in her honour, were in reality her guards.

She was conducted before the Emperor, and openly accused by Mohabit of treason, in having aimed at her husband's death, in order to place on the throne her step-son Shehriar; under whose weak reign she would have exercised supreme control over the Empire. After enlarging upon her treason, and the danger of her pernicious influence, he concluded by demanding the public punishment of so daring an offender. "You who are the Emperor of the Moguls," said Mohabit, "whom we regard as something more than human, ought to follow the example of God, who is no respecter of persons."

Jehangire knew that it was useless to expostulate, and his suspicious mind detected some truth in these accusations: the warrant was therefore signed for the instant execution of the Empress. Her courage, however, only rose with her danger, and she heard her doom without emotion. "Imprisoned sovereigns," said she, "lose their right to life with their freedom; but permit me once more to see the Emperor, and to bathe with my tears the hand that has fixed the seal to the warrant of my death."

Accordingly she was brought before her husband in the presence of her enemy: the tender charm of melancholy gave force to the beauty that exercised so irresistible a spell over her lord; she uttered not a word, and Jehangire being overcome, burst into tears. "Will you not spare this woman Mohabit?" said he, with a voice broken by emotion, "you see how she weeps." "The Emperor of the Moguls," said the chivalrous Rajpoot, "should never ask in vain;" and at a sign from him the guards retired, and Noor-Mahal was restored to liberty.

For more than six months Mohabit reigned supreme; but at the end of that period, with extraordinary moderation, he resigned his power, liberated Jehangire, and dismissed his guards. CHAP. XXII. A.D.1626.

Noor-Mahal now sought her revenge, and laid a plot for his assassination; he barely escaped with life, and fled to the Deccan, leaving his wealth in the Imperial camp. By the interest of the Empress he was declared a traitor, and a price set upon his head; but her bitter hate was tempered by the cooler wisdom of her brother Asiph; who, knowing the value of Mohabit's military skill, persuaded the Emperor to pardon him, and to entrust him with the command of the army in the Deccan.

The Mogul Emperors were in the habit of making progresses through their dominions with an equipage amounting to 20,000 or 30,000 men. The Imperial camp was a moving city, and that of Jehangire was at least twenty miles in circumference. It was divided into squares, alleys, and streets; the royal pavilion standing in the centre, aloof from the other tents, which were not to be raised within a musket shot of it. The portion allotted to the great officers of the court were distinguished by their great splendour, and by the marks which made known the various ranks of the owners. The tradesmen also were arranged according to rule; so that no man was for a moment at a loss to supply his wants.

The camp from a rising ground presented a most agreeable appearance: starting up in a few hours in an uninhabited plain, the idea was realised of a city built by enchantment, filling the mind with delightful wonder and surprise.

Jehangire was the first and last Emperor of the Moguls who trusted his royal person to the waves: attended by his magnificent retinue, he journeyed slowly on to Ahmedabud, whence he proceeded to Cambay; where he had ordered costly barges to be prepared for him, intending to take amusement on the ocean with all his court; he

BOOK II. A.D.1626.

was, however, soon tired of the agitation of the vessel on the waves, and returned to Agra after an absence of five years.

If the welfare of the Empire was occasionally imperilled by the fancies and prejudices of Noor-Mahal; there was, during the first part of Jehangire's reign, one always at hand to strengthen it by his wisdom and intellect. Aiass the Good, the father of Noor-Mahal, raised to the office and title of Actimâd-ul-Dowla, or high treasurer of the Empire, by Akbar, was on the death of the Vizier Murtaza, appointed to the supreme management of the Empire. He had endeared himself to the people by his virtues and his great abilities. In the school of adversity he had early learnt the wholesome lessons of forbearance, and sympathy with the afflictions of others; his gradual promotion to the highest office of the state had made him acquainted with the duties of each station; and his experience of the hardships of poverty made him economise his own pleasures, to have it in his power to relieve with princely generosity the sufferings of the poor. He was revered as well as loved by the people; his benevolence was tempered with justice; and his philanthropy was not of that morbid kind which shrinks from the administration of justice, or the rigour of a necessary law.

Leaving war and conquest to Mohabit Khan and Chan Chanan, son of Byram, and the other great generals of the Empire; he devoted his long life to carrying out to the fullest possible extent the noble theories and beneficent practices of the great Akbar. He bestowed on agriculture the care that had been denied it by many former rulers. Deserted provinces were by degrees repeopled, and made to yield their increase; villages and towns sprang up in solitudes; and forests that had known only the tread of wild beasts were levelled to make way for the care and labour of the husbandman; the property of the farmer was secure, and the industry of the mechanic received its reward. The revenues of the empire gradually increased; to prevent extortion in the collection, the viceroy of every subah[1] was obliged to transmit monthly to court a statement of the improvements and regulations, made in consequence of public instructions from Agra. When the improvements were not in proportion to the amount of taxes levied, the viceroys were either severely reprimanded or degraded. No distinction was made in the administration of justice between Mahommedans and Hindoos; both were worshippers of God, each in his way; both members of the same community, and subject to the same lord.

Aiass was the last minister of the school of Akbar; and lamentable results to the Empire and people of Hindostan followed his death.

Hypocrisy, we are told, is the homage vice pays to virtue. Out of respect to the upright vizier, the Emperor Jehangire, drunken, cruel, indolent as he was, and vicious in every respect, yet managed to preserve the mask of justice; and if not just himself, checked with vigour, often with ferocity, any injustice in his viceroys or public officers.

At his death this mask was cast aside, and the Emperor gave free play to the natural bent of his disposition. Tyranny and oppression began again to flourish; the administration of the country rapidly declined; middlemen were reinstated, and tyrannical governors, so long as they gratified the drunken whims or avarice of the Emperor, were supported; punishments by mutilation, abolished by Akbar, were again added to the sanguinary code of Hindostan; and throughout the country the sharp sword of despotism was wielded with a fierce hand. The Empress was inconsolable at the death of her father, and proposed at once, as a proof of her affection and magnificence, to perpetuate his memory in a monument of solid silver. The Imperial architect soon convinced her that a metal so precious would not be the most lasting means of transmitting the vizier's fame to posterity. "All ages," he

BOOK II. A.D.1626. said, "are full of vanity, and even the empire of the house of Timour, like all sublunary things, is subject to revolution and change." The Empress seeing the wisdom of these words, altered her purpose; and a magnificent fabric of stone retains in Agra to this day the name of Actimâd-ul-Dowla.

Whilst Aiass was cementing the civil power of the empire, Mohabit, and Chan Chanan, the noble son of Byram Khan, the guardian of Akbar, were increasing its extent. In this latter warrior we find united all the virtues and accomplishments that distinguish this golden age—bravest amongst the brave, and of scholars the most learned; generous as Baber or Cuttub-ul-Dien, and accomplished as Feize or Abu-l-Fazl; he was created Khan of Khans, the highest title in the Empire, for his military achievements; and Vakil-e-Sultaneh or Lord-Lieutenant of the Empire, for his successful administration during peace.

From Deccan to Candahar, and from the furthermost parts of Bengal to Cambay, he spread the renown and established the majesty of the Great Mogul.

He was of the blue blood of the chivalry of the schools of Baber and Akbar; amongst endless stories of his brilliant valour, still preserved in Hindostan, the following anecdote will give a truer notion of his noble nature than pages of ordinary panegyric. On one occasion, during the wars in the Deccan, when his troops were broken, and he himself with 300 men was striving fiercely against 6000 of his foes, some of his friends seized his horse by the rein to carry him from the field. He positively commanded them to forbear; and his officers, finding their entreaties and attempts to lead him away ineffectual, demanded of him in despair, in case of defeat, what was to be their rallying point, and where they were to look for him? "Under the slain," was his fierce rejoinder, and returning to the fight, he gained a victory which added glorious laurels to his former crown of valour.

By the intervention of Aiass the Portuguese obtained considerable territory in Bengal, and the seaports of the Deccan and Malabar; in 1612 the firmaun was issued permitting the English to form trading settlements at Surat, Ahmedabad, and Cambay; and two years later James I. sent Sir Thomas Roe as his first ambassador to the court of the Great Mogul.

He gives a most interesting account of his visit to this sovereign. When admitted to the Durbar, he found at the end of the room the pictures of James I., his queen, the Lady Elizabeth, the Countesses of Salisbury and Somerset, and that of a citizen's wife in London; above them was another of Sir Thomas Smith, governor of the East India Company. The Emperor received him favourably; but the Portuguese interest was already too strong for the nascent power of England; and the jealousy of the powerful colony of Goa, assisted by the missionaries at Agra, rendered of no effect the liberality of the Emperor and his ministers.

Among the presents sent by James to his new ally was a gilded coach of the period, in which the portly Jehangire used to delight the eyes of his subjects at Agra, much in the same style, probably, as the natives of the present day love to display their ample proportions in the ponderous coaches of the last century.

Sir Thomas Roe also gives us some very amusing accounts of the private life of an eastern king at that period; he thus describes the day's occupations of the Great Mogul. Every morning he showed himself to his people from a window looking on a plain; at noon he was there again to see the elephants, the officers of rank being under him within a rail; thence he retired to sleep amongst his women. At three o'clock he went to the Durbar, and afterwards proceeded to the Guzaleun, a fair court, in the midst of which was a throne of fire-stone; where he admitted all his most select friends, and discoursed on state matters, and got drunk. All public

BOOK II. A.D. 1626. business was transacted at these two places; and this routine never changed, except in consequence of illness or drink.

The Emperor must be seen every day, and if ill, some one must be admitted to see him; if this were not done, a revolution would be the immediate result.

Following the example of Baber and Humaioon, Jehangire drank very hard, and the following confessions contained in his autobiography are worthy of Jean Jacques Rousseau: "From the age of sixteen," he tells us, "I indulged liberally in wine; and in truth, encompassed as I was with youthful associates of congenial minds, breathing the air of a delicious climate, and ranging through splendid and lofty saloons, every part of which was decorated with the graces of painting and sculpture, and the floors bespread with the thickest carpets of silk and gold, would it not have been a species of folly to have rejected the aid of an exhilarating cordial? and what cordial can surpass the juice of the grape? May it not happen that opiates and stimulants have been rendered habitual to the constitution? For myself I care not to acknowledge that such was the extent to which I had carried my indulgence, that my usual allowance was twenty, and sometimes more than twenty cups, each cup containing about six ounces, and eight cups being equal to three pounds. So far indeed was this baneful propensity carried, that if I were but an hour without my beverage my hands began to shake, and I was unable to sit at rest." Gradually he reduced himself, in six months, from twenty to five cups a day, and never began to drink till after the hour of evening prayer, or two hours before the close of the day. He was familiar in his cups; and he often desired his companions of the bowl to ask no favours of him, lest Selim in his cups might promise what Jehangire on the throne could not perform. Like Haroun-al-Raschid, he was fond of perambulating his capital at night; he would disappear from his palace, and spend the greater part of the night in obscure and low punch-houses in drinking and talking with the lower orders.

Sir Thomas Roe relates the following anecdote of the drinking propensities of this prince: "On one occasion," he says, "having taken some pictures to the palace, the Mogul was delighted, and fell to drinking the Alicant wine that I had presented to him, giving tastes of it to several about him, and then sent for a full bottle for me; saying, 'it began to sour so fast, that it would spoil before he could drink it, and that I had none:' this done, he turned himself to sleep, the candles were popped out, and I groped my way out in the dark." The Persian ambassador was treated with even less respect; for on his departure after a sojourn of some months at court, Jehangire had the meanness to send him in a bill for all his entertainments, and compelled him to pay to the uttermost farthing. The value of the presents were, however, with impartial generosity, deducted from the account.

Though so drunken himself, the vice was strictly forbidden in others, and no one could enter the Guzaleun, where the king sat, till the porter smelt his breath; if he had tasted wine he was not admitted to the king's presence; and on the reason being known, he was whipped. Jehangire was not amiable when drunk; and when sober he used frequently to whip and punish most cruelly his companions in excess.

He was favourable to Christianity; and even allowed two of his nephews, and Mirza-zul-Karmin, who had been born and bred in his own seraglio[2] and circumcised, to become Christians. We are even told that he had figures of Christ and of the Virgin at the head of his bed.

Like his contemporary James of England, he was very partial to religious discussions, and arguments on abstruse subjects. Religion was his hobby, and he used frequently to declare that, "the prophets of all nations were impostors, and that he himself, should his indolence permit

BOOK II. him, could form a better system of religion than any yet imposed on the world."

A.D.1626. Sir Thomas Roe relates that "once the good King fell to disputing on the laws of Moses, Christ, and Mahomet, and in his drink was so kind, that he turned to me and said, "I am a king; you shall be welcome, Christians, Moors, and Jews;" and continued, "that he meddled not with their faith; they came all in love, and he would protect them from wrong; they lived under his protection, and none should oppress them. This he often repeated, but being very drunk, he fell to weeping, and in divers passions, and so he kept us till midnight."

Notwithstanding his professed independence of all prejudice, Jehangire was most superstitious, and paid the most abject respect to the self-constituted saints of either religions. We have already seen that in honour of the saint Sheikh Selim, to whose gracious patronage he was indebted for his birth, he had his ears bored and always styled himself Sheikh Selim's slave. Sir Thomas Roe describes his condescension to one miserable fanatic clothed in rags, crowned with feathers, and covered with ashes, which excites contempt and disgust; this wretch, a true type of the wandering saints who to this day rob and terrify the inhabitants of India, was allowed to sit in his presence, a privilege denied to the son of the Emperor: Jehangire would talk with him familiarly and with much kindness, eat of his cake, and in return, share with him his banquet: on his departure he used to embrace him and give him 100 rupees, picking up himself all that fell from his dirty old hands.

But this liberality was merely the result of drink or policy: we have seen, by his endeavour to persuade Akbar to smite hip and thigh the Hindoo creed, that his toleration was more of the head than the heart.

Sir Thomas Roe does not think that the Mogul was so profuse as he desired to be thought; and that even on his birthday, when his greatest munificence was displayed, "all was not gold that glittered." On these occasions he was weighed first against silver, then against gold, and thirdly against silks, calicoes, spices, and other precious commodities, the whole of which were supposed to be distributed to the multitude.[8] The gold and precious stones being packed, Sir Thomas Roe could not see their quality or certify to their existence: he believed that all the valuable commodities were taken home, and that only the money, the corn, and the butter were actually distributed among the people.

The Emperor was sole arbiter and absolute judge in everything; he was controlled by no laws, and the lives of the meanest as well as the most powerful of his subjects were subject to every passing whim; he was proprietor of all the land in his kingdom, excepting some hereditary districts held by a Hindoo prince, for which he paid, but retained absolute jurisdiction; he was the general heir of his subjects; but when there were children to inherit he seldom deprived them of their father's estate.

Persian was the language of the Court; but the public of course spoke, as now, Hindostani. Jehangire was a good linguist, and spoke Persian, Turki, Turkish, and Hindostani equally well.

The Emperor gave audience twice a day from the throne, when all petitioners without exception, having gone through the proper ceremonies, were admitted; amongst his earliest measures was the following device for ensuring easy access to complainants to his presence. A chain was hung from a part of the wall of the citadel, accessible without difficulty to all comers. It communicated with a cluster of golden bells within the Emperor's own apartment, and he was immediately apprised by the sound of the appearance of a suitor, and thus rendered independent of any officers inclined to keep back information. Notwithstanding the magnificence of the Great Mogul, and the majesty and terror of his presence, some

BOOK II. A.D.1626. of the petitioners exhibited a freedom of speech that appears strange in less autocratic lands. The son of a Banian widow having complained to Jehangire that his father had left 200,000 rupees, and that his mother gave him very little, the Emperor sent for her and desired her to give her son 50,000 rupees and himself 100,000; whereupon she demanded permission to speak, and called out with a loud voice, "God save your majesty! I find my son hath some reason to demand the goods of his father, as being of his and my flesh and blood and therefore our heir; but I would gladly know what kindred your majesty is to my deceased husband, to be his heir?" Jehangire laughed and let her have her will.

The death of this monarch, from asthma, took place at the town of Mutti, between Cashmere and Lahore, at the age of fifty-nine, after a comparatively peaceful reign of twenty-two years. By turns familiar and capricious, garrulous and haughty, pedantic in his learning, and much given to theological discussion (especially when drunk); indolent, and a slave to wine, women, and opium, the character of this son of Akbar bears considerable resemblance to that of his maudlin contemporary, James I. of England. But the Eastern monarch possessed a valuable quality, that was entirely wanting in the character of James —one of the greatest elements of success in the great ones of the world—the power of distinguishing between those who were deserving, and those who were unworthy, of confidence and promotion. These qualities enabled him to escape the impotent injustice of the miserable James; and saved his country from a reign of sensual parasites, who covered the glory of England as it were with a mummer's mask, and made her king a laughing-stock and a bye-word among nations.

From his boyhood Jehangire had been cruel as the grave, and when drunk his ferocity knew no bounds. On one occasion, having commanded one of his servants to be skinned alive, the benevolent Akbar exclaimed bitterly, "that he wondered how the son of a man, who could not see a dead beast flayed without pain, could be guilty of such cruelty to a human being."[5] When sober he affected a love of justice, and when thoroughly roused, would not spare those dearest to him. The story of Seif Alla, the adopted son of Noor-Mahal, affords an illustration of his savage justice. With the pride of high station, Seif Alla refused satisfaction to the parents of a child who had been trodden under foot by his elephant, and on their becoming clamorous, expelled them from the city districts of Burdwan: they proceeded to Lahore to complain before the Emperor, and he immediately commanded Seif Alla to render justice to them. Instead of obeying the Emperor, he threw them into prison; upon their liberation, they returned at once to Lahore, and notwithstanding the efforts of Asiph and Noor-Mahal, they obtained a second interview with Jehangire. The Emperor, without saying a word, ordered Seif Alla into his presence. When he arrived, he desired him to be bound, and having mounted the family of the injured man on an elephant, the driver, received orders to make the animal tread Seif Alla to death. The driver dreading the revenge of the Empress, tried to escape the task; but the threats of the Emperor compelled him at last to obey.

Jehangire buried him with great magnificence, and mourned for him for the space of two months. "I loved him," said he, "but justice, like necessity, should bind kings."

We have seen that under the enlightened rule of Aiass the empire of the Great Mogul flourished exceedingly, and the wealth and prosperity of the people was very great; that a considerable amount of lawlessness still existed may be gathered from a statement of Sir Thomas Roe, that he saw 100 robbers executed at one time at Agra, and eight more left with their heads half severed in the streets. And the following verses, written by a Persian

BOOK II. A.D. 1628.

traveller on his arrival at Agra, show that to the peaceful trader the land of Hindostan still retained its terrors:—

> "I have traversed, through the blessing of him to whom none is accountable, roads of which the ground is saturated with human blood.
>
> Well may he be said to have obtained a renewal of life who had escaped a living man from the perils of Guzerat."

The great queen Noor-Mahal survived her husband eighteen years; 250,000*l.* a year was annually paid to her out of the public treasury; her power, however, ceased entirely at his death: from that day she never wore any colour but white: she was too proud to speak even of public affairs, and gave up her mind to study, retirement, and ease. Scorning to counsel where she had once dictated, she retired altogether from the affairs of state, and amongst the gardens and palaces of the royal residence at Lahore she passed the luxurious evening of a life of glory and vicissitude, that reminds us of the last days of the magnificent Queen of Palmyra in her royal retreat near Tibur.

NOTES TO CHAPTER XXII.

[1] The Empire was divided into fifteen subahs, each governed by a viceroy.

[2] There was no difference between the children born in concubinage and wedlock, the fact of their being born in the harem was sufficient.

[3] On one occasion, when Jehangire went to a feast at Asiph Khan's, the road for the distance of upwards of a mile was carpeted with silks and velvets, sewn together, and rolled up as the king passed.

[4] See *Elphinstone.*

[5] Dost Mahommed being once asked by an English officer if it was true that he had caused 12,000 of his subjects to be flayed alive, replied, "Oh dear no, 300 is the outside!"

CHAP. XXIII.

ACCESSION OF SHAH JEHAN.—CHAN JEHAN LODI.—MUMTÂZA ZEMÂNI.—THE TAJE MAHAL.—GREAT FAMINE.

CHAP. XXIII. A.D. 1628.

SHAH JEHAN mounted the throne of the Moguls at Agra under the high-sounding titles of "the True Star of the Faith," the "Second Lord of Happy Conjunctions," and "Mahommed the King of the World." He was in the thirty-sixth year of his age; his mother was the famous Jod Bae, daughter of Oody the Fat, almost as influential a lady in Jehangire's household as Noor-Mahal herself. Her tomb at Secundra stands close to the mausoleum of the great Akbar.

His accession was opposed by Prince Shehriar, who, by the influence of Noor-Mahal, had been named by Jehangire during his last illness his successor; but by the assistance of Asiph, and Mohabit, Shehriar was soon overcome, blinded, thrown into prison, and soon afterwards murdered.

Jehan inaugurated his reign with the indiscriminate slaughter of all his male relatives; he smote all the house of Baber; and left not of the royal line of the Mogul any male that breathed except himself. Shehriar, we have seen, was blinded and slain; two sons of his brother Chusero were murdered at Lahore; also two sons of Akbar's drunken son Danial, who had been imprisoned during the whole of Jehangire's reign. By dagger and bowstring he

BOOK II. A.D. 1628–57.

destroyed all the males of the house of Timour, he himself being the only remaining descendant.

The accounts of the character of Shah Jehan are so contradictory, that the student of the history of the period is fairly puzzled. Whilst some historians describe him as an ungrateful son; a rebellious subject; and a cruel brother; accusing him, without any doubt, of the murder of Chusero, Shehriar, and indeed all his male relatives; others paint him as one of the most beneficent sovereigns that ever sat on the throne of Hindostan. It being impossible to prove which of these accounts is correct, I have preferred a middle course; which, without imputing to Shah Jehan *all* the crimes charged to his account by his enemies, does not free him from those family murders that in all Eastern monarchies appear to have received the sanction of immemorial custom.

As a rule, the decease of a monarch was the signal for all his children to claim the throne; the succession was never determined by seniority; every prince claiming to have been specially nominated by his father; the door was thus always open to intrigue, to murder, and to civil war. Every prince mounted the throne, as it were, by conquest; and few of them could feel themselves secure whilst any of their male relatives remained alive. Although it is not proved that Shah Jehan murdered his brother Chusero to clear his way to the throne, there is very little doubt he slew Prince Shehriar and all his male relatives to secure it.

Shah Jehan celebrated his release from the dangerous ties of consanguinity by a succession of magnificent fêtes at Agra, that eclipsed in costly extravagance the more than imperial displays of the splendid Noor-Mahal herself.

Asiph Jah was confirmed in the office of vizier, with revenues amounting to upwards of a million sterling; whilst Mohabit was raised to the high office of Captain-general of all the forces, with the title and dignity of Chan Chanan, or first of nobles. Under the equable administration of the former the internal arrangements of the kingdom were fostered and regulated, and the prosperity of Hindostan and the provinces greatly increased; whilst under the latter, the Empire was extended far into the countries of Assam and Thibet, and the titles of the Great Mogul were proclaimed south of the yet debateable land of the Deccan. CHAP. XXIII. A.D. 1628–57.

Shah Jehan was a mighty sovereign, and during his reign the Mogul Empire probably attained its highest pitch of magnificence. Agra and Delhi were at that period the most renowned cities in the East; no others could boast of equal wealth and magnificence, or could exhibit such a throng of gallant cavaliers and noble princes as those who twice a day thronged the presence-chamber of the Mogul. Mounted on magnificently caparisoned elephants, shining with gold; or borne swiftly along in luxurious palankeens, well cushioned with all the costly fabrics of the East; with servants preceding to shout out their rank and titles, and others on either side to bear a toothpick and silver spitting vessel, or to brush away the flies and dust; the proud rajahs and omrahs of the Imperial capital were a brilliant race, unequalled for wealth and display in the known world. The Imperial fêtes exceeded in lavish magnificence the most fabulous narration of Eastern extravagance. On the occasion of the marriage of Dara and Susa, the two elder sons of Jehan, the first with the daughter of his uncle Parvez, and the latter to the daughter of Rustum Suffasi, of the royal line of Persia, 875,000*l.* was expended from the public treasury alone, besides the countless expenditure of competing nobles.

But it was not in fêtes and festivities alone that the time of the great rajahs and omrahs of the court at Agra was passed. Every now and then some deep plot, that had for its object the revival of a former, or the subversion of the present dynasty, would agitate the court and involve the whole capital in blood.

Turks, Usbecs, Tartars, and Arabians, whose ancestors

BOOK II.

A.D. 1628–57.

had resided for three or four generations in Hindostan, were considered a deteriorated race, and seldom employed in high offices. Men like Chan Jehan Lodi, whose ancestors reigned before the house of Timour; and Mirza Abdul Rahin, who boasted his pedigree direct from Timour himself, were amenable to no laws or influences but their own unbridled will; and the following narration, by no means singular in the history of a court by turns childish in its amusements and inhuman in its crimes, illustrates clearly enough the power and temper of the fierce nobles surrounding the throne of the Great Mogul. Chan Jehan was from his youth an opponent of the Moguls; he derived his birth from the imperial family of Lodi, and he had not altogether abandoned the hope of regaining the splendid patrimony of his race. Many Affghans of his tribe served under him; and confiding in their attachment, he viewed with secret pleasure any difficulties that threatened the dynasty of the family of Timour.

This feeling of hostility to the reigning family broke into actual flame at the death of Jehangire. Chan Jehan was then in command of the Deccan, and treated with insult and contempt the messenger of the young Emperor sent to announce his accession to the throne.

The renowned Mohabit was sent against him, but Chan Jehan considering discretion the better part of valour, sent messengers to him to request his mediation with the Emperor, explaining away his conduct by the difficulty there had always existed in deciding in favour of the reigning Emperor against the will of Jehangire. "But now," continued he, "that Shah Jehan remains alone of the posterity of Timour, Lodi cannot hesitate to obey his commands." On making this submission Lodi was apparently received to Imperial favour, but the forgiveness was only nominal. The Emperor had in his youth received an insult at the hands of Lodi, and he was one who *never* forgave: whilst in arms against his father he demanded permission to pass through Lodi's government of Deccan; but was absolutely refused, and insult added to injury by the formal presentation of a thousand rupees, of a horse, and a dress, as to a person of inferior dignity. The messenger of Lodi had not courage to deliver the humiliating present; when he got beyond the walls of Berhampore, where Lodi resided, he gave the rupees, the horse, and the dress to a shepherd, desiring him to return the whole to Lodi, and to tell him that "if the presents were not unworthy for him to give, they were too insignificant for his servant to carry to a great prince." Although Shah Jehan escaped the indignity, he never forgave the intention, and carefully watched his opportunity for revenge. A short time after the accession of Jehan, an edict of immunity was issued in favour of all the omrahs who had opposed his accession to the throne; and Lodi availed himself of the indulgence to go to Court; supposing that his position of one of the first nobles of the land was unaffected; but he was soon undeceived: on his first appearance, the usher obliged him to perform some prostrations inconsistent with his high rank. Unable to resent the treatment, he thought it advisable to obey; but not so his son Azmut Khan, a fierce young warrior of sixteen years of age, who thinking he had been kept too long prostrate on the ground, started up before the signal for rising was given; the usher in a rage struck him over the head with his rod, and insisted upon his throwing himself on the ground again. Irritated beyond endurance, Azmut drew his sword and aimed a blow at the usher's head; all was now confusion, and nothing less than the assassination of the sovereign was expected; the Emperor leaped from his throne, and all present drew their swords. Lodi, and his son, rushed from the presence and shut themselves up in his house with 300 faithful followers, where he was immediately besieged by the Royal Guard. The house was close by the palace, and unwilling to use artillery so near his harem, Shah Jehan

BOOK II. A.D. 1628–57. endeavoured, but in vain, to entice him to a surrender; but Lodi knew how certain was his doom, once in the hands of his enemies, and he determined to escape or die in the attempt. Night in the mean time came on, the enemy were thundering at the gates, and his wives were entreating him to secure his safety by flight; he knew not how to act; to remain was death; to desert his women an act unworthy of life: they saw his grief, and their resolution was at once taken; retiring to an inner apartment, they destroyed themselves with daggers. When Lodi was informed of this act of devotion, fury and desperation took the place of doubt; assisted by his sons he buried his two faithful wives in the inner court; when starting up, with rage in his eyes and terror on his brow, he summoned his retainers in the courtyard, and mounting his horse, ordered his drums to be beaten and his trumpets to be sounded; and himself throwing open the gate, cut his way through the astounded guards, exclaiming, "I will awaken the tyrant with the sound of my departure, but he shall tremble at my return."

Disturbed by the noise, the Emperor started from his bed, and furious at the escape of his enemy, ordered ten of his chief nobles to pursue him. Lodi rode forty miles without drawing rein; when he was stopped by the river Chambul, which was so high that he could not cross it without danger; here he was overtaken by the imperial troops and a desperate combat ensued. He defended himself till scarce one hundred of his men remained unhurt; he was wounded, and could scarce sit his horse, when his sons Hussein and Azmut conjured him to attempt the river, and leave them to guard his retreat. Unwilling to lose both his sons, he insisted that one should accompany him, and a contest of generosity now arose between them as to which should have the honour of devoting his life to save that of his father. The enemy were pressing them hard, and every moment was of consequence, when at that instant Perist, the usher who had struck Azmut in the presence appeared in front of the Imperialists. "Hussein," exclaimed Azmut, "the thing is determined; dost thou behold that villain and ask me to go?" He returned with his shattered band to the strife, whilst his father and brother plunged in the river.

The obnoxious usher was a Calmuc Tartar of great personal strength, and the moment he saw the young warrior advance into the plain, he started from the ranks to meet him; superior skill alone saved this youthful David from his gigantic foe; he advanced with his bow ready bent, and aiming an arrow, smote him in the forehead, and laid him dead at his horse's feet. But Azmut did not long survive his exploit; the Imperialists closed around him and his gallant band; and before his father and Hussein had gained the further shore, his soul, and those of his daring comrades, had winged their way to the heroes' paradise.

After a series of exploits and hairbreadth escapes worthy of the Bruce himself, Lodi found safety with the Nizam at Dowletabad; but the Emperor was disturbed at the escape of his noble foe, and he used every argument to induce his protector to deliver him up; he even advanced into the Deccan at the head of 100,000 horse, to compel his surrender. In the meantime Lodi marshalled the united forces of Golconda and Beejapore to resist the Mogul, and everywhere war desolated the table-land of the Deccan.

Shah Jehan felt it beneath his dignity himself to head an army against a rebellious subject; but his place was ably supplied by his vizier Asiph Jah; and Lodi was at length utterly defeated and his army scattered to the winds. Again he was forced to fly; and after innumerable sufferings, only varied by unceasing strife, he was overtaken by a detachment of 5000 Imperial troops; his followers were reduced to only thirty men; he begged them to leave him, and as a last act of friendship to save themselves by flight. They refused, with the noble answer,

BOOK II. A.D. 1628–57.

that that was the only command they could not obey; he made no reply, but advanced sword in hand against the enemy. The Imperial general was thunder-struck when he saw thirty men advancing against five-thousand, and supposed they intended to surrender; but was soon undeceived; and when at a short distance from his line he gave orders to his men to fire, Lodi fell dead at the first shot, and his thirty paladins died to a man. Thus died the last representative of the line of Affghan princes who ruled Hindostan before the advent of Timour. A warrior of the true stamp of Bayard or Baber, his mind was noble as his descent, and his courage equal to his ambition. The rolls of Indian chivalry can boast names as illustrious as any that gild the page of European history; but not one more noble appears in either than that of Chan Jehan Lodi of Malva.

Blessed however as Shah Jehan was during many years in the wisdom of his ministers and the successes of his arms; it was in his wife he possessed a jewel that threw all other sources of happiness into the shade. Heaven had vouchsafed to him its greatest earthly blessing, in giving him one whose beauty was only equalled by her virtue; and who obtained, by the noblest and purest attributes of her sex, the influence that is often conceded to less excellent qualities.

The incident by which this inestimable jewel came into the possession of the Mogul, affords an illustration of the romantic, though not always creditable, circumstances, that frequently attended the rise of the favourite of an Eastern king.

Whilst residing at his father's court at Agra, Jehan, with all the other princes and nobles, took great delight in attending the fête days of the Noroze, when the ladies of the Court displayed their beauty, and their merchandise, to all comers; and sold to the highest bidder; on this occasion the Emperor Jehangire, for a freak, had desired all the ladies to provide precious stones; and the noblemen were desired to purchase at whatever price the ladies chose to put upon them. The ladies obeyed the Imperial injunction, and took and arranged their booths according to their fancy. In order to inaugurate with especial honour the newly erected market of the royal palace, the King himself announced his intention of becoming a buyer; and on the appointed day attended with all the gallants and nobles of his court, to purchase the jewels and other trifles the ladies had to dispose of. During the fair, Prince Jehan coming to the booth of Arjemund Banu, daughter of the vizier Asiph Jah, and wife of Jemal Khan, asked her what she had to sell; and was promptly answered, she only possessed one large diamond, and that its price was very high; he desired to see it; when she showed him a piece of fine transparent sugar candy, of a tolerable good diamond figure. On enquiring what price she set upon it, she told him with a pleasant air it was worth a lac of rupees, 12,500*l.*; he immediately paid the money; and getting into conversation with her, found her wit was as exquisite as her beauty, and invited her to the palace; she accordingly went thither and remained two or three days. Strange to say, on returning to her husband, she was not so well received as she desired; whereupon she made complaint to Jehan, who with princely vehemence, ordered him to the elephant garden, there to be destroyed by an elephant.

Jemal Khan, however, the luckless husband of this frail fair one, desired to speak to the king before his execution; and being graciously allowed the favour, he explained that his coldness to his wife, far from being designed as an insult to the heir apparent, was intended as the highest possible compliment. It was not that he was angry with her for her favourable reception of the royal advances; but that he himself felt unworthy to receive back to his bosom one who had gained the affections of the son of the Mogul!

Jehan was highly pleased with his judicious homage;

BOOK II.

A.D. 1628–57.

gave him a royal suit, with the command of 5000 horse; and relieved him from his domestic difficulty by taking the lady into his seraglio, where she soon became his favourite wife and the mother of his children.

When Shah Jehan mounted the throne, Arjemund Banu was dignified with the title of Mumtâza Zemâni, the Most Exalted of the Age. She united in her mind and person, much of the exquisite beauty and fascination of her aunt, Noor-Mahal, with the wisdom and integrity of her grandfather and father.

Notwithstanding the very questionable incident that caused her elevation to the throne, the subsequent conduct of Mumtâza Zemâni fully warranted the deep and lasting affection of Jehan. A virtuous woman, we know, is a crown to her husband, and during the greater part of his reign did this priceless chaplet adorn the brow of Shah Jehan; during the whole of her life he had no other wife; and for twenty years he was that Phœnix of Eastern married life, that almost imaginary being of Mohammedan history, the husband of one wife.

Mumtâza bore him a child almost every year, and when at length she died in child-birth, and to charm death's fatal power no herb was found; when "the silver cord was loosed, and the bowl broken at the fountain," Shah Jehan was amongst the number of those who, at the end of life, are brought to acknowledge, that of all the good gifts that providence has spread in their path, the love of woman has been the most delicious, the most intoxicating, the most durable, and even the least deceitful.

The tale of Mumtâza's death is thus told by the native historian: "In the fearful agonies of a prolonged labour, the queen imagined she heard the child crying in her womb; she sent immediately to her husband Shah Jehan. 'No mother,' said she, 'ever survived who had heard her child cry before its birth. I am about to die. I cannot doubt it; but before I quit this life, I have two requests to make to you. Promise me that you will never marry again, that no more of your children may dispute with mine your love and your riches; swear to me, moreover, that you will raise over my remains a tomb that will render my name immortal.' Her presentiments were true, and she died immediately after in giving birth to a daughter." CHAP. XXIII. A.D. 1628–57.

From the days of Herodotus down to the present time, great princes; distinguished statesmen; conquerors, and poets; and even the "homunculi," the small fry of the human race, have sought to perpetuate in their tombs the notice they enjoyed, or coveted, during their lives. The return of dust to dust; of flesh to its parent earth; has from time immemorial been commemorated by the conversion of gold into stone; the victory of death recorded by the labours of the living.

Amongst Eastern monarchs especially, the erection of splendid tombs for themselves or their relatives, or even for the dissevered members of their living bodies, has always been considered a sacred duty.[1]

Shah Jehan observed to the letter the last request of her he had loved so well. He took no other wife; and at his bidding there arose on the banks of the Jumna at Agra the most costly tomb that ever covered mortal clay. To this day may be seen, sharp and beautiful, as if chiselled but yesterday, the marble walls and priceless mosaics, the lofty minarets and polished dome of the "Queen of edifices," reposing amid luxuriant gardens, marble fountains, and waving cypresses; and affording a precious proof of the affection and magnificence of the Emperor of Hindostan and of the worth and influence of his beautiful wife.

The labour of twenty thousand men, during twenty-two years; an expenditure of nearly a million sterling; the mines of Golconda; the precious stones of Ceylon; the jasper and lapis-lazuli of Caubul; the genius and skill of Italy; combined to raise this testimony of affection, and

BOOK II. A.D. 1628–57.

emblem of mortality; and to add another costly monument to commemorate the sting of death; the victory of the grave; the harvest of the angel Azrael; the unerring stroke of the rider on the white horse.

The Taj Mahal is the most perfect specimen of Saracenic architecture in the world; it was more costly than the whole of those immortal temples raised by the princely Pericles on the Acropolis of his native city, to astonish succeeding ages by their marvellous beauty, and to mark as it were the limits of the beautiful in art, beyond which imperfect man is not destined to arrive.[2]

The exquisite finish of the whole building removes it far beyond the realms of criticism or comparison. It bears to the cathedral of Milan about the same resemblance that a highly finished miniature of Thorburn does to a life-size portrait of Vandyke.

The remark of the famous Italian architect Zaffani, that all that was required to render it perfect was a glass case sufficiently large to contain it; conveys some idea of its apparently fragile and exquisite beauty; whilst the exclamation of the impulsive Frenchman, "Je consentirais mourir à l'instant même si j'étais sûre d'avoir un semblable tombeau," shows the strange effects of its beauty on some enthusiastic natures. It was built some hundred years after the palace of the royal race of Grenada had been destroyed by the bigoted churchmen of Isabella of Castille; and it has ever since been to the travellers and architects of the East, what the remains of the palace of Boabdil still are to the dilettante of the West; a miracle of beauty and skill.

The years 1631 and 1632 were marked by public calamities of various kinds; a famine of more or less severity raged over the greater part of Asia; an extraordinary drought dried up all the rivers, and the chapped ground refused her increase; starvation, followed by disease and death, ravaged the finest lands of India, Persia, and Western Tartary; in the latter country no rain fell for years; and populous and flourishing provinces were converted into arid and howling solitudes.

At first Shah Jehan did all he could to alleviate the sufferings of his people; he remitted taxes to the amount of three millions sterling, and opened the public treasury for the relief of the poor; but money could not purchase that which did not exist, and the harvest of death was unstayed.

At length he got impatient at the apathy of those who in their extremity sought relief at the shrine of their gods rather than in more energetic exertions; and he was enraged with those who prayed for assistance they were too lazy to afford themselves. "If they have a thousand gods," said he, "yet the thousand have not been able to guard them from famine; this array of divinities, instead of being beneficial to their votaries, distracts their attention by its numbers; and I am therefore determined to expel them from my empire." He unsheathed the sword of religious persecution against them, and gave orders for breaking the graven images, and destroying their temples with fire: but, as ever has been the case in India, persecution merely augmented the evil it was intended to destroy; fanaticism took the place of credulity; and thousands who had thitherto sought relief in the harmless adoration of stocks and stones, sprang to arms, and died in defence of their outraged gods. Jehan saw the impolicy of his act; and the abhorred edict was recalled with the cutting sarcasm, "that a prince who wishes to have subjects must take them with all the trumpery and trouble of their religion."

These were sad days for the natives of Hindostan: the march of armies, and the sword of persecution, devastated even the scanty harvest that providence had vouchsafed, and added to the number of those whom famine and disease had spared; and whilst the Emperor smote hip and thigh his own starving subjects, Asiph Jah carried the war into the Deccan and Telingana, and laid waste with fire and sword the fairest provinces of the kingdom of Beejapore.

BOOK II. A.D. 1628-57.

In the year following the European and Mogul armies first clashed on the banks of the Hooghly. Shah Jehan had a particular cause for animosity against the Portuguese, who had settled in Bengal during the reign of his grandfather. Whilst in arms against his father, he applied for assistance to Michael Rodriguez, who commanded the Portuguese troops in Bengal, and was refused with the insulting remark, that it was contrary to Christian principles to assist a rebel who had wantonly taken up arms against his father and sovereign. Jehan never forgave the reproof, and it scarcely required the instigation of his favourite sultana, Mumtâza Zemâni, whose orthodox deism was grievously insulted by the worship of saints and images, to induce him to seek the first opportunity of revenging his insulted honour.

The pretext was not long wanting. Casim Khan, governor of Bengal, sent to Agra to complain of the insolence and exactions of these strangers, who, instead of confining themselves to trade, fortified their factory, and exacted heavy tribute from all the ships that passed under their fortress. The laconic injunction, "expel these idolators from my dominions," was not so easily executed as expressed. The Portuguese defended themselves bravely; but at length the fort was taken by assault, and 3000 Christians fell into the hands of Casim; their lives were spared, but their obnoxious images were destroyed and their trading privileges annulled.

NOTES TO CHAPTER XXIII.

[1] Mohammed Toghlak buried one of his teeth and erected a magnificent tomb over it.

[2] Dow quotes the cost at 750,000*l.*, Thorne at 960,000*l.*, Sleeman at 3,174,802*l.* St. Paul's cost a little over 700,000*l.*, whilst the whole cost of the immortal buildings raised by Pericles on the Acropolis of Athens was under 700,000*l.*

The white marble was brought from Kandahar, more than 600 miles distant, and from Jeypore, 200 or 300 miles distant; the red from Futtehpore and from the neighbouring Mewat hills. One single mosaic flower in the screen contains a hundred stones, cut to the exact shape necessary, and highly polished.

CHAP. XXIV.

SHAH JEHAN'S SONS, DARA, SUJAH, AURUNGZEBE, AND MORAD.—HIS DAUGHTERS—INTESTINE WARS.—MAGNIFICENCE OF SHAH JEHAN.—HIS DEATH.—AURUNGZEBE MOUNTS THE THRONE.

CHAP. XXIV.

A.D. 1628-57.

The first years of the reign of Shah Jehan were blessed by the triple possession of a good wife, a sound constitution, and a faithful vizier; but his latter days were embittered by the jealousies and ambition of his children. In a sketch like the present it is useless to attempt to unravel the endless intricate plots of which the Imperial throne of Delhi was the object during the last years of the reign of Shah Jehan; but a glance at the tortuous path by which Aurungzebe mounted the Musnud of the Mogul, is necessary to an appreciation of his character, and to the correct understanding of the state of Hindostan at that period.

Of the numerous children born to Shah Jehan by his wife, the daughter of Asiph Jah, four sons and two daughters only had survived. Of these, Dara, the eldest son, was without doubt, one of the most accomplished and enlightened princes that India ever produced. He was agreeable, witty, and liberal; and his misfortunes arose chiefly from too much self-reliance, and a haughty indifference to the opinions of others; he was occasionately passionate; but his temper passed away like a fire of straw. Inheriting the strong intellect of his family, he was the most highly educated man in his dominions; and not content with cultivating the learning of Persia and Arabia, he drank deep at the ancient streams of Hindoo

BOOK II. A.D. 1628–57.

philosophy, and even studied the history and religion of Europe under Père Buzee, principal of a community of Jesuits, whom his liberality had induced to settle at Agra.

Bernier gives but a very indifferent account of the faith of Prince Dara; he describes him as a lax Mussulman, a pagan with pagans, and a Christian with Christians. But nearly every one of the race of Timour were deists; and in displaying perfect liberality in all matters of faith, and listening with the same interest and curiosity to all the various religious disputations of his subjects, he was only following in the steps of Akbar, and the other liberal thinkers of his race.[1] Aware that his liberality in religious matters had alienated the affection of the great Mussulman nobles of his father's court, and alive to the impending struggle for the throne, he cultivated Mammon in the persons of his Christian and Hindoo subjects. He was especially opposed to those bitter religious animosities, that in all ages have prompted and excused so much cruelty and injustice; and not satisfied with mere professions on the subject, he wrote a treatise, in the vain hope of reconciling the Hindoo and Moslem creeds. These liberal tendencies gave rise to many bitter enmities on the part of rigid Moslems; but on the whole, they rendered Dara popular with the great mass of his subjects; and combining, as he did in a remarkable degree, the frank generosity of the soldier with the polished cultivation of the man of letters, he was at the time of his father's dethronement the most illustrious of the noble race of Baber.

Sujah, the second son, much resembled him, but he was more secret and more firm; fearless as a soldier, he was yet more fearless in debauchery; prudent in all the concerns of life, in pleasure he knew no master but his will. Although his father and brothers were Sunnees, he favoured the Shiahs, the dominant sect of Persia; and it was to the great Persian nobles, who, since the return of Humaioon, had been all powerful in Hindostan, that he looked for support. The third son, Aurungzebe, whose name is as distinguished in Eastern history as that of any sovereign who ever occupied the throne of Hindostan, was one of those characters who in every age and in all countries will rise to distinction. A stranger to the noble generosity and liberal nature of Dara, and inferior to Sujah in personal appearance and prowess, he yet eclipsed them both in those solid qualities that exalt man above his fellows; ambition was his god, success in life his study, and every gift of his nature, every acquirement of his understanding, were bent to the attainment of these objects.

Selfish, cruel, and exceedingly well versed in the arts of dissembling, he allowed no generous impulse to thwart his ambition; no mercy to temper his will; no compunction to interfere with the execution of his plans. Ascetic by nature, and a hypocrite by policy, he combined in the imprisonment of his father, and the relentless extermination of his brothers, the venomous craft of Louis XI. with the merciless ferocity of Cæsar Borgia. Under the humble garb of a fakeer he concealed the pride and cruelty of an ambitious and pitiless tyrant; and whilst a hermitage was the professed object of his desires, a throne was the real aim of his life.

The Emperor Aurungzebe occupies the same position in Eastern history that Louis XI. does in that of Europe; unforgiving and crafty in all the relations of private life, he yet ruled his country with marked success, and paralysed his foes as much by his energy as by his deceit.[2]

Morad, the fourth and youngest son of Shah Jehan, was haughty, imperious, daring, and thoughtless; a slave to wine, women, and the worship of the wind, he despised cabals and the intrigues of the cabinet, and gloried in keeping nothing secret; he delighted in athletic exercises, and boasted loudly that he trusted only in his arm and sword to enforce his claim to the throne. He was unfit to hold imperial power himself; but he promised to become

BOOK II. A.D. 1628–57.

a most dangerous instrument in the hands of his more diplomatic brother Aurungzebe.

The daughters of Shah Jehan were no less conspicuous than his sons; Jehanara, or Begum Sahed, the eldest, was very beautiful, and a great wit; she was passionately devoted to her father, who had every confidence in her, and in most cases was the servant of her will. This influence gained her vast and costly presents, which she spent in generous and liberal donations; she supported Dara in all his intrigues, and openly proclaimed her solicitude for his welfare. Bred up in the vicious atmosphere of a harem, her mind did not escape the low morality that typifies the female sex in the East. In countries where the primrose path of love is hedged in with death, and where the sack and bowstring are the penalty of violated chastity, the ruling passion is yet as omnipotent and irresistible as in more sober climes, where similar difficulties are settled by a cheque on the bankers, or an appeal to the new divorce court.

Jehanara was a slave to love, although aware that death and disgrace would attend discovery. On one occasion she had admitted a suitor to her chamber, when she was surprised by a sudden visit from her father; at her wits' end to secure the escape of her lover, the only place of concealment that offered itself was one of the great cauldrons, made to hold water for the bath, into which he was immediately hustled; but Shah Jehan, who was fully aware of his daughter's free and easy morality, and had come with the intention of convicting her, suspected the truth. After greeting her affectionately, and conversing agreeably on various matters, he enquired why he found her less neat and becomingly arrayed than usual; adding politely the very disagreeable remark, that she did not make sufficiently frequent use of the bath; and regardless of her excuses, he commanded the fires to be lighted under the cauldron, in order that she might at once perform her ablutions. Apparently unconscious of her terrible agony during her lover's boiling, he continued cheerfully conversing till his eunuchs brought him word that the wretched lover was done, when he departed without a frown or a word of reproach:[3] on another occasion, suspecting an omrah of high rank of enjoying the fatal distinction of his daughter's love, he treated him with marked attention, and gave him from his own box betel so highly poisoned, that on eating it he fell down dead.

Ranchenara Begum, his second daughter, though neither so handsome or spirituelle as Jehanara, was yet cheerful, graceful, and ambitious, and was not far behind her sister in the pursuit of doubtful pleasures. She was devoted to Aurungzebe, and it was by her assistance that he managed so completely to checkmate the bold diplomacy of his brother Dara.

Shah Jehan, with the natural affection of a father for his first-born, associated Dara with him on the throne; and feeling the impossibility of keeping his four sons at court together, with the certainty of their destroying each other or of being himself the victim of their cabals, he despatched them to satrafies in the most opposite districts of his empire; Sujah was sent to Bengal, Aurungzebe to the Deccan, and Morad to the small but important province of Guzerat.

To calm the jealousy of his brothers Dara was nominally appointed to Caubul and Moultan; but being the eldest and heir to the throne, he did not in reality quit Agra.

Dara was the favourite son of Shah Jehan; but he could not fail to discern the superior capacity of Aurungzebe for empire, and frequently sought from him counsel and advice. This was very evident to Dara, who could not refrain from saying occasionally to his friends in private, that of all his brothers he feared "only the bigot, that great praying man."

Whatever influence the right of paternity might have exercised over the younger sons of the Mogul, that

BOOK II. A.D. 1628–57.

of primogeniture had none at all, and the decided preference of Shah Jehan for his eldest son was in itself sufficient to unite his brothers in enmity against him.

In the year 1657, in the twenty-ninth year of his reign, Shah Jehan was seized with paralysis, and no sooner was his illness known than the kingdom was thrown into commotion; for four days the shops were closed, and every one prepared themselves openly for war. In his imbecility Jehan began to dread the power and hasty nature of Dara, and lived in perpetual terror of poison. In anticipation of his decease, his affectionate children quitted their respective governments of Bengal, Guzerat, and the southern provinces, and marched with all their forces straight on Delhi, intent on expelling their elder brother, and of subsequently contending for the throne amongst themselves.

It was to no purpose Jehan wrote with his own hand to say he was alive and doing well, and desired them to return to their governments; they pretended not to believe it, and insisted that he was dead; but said if he was alive, they were determined to free him from restraints, kiss his feet, and then obey his commands. In execution of this filial determination, Aurungzebe formed an alliance with Meer Jumla, a Persian of enormous wealth and experience, lately in the service of the king of Beesepore; and uniting with Morad and his army from Guzerat, he proclaimed Dara a kaffir or infidel, and Sujah a kafizy or heretic, equally unfit to rule over the faithful, and commenced his march towards Agra. Sujah in the meantime continued to advance towards the capital, unwilling to leave the field entirely to his brothers; Dara despatched against him his son Soliman Chekoh, a youth of great promise, who gained a considerable victory, forcing Sujah to retire: after some time spent in a useless pursuit, he returned in triumph to Agra, but too late to save his father from the superior genius of Aurungzebe.

The first army sent by Jehan and Dara against the

united forces of Morad and Aurungzebe was commanded by Jesswunt Singh, a Rajpoot chief of distinguished fame. The contest was long doubtful, but at length terminated in favour of the brothers, partly owing to the irresistible gallantry of Morad, and partly to the treachery of Cosim Khan, the chief of Jesswunt's artillery, who adopted the strange device of burying the ammunition in the sand.

After a halt of a few days, Aurungzebe marched on to meet the bulk of the Imperial forces that were awaiting the arrival of Dara to take command. Jehan tried in vain to stop this cruel war; but finding at length that it was impossible, he commissioned Dara to defend his throne. The aged monarch melted into tears when he despatched his son with this very questionable blessing: "Go, Dara," said he, "God bless thee; but remember well my words; if thou losest the battle, take heed if thou ever come again into my presence."

The army of Dara numbered 100,000 of the finest horse in Hindostan, 20,000 infantry, and 4000 pieces of cannon: whilst that of Aurungzebe scarcely amounted to 40,000 men, who were nearly worn out with long marching. Notwithstanding the discrepancy in numbers, Dara was from the very first out-manœuvred by Aurungzebe; but his valour made up for his want of generalship; mounted on a proud Ceylon elephant, he out-faced the fierce artillery of Aurungzebe, and at the head of his troops broke through the chained elephants, and entered his brother's camp.

Meantime the courage of Aurungzebe did not quail; notwithstanding the victorious rush of Dara, he stood firm and attempted to arrest the fugitives by his manner. Calling by name to those of his great omrahs who were about him, he cried out, "Courage, my old friend, God is! what hope is there in flying? Know you not how far off is our Deccan; God is! God is!" and that they might see that he at any rate would not turn, he commanded

BOOK II. A.D. 1628–57.

before them all to have his elephants' legs chained; and thus immoveable amidst the fluctuating waves of the fight, he remained a conspicuous rallying point for his friends and a mark for the onslaught of his foes.

Fortune however still declared itself for Dara, and but for a circumstance as unforeseen as it was unfortunate, the defeat of Aurungzebe would have been complete. Callil-ullah-Khan, one of the chief officers of Dara's army, was his enemy; he owed him a grudge, and now was his time to revenge it. Riding hastily up to Dara, he greeted him with victory, "God save your Majesty, you have gained the victory; what will you do any longer on your elephant? what remains now to be done but to take horse and pursue these runaways? let us do so, and not suffer them to escape our hands." Blinded by these sweet words, Dara allowed himself to be tempted down from his elephant, and joined fiercely in the pursuit; no sooner was he missed from his howdah than alarm spread through his army, and Callil-ullah-Khan proclaiming aloud that he was dead, a panic seized his victorious troops, and every one sought safety in flight. Never was fortune so fickle, or great events so regulated by the turning of a straw; a hasty act was sufficient to convert victory that even then hovered over the head of Dara into ruin and disgrace, and to place on the brow of Aurungzebe the crown of Hindostan. Taking advantage of the confusion his treason had caused, Callil-ullah-Khan now joined Aurungzebe with 30,000 cavalry, and the victory was complete. Dara fled to Agra, but mindful of his father's parting injunction, dared not enter the presence. Jehan however felt for him, and sent a trusty servant to comfort him, desiring him to go to Delhi, where he would find troops, &c., and assuring him that in the meantime he would do his best to circumvent Aurungzebe.

How was the mighty fallen; he who scarcely a week before had marched through the streets of the capital at the head of the armies of the Mogul, now quitted it a fugitive with 300 followers. The unfortunate Dara was not the only person of renown whose return home after this fatal defeat was attended with difficulty; seeing the hopelessness of the cause, Jeswunt Sing, after displaying prodigies of valour, returned to his own capital of Oodifore, with only 400 men, the sole survivors of a body-guard of 8,000 who had attended him to the field; instead of receiving him with the welcome his misfortunes deserved, his wife, a descendant of the Rana of Oodipore, the oldest aristocracy in India, or in the world, ordered the gates to be shut, and refused to let him enter; she fiercely denied that he was her husband. "The son-in-law of the great Rana," she said, "could not have so low a soul as to venture to leave a field of defeat alive." In war she said, a Rajpoot Prince must either vanquish or die, and having ventured to marry into so illustrious a house, he must, without regard to consequences, imitate its virtues; adding that even though her husband was base enough to avoid death by dishonour, it did not befit her high blood and lineage to endure the same. She ordered her funeral pile to be raised, and it was only on the distinct promise that he would raise another army to avenge his defeat, that she consented to live and to see her astounded lord.

Aurungzebe marched direct to Agra, proclaiming openly the incapacity of his aged father, and his determination to free him from the thraldom of evil counsellors. Arrived at Agra, he seized the palace and placed his father Jehan under close restraint, together with his sister Jehanara, and the wife and son of the defeated Dara.

Finding he could not arrest his advance, Shah Jehan sought to inveigle Aurungzebe into his power; on one occasion he nearly enticed him into the palace, where he had several lusty Tartarian women concealed, ready to seize and strangle him at a given signal; but the fox was not so easily trapped. Aurungzebe doubted the sudden

BOOK II. A.D.1658.

growth of affection in the bosom of his father, and knew too well the hatred concealed in that of his sister Jehanara. Moreover all the plots and secrets of the Court were carefully confided to him by his younger sister Ranchanara Begum. Although master of the capital and of the throne, Aurungzebe had yet many dark deeds of blood to perpetrate, before his power could be considered firmly established. Dara indeed was defeated, but yet lived; and Morad, his ally, now alive to the selfish designs of his brother, was already asserting his right to the lion's share of the spoil; whilst Sujah was rapidly advancing on the capital, fierce at being thus supplanted by his younger brother, and professedly indignant at the imprisonment of his father and sister.

The inflexible determination of Aurungzebe, however, soon freed him from the horns of this triple dilemma. The murder of a brother in his discontent was not a deed of sufficient magnitude to retard for any length of time the unhesitating ambition of one who could imprison his father in his old age; the death of Morad was decided upon the moment he became urgent for regal power. Aurungzebe, with the bold determination and unflinching purpose of a daring mind, recognised an opportunity of killing two birds with one stone, and perceived that the destruction of his younger brother might be made the means of striking terror into his other foes. Morad was a great favourite with the troops, and if Aurungzebe dare to slay him with impunity, openly and in the face of men, who that he desired to kill could after that be considered safe? Aurungzebe had always professed the greatest frendship and affection for Morad, calling him, whether in public or private Hazaret, King or Majesty; and reiterating, without causing suspicion, his asseveration that the kingly title had no attraction for him, who desired only to live and die a holy fakir.

The natural disposition of Morad assisted his brother's plots against his liberty and life; he was reckless, given to wine and other sensual indulgences. Aurungzebe knew his weak points, and made of his pleasant sins a rod to scourge him; he invited him to supper, when he offered him a beaming goblet of Shiraz wine and some very choice bottles of the Caubul vintage. Morad drank and was merry, and, to crown the joys of the evening, some of the graceful dancing girls of Hindostan were introduced, to display their accomplishments and the elegant symmetry of their limbs. Aurungzebe, in accordance with his character of a strict Mussulman, rose, and, exhorting his brother cheerfully to make merry, left the apartment.

The mirth then waxed wild and furious. Morad soon got drunk, and fell asleep on a sofa, and in this condition was disarmed; when Aurungzebe entering the apartment, as if enraged with this unwonted debauch, awoke him with a sharp kick, saying, "What means this shame and ignominy, that such a king as you are should have so little temper as thus to make himself drunk? What will be said of both of us? Take this infamous man, this drunkard," said he to his attendants, with well-feigned indignation, "tie him hand and foot, and throw him into that room to sleep off his wine." Upon this he was seized, and immediately after sent in close confinement to Delhi.

Once in his power, Aurungzebe was content to try the ordinary course of the law to effect his destruction; he ordered him to be tried by the chief magistrate, for putting a man to death without sufficient cause; but the just judge acquitted him, saying that "putting a man to death for a crime in the exercise of his authority, was not punishable by law." Aurungzebe immediately displaced him, and appointed a more subservient judge, who sentenced Morad to prison, where he remained for several years; at length he attempted his escape by means of a rope, and would have succeeded had not the lamentations of a Hindoo concubine he was leaving aroused the guard,

BOOK II. A.D. 1658.

and caused his discovery; he was immediately beheaded in prison.

Aurungzebe, now actually baptized in the blood of his kinsmen, cast aside the cloak of hypocrisy under which his dark schemes of ambition had been concealed and matured; and, under the proud title of Alemgire, or "Conqueror of the World," openly proclaimed himself Sultan of Hindostan.

After the defeat of Dara, and the confinement of Morad, his intimate friends and followers urged him to seize the crown and proclaim himself Emperor; he refused with well-feigned humility, but at length suffered himself to be persuaded. "You are determined," said he, "to sacrifice my love of retirement to your own ease. Well, be it so; God will perhaps give me that tranquillity on a throne which I hoped to find in a cell; and if less of my time will be spent in prayer, more of it will be employed in good actions; I should only have an inclination for virtuous deeds in my retreat, but as the Emperor of the Moguls I shall have the power of doing them; it is this consideration, and not the vain pomp of greatness, which induces me to assume the Empire."

He accordingly ascended the throne of Delhi 1658 A.D., in the 40th year of his age. Shah Jehan was at that period in his sixty-seventh year, and had reigned altogether thirty years.

After the defeat of Dara, one more crisis of fate remained to be surmounted: Sujah, at the head of the forces, and rajahs of Bengal, and backed by the undisguised sympathy of the great mass of the nobility, who dreaded from the sanguinary inauguration of the reign of Aurungzebe, the future cruelty of his career, was marching in hot haste on Agra, determined to reinstate his father or to establish himself on the throne of his ancestors.

"The wars of brothers are cruel," says the Stagirite; and never in the history of Hindostan did two armies contend with greater fury than did those of Sujah and

CHAP. XXIV. A.D.1659.

Aurungzebe, on the plain before Allahabad, "the City of God." During the battle the elephant of Aurungzebe was charged by one of the nobles of Sujah and forced on its knees; Aurungzebe had one foot out of the howdah ready to alight; one step more, and the crown of Hindostan would probably have fallen from his brows; but in the person of his great Persian general, Meer Jumla, he possessed a good genius, that was wanting to his brother on a similar occasion.

"Stop," said he, turning sternly to Aurungzebe; "you descend from the throne." The Emperor resumed his place, and unmoved remained a mark for the shafts and arrows of his foes.

The same presence of mind was wanting to his brother Sujah in a like extremity; finding his elephant disabled, he descended, and mounting a horse joined fiercely in the fray; the empty howdah returning to the rear was again received as evidence of the fate of the Sovereign, and changed the destiny of the crown of Hindostan; his army was totally defeated, and his brother left undisputed master of the field.

The power of Aurungzebe was now founded on the firmest base; and when, a few years afterwards, he perfidiously seized and slew the unfortunate Dara, and instigated the cruel slaughter of Sujah and his family, in the inhospitable regions of Arracan, there remained nothing but the remembrance of his perfidy, the bitter reproaches of his imprisoned father, and the damning spot of his brother's blood, to disturb the enjoyment of his illgotten crown.

There are few narratives in history more touching than the adventures and misfortunes of the two eldest sons of Jehan. Their devotion to their wives, the chivalry of their defence, and the heroism of their death, proclaim them worthy descendants of Baber and Akbar; and prove that notwithstanding the perfidious cruelty of Aurungzebe, generosity and a noble nature were

BOOK II. still the characteristics of the Princes of the house of Timour.

A.D.1659. After his defeat, Dara fled beyond the Indus, where, although at first secure, he was at length seized and sent to Delhi for execution. During his retreat his favourite Sultana was taken ill, and notwithstanding her earnest entreaties, he refused to leave her; when at length she died in his arms, the spirit of the haughty Dara broke out into a great and exceeding bitter cry, that all his past misfortunes were nothing, but that now, indeed, he was alone upon the earth.

When Nadina Bana died, Dara was almost alone; he tore off his magnificent robe and threw the Imperial turban on the ground and clothing himself in a mean habit lay down by his departed consort. In the evening Gal Mahommed, a faithful follower, joined him with fifty horse. Dara was overjoyed at his arrival; starting up, he ordered his wife's body to be embalmed, and taking Gal Mahommed's hand begged him as a last favour to escort her with his fifty horse to Lahore, to the sepulchre of her great ancestors: adding bitterly, "Aurungzebe himself will not refuse a sepulchre to the family of Dara."[4]

Shortly after, Dara was betrayed, and carried in ignominy to Delhi, where, by order of Aurungzebe, he was assassinated. The head was taken to Aurungzebe, who commanded it to be put into a dish, and having sent for water he washed it clean, and wiped it with a handkerchief. When fully satisfied that it was the very head of his beloved brother, he began to weep; and exclaiming, "Oh! unfortunate man," he ordered that it should be buried in the tomb of Humaiun, and retired to his harem.

Sujah was slain in Arracan, after a defence that for gallantry and determination is almost unequalled. Piâra Bana, his only wife, still famed by the poets of Bengal for her wit, beauty, and grace, was taken to the zenana of the Rajah of Arracan, where, after disfiguring herself with her own hands, she committed suicide by dashing her head against a stone.

Thus ended the cruel war which had lasted five years and spread sorrow and destruction throughout Hindostan. But Aurungzebe had yet another duty to perform before he could reap the full reward of his unrelenting treachery. Having got rid of the immediate competitors for the throne, he had now to destroy all who might subsequently annoy him.

His whole history supplies a parallel to the conduct of crooked-back Richard towards Clarence and his nephews in the tower. Soliman, the son of Dara, and Sefe, his grandson, and the child of Morad, were confined in the fortress of Gwalior, and destroyed by drinking "poust," an infusion of poppy-heads, the usual method of removing the Princes of the house of Timour in Hindostan. The person destined to death by this cruel process was forced to drink the poust the first thing in the morning, and was allowed nothing to eat till he had swallowed a large cupfull. Losing little by little their strength and understanding, and growing torpid and senseless, the travellers on this royal road to the other world wasted gradually away and died insensibly.

Although the perfidy and cruelty by which the treacherous Aurungzebe waded to the throne through oceans of kindred blood carries us back to the worst days of the Affghan dynasties, the sagacious policy by which he secured peace and security to his subjects remind us no less of the most prosperous years of the reign of Akbar; and during the eighteen years of profound peace that succeeded to the devastating tumults and contentions of his accession he sought, apparently by a singular moderation in the exercise of his power, to obliterate the remembrance of the savage acts by which he had obtained it.

Aurungzebe was now the greatest potentate of the Eastern World; and the Shah of Persia, the Shereef of

BOOK II. A.D. 1659-77.

Mecca, the Emperor of China, and even the sovereigns of Europe, sent to congratulate him upon his success and to solicit his friendship.

In the year 1666 the Emperor Shah Jehan died in the Palace at Agra, at the age of seventy-five. For nearly eight years he had been kept in restraint by Aurungzebe, and his existence was almost forgotten throughout his empire. He preserved indeed all the insignia and pomp of royalty, but was denied the sweets of power. A lax Mussulman in his youth, the misfortunes of age brought with them a craving for the support that is not of this world; and he gave scope to the intolerance of his creed. The Church at Agra, where the Jesuits had a congregation of thirty or forty Christian families, was pulled down, and the steeple bell, that could be heard al over the city, broken up with every possible insult. The Koran was constantly read in his presence, and his former toleration of Brahmins and Christians was bitterly repented of.

Tenderly nursed by his daughter Jehanara, who had divided his affection with his son Dara, since the death of her who had for twenty years engrossed it all, his time was passed chiefly in long fits of melancholy, or in the pageantry and childish amusements of an Eastern Court.

Bitter and constant were his complaints against Aurungzebe; he never forgave him, and could not hear his name mentioned without a curse. "Fathers have been dethroned by their sons," he used to say, "but to insult the misfortunes of a parent was left for Aurungzebe."

Interrupted in the completion of a tomb for himself, which he intended to equal the one erected over his wife, his last request was to be laid by the side of her he had loved so dearly; and to this day may be seen, side by side, enclosed within a screen of elaborate tracery, the tombs of "the most exalted of the age" and of the "King of the World," her husband.

Shah Jehan was an able monarch, and although given to fits of intemperate anger and oppression, his usual strong love of justice, his great energy, and real desire for the welfare of his subjects, enabled him to maintain in all its unequalled splendour the noble dominion handed down to him by his father.

Much as we may detest the inhumanity of the son, who could bring down his father's "grey hairs with sorrow to the grave," we must remember that the sin of disobedience he learnt from that father himself; and when sympathising with the complaints and curses of Jehan, at the cruelty and tyranny of Aurungzebe, we must not forget that exactly the same disobedience and rebellion on his part had embittered his own father's dying hours, and the same indiscriminate slaughter of all who opposed his road to power had marked the commencement of his reign.

"The perishable pilgrim," Jehanara Begum, survived her father many years, and was reconciled to her brother Aurungzebe; she was buried in the Moti Musjid, or Pearl Mosque, at Delhi, built at her request by her father Jehan, where amidst ruin and desolation may still be deciphered the last injunction of this daughter of the house of Timour. "Let not any person desecrate my tomb with any other things than earth and flowers, for these are fitted for the resting-place of a Holy Spirit."

Possessed of all the provinces of his grandfather Akbar, and with a revenue of forty millions sterling, Shah Jehan was in the fullest sense of the words a magnificent monarch, boundless in his expenditure, glorying in regal pomp and display. No part of his dominion was excluded from the advantageous effects of his lavish prodigality; and whilst he stored the citadel of Caubul with thousands of costly suits of steel armour, inlaid with gold and tissues, and with fine dresses in sufficient quantities to have afforded every one of his omrahs a fresh dress of honour for every day in the year; he also beautified Agra with the Tage,

BOOK II. A.D. 1659-77.

and constructed at Delhi those matchless gardens which have so often illustrated the stories of Indian romance and Eastern song.

The grandeur and magnificence of this Emperor far exceeded all that had hitherto shaken the credulity of an ignorant world. His progresses through his dominions were accompanied by an army of 80,000 or 100,000 men; and his daily exercise in his capital was attended by a hundred young omrahs, of the noblest rank, mounted on the finest Arabian horses, and armed with golden helmets, and swords and shields inlaid with the same precious metal.

He was the great Mogul of whom Eastern travellers relate, that on the birth of a grandson he seated himself on the famous golden throne, surmounted by a parrot as large as life, cut out of a single emerald; and backed by two peacocks, the jewels in whose tails amounted to a million and a quarter sterling—the most costly seat of Empire ever devised by man's extravagance.

The report of the wealth and power of this country of the Moguls began about this time to attract the attention of merchants and adventurers in all parts of Europe; and the increased facilities of navigation afforded them a comparatively easy means of visiting those regions of unknown wealth.

It was in this reign, also, that the splendour of the Court, the fabulous wealth, the number of the retinue, the equipment of the troops, and the glory of the Empire of the great Mogul, became familiarised to European ears through the entertaining works of Bernier and Tavarnier: in the year 1662, in consequence of the island of Bombay, together with Tangier, being ceded to the English, as part of the dower of the Infanta of Portugal on her marriage with Charles; the Earl of Marlborough, with a fleet of five ships and five hundred men, arrived in India, and the first English soldier in arms landed in the Mogul Empire.

Six years afterwards it was ceded by the Crown to the Company, on a nominal rent of ten pounds of gold, payable on the 10th of September in each year. A few years before the termination of his reign, Jehan gave the English permission to trade without restriction throughout his dominions. The cause of this grant, as showing the small causes by which Providence occasionally works out the greatest effects, is worth recounting.

A Doctor Boughton, anxious for adventure, had penetrated from Surat to Agra, where, the success of his practice being noised abroad, he was callėd in to attend the daughter of Shah Jehan, through a severe illness. When desired to name his reward he requested the privilege of free trade for his countrymen, and on this being granted he repaired to Bengal, where, with the consent of the Rajah, he established a Company's factory on the Hooghly. Thus was sown the small seed from which sprang the spreading tree of British rule in India.

The death of Shah Jehan made no difference to Aurungzebe; he had for many years been the actual Emperor of Hindostan; the khutba was read in his name, and the coin of the realm bore his image and superscription.

Ascetic as he was, his pomp and display equalled in every way that of his father, in the height of his magnificence; and the accounts of the splendour of his progresses through his kingdom furnish some of the most striking pictures of the dazzling majesty of the Mogul in his pride.

Whilst he himself, with a guard of 50,000 men, and accompanied by his whole Court, proceeded to Cashmere for the benefit of his health, his generals invaded Assam, and threatened China, reduced the rebel Rajpoots of Agimere, and effected considerable conquests in that quicksand of the Mogul power, the Deccan.

The immense wealth and prosperity of the kingdom at this period had greater power to attract the cupidity and

BOOK II. A.D. 1659–77. ambition of his neighbours than his might had to awe them; and all along his northern and western frontiers, needy chieftains of hardy mountain warriors were watching eagerly for any opportunity that should favour an inroad into the flourishing territories of the Mogul. The desired pretext was soon furnished by the carelessness of a secretary of Aurungzebe, who, in addressing the Shah of Persia, omitted some of his many titles of honour, and thus raised the ire of the wine-bibbing monarch Abbas.

Heaping indignities on the ambassador of the Mogul, he sent him back to Delhi with a present of three hundred horses, and the insulting message, that as his master might soon require swift horses to fly from the Shah of Persia's resentment, he had sent him three hundred from the Imperial stable whose speed would not disappoint the expectations of his fears.

Uniting his forces with the Affghans, the bitter and hereditary enemies of the Moguls, Abbas entered the Punjaub with fire and sword; but death also accompanied him, and claimed him for his prey at Lahore, before he had had time to wreak his vengeance on the unfortunate subjects of Aurungzebe.

The Persian army retired on the death of Abbas, but not so the Affghans; this race of hardy warriors, who prided themselves on the deeds of their ancestors from time immemorial, were not likely to stay their hand when they saw the slightest chance of recovering their lost patrimony; and so firmly imbued were they with the hope of regaining the noble kingdom wrested from them by the daring Baber, that the ordinary oath of an Affghan noble of those days was, "May I never be King of Delhi if it is not so." Encouraged by some slight success, and the fortuitous appearance amongst them of a soldier bearing a strong resemblance to the deceased Prince Sujah, the brother of Aurungzebe, they made a fierce inroad into the Punjaub under a leader of fortune called

Mohammed Shah, who proudly claimed descent from Alexander the Great, and the daughter of a King of Trausoxiana.

Aurungzebe marched against them with a very large army, and forcing them back across the Indus, carried the war into their own country, and with fire and sword scourged and devastated the fair valleys of Affghanistan.

At the foot of these renowned passes, since become so ominously famous as the scenes of the defeat and massacre of many thousands of England's sons, Aurungzebe halted; he was not mad enough to expose his troops, numerous and victorious as they were, to the almost certain destruction that hovers over the dark portals of the Khyber and Bolan.

The means by which Cossim Khan, the lieutenant of Aurungzebe, eventually freed his master from the constantly recurring danger of Affghan invasion recalls the days of Scottish feudal power, when, in the midst of the feast, the introduction of the boar's head was the signal for the immediate destruction of the guests.

Having invited, in his master's name, all the leading chiefs who had supported the claims of the supposed Sujah to a banquet at Peshawur, soldiers were concealed around the apartment; and when the guests were drunk with wine they emerged, and slew them all.

With the exception of these distant wars on the frontiers of the kingdom, the first eighteen years of the reign of Aurungzebe were marked throughout the central provinces of Hindostan by peace as prosperous as it was unusual; but during the last fifteen years of his life, events of a very different character mark the history of his reign; he lived almost entirely in camps; and the unceasing inroads of Rajpoots, Affghans, Seiks, and Mahrattas, showed how numerous were the enemies of the Mogul race, and gave ominous portent of a rapid fall, whenever a master-hand should fail.

NOTES TO CHAPTER XXIV.

[1] Akbar himself wished to form a religion of his own; and Jehangire used to say, when drunk, that all prophets were equally false. Mumtâza Zemâni, the daughter of Asiph, the mother of Dara, was a notorions Deist.

[2] The early character of Aurungzebe will be best appreciated by studying that of Rashleigh Osbaldistone, in "Rob Roy." The great novelist would almost appear to have had, in the character of the Mogul Emperor, the original of that masterly sketch.

[3] The Begum Sumro, mother of Dyce Sombre, suspecting an intrigue between her husband Somers and one of her handmaids, determined to starve the wretched girl to death, and had a pit dug under her own and husband's bed, so that she might at the same time gloat over every sigh and gasp of her rival, and the agony of her faithless spouse.

[4] "See now this cursed woman and bury her, for she is a king's daughter:"—aristocratic to the backbone.

CHAP XXV.

THE RISE OF THE MAHRATTAS.—HISTORY OF SIVAJI.—IS PROCLAIMED MONARCH OF THE CONCAN.—HIS CHARACTER AND DEATH.—JESWUNT SINGH.

CHAP. XXV. A.D. 1659–77.

THE decay of an Empire is never more surely indicated than by the rise of intestine foes in its body politic, the rebellion of the members against the head; like the parasites that flourish on the decay of an old tree, they typify at the same time its exhausted vitality, and assist to complete its ruin.

The sudden rise to great power of the Mahrattas, Seiks and Jats, was unerring evidence of the diseased condition of the Empire of Aurungzebe.

The decline of nearly every nation in history has been precipitated by the insensate prosecution of some conquest which nature or destiny appears to have forbidden. What the invasion of Rome was to Carthage, of Greece to Darius, of China to Genghis Khan and Timour, and the plains of Italy to Francis I., and of Russia to Napoleon, that was the conquest of the Deccan to the Mogul dynasty of Hindostan.

It was the *ignis fatuus* of their fortunes, whose deceptive brilliancy lured them to repeated destruction; the treasure they wasted, and the armies they sacrificed, together with the constant absence of the chief power from the capital of Hindostan, were not the least important causes of their downfall.

The Emperors of Hindostan overlooked the immense

BOOK II. A.D. 1659–77.

distance between their capital and the seat of war; and ignored the very distinct boundaries by which nature had marked out the Deccan and the plains of Hindostan as destined for different habits, races, and rulers.

In the year 1344, nearly fifty years after the invasion of the Deccan under Alla the Sanguinary, Ibn Batuta, a native of Tangier, who travelled through the country, describes the Mahrattas, or natives of Marashta, a district comprising the greatest part of the Deccan, as a people well skilled in the arts, medicine, and astrology, whose nobles were Brahmins; from that period their name is scarcely mentioned in Mahommedan history, but their state, though unnoted, was one of transition and growth, and it needed but the head and energy of a great leader to rouse and render terrible a nation whose inactivity had hitherto excited contempt.

Although the nominal sovereignty of the several kingdoms of the Deccan had been vested in the Mussulman nobles who founded the several dynasties of Golcondah, Ahmednuggur, and Bejapore, the actual power was still to a considerable extent retained by the Brahmins and native Rajahs.

The Mussulman rulers of those kingdoms being in a state of almost constant warfare with the Mogul Emperors of Delhi, had been forced in self defence to propitiate as much as possible their Hindoo subjects; from this cause they soon became tolerant in matters of faith, and assimilated and identified themselves in many respects with their Mahratta subjects.

The superior education and hereditary influence of the Brahmins soon raised them to the highest offices in these States; everywhere they became the chief ministers, and the entire management of the revenue and civil government was under their direction; thus the dominant power of the Deccan, although nominally Mussulman, was in reality still Hindoo; and all that was required to enable the inhabitants of the country of Mahrashta, or indeed of the whole Deccan, to cast aside the foreign yoke, and take their places in the Peninsula of India, as a great and powerful Hindoo nation, was a leader endowed with sagacity to organise, and energy to direct their efforts. When they suddenly emerged from obscurity in the reign of Aurungzebe, the Mahrattas numbered about six millions, inhabiting a belt of country embracing a considerable portion of the Deccan and Concan.

CHAP. XXV. A.D. 1659–77.

This country, although not the most fertile, was the most salubrious of the whole peninsula of India, and the peculiar formation of the Western Ghauts, the precipitous mountains, inaccessible valleys, and impregnable hill forts, rendered it at once the country of all others the most favourable for defence, and the most dangerous to the invader.

The Mahrattas had from time immemorial been an agricultural people amongst whom trade was held in contempt; they loved rather to hear the lark sing, than the mouse squeak; they were a nation of hereditary marauders, who had no other name for victory but that which signified the "plunder of their enemy;" war was with them a trade rather than an art. Clothed in short drawers, half down the thigh, a turban, and sometimes a cotton frock, a cloth round their waists, which answered the purpose of a shawl, ignorant of any baggage but booty, and able with ease to perform marches of thirty to forty miles a day, for twenty or thirty days consecutively;[1] armed with matchlock, sword and shield; excellent as marksmen and famous hand to hand; able to scale with perfect ease, and thread with infallible instinct the precipices and jungles, impassable to all save the goats and bisons of their native mountains, the Mawullees or peasants of the Concan, were for all purposes of predatory and guerilla warfare, the most excellent infantry in the world. The cavalry were scarcely inferior in endurance and daring to the infantry; and anyone who has seen the long easy seat of the Mahratta horsemen; the perfect skill and grace with which

BOOK II. A.D. 1659–77.

they handle sword, shield or spear, the comfort and convenience of their saddles and accoutrements, the sharp bitting of their active horses, will acknowledge them to be, to all appearance, the most wiry workmanlike looking cavalry in the world. Although of course not equal in weight to the heavy Mussulman cavalry mounted on the large horses of Caubul and Lahore, they so far excelled them in the rapidity of their movements and marches, that they were never compelled to engage against their will, and were often able to pillage and burn under the very beards of their enemies, and get clear off with their booty, almost before their presence had been discovered. In all ambuscades the Mahrattas rode mares to avoid the danger of neighing; and when proceeding on a distant expedition, where speed and surprise were the necessary materials of success, each horseman after the manner of the Tartars, and the wild Indians of the Pampas, was accustomed to lead or drive one or two loose mares, in order to be able frequently to change the weight, and to have ready transport for their anticipated plunder; the length and rapidity of marches thus organised appear incredible in these days of four-year-old chargers, and twenty-four stone warriors; indeed the difference between a twelve-stone man with two horses, and a twenty-stone man with one horse is too remarkable to require much notice.

A country like the Deccan, peopled by a hardy, enterprising and marauding race, cherishing as their dearest traditions the narrations of the predatory excursions and adventures of their ancestors, and ready at any moment to turn their ploughshares into swords, must always offer a promising field for the enterprise of any energetic or ambitious soldier of fortune; and whenever the blast of war was sounded amidst the hills and valleys of the Concan, or the mystic chuprattie circulated with lightning speed amongst the villages of the Deccan, the hardy Deccanee or Mawullee found little difficulty in persuading himself to join any raid or party contest that might be afoot; he had but to reach down his shield, burnish up his paternal lance or sword, borrow or steal a horse, and he was at once ready to follow any leader in the game of taking cities or driving cattle, harassing a Mussulman army or pillaging a Hindoo prince.

The Mussulman sovereigns of the Deccan, although not constantly engaged in open warfare, indulged in a continued rivalry, that decorated indeed their capitals and increased the splendour of their courts, but that also encouraged the turbulent dispositions of their subjects; an incessant system of spoliation and border warfare kept alive the military spirit of the country, and offered constant encouragement to the bold and adventurous on both sides, to take arms under any energetic leader who might enter the field.

We have seen that for a hundred years the Moguls had been unceasing in their efforts to occupy the Deccan, and although protracted campaigns carried on at a great distance from the seat of power, were naturally weak in their results, they afforded the Mahrattas a fine opportunity of acquiring the improved arts of war, till a knowledge of their power, and a suspicion of the weakness of their enemies, originated expeditions of greater importance than the collection of booty; and by degrees the spirit of predatory warfare, the hereditary occupation of the Mahratta people, yielded to the nobler but more dangerous lust of conquest. Each individual of the Mahratta community had his particular duty to perform in the endless wars of the period; every caste and every occupation supplied its quota to the predatory armies of this marauding people; the horse and foot soldiers, the sutlers and spies, were all distinct castes, ready at a moment's notice to play their particular part in defence or conquest: the Remosy or robber caste, who supplied the best spies to the Mahratta chiefs, deprived by English domination of their hereditary means of living, unable to

BOOK II. A.D. 1629–80.

dig, and ashamed to beg, are at present employed by the English residents in the Deccan to keep off any erratic thief from their property.

It was at this period, 1629 A.D., that Sivaji Bhonslay, the son of Shahji Bhonslay, first taught his countrymen, that the Mussulman race of their day were of far different metal from those indomitable warriors, before whom their ancestors three hundred years before, had fled like sheep; and that all that was required to ensure liberty and even dominion for the Hindoo people was union, energy, and daring.

Sivaji, the son of Shahji, the founder of the Mahratta power, was one of the greatest freebooters in history; and his fiery spirit fanned into a flame the latent energy and ambition of the Hindoo races of India: he was, as we have said, the son of Shahji Bhonslay, a Mahratta noble of high standing in the service of the King of Beejapore; his mother was the daughter of Jádu Ráo, a Mahratta who claimed the purest Rajpoot descent. Shahji was Zemindar of Tanjore, and lord of an extensive jagheer in the neighbourhood of Poona.

Sivaji claimed to be a Hindoo of the Tchatrya, or warrior class, and indeed traced his descent from the warriors of Oudipoor, acknowledged to be the oldest family in India; but his lineage was not without flaw, and when late in life he was desirous of obtaining the recognition of his high caste by the Brahmins, he had to pay very freely for the privilege; he was the unflinching foe of the Moslem faith, and the fact of the birth of his father Shahji, being attributed to the energetic prayers of a Mussulman devotee, shows how unsearchable are the ways of Providence, and how even the most devout may be made the instrument of the destruction of his cherished creed. The miraculous birth of Shahji and the unwonted combination of the Mussulman title of "Shah," which is one of nobility, with the Mahratta termination of "ji," which is one of respect, is rather amusing; it exhibits a sinking of religious differences, between the bigoted professors of hostile creeds, that is worthy of praise and imitation.

Malloji Bhonslay, the father of Shahji, was a member of a respectable Mahratta family, living near Dowletabad; not having any children for many years, which strange to say is considered a misfortune by the Hindoos, and no substitute for the waters of Ems or Kissingen existing in the Deccan, he offered up his prayers to Mahdeo Vishnu,[2] and to all the other three hundred and thirty million gods of the Hindoo calendar, to send him a son. Meeting with no success, and dispirited by the indifference of his own deities, he imitated the example of Akbar under the same circumstances, and sent his wife to a Mussulman faqueer named Shah Shereef, begging him to intercede in her behalf; with admirable generosity the worthy faqueer immediately consented, and prayed so effectively that the wife of Malloji in due time gave birth to a son, who out of compliment to the holy saint was called Shah; and a second being added to the family of Malloji by the same miraculous intervention was called Shereef.

Strange to say Malloji quarrelled with his wife, after this rare instance of marital obedience, and sent her together with her son Shahji to reside at Poonah, whilst he himself married a second wife, also a Mahratta, by whom he had a son named Ekoji, of whom he became very fond: he went to reside at Beejapore, and soon became one of the leading chiefs of that kingdom.

Shahji being constantly absent on warlike expeditions, Sivaji was carefully educated by Dadoji, a Mahratta Brahmin. He instilled into him the love of his country; but military fame was his ambition; at a very early age he displayed his marauding predilections, and when only entering his teens, the proprieties of the Deccan were shocked by reports that the son of the respectable Shahji was connected with many a distant raid and midnight foray: finding his opportunity in the disturbed state of the Deccan, owing to the invasion of the Moguls, he raised

BOOK II. A.D. 1629–80.

banditti, made war, and exacted tribute from neighbouring zemindars: he soon repudiated a father, and advisers not quite suited to his enterprising nature; and gradually insinuating himself with wily cunning into the supreme control of the jagheer, he secretly got possession of some hill forts, and established himself as polygar of the district, paying revenue to none, but exacting it from all he could; in the course of three years he rose from the condition of a zemindar to that of the most powerful Hindoo prince in India, his authority extending over almost the whole region of the Concan and Deccan. But bold as were his ultimate designs and intentions, all his plans were conducted with the greatest secrecy; and neither his sovereign at Beejapore, or his father whom he had supplanted in his jagheer, were in the least aware of the deep-seated ambition of the young Mahratta.

The history of Sivaji, for the first fifteen years of his independent career, is one of the most exciting and romantic it is possible to conceive: his sword was never out of his hand, and whether the enterprise that engaged his attention was in the neighbouring districts, or hundreds of miles distant in Hindostan or the Carnatic:—whether it was the conquest of a kingdom, or the plunder of a few hundred head of cattle, he was ever the leader in person, and was a model of daring and cunning to the warriors of his army.

The whole country was covered with hill forts, of various degrees of strength and security; and the endless surprises and stratagems, by which he obtained possession of them one after another, the fabulous speed of his midnight marches, and his sudden appearance in far off districts, before his absence from home was even suspected, read almost like a romance, and recall the charming narratives of the exploits of Robert Bruce, and his dauntless lieutenants Douglas and Randolph.[3]

Before attacking any city, Sivaji sent spies, or visited it himself for the purpose of finding out the number and condition of the inhabitants, and marking the houses of all the wealthy citizens. The whole population of the Deccan and Concan were turned by this restless marauder to the great ends of rapine and conquest.

When Aurungzebe, who had been appointed viceroy of the Deccan by Shah Jehan, began to meditate his treason against his father and brother, he saw in Sivaji one who could assist him in his ambitious projects.

He encouraged him to attack the kingdom of Beejapore, and made over to him two or three forts to assist his plans; promising at the same time that he should hold exempt from all tribute to the Mogul any district he might conquer.

The first actual contact of Sivaji with the powers of Beejapore was one likely to make his name ring through the length and breadth of India:—annoyed beyond measure at the excesses of the youthful marauder, and unable to get any satisfaction from his father, who had openly repudiated him, the government of Beejapore despatched against him a considerable army under a general named Afzal Khan. Sivaji with Indian guile, now wrote expressing his contrition, and imploring pardon for his crimes, at the same time inviting the general to come and receive his submission; it was settled that Afzal should meet him in a tent, with his followers, Sivaji stipulating that only five should accompany him. When they met to embrace, Sivaji struck him in the abdomen with an instrument called the "tiger's claw," which, formed of sharp ripping hooks, lies concealed in the hand till required;[4] before he recovered from his surprise, he despatched him with his dagger, when at a given signal his men rushed from their ambuscade, and putting the Beejapore troops to flight, plundered their camp.

By this daring act Sivaji became master of the greater part of the Concan. The next object of his attack was Panala, one of the strongest fortresses in the Concan; and

BOOK II. A.D. 1629–80.

the wily manner in which Sivaji acquired possession of it, gave him at once an immense reputation, and brought hundreds to his standard.

He confided his design to several of his best officers, and when all was prepared, he pretended suddenly to quarrel violently with them, and to affront and chastise them. In consequence of this conduct, they immediately left his service, accompanied by seven or eight hundred picked troops, and entered that of the governor of Panala. Shortly after Sivaji marched to besiege the fortress, when on a certain night his confidants within admitted their comrades from without, by some trees that grew as high as the wall, and then opened the gates.

These continued successes soon spread his renown through the country; adventurous Hindoos from all parts of the Deccan and Concan now joined his standard; he became more daring as his numbers increased, and soon his wild horsemen were seen plundering within sight of the walls of Beejapore.

When the King of Beejapore sent messengers to Sivaji, requiring him to submit, he answered proudly: "What superiority has your master gained over me, that I should consent to your mission? begone speedily lest you be disgraced." For these wild freaks of his son Shahji was imprisoned at Beejapore, but after two years was liberated, when he went to visit the author of his misfortune at Rairee: Sivaji notwithstanding his entreaties, insisted upon running ten miles by the side of his palanquin, and afterwards seating him upon the Musnud, took off his slippers, and stood amongst his menial servants, an act of filial reverence that gained him great renown.

The King of Beejapore then sent against him the bulk of his army, and besieged him in Panala. At this time the three chief districts of Beejapore were governed by Abyssinians or Seddees, and the army was commanded by Siddee Johar, an Abyssinian of great repute, and governor of Dunda Rajapore, an important fortress in the Concan.

Sivaji made a gallant defence, but finding at length that success was hopeless, he availed himself of the following daring ruse: he entered into negotiations with Siddee Johar, and openly engaged to give up the fortress under certain conditions; and whilst the Abyssinians were thus thrown off their guard, he secretly left the castle, and having arranged his plans was immediately joined by troops from his other stations, when he marched with extraordinary speed on Dunda Rajapore, and delivered a forged letter from Siddee to his lieutenant, commanding him to give up the place as a condition of the surrender of Panala: the supposition that he could not have left Panala, without the consent of Siddee Johar, and the knowledge that negotiations had for some time been in progress, prevented any suspicion: the town was at once given up to him, and he returned in triumph to raise the siege of Panala. Siddee Johar thus disgraced, was after a short rebellion, assassinated by order of his master the King of Beejapore.

When Aurungzebe was preparing to march towards Agra to dethrone his father, he sent officers of high command to Sivaji, to request him to join him: but Sivaji with well-feigned astonishment, having himself already repudiated his father, pretended to be struck with horror at the prospect of so unnatural a rebellion: he received the prince's messenger with indignity, drove him from his presence, and ordered the letter he had brought to be tied to the tail of a dog: Aurungzebe never forgave him, and from that moment vowed the destruction of this "mountain rat," as he insultingly styled him.

He next turned his arms against Surat, called the Port of Mecca, from the number of pilgrims who thence took ship to visit their Holiest of Holies, a deadly insult no true son of the Prophet could ever forgive: he entered

BOOK II. A.D. 1629–88.

the city in disguise, and spent three days in discovering the houses of the wealthy inhabitants:—he then formed his camp into two divisions, one of which he placed before Bassein near Bombay, the other before Choul, some fifty miles lower down the coast, as though he intended to besiege those places. He suddenly took 4000 cavalry from Bassein, and advancing through unfrequented tracks which he had himself explored, and with a speed that only a Mahratta horseman could accomplish, he appeared unexpectedly before Surat: defence was hopeless, and entering the city he plundered it at his leisure for six days. Sivaji was content with the plunder of the Mussulman merchants, and left the Dutch and English factories unmolested.

Surat was at that time overflowing with the gold of Araby and Persia, and contained some of the richest merchant princes in the world. At the commencement of hostilities with Aurungzebe, Sivaji signalised himself by an exploit so congenial to the temper and enterprise of his people that to this day they celebrate it as the most chivalrous act of their history. Indignant at the rebellion of one whom he was accustomed to consider a freebooter, Aurungzebe sent special orders to Chaest Khan to exterminate him. In obedience to these orders he recaptured many of Sivaji's forts, but the numerous sieges so delayed him, that the more complete subjection of this ubiquitous enemy had to be postponed till the following year. Next spring Chaest marched from Aurungabad, and after a successful campaign of several weeks occupied Poonah, in Sivaji's own country, and only twelve miles from Singhar, the hill fort of his jagheer.

Sivaji had grown up to manhood at Poonah, and every hole and corner of the city was familiar to him: and he took advantage of this circumstance to strike a blow that rang to the very limits of Hindostan. The house occupied by Chaest Khan, either accidentally or from a design to insult, happened to be that in which Sivaji had passed his early days. At the time of this invasion of his jagheer he was forty miles distant; but no sooner did he hear of it than, accompanied by fifteen trusty men, he rode in one night to Poonah: here, having disguised himself and followers as minstrels, he joined a marriage procession that was allowed to enter the forts to visit a famous shrine sacred to Siva; once within the guards he made his way to the palace and surprised Chaest Khan in his harem. His son and several women were cut to pieces, but the Khan with the loss of his hand managed to escape through the window.

Sivaji's retreat was as rapid as his attack; before the Mogul troops were thoroughly aroused he was half way to Singhar, where the firing of guns and the blaze of thousands of torches announced to the inhabitants of the Deccan some new exploit of their prince.

In the next campaign Chaest Khan was joined by the Maharajah, Jeswunt Sing of Judpore, for whom Aurungzebe had conquered the kingdom of Guzerat:—but these two generals did not agree, and this soon coming to the ears of Sivaji, he determined to make matters safe by tendering his services to the Maharajah to kill the Khan. This offer was accepted and the deed was done, but whether Sivaji did it in person or not is uncertain.

Aurungzebe and Sivaji were nearly the same age, and in many points displayed a very marked similarity of character; both were energetic, crafty and ambitious, and both stern bigots of their separate creeds:—Aurungzebe did all that Mahommed himself could have desired to extend the Moslem creed, whilst Sivaji styling himself "the Champion of the Gods," made it his especial boast to protect "Brahmins, kine, and cultivators," and to preserve from all insult the Hindoo temples.

Sivaji with all his ambition, and desire to take to himself some of the rival provinces of the kingdom of Beejapore, was mistrustful of the growing power of the Moguls; and he soon perceived that the power of the Brahmins and

BOOK II. A.D. 1629–88.

the glory of the Mahratta nation, could be but little augmented by the substitution of the omnipotency of the Mogul arms for the Mussulman kingdom of the Deccan. No sooner therefore had Aurungzebe left the Deccan, than all Sivaji's energies were directed against the Mogul generals that were left in command, and a fierce war waged with great cruelty on both sides was the result.

At length in consequence of the professed friendship of Aurungzebe, a treaty was concluded with Sivaji, and invited by an autograph letter of the Emperor, he set out for Delhi accompanied by his son.

He entered Agra attended by 500 nobles on horses splendidly caparisoned, and with about the same number of infantry; the whole city turned out to meet him, but when he went to court, he found that he was the dupe of Aurungzebe, who desired his presence merely to humble and disgrace him in the eyes of his subjects.

He was very coldly received, and placed among the inferior omrahs, who at a considerable distance surrounded the throne of the Great Mogul. The proud Mahratta is said to have shed tears of indignation and anger at this public insult; and to have hurled words of defiance and threats of vengeance at the "Conqueror of the World," that must have sounded strange to the silken courtiers of Delhi.

It is said that a daughter of Aurungzebe, looking through the grated window that opened from the terrace into the court of audience, was struck with admiration at the bold and undaunted indignation of the Mahratta, and that her intercessions alone saved him from the fury of the insulted monarch: but although he did not punish him with the death his bold speech had merited, he determined to detain him a prisoner, and for that purpose set close watch over his movements: but the Mogul, crafty as he was, was no match for the wily Mahratta.

After remaining a few months in restraint, Sivaji

feigned sickness, saw doctors, took physic, lay in bed, and did the business of a regular invalid; but soon pretending to recover, he made it a custom every Thursday to distribute amongst the poor who crowded in large numbers to his gates, great quantities of sweetmeats and pastry, which were brought in large baskets, each of which required three or four men to carry it; these when emptied were taken back to the confectioners, and at length, when the frequency of the presents had disarmed attention, and when everything was ready, Sivaji, one Thursday evening, having acquainted his confidants with his design, ordered a slave to take his place on the bed, and leaving the customary attendants in the room he emptied the sweetmeats, and putting his son into one basket and himself into another, they were carried out of the house: when he got clear of the city he mounted his son on a sorry horse, and led him by the bridle towards Muttra; arrived there he shaved his beard, his moustachios, and his long side locks, and committing his son to a Brahmin, to be conducted to the Deccan, he travelled as a pilgrim by Allahabad and Benares to Gerar.

Being much fatigued he ventured to buy a wretched horse, but not having silver he incautiously opened a purse of gold. As his escape had been noised through Hindostan, the owner of the horse, who was suspicious at seeing so much money in the hands of one in the dress of a beggar, said, "surely thou must be Sevaji." The latter made no answer but gave the purse, and mounting the horse, pushed on with all speed to the sacred shrine of Juggernauth, where stood the magnificent temple of the Sun, whose costly erection had consumed the whole revenues of India for twelve years.

Another account states, that by his orders his army advanced by detachments towards Agra, and that a body of Mahratta horse actually approached the walls of the city; that Sivaji and his son were carried out in two

BOOK II. A.D. 1629–88.

large baskets to the river side, where a boat as for common passengers was awaiting him; that upon reaching the shore Sivaji sprang from his concealment, and giving the boatman a gold mohar, told him "to go back and tell Aurungzebe, that he had ferried over Sivaji and his son:" when mounting fleet horses, they rode by unfrequented roads to Guzerat. This account however is not correct, for it states that the speed was too great for the son who died of it; whereas Sumbhaji lived many years.

From this time Sivaji was ever in arms against the Moguls. The rancour of religious animosity and political rivalry was increased by personal hatred; and whilst Aurungzebe professed to treat with contempt the power of the "mountain rat," as he termed Sivaji; the fierce Hindoo equally haughty, compared the annual tribute which he sent to Delhi, to the "oil-cake he gave his cow to make it give more milk." Unable to take the field in person, Aurungzebe despatched his son Prince Mahomet Mangam to the Deccan with instructions to effect by stratagem what was hopeless by force or assassination.

When he marched at the head of his army into the Deccan, Sivaji, disguised as a peasant, awaited his passage through a village near Brampore, and presented a plate of cream, which from its appearance, Mangam ordered to be served at his own repast; within was a note enclosed in wax, written by Sivaji, declaring that "curiosity had led him to view the mighty prince who condescended to become his antagonist in the lists of fame."

The craft of Aurungzebe is in no instance more conspicuous than in this deep-laid intrigue; his instructions to his son were to allow Sivaji to get head until his own troops should grumble and be discontented, when he would naturally be reproached from home, and so be obliged to make his father's severity an excuse for rebellion; he pretended to quarrel with the great officers of his army, and then applied to Sivaji for assistance; but the latter knew through his spies the innermost secrets of the camp of Mangam; he knew that it was altogether a farce, and in answer said that the Sultan was strong enough without him, that he would protect the Deccan in his absence, and promised him refuge in case of defeat, &c. &c. &c. CHAP. XXV. A.D. 1629-88.

At length after thirty years of almost uninterrupted warfare, during which his sword was never sheathed for a longer consecutive period than eight months; having made considerable conquests, and accumulated very great wealth, Sivaji, who seems to have aspired to be the restorer of the Hindoo faith, as well as of the national independence, thought himself entitled to be formally enthroned monarch of the Concan, and the northern portion of the Deccan. He professed to trace a direct lineage up to the most ancient of the Rajpoot families of India, but unfortunately for himself, and also probably for his subjects, the Brahmins detected some flaw in his genealogical tree, and the mésalliance of one of his ancestors, many centuries before, cost him a fabulous treasure to erase.

Before the Brahmins would allow him the religious rights of an absolute and undoubted prince of the Cshatrya caste, he was forced to perform several costly ceremonies, that however attractive to the priesthood, must have appeared dull and unprofitable to him; he was weighed against pure gold, and the result—ten stone—valued at sixteen thousand pounds, with one hundred thousand more, were distributed to the wily ministers of his faith, and the titles of the head ornament of the Cshatrya race: "His majesty the Rajah," "Siva, Possessor or Lord of the Royal Umbrella," were proclaimed through the length and breadth of his newly acquired dominions.

Sivaji is not the only Hindoo, who by a lavish expenditure has re-established a doubtful lineage; it is not many years ago, that the Rajah of Tanjore, wishing to establish his right to the Brahminical caste, was commanded by the priests to make a cow of gold, afterwards

BOOK II. A.D. 1629-80.

of course to be given to the priests, large enough for him to creep through from the mouth to the tail; by this new birth all impurities in his lineage were washed away, and he became a Brahmin of pure descent.

Assisted by the Siddees, and coasting mariners of the Concan, Sivaji made one nautical expedition with a fleet of eighty vessels, down the coast of Malabar; but fortunately for his enemies, the motion of the mighty deep did not agree with him, and having reached land in safety, his tutelary deity wisely forbade his ever again tempting fickle fortune on the ocean.

In the year 1680, at the age of fifty-three, Sivaji fell a victim to the excessive energy, that had from his earliest youth distinguished his career; he died from inflammation of the chest, arising from fatigues endured in a distant foray on the Moguls.

Sivaji is certainly one of the greatest princes of Hindoo history; he revived the ancient glory of a race, that centuries of subjection had tended to debase; and during the very height and power of the Mogul dynasty, he founded and raised to empire the most powerful native kingdom yet seen in Hindostan.

He possessed every quality requisite for success in the disturbed age in which he lived; cautious and wily in council, he was fierce and daring in action; he possessed an endurance that made him remarkable, even amongst his hardy subjects, and an energy and decision that would in any age have raised him to distinction. By his own people he was painted on a white horse going at full gallop, tossing grains of rice into his mouth, to signify that his speed did not allow him to stop to eat.

He was the first Hindoo prince who forced the heavy Mogul cavalry to fly before the charge of the native horse of India; his strength and activity in action were the glory and admiration of his race; and long after his death, the proudest boast of the Mahratta soldier was to have seen Sivaji charge hand to hand.

He spared neither gold or exertion to obtain accurate information concerning the motions and intentions of his foes. He not only knew every opulent house in the town he was besieging, but often the very cell in which the treasure was concealed. He waged war with the commanders of opposing armies as much as with the armies themselves; and whether gold or steel was the means he adopted to conquer them, he generally succeeded; scarcely a viceroy of the Emperor, or a general of the kings of Beejapore, or even the son of Aurungzebe himself, were free from the suspicion of having touched Mahratta gold.

He was almost worshipped as a god, and the renown of his deeds, his eagle glances and long arms, his rapid marches and secret forays, are to this day the most popular themes of the wandering Gursees, or minstrels of the Deccan.

Even his weapons were reverenced as holy, and his good sword Bhowanee has been to the bards of the Deccan what the Joyeuse and Durandel of Charlemagne and Roland; and the Askalon of our own patron saint, were to the wandering troubadours of Europe. The best parallel for the great Mahratta will be found in the character of the Sultan Baber; possessing to a considerable extent the polished mind and personal prowess of that noble prince, he excelled him in foresight and stratagem; bold and reckless of danger as the most daring warrior that ever lived, he never attempted force where stratagem could avail.

The character of Baber reminds one of the bold open daring of the lion, while that of Sivaji resembles more the wily cunning of the tiger of his own native hills. Always in ambush till the time of action arrived, he crept stealthily on his foes, and seldom failed when once his spring was really made; always pretending to do that which he never intended, no one was acquainted with his plans but by the success of their execution. So completely

BOOK II. A.D. 1680.

were his movements kept secret, and so often had he circulated false reports of his death, to account for his sudden disappearance on some distant expedition, that for several days after his body was actually consumed, according to the Hindoo rites, he was supposed by his enemies, and even by his troops, to be commanding in person under the walls of Surat; and it was months before Aurungzebe knew that death had removed the great enemy against whose unflinching front the Mogul forces had dashed as hopelessly as the waves upon a rock-bound coast.

"He was a great captain," said Aurungzebe, when he heard of his death, "and the only man who has had the power to raise a new kingdom, whilst I have been endeavouring to destroy the ancient sovereignties of India. My armies have been employed against him for nineteen years, and nevertheless his state has been continually increasing." He was mild and merciful, and although a bigoted worshipper of Brahma, he scorned to retaliate on the Moslems the cruel persecution which they had inflicted on the followers of his faith.

Anecdotes of his personal intrepidity are still current throughout the Deccan; he would at any moment risk his life and jeopardise his crown to gratify a whim or to fulfil a ceremony. On one occasion he entered Bombay by stealth, when he was besieging it, on purpose to ascend the natural chimney of rock on Malabar hill, that is supposed to purify from sin all who enter below and emerge above. His love for music often led him into dangers from which only his activity and daring released him; many a time did he in disguise enter the very strongholds of his enemies, with no other purpose than to listen to the inspiriting narrations of the deeds and exploits of the Hindoo gods, as sung and recited in the Kuthas at the numerous Hindoo festivals.[6]

Sivaji left immense wealth, and at his death was absolute sovereign of a territory in the Deccan, upwards of four hundred miles in length by one hundred and twenty in breadth, and three hundred miles away in the far south of India he possessed the district of Tanjore, equal in extent to many of the native sovereignties.

CHAP. XXV. A.D.1680.

Every part of India, from the Nerbudda to Tanjore, and from the Concan to Madras, at some time or other had to purchase the friendship of Sivaji, or to pay heavily for their temerity in neglecting it; so great and so constant was the influx of gold to his mountain capital of Rairee, that "the caves of Rairee" became a proverb, as a depository from which nothing ever returned.

He had no rival in Deccan; in energy, personal activity, rapidity of thought and action, he far excelled all the officers of his day; beloved and respected as the guardian of the nation, and as the first leader who had for many hundred years enabled the Hindoo to contend with the fierce and ruthless Moslem, he moved everywhere in perfect security, and often alone: it was owing to his having friends in the multitude that his daring visits to the strongholds of his foes were successful.

A few months after the death of Sivaji, Aurungzebe was relieved by death from a great subject, equally dangerous as friend or foe, in the person of Jeswunt Sing, the renowned chief of the Rajpoots. Jeswunt was one of the most remarkable men of those turbulent days; for forty-two years, from his first contest with Aurungzebe on the Nerbudda to the day of his death at Caubul, there was not an event of importance in which he was not deeply engaged. He held by turns the viceroyalty of Guzerat, Deccan, Malva, Ajmere, and Caubul: he was always plotting against the Mogul power, and although at various times he supported one brother against another, it was from no friendly feeling, but merely in the hope that they would ultimately destroy each other, and the inheritance be his. Had Jey Sing of Amber, the Rana Raj of Mawar, Sivaji, and the other great native princes of his time coalesced with Jeswunt, the Mogul power must have fallen. Aurungzebe professed great friendship for Jeswunt, but his

BOOK II. A.D. 1680.

real feeling was one of intense hatred. "Sighs," says his historian, "never ceased to flow from Aurungzebe's heart whilst Jeswunt lived;" and the surest evidence of the dread the Rahtore had inspired him when alive, will be found in the ruthless animosity with which he pursued his family when dead.

Jeswunt died beyond the Attock whilst viceroy of Caubul. His wife was at that time seven months advanced in pregnancy. She wished to attend her lord to heaven, but her Suttee was forcibly prevented; three other wives and six concubines, however, celebrated that fearful rite. As soon as the queen could travel, the Rahtore contingent set out for their own country; but Aurungzebe was not inclined to allow a scion of the old stock to escape him if he could help it; and when they reached Delhi, he commanded them to give up the infant prince: they refused. He offered to divide the whole of Mawar amongst them if they would accede to his request: they still refused. "Our country," said they, "is with our sinews, and these can defend both it and our lord." Their quarter was surrounded by the legions of Aurungzebe, and the infant Azit was, with difficulty, smuggled out of the city in a basket of sweetmeats. The chief object of their devotion thus secure, they mounted their steeds, and placing their women in the centre, attempted to cut their way through the Mogul troops; they were, however, overpowered, and forced to retreat. Finding their case hopeless, they adopted the usual means to save their own and their deceased lord's honour.

The widow of Jeswunt, together with their own wives and daughters, were enclosed in a room filled with gunpowder and all sent to heaven. Having thus performed one of the great ordinances of their caste, they took a double dose of opium, and donning the saffron robe, issued out into the city with the desperate hope of cutting their way through.

Delhi has seen many fierce combats in her streets, but none that ever equalled the deeds of this handful of heroes. Doorga-da, the uncle and guardian of Azit, and a few other warriors, succeeded in hewing their way through the opposing ranks; they rejoined their infant prince outside the city, and regained their own country. This battle, fought on the seventh day of the month of the Monsoon 1680 A.D., is still a sacred day in the calendar of Mawar.

Doorga-da now assumed the place of his brother Jeswunt, and soon became an equal terror to the Moguls. Aurungzebe had a great dread of this famous leader of the Rahtores; he had pictures drawn of him and also of Sivaji, the latter sitting cross-legged on cushions, in the ordinary position of Hindoo princes, the former on horseback, toasting bawtres or barley cakes with the point of his lance on a fire of maize sticks.

The Emperor used to say, "I may entrap that fellow," meaning Sivaji, "but this dog is born to be my bane." Aurungzebe was not one to give up the quarry because his first swoop missed; his enemy might escape him for the time, but his plans were always laid for future revenge. By the devotion of Doorga-da and his brave Rahtores, Prince Azit had once escaped him; but it only made him more determined to indulge his revenge later. It was years before that opportunity occurred, but there is no summer like a late summer, and no revenge is so sweet as that which has been long delayed.

A few years before Aurungzebe's death, he commanded Prince Azit's attendance at court. The young prince obeyed him, and was received not only with all the distinction that was his due, but with the most specious courtesy. One day with unusual familiarity the King desired him to advance, and grasping firmly his folded hands (the usual attitude of deference in one of his rank), said "Well Rahtore, I am told you possess an arm as nervous as your father's: what can you do?" "God preserve

BOOK II. A.D. 1680. your Majesty," replied the Rajpoot prince, "when the sovereign of mankind lays the hand of protection upon the meanest of his subjects, all his hopes are realised, and when he condescends to touch both my hands, I feel as if I could conquer the world." His vehement and animated gesture gave full force to the words, and Aurungzebe bitterly exclaimed, "Ah! here is another hero." Yet affecting to be pleased with his boldness of speech, he ordered him a dress of honour, which, according to custom, he put on in the presence, and having made his obeisance, left well pleased. That day was his last; he returned to his quarter and died in great torture: the robe was poisoned.

NOTES TO CHAPTER XXV.

[1] An Indian messenger can easily perform from forty to fifty miles a day for thirty or forty days consecutively; at the commencement of the last rebellion the Sikhs marched from Peshawur to Delhi at the rate of thirty miles a day.

Septimus Severus marched from the neighbourhood of Vienna to Rome, a distance of 800 miles, in forty days.

[2] The Brahmins say that the gods of the earth, great and small, number three hundred and thirty millions.

[3] The stratagem by which the Douglas surprised the castle of Roxburgh was very nearly identical with the one by which Sivaji obtained possession of a hill fort of the Deccan. "On the eve of Shrove Tuesday," says Sir Walter Scott, "on the 6th of March, 1312, when the garrison were full of jollity and indulging in drunken wassail, Douglas and his followers approached the castle, creeping on hands and feet, and having dark cloaks flung over their armour. They seemed to the English soldiers a strayed herd of some neighbouring peasant's cattle, which had been suffered to escape during the festivity of the evening. They therefore saw these objects arrive on the verge of the moat and descend into it without wonder or alarm; nor did they discover their error till the shout of Douglas! Douglas! announced that the wall was scaled and the city taken.

[4] Il fit attacher un bistouri des mieux acquisez à une bague qu'il portoit au doight; le bistouri tournoit aisément autour de la bague, et pour lors il était caché dans l'ombre de sa main.—See account of Cæsar Borgia's Ring.

[5] When George he shaved the dragon's beard, and Askalon was his razor; Joyeuse name of Charlemagne's sword, Durandel that of Roland.

* The Deccan ballads are still pretty enough, as the accompanying fragment shows. About fifty years ago Trimbukjee, a Mahratta of note, escaped from prison by the following device: while in confinement a common looking Mahratta offered his services to the commanding officer; he was accepted, and had to keep his horse under the windows of the prison: nothing was remarked about him but his attention to his horse and a constant habit of singing. Upon the disappearance some time after of both Trimbukjee and the groom, it was remembered that the words of the song were these:—

"Behind the wood the bowmen hide
The horse beneath the tree;
Where shall I find a knight will ride
The jungle path with me?
There are five and fifty coursers there,
And four and fifty men,
When the fifty-fifth shall mount his steed,
The Deccan thrives again."

CHAP. XXVI.

RELIGIOUS PERSECUTION AND INTOLERANCE OF AURUNGZEBE.—RELIGIOUS WAR IN RAJPOOTANA.—AURUNGZEBE MARCHES TO OUDIPORE.—FORCED TO RETIRE BY FAMINE.—HIS LATTER YEARS EMBITTERED BY CONDUCT OF HIS SON.—HE QUELLS REBELLION IN DECCAN AND SUBDUES ALL HIS FOES.—HIS DEATH AND CHARACTER

BOOK II. A.D. 1688 to 1707.

TOLERANT as Aurungzebe was at the beginning of his reign towards all sects in his dominions, it appears that as he advanced in years he displayed a considerable spice of the merciless spirit of persecution that distinguished Mahmoud of Ghizni, and that he sought, by a forced conversion of the Hindoos, to add the distinction of Mohi-eddin, the "reviver of religion," to his many illustrious titles.

On account of the great loss to agriculture, by the slaughter of kine during the famine in the last reign, the Brahmins had obtained an edict from Jehangire that no cattle should be killed, and they offered enormous sums to Aurungzebe to renew the injunction; but he refused, with bitter insults, to show any toleration whatever to the prejudices of his idolatrous subjects, and answered their petition by levying a capitation tax on every Hindoo throughout his dominions who would not immediately abjure his faith. By his orders the Hindoo pagodas were desecrated and destroyed; ancient and beautiful sculptures were defaced; mosques rose on the ruins of holy temples; the most hallowed shrines of Muttra, Benares, and Ahmedabad, were polluted by the slaughter of cows and other sacred animals; and his high-caste prisoners were compelled at the sword's point to swallow the dust of the marble statues of their gods, pounded up for the purpose.

"But whoso breaketh an hedge the serpent shall bite him;" and the Emperor found to his cost, that in breaking down the hedge of absolute toleration, planted by his ancestor Akbar and preserved by his descendants, he had roused a nest of snakes, that, little heeded at first, soon threatened the very existence of his power.

The Hindoos, perfectly tolerant themselves on all religious matters, never interfering with the creeds of others or attempting to make proselytes to their own, yet possess certain articles of faith and certain traditions of caste, which they cherish in life and cling to in death; and again a bitter spirit of enmity arose between the followers of Brahma and Mahommed, and the fanaticism of religious hatred added tenfold to the resuscitated spirit of hereditary animosity.

All Aurungzebe's efforts at conversion, however, failed most signally; a few petty rajahs indeed were tempted by his offers, but the people generally clung to their pagodas and their ancient faith. Everywhere discontent and uneasiness prevailed; labour forsook the field and industry the loom; whilst bands of robust faqueers, taking advantage of the general uneasiness, ravaged the country, under the excuse of defending the Hindoo faith; and an old female faqueer led such a multitude in arms from Agra to Delhi, that it required the presence of Aurungzebe himself to subdue it.

These symptoms of rebellion, however, did not change the conduct of Aurungzebe; and when at length the decrease of the revenue brought representations from the governors of the provinces, and caused him to pause in his suicidal career, it was only to enable him to take measures to renew it at a more favourable season with tenfold zeal and intolerance.

BOOK II. A.D. 1688 to 1707.

This persecution, that caused only discontent amongst the peaceable rajahs of Bengal, was received in far other guise by the warlike tribes of Rajpootana, who, fierce and bigoted as the Moguls themselves, prided themselves on a direct descent from those who defeated Alexander on the banks of the Indus, and claimed to be endowed with courage from the heart of Brahma himself.[1] When therefore, in the madness of his pride, Aurungzebe sent an ambassador to the Rana, proffering as a compromise to the capitation tax, that he should no longer strike coin in his own name but in that of the Mogul; that kine should be killed in his dominions; that pagodas should be demolished or converted into mosques; and that justice should be administered according to the Koran, the insulting proposals were received in the same spirit of arrogant contempt in which they were made.

A close alliance was immediately contracted between the three great chieftains of Rajpootana, the rajahs of Abnir, Chitore, and Joudpore, and before many weeks 200,000 Rajpoot warriors were in the field, ready to shed the last drop of their blood in defence of their gods and of their ancient faith. A noble letter from the Raja Sing of Joudpore to the Emperor, will long live as a bold and eloquent protest against the bigotry and intolerance on religious matters of the mighty ones of the earth.

"May it please your Majesty, your ancestor Mahommed Jelal-ul-Dien Akbar, whose throne is in heaven, conducted the affairs of the Empire in equity and firm security for the space of fifty-two years; he preserved every tribe of man in ease and happiness, whether they were followers of Jesus or of Moses, of Brahma or Mahommed; of whatever sect they might be, they equally enjoyed his countenance and favour, insomuch that the people, in gratitude for his indiscriminate protection which he afforded them, distinguished him by the appellation of the "Guardian of Mankind."[2] His

Majesty Mahommed Noor-ul-Dien Jehangire likewise whose dwelling is now in paradise, extended for a period of twenty-two years the shadow of his protection over the heads of his people, successful by constant fidelity to his allies, and a vigorous exertion of his arm in business. Nor less did the illustrious Shah Jehan, by a prosperous reign of thirty-two years, acquire to himself immortal reputation, the glorious reward of clemency and virtue. Such were the benevolent inclinations of your ancestors; whilst they pursued their great and generous principles, wheresoever they directed their steps, conquest and prosperity went before them, and thus they reduced many countries and fortresses to their obedience. During your Majesty's reign many have been alienated from the Empire, and further loss of territory must necessarily follow, since devastation and rapine now universally reign without restraint; your subjects are trampled under foot, and every province of your Empire is impoverished; depopulation spreads and difficulties accumulate; when indigence has reached the habitation of the sovereign, what can be the condition of the nobles? as to the soldiery they are in murmurs; the merchants complaining; the Mahommedans discontented; the Hindoos destitute; the multitude of people wretched, even to the want of their nightly meal, are beating their heads throughout the day in rage and desperation. How can the dignity of the sovereign be preserved, who employs his power in exacting a heavy tribute from a people thus miserably reduced? At this juncture it is told from East to West that the Emperor of Hindostan, jealous of the poor Hindoo devotee, will exact a tribute from Brahmins, Samorahs, Joghies, Byrajhees, and Sonassees; that regardless of the high honour of his Timourian race, he condescends to exercise his power over the solitary inoffensive anchorite! If your Majesty places any faith in those books by distinction called divine, you will there be instructed that God is the God of all mankind, not the God of the Mahommedans

BOOK II. A.D. 1658 to 1707.

alone! The Pagan and Mussulman are equal in his presence; distinctions of colour are of his ordination; it is he who gives existence; in your temples, to his name, is raised a prayer; in a house of images where a bell is shaken, still he is the object of adoration; to vilify the religion or customs of the men is to set at naught the pleasure of the Almighty. When we deface a picture we naturally incur the resentment of the painter, and justly has the poet said, 'Presume not to arraign or scrutinise the various works of power divine.' In fine, the tribute you demand from the Hindoo is repugnant to justice; it is equally foreign to good policy, as it must impoverish the country; moreover it is an innovation, an infringement of the laws of Hindostan. But if zeal for your own religion has induced you to determine on this measure, the demand ought by the rules of equity to have been made first on Ramsing, who is esteemed the principal amongst the Hindoos; then let your well-wishers be called upon, with whom you will have less difficulty to encounter; but to torment ants and flies is unworthy an heroic or generous mind. It is wonderful that your ministers should have neglected to instruct your Majesty in the rules of rectitude and honour!!"

A wise man would have paused and counted the cost of arousing the fanatical enmity of so formidable a power, but age had warped the judgment of Aurungzebe; he was distrustful of his fitness for the next world, and he sought to obliterate, in the blood of an infidel race, the unnatural murder of many true believers, thus following the example of Timour the Tartar.[3] He remembered that his numerous wars had not been carried on without causing the destruction of many of God's creatures, and *similia similibus*, he resolved to wipe out the remembrance of past crimes by others of a like nature.

Moreover Aurungzebe had an insult to avenge on the House of Mawar, that in the mind of an Emperor of Hindostan would outweigh all considerations of policy and even safety; his addresses had been slighted by a Rajpootni princess, and not only slighted, but treated with scorn and derision. A few years before, Aurungzebe, who with all his professed asceticism, appears to have fully inherited the Aphrodisiac character of the race of Timour, demanded the hand of the Princess of Roopnagurh, a junior branch of the House of Mawar, and without waiting for a reply, sent 2000 horse to escort the lady to his court. However willing she might have been under ordinary circumstances to become the favourite sultana of the Mogul, her royal blood rebelled at the notion of being thus delivered on demand, without her own consent; and moreover she was already fascinated with the gallantry of Raj Sing, the paladin of her race, and she determined to reject with scorn the demand of Aurungzebe, and to entrust her cause to her lover, with the promise of herself as the reward of protection. Her resolution once taken, no time was to be lost, but the natural delicacy of the high-caste lady shrank from openly soliciting the protection she desired. As usual on such occasions the family priest was called in, who soon devised a plan that would ensure the desired succour, without any infraction of the strictest decorum: by his advice the following laconic note was penned and despatched by a trusty messenger to Raj Sing. "Is the swan to be the mate of the stork, a Rajpootni pure in blood to be the wife of the monkey-faced barbarian?" Ere the note could be delivered, she was compelled to accompany the Mogul troops to her Simian admirer; but once acquainted with the wishes of the fair Princess of Roopnagurh, Raj Sing flew like a true knight to her rescue: before she had proceeded many leagues, he crossed the foot of the Aravulli with some picked troops, attacked the Imperial guard, and delivered the distressed princess from the hand of her despoilers. All applauded this gallant act, and without exception the leading chiefs of Mawar gathered round the red banner.

BOOK II.

A.D. 1688 to 1707.

Native chivalry was at its height amongst the Rajpoots of this age; they breathed an atmosphere of battles, and for more than thirty years scarcely a chieftain of any note had died on his pallet.

Aurungzebe always more or less dreaded the fiery natures of these haughty chiefs, and lost no opportunity of teaching them a lesson of humility. For some slight want of respect he had commanded Nahur, a famous chief of Oudipore, to enter a tiger's den alone and unarmed; he obeyed without trepidation, and approaching the tiger, who was pacing backwards and forwards, thus contemptuously addressed him: "Oh! tiger of the 'Meah,'" a term given by Hindoos to Moslems, "turn and face the tiger of Jeswunt." The tiger unaccustomed to such unceremonious salutation, looked at him and walked away; when Nahur, turning to the Emperor, said, "you see he dare not face me, and it is contrary to the oath of a Rajpoot to attack an enemy who dare not confront him."

On another occasion Soortan, a gallant warrior of Aboo, the sacred mountain of the Rajpoots in the Aravulli, was brought prisoner before Aurungzebe; he refused the regular prostrations; he said, "his life was in the King's hands, his honour in his own; he had never bowed the head to mortal man, and never would." They tried to introduce him into the presence through a low portal, but he came in feet and stomach first; and Aurungzebe who could not help admiring him, permitted him to depart, asking him at the same time what favour he could grant him. "Nothing," replied he, "but to suffer me to return the Paradise of Aboo."

The mountainous provinces that at this period acknowledged the supremacy of the Rana, or great chief of the Rajpoots, formed a kingdom about half as large as France, and about as populous as Switzerland; attached to their soil, as the ground on which their deities as well as their ancestors had lived, and enabled amid their rugged mountains and narrow defiles to defy all but a nominal subjection to the most powerful monarchs of Hindostan, the Rajpoot races combined in a rare degree the love of country and the stern fanaticism that so frequently constitute the sole though priceless birthright of mountain races.

They are without exception the finest race of men in India, if not in the whole world; their muscular power and extraordinary endurance, their contempt of death, and the devotion with which they have always resisted religious persecution or defilement of caste, render them when fairly roused and well commanded, the most valuable of friends or the most dangerous of foes. To this day a company of Rajpoot soldiers of Oude or Rajpootana present much the same contrast to the low-caste men of Madras or Bombay that a troop of life-guardsmen would to a regiment of Mexican irregulars.

Aurungzebe's invasion of this formidable region was conducted on a scale equal to the magnitude of the undertaking; he summoned all his troops from Caubul, Bengal, and Deccan, and assembled a field-train consisting of 70 pieces of heavy ordnance, 60 of horse artillery, and a dromedary corps mounting swivels 300 strong; an armament far surpassing at that period any owned by the most potent sovereigns of Europe. On the approach of this overwhelming force, the Rana Raj Sing deserted the plains and collected his forces within the natural fortresses of the Aravulli range, whence he watched in perfect security the movements of his foe.

Aurungzebe marched through the Dobarri pass with a magnificent force of 50,000 picked troops without opposition, and advanced straight to the capital of Oudipore; here palaces, gardens, lakes, and isles, and all the elaborate splendour of a luxurious capital met his eye, but not a living thing; all was deserted and silent as the grave. Confident in his numbers, the Mogul encamped in fancied security, but the third night his army was attacked by Raj Sing; some were at chess, some praying, some feasting;

BOOK II. A.D. 1688 to 1707.

"they came to steal and fell asleep." They were dispersed with terrific and unrelenting slaughter, and Oudipori, the favourite Rajpootani wife of Aurungzebe, who had accompanied him in this arduous war, fell into the hands of her countrymen.

As we have before remarked, the Rajpoots, of all races in India, are the most sensitive about the honour of their women, and the most delicate in their treatment of those of their enemies. It is only when animosity is heightened by the desire of revenge, when they wish to disgrace and degrade their foes, that they enact such scenes of atrocity as those lately witnessed at Delhi and Cawnpore.

Oudipori was carried to the Rajah, who treated her with every attention, and immediately sent her back under a strong escort to Aurungzebe, with the sole request that in return he would spare the sacred animals that might be left in the plains; but the Emperor could not credit generosity so foreign to his own nature, and attributed to fear what was merely the impulse of a noble and chivalrous character. He continued the war with fire and sword, but although he again took Chitore the Immaculate, the result of the campaign was altogether unsatisfactory; everywhere the inhabitants deserted their homes and drove their flocks and herds to the mountains; all the passes were closed against the Mogul reinforcements, and in addition to the unrelenting enmity of an outraged nation, the Emperor soon had also to contend against famine, and after several months of calamity and disgrace, he was not sorry to leave the barren battle-field of Mawar to his sons and generals.

The latter years of Aurungzebe were full of great and deserved anxiety; his children one after another turned against him, and always found in the Mahrattas and Rajpoots allies able and willing to súpport them. He now in his turn encountered that marble-hearted fiend, filial ingratitude, and felt "how sharper than a serpent's tooth it is to have a thankless child." His eldest son

Akbar had formed an alliance with Sumbhaji, the reckless son of Sivaji, and frequently his banner flaunted side by side with that of the Mahratta in the hard-fought fields of the Deccan. Aurungzebe never suffered natural affection, or the ties of blood, to interfere with policy or success; for some time he dissembled his wrath, and feigned even more than ordinary affection for his rebellious son; and a truce being concluded between the contending parties, he sent him a dress of honour, a fine horse richly caparisoned, and a vest beautifully embroidered.

Akbar received these tokens of affection with all outward respect, but mistrusted his father even when sending gifts; he did not immediately don the gorgeous attire, as was customary; but kept it, with the excuse that he wished to inaugurate the honoured vestments with greater solemnity. In the meantime he put it on a slave, who died in two days; like that given to the son of Jeswunt, it was perfumed with poisoned powder. Naturally this affair did not greatly tend to the reconciliation of either party. Akbar now feeling that all hope of forgiveness was past, threw himself heart and soul into the contest on the side of the Deccan princes, and the war that had before halted for a season, was resumed with increased vigour on both sides.

The rebellion in the Deccan was now general; the kings of Beejapore and Golconda, supported by the other Deccanee rajahs, and swayed and directed by Sumbhaji, united their hitherto opposing forces, and raised an impenetrable bulwark against the advancing power of the Mogul. This hostile array was greatly strengthened by the active alliance of the Siddees, or descendants of Abyssinian adventurers, who during many centuries had exercised great power and influence in the Deccan; and whose present descendants, known by the general term of Arabs, constitute the fierce and fanatical mercenaries and robbers of the provinces of the Nizam of Hydrabad.

Aurungzebe conducted the war in person; but his continued absence from his capital and the great distance of

BOOK II.

A.D. 1688 to 1707.

the seat of war from the centre of his resources, considerably impaired the efficiency of his armies, and brought upon his subjects the miseries inseparable from absentee domination. Fully occupied for many years in conducting warlike operations in a distant corner of his dominions, he was unable to exercise the supervision indispensable to good government; and compelled to entrust immense provinces to lieutenants, who were indifferent or unable to control them with strict justice, anarchy and oppression rapidly raised their heads in districts that for the last 150 years had been blessed by a firm and stable government.

But towards the end of his long reign the cloud that hung with dark portent over the departing glory of the Moguls rose for a season, and allowed the sun of their prosperity to shine once more with its wonted splendour. The storms that had darkened the horizon passed away; and at length, after six years of harassing warfare, the star of Aurungzebe was again in the ascendant. His arms were everywhere victorious; the proud monarchs of Golconda and Beejapore were forced to surrender their capitals to his victorious troops, and his son Akbar to seek in an English ship a distant asylum at the court of Ispahan; and to complete his triumph, the fierce and cruel Sumbhaji after excluding himself from all hopes of mercy by poisoning tanks, and other barbarous modes of warfare, was betrayed into the hands of the Mogul, whilst in a state of intoxication, and subjected to fearful tortures by his inhuman captors. He was offered life and fortune if he would turn Moslem; and on refusing, he was clothed in a dress derogatory to his caste, and paraded through the Mogul camp, sitting backwards on a camel, and treated with the most brutal indignities; but cruelty could not bend the bold spirit of the fierce Hindoo; and when Aurungzebe again sent him an offer of pardon on the same terms, he burst into a scornful laugh. "Tell the Emperor," said he, "that if he will give me his daughter, I will become a Mussulman." This taunt, the most insulting it was possible to make to a

Mussulman, was cruelly expiated; by the emperor's commands his tongue was torn out by the roots, his eyes seared with hot irons, and he was finally put to death in the most degrading manner. Sumbhaji possessed much of the courage and activity of his father, but he was a slave to his passions; his intemperance knew no bounds, and his presence in the neighbourhood was always enough to cause a panic amongst the fairer portion of his subjects.

CHAP. XXVI.

A.D. 1688 to 1707.

He was as cruel and revengeful as his father (for a Mahratta) was merciful and forgiving; he was a monster, whose meteor course was marked with the blood of his subjects more than with that of his foes; the vast treasures of Rairee were squandered in idleness and debauchery; his troops were unpaid, his subjects over taxed; he knew no god but his lust; and the brutal murder of his father's favourite wife, the trampling under foot of his ministers by elephants, and the cruelty exercised towards the holy order of the Brahmins, and the actual murder of one of them, soon alienated from him all that was respectable amongst his nation, and raised a spirit of discontent that relaxed the military organisation of the nation, and reduced his regular armies to bands of independent freebooters.

Sivaji had tried hard to bring up this wayward youth in a course more befitting the future sovereign of so powerful a nation; and on one occasion, being enraged by the representations of a Brahmin, whose domestic felicity was much disturbed by the nightly visits of the erotic prince to his wife, he gave orders that the next time Sumbhaji attempted to leave the fort after watch time, the guard should cast him head foremost from the rocks; but the impetuous prince was not one to forgive such a threat even from a father: he forthwith withdrew from Rairee, and joined Prince Mangam, at that time commanding the Mogul troops in the Deccan; and on one occasion his banner was displayed side by side with the Mogul against his father, and for the first and last time in his life Sivaji was defeated.

BOOK II.

A.D. 1688 to 1707.

Thus apparently delivered from all his foes in the Deccan, the cruelty and intolerance of Aurungzebe kept pace with his success. Abou Houssein, King of Golconda, was publicly scourged, to extort confession of his wealth; and his brother in misfortune Adil Shah, the proud monarch of Beejapore, was paraded in silver chains before his conqueror. Neither did the capitals of Deccan fare any better than the sovereigns; the palaces, the caravansaries, and the mosques, that for more than a century had made Beejapore the glory of Southern India, were levelled with the dust, and in a few days one of the most flourishing capitals of the East was reduced to the condition of the Palmyra of India.[4]

Nothing will give a better idea of the wealth and prosperity of Southern India, during the latter days of the Mahommedan kings, than the rapid growth and unequalled splendour of the city of Beejapore; it was only commenced in A.D. 1500; in rather less than fifty years it equalled, in the size and magnificence of many of its buildings, the imperial cities of Agra and Delhi.

The red marble mausoleum of Mahommed Adil Shah, larger than the Pantheon or St. Paul's, and but little inferior to St. Peter's itself, may be distinguished from the village of Kunnoor, a distance of fourteen miles; whilst there may still be seen the remains of the tomb of a favourite sultana, that with more than eastern extravagance, was covered with chunam made of powdered pearls![5] What was the vaunted profusion of a loving queen of Egypt to that of a doting monarch of Beejapore!

Thus fell the last Mussulman kingdoms of the Deccan; both were offshoots of the great Bhaminee dynasty, that owed its existence to Alla the Sanguinary, and both owed their independence to the Turkish race. Eusuf Adil Shah, first monarch of Beejapore, was a son of the Sultan of Turkey; and Koolli Koothub Shah, first monarch of Golconda, was also a prince of that adventurous race.

Henceforth the Deccanee kingdoms were united in the

great sovereignty of Hydrabad, nominally a province of the Mogul empire, but governed by a race of hereditary princes, distinguished by the title of the Nizam, who paid the same amount of real homage to the monarch of Delhi that the Pasha of Egypt does to the Sultan of Constantinople.

A.D. 1608 to 1707.

The death of Sumbhaji again united the rising power of the Mahrattas. They had no great cities to lose, no valuable territory to guard; and whilst Aurungzebe with much labour besieged and occupied their detached hill forts, they in their turn continued to pillage and destroy, and under their chief, Sakojee, carried their arms into the Mogul territory, and levied their wonted chout through the most fertile provinces of Hindostan. The gleam of success that had brightened the declining years of Aurungzebe, did not continue very long; he himself was too old to direct in person a war against foes so active and restless as the Mahrattas; and the indifference of his generals, who regarded the opening splendour of the rising sun, in the person of his successor, more than his own setting glory, enabled the Mahrattas to maintain a successful predatory war, as honourable and profitable to themselves as it was disgraceful and ruinous to the Moguls.

At length in the city of Ahmednuggur, in the Deccan, in the year 1707, in the fifteenth year of his reign and the nineteenth of his age, Aurungzebe was summoned to the regions of death, to meet that God in whose name he had committed many atrocities, and whose laws he had fearlessly defied.

His last moments appear to have been considerably tinged with the bitter spirit that marks the dying words of the great Preacher of Israel.

"Vanitas vanitatum et omnia vanitas" was the desponding wail of his parting life. "I came a stranger into the world," he writes mournfully, in a letter to his son Azim Shaw, "and a stranger I depart. I know nothing of myself: what I am, and for what I am destined; the

BOOK II. A.D. 1707.

instant which passed in power has left only sorrow behind it. I brought nothing into the world, and except the infirmities of man, I carry nothing out. Though I have a strong reliance on the mercies and bounties of God, yet regarding my actions, fear will not quit me. Come then what may, I have launched my vessel to the waves." There is a touch of nature in this letter that is amusing: "the Begum *appears* affected; but God is the only judge of hearts. The foolish thoughts of women produce nothing but disappointment." This querulous complaint of his nurse is so natural in a senile invalid! Another letter to Prince Kambush, the son of his old age and his favourite wife Oudipori, is much to the same purpose.

It is related that by the orders of the great Saladin, a winding sheet was carried before his corpse at his funeral, and an herald proclaimed in an impressive voice: "this sheet alone, of all his victories, could Saladin take with him to the grave." In like manner Aurungzebe left strict orders that no gorgeous tomb, like those that covered the ashes of his ancestors at Secundra or Agra, should be raised over his grave; as his personal habits had been simple, so did he desire should be the monument that was to perpetuate his memory. The utter worthlessness of worldly wealth to secure the happiness of a future state, and the senseless vanity of seeking to perpetuate in enduring structures the shortness of a fleeting career, was fully present to his mind: a shroud for his vesture, and a coffin for his chamber, was all the paraphernalia that Aurungzebe desired to take with him to his grave; and in the humble wooden tomb at Rauzah, "the place of tombs," near Ellora, far eclipsed in splendour by the neighbouring mausoleum of a Mussulman faqueer, few would seek to recognise the last resting-place of the magnificent sovereign of Hindostan.[6]

The character of Aurungzebe is by no means a rare one amongst mankind; and Richard III. of England, Louis XI. of France, and Philip II. of Spain, furnish us with kingly parallels. A bad man, and a successful ruler, his good acts were the result of policy, his bad ones of his disposition. Ascetic by design and temperate by inclination, expediency alone tempered his cruelty, and necessity his zeal; superstition and intolerance were the chief characteristics of his mind. He was a bad son, a cruel brother, and an unjust father; but he was yet the author of many wise and excellent regulations of public policy; and his liberal patronage of learning and science, the wisdom of his laws, the encouragement he gave to commerce and agriculture, the restraint he imposed on the oppression of his nobles, and the attention he bestowed in regulating the courts of justice, must ever be remembered to his honour. Blessed with an iron constitution, a long life, and untiring energy, his want of toleration marred the success of his reign; and whilst his empire increased in extent, his revenue was materially diminished.

Possessing undaunted resolution, and a personal intrepidity that never wavered, he yet trusted to intrigue, rather than to the exercise of the more generous qualities, for the success of his projects. The fox's skin was that most suited to his nature; but when that failed, no prince in history ever donned with fiercer determination that of the lion. He combined "the soft tongue that breaketh the bone," with "the much fair speech of the strange woman," and never lacked the devout visage and pious action that could sugar over the most ghastly deeds.

As a ruler he was as great as Akbar, as a warrior as brave as Baber, as a monarch more magnificent than either; but those are few, we fancy, who would not have preferred the dinner of herbs with either of these noble men to the stalled ox with Aurungzebe.

His revenue amounted to nearly forty millions sterling, a sum that appears enormous, when we remember that in India the products of the earth are, at most, one sixth of the price they cost in England.[7]

His state far exceeded that of any of his predecessors,

BOOK II. A.D. 1707.

even that of the splendid Akbar himself; and the fabulous splendour of the Farrah-Bagh, or Palace of Delights, which he built at Ahmednuggur, to signify the perpetuity of his occupation of the Deccan; the armies of attendants that followed his camp; the extent of the canvas walls of the royal tents, enclosing a space nearly three-quarters of a mile in circumference; the separate establishments for cooling water with saltpetre, preparing betel and sweetmeats, and for keeping the rarest fruit in condition for the royal palate, appear fabulous even to those who have themselves experienced the luxurious arrangements of Eastern life.

Aurungzebe was indefatigable in business, and received with scorn the advice of his omrahs to be more careful of his health. "All men," he said, "have a natural inclination to a long, easy, and careless life, and need no councillors to shake off business and trouble; besides, our wives that lie in our bosoms, do too often, beside our own genius, induce us that way. There are," added he, "times and conjunctions so urgent that a king ought to hazard his life for his subjects." His strong sense is strikingly exhibited in an admirable letter, written to Mallah-Sale, his old tutor, who had come to court in the hopes of being made an omrah by his grateful pupil.[8]

In many respects Aurungzebe displayed a very marked contrast to the tastes and desires of his ancestors; contrary to the custom of every sovereign of the House of Timour, he refused to have the history of his reign written, saying that he preferred the cultivation of inward piety to the ostentatious display of his actions: the history was however written in secret, by Khafi Khan, a native of Delhi,[9] and with the exception of that of Ferishta, is, without doubt, the most exact and reliable of the histories of Hindostan.

NOTES TO CHAPTER XXVI.

[1] The Brahmins came from the head of Brahma, and are endowed with wisdom. The Sittri or Cshatrya, the warrior caste, from his heart, as emblematical of courage. The Bice from his belly, as emblematical of agriculture and trade. The Sudras from his feet, to signify menial subjection.

[2] All Mussulmans may take the name of Mahommed.

[3] This was Timour's ostensible reason for invading China.

[4] At Beejapore the Emperor gained possession of the largest gun in the known world, called Mallek-i-Maidan, "the monarch of the plain;" this gigantic piece of ordnance was cast at Ahmednuggur, and was taken from Houssein Nizam Shah by Mahommed, king of Beejapore: the muzzle was 4 ft. 8 in. in diameter, calibre 2 ft., length 15 ft., and the weight 40 tons. It was cast by an officer enjoying the appropriate name of Roomi Khan; on it was this inscription: "the Prince Mahommed Ghazi, in splendour like the sun, under whose umbrella the world sought a shelter (and didn't find it), by the force of his all destroying sabre, in the twinkling of an eye took the monarch of the plain from Nizam Shah." The Emperor Aurungzebe substituted this: "Shah Alumgeer Ghazi, Emperor of Kings, who restored justice and conquered the sovereigns of Deccan, reduced Beejapore; good fortune on him daily smiled, and victory exclaimed, 'he hath subdued the monarch of the plain.'"

[5] Probably chunam made from the shell of the pearl-oyster.

[6] "Oh you, who have seen the glory of Alf Arslam exalted to the heavens, repair to Maru and you will see it buried in the dust!"—*Gibbon*, vol. v. p. 668.

[7] Ragi is the chief article of food of the poorer classes in Southern India; sufficient for a meal can be bought for the sixth of an anna, or one farthing sterling. The banana is also a plentiful food in India; it is forty-four times as prolific as the potato; one hundred and thirty-three times as wheat. One acre will support fifty persons.

[8] "What is it that you would have of me, doctor? Can you reasonably desire I should make you one of the chief omrahs of my court? Let me tell you, if you had instructed me as you should have done, nothing would be more just; for I am of persuasion that a child well educated and instructed, is as much at least indebted to his master as to his father; but where are those good documents you have given me. In the first place, you have taught me that all Frangastan, or Europe, was nothing, but I know not what little island, of which the greatest king was he of Portugal, and next to him he of Holland, and after him he of England; and as to the other kings, as those of France and Andalusia, you have represented them to me as our petty rajahs, telling me the kings of Hindostan were far above them altogether, and that they were the only true Humaioons, Akbars, Jehangires, Chah Jehans, the fortunate ones, the great ones, the conquerors and kings of the earth; and that Persia, Usbec, Kashgar, Tartary, and Cathay, and China, tremble at the name of the king of Hindostan — amirable geography You should rather have taught me to distinguish all those different states of the world, and well to understand their strength, their way of fighting,

BOOK II.

their customs, religion, government, and interests; and by the perusal of solid history, to observe their rise, progress, decay, and whence, how, and by what accidents and errors, those great changes and revolutions of empires and kingdoms have happened. I have scarce learnt of you the names of my grandsire, the famous founder of this empire; so far were you from having taught me the history of their life, and what course they took to secure such great conquests. You had a mind to teach me the Arabian tongue to read and write; I am much obliged to you, forsooth, for having made me lose so much time upon a language that takes ten or twelve years to attain to perfection—as if the son of a king should think it an honour to be a grammarian, or some doctor of the laws; and to learn other languages than those of his neighbours, when he cannot well be without them—he to whom time is so precious, for so many weighty things which he ought by times to learn; as if there were any spirit that did not with some reluctance, and even with a kind of debasement, employ itself in so sad and dry an exercise, so wearisome and tedious as is that of learning words! Know you not that childhood well governed, being a state which is ordinarily accompanied with a happy memory, is capable of thousands of good precepts and instructions, that remain deeply impressed the whole remainder of a man's life, and keep the mind always raised for great actions; the law, prayers, and sciences, may they not as well be learned in our mother tongue as in Arabic? You told my father, Shah Jehan, that you would teach me philosophy; it is true I remember very well that you have entertained me for years with airy questions of things that afford no satisfaction to the mind, and are of no use to human society; empty notions and mere fancies that have only this in them, that they are very hard to understand, and very easy to forget; only capable to tire and spoil a good understanding, and to breed an opinion that is insupportable. I still remember that after you had thus amused me, I know not how long with your fine philosophy, all I retained of it was a multitude of barbarous, dark words, proper to bewilder, perplex, and tire out the best wits, and only invented the better to cover the vanity and ignorance of men like yourself, that would make us believe they know all, and that under those obscure and ambiguous words are hid great mysteries, which they alone are capable to understand.

"If you had seasoned me with that philosophy, which forms the mind to ratiocination, and insensibly accustoms it to be satisfied with nothing but solid reasons; if you had given me those excellent principles and doctrines, which raise the soul above the assaults of fortune, and reduce her to an unshakeable and always equal temper, and permit her not to be lifted up by prosperity, nor debased by adversity; if you had taken care to give me the knowledge of what we are, and what are the first principles of things; and had assisted me in forming in my mind a fit idea of the greatness of the universe, and of the admirable order and motion of the parts thereof; if, I say, you had instilled into me this kind of philosophy, I should think myself incomparably more obliged to you than Alexander was to his Aristotle, and believe it my duty to recompense you as he did. Should you not, instead of your flattery, have taught me of that point so important to a king, viz. what are the reciprocal duties of a sovereign? and ought not you to have considered that one day I shall be obliged with the sword to dispute my life and the crown with my brothers? Is not that the destiny of almost all the princes of Hindostan? Have you even taken any care to make me learn what it is to besiege a town or set an army in array? For these things I am obliged to others, not at all to you. Go and retire to the village whence you came, and let nobody know who you are and what has become of you." CHAP. XXVI.

[9] He left a most voluminous correspondence, afterwards collected by his secretary.

CHAP. XXVII.

THE DISSENSIONS OF THE SONS OF AURUNGZEBE.—BAHADAR SHAH.—THE ENGLISH OBTAIN A FOOTING IN BENGAL.—THE RAPID DECLINE OF THE MOGUL EMPIRE.—THE FIERCE CAREER OF NADIR SHAH.—MASSACRE OF THE INHABITANTS OF DELHI.—THE ASSASSINATION OF NADIR SHAH IN A.D. 1747.

BOOK II. A.D. 1707.

In the year 1686 the English in Bengal made an attempt to establish by force of arms a settlement which had been denied to their diplomacy; the ill success attending this, and in fact all the early attempts of England in India, foreshadowed but very slightly her subsequent unequalled success.

The English were entirely driven out of Bengal, and obliged to seek refuge in Madras; but the evil did not stop there; the violence and arrogance of Sir John Child had irritated Aurungzebe, and by his orders the factory at Surat and the island of Bombay were attacked by the fleet of his Abyssinian Siddees. The factories at Masulipatam and Viziagapatam were seized and destroyed; and it was only by the most abject submission that the English saved themselves from utter expulsion.

In the meantime the French had formed a strong settlement at Pondichery, and these versatile adventurers were spreading through the various courts of India.

From the period of the death of Aurungzebe, the honourable senators and councillors, that for upwards of 160 years had more or less swayed the destinies of Hindostan, were unknown in the councils of the Moguls; and the reign of boys and women soon brought to utter ruin the magnificent Empire of Akbar.

Notwithstanding their long residence, the Moguls were never thoroughly naturalised in India; they were still exotics, and want of energy, arising from a residence in an enervating climate unsuited to their nature, was plainly perceptible: all those who now rose to great power in India, whether in the service of the Emperor, or in that of his enemies, were recently imported foreigners, or the aboriginal inhabitants of India itself. The greatest officers of state, as well as the most successful generals, were now either Persians, or the Tooranee Moguls, Tartars just come over with fresh blood and undiminished vigour, from the countries north of the Indus.

Meer Jumla, the greatest of Aurungzebe's generals, and the most dangerous of his subjects, was a Persian; whilst his most successful enemies, who now defeated on equal terms the formerly irresistible Moguls, were the Hindoo princes of the Deccan or Rajpootana. Except in name the Moguls were no longer the dominant race in Hindostan. Aurungzebe wished to divide his empire between his two sons, Kambush and Azim; and for that purpose wrote a very interesting state paper, reminding them of the existence of the two capitals Delhi and Agra, and of the possibility of making each the centre of a very considerable and flourishing empire. He advised them to unite the southern and western provinces of the Deccan, Malwah and Guzerat, in one kingdom, having its seat of empire at Agra; whilst Delhi should be the capital of the northern provinces, including Caubul, Cashmere, and other recently acquired countries; but in all these plans for the amicable partition of his dominions, the insatiable nature of the lust of empire did not enter sufficiently into his calculations. "Ten dervishes," says the Tartar proverb, "may sit on one carpet; but the same climate will not hold two kings;" and no sooner had he "vanished in the regions of death," than his three sons advanced from their

BOOK II. A.D. 1707-12. separate governments at the head of their several powers, to lay claim to the splendid patrimony of their race. They fought for the crown with the same bitter spirit that had been exhibited by their father in his contests with his brethren; again did the Erinnys of the soil of Hindostan daub her lips with her own children's blood; and again were the scenes of civil discord, that marked the fierce wars of Dara, Sujah, and Aurungzebe, enacted between Azim, Kambush and Shah Allum; but after many severe actions, Shah Allum, the eldest son, was finally victorious; and his brothers having been despatched "to the shades," by some means or another, he mounted his father's throne under the title of Bahadar Shah.

Bahadar Shah was a prince of some ability, and of a far more generous nature than his father Aurungzebe; but the unsettled state of his empire, and his numerous and increasing enemies, did not afford him much opportunity for beneficial legislation. His desire to subdue the rebel Rajpoots, and to establish on a firmer foundation his father's costly conquests in the Deccan, was defeated by the renewed attack of his ancient enemies the Sikhs; who, notwithstanding the severe handling they had received from the generals of Aurungzebe, the expatriation of one of their leaders, and the cruel death of the other, had rapidly gathered head, and under their patriarch Banda, had openly taken the field, with disciplined troops, and after ravaging the provinces of Lahore, had advanced almost as far as Delhi itself.

Those who could bear the exposure and hardships of a life so trying as that of an Eastern faqueer, would naturally make the most hardy and enduring soldiers in time of war. In the East these lusty devotees are ever numerous, contenting themselves with begging and soliciting alms, when awed by a strong government; but always ready to band together and take up arms, the moment the hand of power and justice is weakened by impotent rulers or intestine commotions. The Sikhs were of this order; and the insults and atrocities they committed through the North-West, during the time of Aurungzebe and his successors, were only equalled by those perpetrated by the Gosaeens and Byragees, the Mahratta fanatics of the South.

Under the cruel religious persecution of Aurungzebe the Sikhs had become purely Hindoo, and had practised most atrocious cruelties on all true followers of the Prophet; the subversive nature of their doctrines, and their dangerous proximity to the capital, admitted of no delay: and no sooner had Bahadar Shah set the crown of the Moguls firmly on his head, than he proceeded hastily to the North, to effect their suppression. But the power of the Emperor, although sufficient to arrest, could not extirpate this warlike sect; when utterly beaten and their chief taken, they retreated to the mountains, where they remained, adding continually to their numbers, and offering a rallying-point to all the discontented spirits of the North-West. In about eighty years their leader, Maha-Singh, was able to take the field at the head of sixty thousand horse; and a few years later it was found advisable, if not necessary, for the British Government to form an alliance, offensive and defensive, with his son Runjeet Singh, the "Lion of Lahore," whose troops under his successor, gave English supremacy so severe a blow on the hard-fought fields of Punjaub.

We have seen that the indiscretion and want of diplomacy of the English merchants in Bengal inflamed the enmity of Aurungzebe, who banished them entirely from that district, and threatened them with total expulsion from India; but during a short reign of five years, the liberality of Bahadar Shah, or as is more probable, the cupidity of his second son Azeem Ooshaun, viceroy of Bengal, enabled the English to re-establish themselves on a permanent footing, by the purchase of the zemindaries of Calcutta and the surrounding districts.

In 1713, two agents of the company started from Calcutta for Delhi, to try and negotiate a treaty to enable them to extend their territory and power in Bengal: they

BOOK II.

A.D. 1707–12.

were, however, utterly unsuccessful, and were about to return in despair, when the fortunate indisposition of the Emperor[1] enabled an English medical gentleman of the name of Hamilton to make known the power of European science, by curing in a short time an attack that had baffled the attempts of all the hakeems and astrologers of Agra.

Gratitude for his cure; an openly expressed admiration and a secret dread of the power of these white-faced infidels, impelled the Emperor to grant them permission to purchase thirty-seven large zemindaries around Calcutta; by this means they obtained a valuable district, extending fourteen miles on each side of the Hooghly, and thus the pill-box, that in the reign of Shah Jehan had first established the English company in Bengal, was the means of re-establishing its fallen fortunes. Certainly the heraldic device of "three pills passant," that denote the pharmacopœian ancestry of the princely house of the Medici at Florence, might have been fairly adopted by the enlightened community of Leadenhall Street.

In the meantime, whilst the shadow of England, stealthily spreading over the land of India, was heralding the coming event of her supremacy, the Mogul dynasty was struggling in hopeless inefficiency, and the Empire sinking into a state of anarchy and confusion, worse even than that existing under the later monarchs of the Affghan dynasty.

Some idea may be formed of the confusion worse confounded that afflicted that unhappy country from the fact that, during the eleven years, 1707 to 1718, succeeding the death of Aurungzebe, five sovereigns actually sat on the Musnud of the Moguls; two of whom, together with six unsuccessful competitors for the crown, died in the field, or were otherwise slain.

This period is unmarked by any event but the rank growth of anarchy and tyranny, and the unmistakeable signs of rapid decay and impending dissolution.

In all directions the discordant portions of the Empire were arming against the supreme authority; and the several members of the body politic, whose union alone would ensure the duration of the Empire, were in arms against each other; everywhere the Zemindars aimed at independence, and the country was overrun with banditti; the Sikhs in the north-west, already quite rallied from their defeat by Aurungzebe and Bahadar Shah, attacked successively the generals of Feroksere; and the Mahrattas under Sahojee, the son of the wretched Sumbhajee, built forts and burnt villages at will, throughout the viceroyalty of the Deccan, and levied chout and imposed taxes on inland trade, in the very centre of Hindostan itself.

Such was the utter degradation of the sovereign, and his not unreasonable dread of the overgrown power and ambition of the viceroys and lieutenants of his Empire, that he was obliged to cement the illwill existing between the various races in his dominions, and to form alliances with some of his subjects to defeat the ambitious designs of others; and to such an extent was he forced to adopt this suicidal policy, that in order to humble the dangerous power of his southern viceroys, he secretly urged the lawless Mahrattas to levy their black mail in defiance of the armies commanded by his own officers, who imagined they possessed the Emperor's orders for putting an end to these exactions.

This intestine war could only terminate in the utter annihilation of the imperial power, and the rapid rise of all who could profit by the ruin of the Empire: accordingly we find that in proportion to the decline of the Moguls was the rise of the Mahrattas to power, till at length, not content with levying the chout, or fourth part of the revenues, of the six provinces of the Deccan, they had the amazing impudence to insist upon receiving an additional tenth part as an immunity for the expense of raising the original or other fourth part. In addition to this double exaction, the wretched subjects of the Mogul

BOOK II. A.D. 1714–44. had to pay their regular land-tax to the Government; and the misery and desolation that soon pervaded districts exposed to this treble imposition, was one of the causes of the rapid growth of the native Hindoo powers.

"He whose house is burnt," says the Scotch proverb, "must become a soldier;" and throughout the Mogul Empire, the oppressed inhabitants, deprived of all the hard-earned fruits of their labour, found no other resource left them but to turn their ploughshares into swords, and in marauding expeditions against their neighbours, to recover from the weak the losses they had sustained from the strong.

1713–18. During the reign of Feroksere, the great grandson of Aurungzebe, the patronage and power of the Empire had been usurped by two Syed Omrahs, Hassan and Abdalla; and again we find the lineal descendants of the Prophet in possession of the throne of Hindostan. For many years the Syeds exercised supreme power, and dethroned the Emperors one after another with indefatigable celerity. In the meanwhile Cutterlick Khan, a powerful chief of the Tooranee Moguls, established himself firmly in the Deccan, where some years afterwards he defeated the combined power of the Syeds and their puppet Emperor, and established for himself the kingdom that his successors, under the title of Nizam-ul-Molk, "Composer of the State," have held ever since.

1720. On the death of Hassan and Abdalla, who were defeated and slain by the Nizam in a fierce action in the Deccan, the Emperor Mahommed, freed from their influence, solicited and obtained the friendship and submission of this powerful and dangerous subject; and having invested him with the Viziership, he induced him to quit his sovereignty of the Deccan for the capital of Hindostan, whither he proceeded with a following of 20,000 men to take the supreme direction of affairs. Even at this, the eleventh hour, the wise counsels and strong will of the Nizam might have revived and saved the Mogul Empire; but the seal of destruction was set on that kingdom, and the maudlin sovereigns who succeeded each other on the throne were only the instruments of its more complete and rapid fall.

The wisdom of the Nizam was insulted, his experience ignored, and his power not a little dreaded; and finding himself in danger of losing his kingdom by his absence from the Deccan, and his life by a residence at Court, he very shortly retired to his dominions, where he found that the treachery of Mahommed had armed his own son against him, and had promised his kingdom to another as a reward for taking his life. Naturally irritated at such conduct, he openly made war against his sovereign, and seizing Guzerat and Malwah, ravaged the provinces of the Empire without mercy; and in 1735, having secured the alliance of the leading Mahratta chiefs, he invaded Hindostan, and his lawless allies plundered up to the very gates of Agra and Delhi: the humiliation of the mighty race of Timour was now complete, when its representative was forced to pay ransom to his own subjects in the very palaces of his haughty ancestors, Akbar and Aurungzebe.

In the meantime an event was impending that was destined to complete the overthrow of the remnant of the Mogul Empire, and the keystone that was to complete the arch of ignominy that now overshawdowed the Mogul race was being fashioned in the neighbouring land of Persia. It was impossible that the corruption and decay visible in every province of Hindostan should escape the notice of that warlike nation of Asia. The sight of Rajpoots, Mahrattas, Sikhs and Jaats all contending amongst each other, or united against their nominal sovereign, would alone have created a conqueror, had there not been one ready at hand, as fierce as Timour and as daring as Baber, who was only waiting an opportunity to dash in and appropriate with a strong hand the prize for which the others were contending with so much animosity.

BOOK II. A.D. 1714–44.

Nadir Kouli, "the slave of the wonderful," called Nadir Shah, the last Asiatic conqueror who overran Hindostan, is without question one of the most remarkable characters of Eastern history; with Timour and Genghis Khan we must number him amongst the most famous of the princes of the sword, and it is in the annals of blood that we must search for deeds such as those that have handed down his name to posterity.

Nadir Shah was of low origin and family, the son of a man who "had wiped his nose with his elbow,"[2] and in his youth earned a livelihood by making coats and caps of sheepskin; but he possessed the dauntless spirit that breaks through all the trammels of caste with scarcely an effort. Unlike the great Mahratta Sivaji, who underwent severe penances and spent vast treasures to erase a flaw in his descent, Nadir treated the whole subject of birth and lineage with utter contempt. Like all the great conquerors of the East, his empire was acquired by the sword, and it was with that unanswerable argument that he replied to all who were inquisitive regarding his lineage and his right. "This," said Moez, one of the most daring of the caliphs, when questioned about his family, "This," drawing his sword, "is my pedigree, and these," casting a handful of gold amongst his soldiers, "are my children and my kindred." In a like spirit Nadir dismissed the ambassador of the almost nominal sovereign of Hindostan, who required that his son should prove a male pedigree extending through seven generations before he would allow him to marry a daughter of the race of Timour: "Go," said he, "tell your master my son is the son of Nadir Shah, the son of the sword, the grandson of the sword, and so on till he has a descent of seventy generations instead of seven."

From an early period of his career, Nadir Shah was a freebooter on a grand scale, sparing his own countrymen, but making daring and increasing excursions into the frontier lands of his neighbours; by degrees his band attained considerable power and influence in a country so shaken with anarchy and revolt as Persia; and as the Mahrattas under Sivaji rose to empire on the decay and corruption of the Mogul Empire, so did Nadir flourish on the weakness of the declining dynasty of Sophi.[8]

Shortly after the threatened invasion of Hindostan by Shah Abbas, the Affghans, completely foiled by the great power of Aurungzebe, and defeated in all their attempts on Hindostan, turned their arms against their former allies, and in a few years seized and monopolised the whole government of Persia; Nadir Shah, although a subject, was not one to submit tamely to a foreign yoke, especially that of a race so fierce and relentless as the Affghans: he vowed their destruction, and by a series of daring exploits and an almost unequalled display of energy and physical endurance, he entirely expelled them in the short space of two years.

It frequently happens that the subject who undertakes and brings to a successful termination the work that should have been performed by the sovereign himself, becomes a dangerous rival in the respect and admiration of the people; this was exemplified in the case of Nadir, his glory and success were extolled to the heavens, whilst the inefficiency and cowardice of the sovereign exposed him to contempt. Nadir was the Bolingbroke of the last effeminate representative of the house of Sophi. The "slave of the wonderful" was not blind to his position, or slow to avail himself of it; he dethroned the sovereign; but satisfied with the substance, he scorned the emblems of royalty, and firmly refused to accept the crown.

It was not till some years later that—assembling the chiefs and nobles of the Empire to the number of one hundred thousand on the plains of Mogan, on the eastern shore of the Caspian Sea, the favourite camping ground of oriental princes, which had seen the victorious tents of Heraclius and the fierce legions of Tamerlane—Nadir accepted the proffered distinction. The circumstances

BOOK II. A.D. 1714–44.

attending his acceptance of the crown illustrate the extraordinary power he already possessed over his countrymen, and show how completely a matter of indifference must have been any outward distinction to one so powerful. He consented to mount the throne solely on condition that the Shia creed of Mahommedans, comprising by far the greater number of the Persian race, should be abolished, and the Sunee established in its stead.

Nadir himself, like his prototype Genghis Khan, had no religion whatever, and scoffed at and derided all with equal bitterness; this subversion of the established worship of an entire nation was no effort of conscience, but merely the result of a whim, or an act of political expediency. That he should have effected this startling revolution between sects so bitterly opposed as these two great divisions of the Mahommedan religion without striking a blow, and merely by urging it as a condition of his accepting a crown, illustrates a degree of national degradation and the power of a strong will unequalled in history.

Not satisfied with driving the Affghans out of Persia, Nadir Shah followed them with fire and sword into their own prosperous kingdom. He marched through Candahar to Ghizni and Caubul, where plucking the muzzle of curbed licence from his troops, he hounded them on to slaughter, and for seven months the wild dog of Persia did flesh his tooth in every innocent of Affghanistan.

The barbarous atrocity with which his men burnt and destroyed everything that came into their power, was the forerunner of the career of cruelty that was to mark his invasion of Hindostan.

Greedy for the blood of his enemies, and unwilling that any should escape, he sent a command to the Emperor Mahommed at Delhi to kill every Affghan who fled to him for protection. The refusal to comply with his command, and the accidental destruction of his envoy and suite by the inhabitants of Jellahabad, gave Nadir the pretext he so much desired for invading Hindostan. In 1738 he crossed the Indus with an army of two hundred and seventy thousand Persians, Georgians, and Kizzilbashes; and again did "trenching war channel the fair fields of Hindostan, and bruise her flowerets with the armed hoofs of hostile forces."

The Emperor Mahommed made a feeble attempt to defend his empire, but his troops being defeated with great ease, he sought safety in flight, and Nadir advanced unopposed to the walls of Delhi.

Without any design of annexing Hindostan, and attracted more by the ease with which the conquest could be effected, and the probable amount of booty to be obtained than by any idea of subjugation, Nadir was willing to retire on the payment of two millions sterling; but the treachery of the old Nizam of the Deccan, and the intrigues of the numerous and powerful body of Persian nobles inhabiting Delhi offered him the prospect of such a golden harvest, that after a short delay he entered the city, the gates of which were opened to receive him.

For two days the army of Nadir Shah remained at Delhi, maintaining the most perfect order and restraint; and the proffered ransom of two millions having been increased to the more tempting sum of thirty, he was again on the point of retracing his career of pillage and destruction to the Indus, when an event occurred to prevent his return which will long be remembered as furnishing the material of one of the most bloody of the blood-stained pages of Indian history.

On the third day of the occupation of the Persians, rumour, that hundred-mouthed monster, whispered it through the streets of Delhi that Nadir Shah had been assassinated in his harem by a Calmuck woman at the instigation of Mahommed; when the natives, rising *en mssse*, slew every Persian who happened at that time to be within the walls.

BOOK II. A.D. 1714–44.

Nadir was encamped outside the city, and it was midnight when the news reached his camp; proceeding instantly to the mosque of Ruschid-ud-Dowlah, he remained there surrounded by troops till the morning, when mounting the roof, he drew his sword and gave orders to commence a general slaughter and pillage, and to smite hip and thigh the inhabitants of every street in which was found a dead Persian. "Allez, mes enfans," said the Maréchal de Luxembourg to his troops at a siege in Holland in 1671, "pillez, volez, tuez, violez, et s'il y a quelque chose de plus abominable, ne manquez pas de la faire, afin que je voye que je ne me suis pas trompé, en vous choisissant comme les plus braves des hommes;" and in other words, but with as cruel a heart, did Nadir hound on his troops to the slaughter. From sunrise to mid-day the streets ran with blood, and the cruelties of the Moguls of Timour were enacted with equal ferocity by the vengeful Persians. During these many hours of slaughter Nadir Shah was seated on the mosque; none dare approach him, for his countenance was very terrible to behold, and the outward calm of his manner concealed a heart as ruthless and cruel as any ever set in mortal clay.

At length, when the streets were red [4] with blood, and the arms of the smiter were wearied, Mahommed and his omrahs appeared before him; he asked what they wanted. "Spare the city," said they; he answered not a word; but when he looked on Mahommed bathed in tears, he repented and gave orders to spare all that remained.

The power that could arrest in full career the headlong course of rapine and murder of an army fierce and merciless as that of the Persians, was scarcely less remarkable than the iron will that could without opposition divert the national religion of a whole people from its established course; but the will of Nadir Shah was of that fierce, impetuous nature that admits no argument and knows no delay. Frequently, during his many wars, he was known to halt his army and send an officer to give some general of division whose conduct had displeased him four dozen on the spot.

Although the general massacre of the citizens of Delhi ceased at the beck of Nadir, his own private revenge was not so quickly satisfied. For days he sat in judgment in the city, and hundreds of the chief inhabitants were brought before him to account for their participation in the outbreak; numbers were barbarously executed, and others more cruelly mutilated. He levied an enormous fine on all the officers, bankers, &c. in the city; and many put themselves to death to avoid the punishment inseparable from their inability to pay. He beat with sticks the Vaqueel of Bengal for not expediting the collection of the fine imposed in the city, and when the vizier pleaded his inability to pay the enormous sum of two and a half millions sterling, he had all his effects sold, and seizing three of his daughters and seven of his most beautiful women, forced them into his own harem.

Fearful as were the atrocities committed by Nadir and his troops, they were disregarded by those who managed to escape them; and to this day the lingering tortures of their own countrymen, the licentious excesses of the Persian soldiery, and the fierce presence of Nadir himself, form the chief staple of amusing anecdote amongst the low-caste frequenters of the bazaars at Delhi, and compose the greater part of the comic songs of the wandering minstrels of Hindostan.

It is probable that no city in the world has witnessed such appalling scenes of bloodshed as Delhi; for hundreds of years it has been the sanguinary centre around which have fought and died the invaders and defenders of the coveted land of India. It was the familiar account of scenes such as those enacted by the soldiers of Nadir and Timour, and the tradition of others almost as atrocious, that prepared the minds of the inhabitants of Delhi for the conception of those hellish orgies by which they have lately announced their contempt of our rule, and which have

BOOK II. A.D. 1714–44.

associated for ever the name of the capital of India with deeds of ferocity that history can certainly equal, but for which history nowhere recounts a speedier retribution.

After retaining possession of Delhi for thirty-seven days, Nadir commenced his return march to Persia, hampered with spoil and prisoners, and laden with treasure, variously stated at thirty, and one hundred and twenty millions sterling.[5] Amongst his spoils were the peacock throne of Shah Jehan, on which the richest jewels of the East had been arranged by the most skilful artists of the West; and the Mountain of Light that, so often and so fiercely contested, is now the most precious gem in the crown of the Empress of India. His progress was naturally slow; but this tardiness only gave greater leisure to his fierce Persians to burn, ravish, and destroy to the full bent of their savage natures; for miles on either side of his line of march the country was a desert, and two hundred thousand Hindoos are supposed to have expiated with their blood the fortuitous crime of their birth.

There can be no doubt that, had he been so inclined, Nadir could have retained possession of Delhi and established a Persian dynasty in Hindostan; that he did not do so was owing to the wise conclusion that an empire with two capitals so far apart as Delhi and Ispahan could never stand. He felt that although he had the absolute power to select whichever of the two he chose, he could not enjoy them both, and preferring the land of his nation and kindred to that of the Hindoos and Moguls, he returned to Persia.

He made a merit of this political necessity, and claimed the praise of the highest magnanimity for relinquishing his hold on India to return to his native country.

Before he quitted Delhi he replaced the degraded Mahommed on the throne,[6] and announced the event by proclamation to all the princes of India, exhorting them to obey his rule, and at the same time threatening to return immediately with increased power, and visit with terrible punishment those who disregarded his commands. It is probable that Nadir fully intended to fulfil this threat, and that, even in the absence of any particular necessity for his interference, he would ere many years had elapsed have returned to reap another abundant harvest of treasure and blood, had not the knife of the assassin suddenly cut short his career.

His end, like that of Domitian, Caligula, and other similar characters in history, had become a matter of necessity to his subjects; so insatiable was his thirst for blood, that self-preservation compelled his nobles to terminate the existence of one whose sole pleasure lay in the destruction of his species.

The immediate cause of his assassination was the inhuman treatment of his own son, and the sanguinary remorse that caused him to seek to wash out, in the blood of the noblest of the land, his own participation in the crime. Suspecting his son of having attempted his life, he ordered him into his presence and put his eyes out; but so maddened was he by the consciousness of his own cruelty, that he sought comfort in decapitating fifty noblemen because they had not sacrificed themselves for his son. Several nobles of the highest rank in the kingdom having ascertained that their names were on the proscribed list, took the law into their own hands and assassinated him in his tent near Mushed.

Nadir Shah must be ranked with Genghis Khan and Timour in modern history, and with Nero and Cambyses and other monsters of more ancient days. He occupies a prominent position in history as one of the greatest destroyers of the human race. He equalled all his prototypes in his fury and his lust for shedding blood, and excelled not a few in energy and vigour. The history of his destructive career proves how inappreciable has been the progress of civilisation or the ameliorating influences of increased intercourse amongst the princes and nations

BOOK II. A.D. 1714–44.

of the East; the eighteenth century sent a monster of cruelty and wickedness more fierce and more ruthless than any that had preceded him in the history of the world.

The character of Nadir as summed up by the historian will best explain his nature, and account for the extraordinary influence exercised by this mighty destroyer of his species.

"Courage, which he possessed in common with the lion, was his only virtue, and he owed his greatness to the defects of his mind; had his eyes melted at human miseries, had his soul shuddered at murder, had his heart glowed once with benevolence, or had his heart revolted at injustice, he might have lived to an old age; but he would have died without the name of Nadir or wonderful."

In 1744 war broke out between France and England, and whilst Nadir was sacking Delhi, the territory of Madras was the scene of a series of bitter contests between the powers of England and France; and on the surf-beaten shores and burning plains of the Carnatic, ten thousand miles distant from the parent states, were revived the fierce antipathies of Agincourt and Blenheim.

Everywhere in these contests the French were victorious; their hold on the country was stronger, their resources greater, and their generals and statesmen far superior to those of England; and the energy and military capacity of Bussy and Labourdonnais, and the successful diplomacy of Dupleix, assisted by the local knowledge and polyglot capacity of his half-caste wife, Jeanne de Castro, everywhere established the power of their arms and attracted the alliances of neighbouring princes.

After a bloodless contest, in which the French lost none and the English only five or six men, Madras yielded to the French troops, and, in the face of India, the lilies of France were hoisted over the leopards of England on the citadel of Fort George.

The French were the first to establish the boundless

superiority of European over native arms and discipline, and to recognise and avail themselves of the facility of imparting the military science of Europe to the Sepoys of India, thus rendering them the means of their own subjugation; and there is little doubt that, had the French East India Company received the support they were entitled to expect from the mother country, the remarkable talents and enlarged ambition of Dupleix would have raised for France an empire as great as that now enjoyed by her rival.

But in 1754, whilst Dupleix was successfully combating the English in the Carnatic, and his Lieutenant Bussy was pursuing a career of conquest on the upper waters of the Godarey and the Nerbudda, he was suddenly recalled to France; not to receive the honours and rewards his genius and policy had so worthily earned, but to meet with the same foul calumny and persecution that, a few years later, drove to despair and ruin the two most distinguished officers of the rival power.

France was desirous of peace, and England would only grant it on condition of Dupleix's recall: thus whilst England ceded a few insignificant cities, France resigned an empire. Well may the historian[7] exclaim, "Never did a country make so great a sacrifice from a love of peace."

From the day of Dupleix's departure from India, French domination ceased; the impetuous though unfortunate Lally, and the eager and determined Bussy, were no longer a match for the English agents of the company, who, liberally supported from home, and strengthened by the alliances that success will always command from the native powers of India were soon complete masters of the field; the French were everywhere defeated; and the English commenced, on the foundation their enemies had laid, the erection of the present marvellous structure of Indian empire.

There was at this time no great power in Hindostan to

BOOK II. A.D. 1714–44.

conquer; no powerful dynasty to subvert; the power of the Moguls was extinct, whilst that of the Hindoos was divided against itself. In this state of universal war the assistance of the drilled soldiers and practised artillery of England was eagerly sought by all the contending parties. It was soon perceived that the tactics and discipline of the Europeans invariably turned the scale against any odds; and dragged as it were into innumerable quarrels, often unwillingly, and generally without any defined object, the company gradually found themselves actual possessors of extensive kingdoms they had originally only intended to defend for their native princes. British influence rapidly became paramount; the nation, startled and almost alarmed at her sudden fortune, found herself unexpectedly the parent of a gigantic offspring, docile indeed to all appearance, but portentous in stature and unknown in disposition and resources.

Mahommed Shah survived the destruction of his capital by the Persians nine years, and died in 1748 after a disastrous reign of thirty years. In many respects the miserable government of this prince reminds one of that of his namesake Mahommed III., whose "continued infancy" some three hundred years before had wooed the onslaught of the fierce Timour:—again had the same causes produced the same results, and the imbecility of the sovereign and the rottenness of the state been the inciting cause of foreign aggression. Another cycle in the history of Hindostan was completed; the power that had arisen and flourished on a former condition of weakness was now in its turn enfeebled and supplanted by one animated with more health and vigour.

Mahommed was succeeded at his death by his son Ahmed Shah: but here let us drop the veil over the closing history of the Mogul race; from this period to the year 1803, when the Great Mogul became finally the pensioner of English merchants, all is uninteresting and unprofitable. "A succession of nominal sovereigns, sunk in indolence and debauchery, sauntered away life in secluded palaces, chewing bang, fondling concubines, and listening to buffoons. . . . . The Afghan soon followed to complete the work of devastation which the Persian had begun. The warlike tribes of Rajpootana threw off the Mussulman yoke. A band of mercenary soldiers occupied Rohilcund. The Seiks ruled on the Indus. The Jauts spread dismay along the Jumna."[8] The solitary province of Delhi was all that remained of the mighty empire of Akbar; and in less than a hundred years from the death of Aurungzebe, the nominal possessor of a revenue of forty millions sterling was forced to sell the marble and inlaid ornaments of the imperial palace at Delhi, to supply food for his own children, and to descend from his kingly state to grind rice for princely infidels.[9]

Already the spider had woven her web in the palace of Akbar, and the owl had sung her watch-song on the towers of Aurungzebe; and the picture of the descendants of these mighty sovereigns humiliating themselves in their own palaces before the ministers of those nations whose very sovereigns had scarce dared to enter the presence of their ancestors, may point the moral, but will scarcely adorn the tale of fallen majesty.

The Great Mogul was now a mere "nominis umbra;" his titles were but sounding brass, his glory the smoke of an expiring flame, and his power a fire choked amongst the thorns of rebellion and discontent. The brilliant star of the great race that had swept with such dazzling splendour across the broad arch of Eastern history had gradually lost its brilliancy, till, like the nebulous lustre that survives the passing meteor, a few sparks of light alone remained to indicate rather the course it had pursued than the splendour it had displayed.

BOOK II.

NOTES TO CHAPTER XXVII.

[1] Feroksere succeeded Jehander Shah, who succeeded Bahadar Shah.

[2] "I am the son of a man who wiped his nose with his elbow," said Antisthenes when questioned about his lineage.

[3] The Sophi dynasty ruled in Persia for two centuries, an age that may be considered Augustan; their names were as follows:

Shah Ismael Sophi,	Sophi the Cruel,
Tahmasp,	Abbas,
Ismael II.	Soliman,
Mahommed,	Hassyn,
Abbas the Great,	Tahmasp.

The Sophis were displaced by the Affghans, who took the title of Sultan; in their turn they were displaced by Nadir Shah, 1736. The descendants of Nadir Shah were overturned by the Zend family, who were succeeded by the Cajars or Turki tribe who rule at present.

[4] The number slain is variously stated between 100,000 and 8,000; such figures baffle even an approximate computation.

[5] His own treasure is stated at 87,000,000*l.* sterling; that of his army, at 12,000,000*l.*; besides 25,000,000*l.* paid in ransom before he entered the city. He also took 1,000 elephants, 7,000 fine horses, 10,000 camels, 120 writers, 200 masons, 300 stone-cutters, 200 carpenters. (Col. Luard, *Views on India.*) Other writers put it at about one quarter.

[6] On one occasion Nadir Shah was seated with Mahommed Shah, when coffee was introduced, and the servant, doubtful how to act so as not to hurt the dignity of either monarch, presented the cup to the vizier, who presented it to Mahommed Shah his master, requesting him to present it to the conqueror, by which he avoided giving offence to either party.

[7] Macaulay.

[8] Macaulay.

[9] In 1802, when Lake relieved the Mogul from the Mahratta under Scindia, their condition was miserable in the extreme. The yearly stipend allowed to each of the surviving princes of the blood was only 22*l.* per annum, and the whole allowance of the emperor for personal expenses, family and dependents, &c., and his harem, did not exceed 24,000*l.* per annum. In 1803 Shah Allum II. had to sell the ornaments of his palace at Delhi to find food for his children.

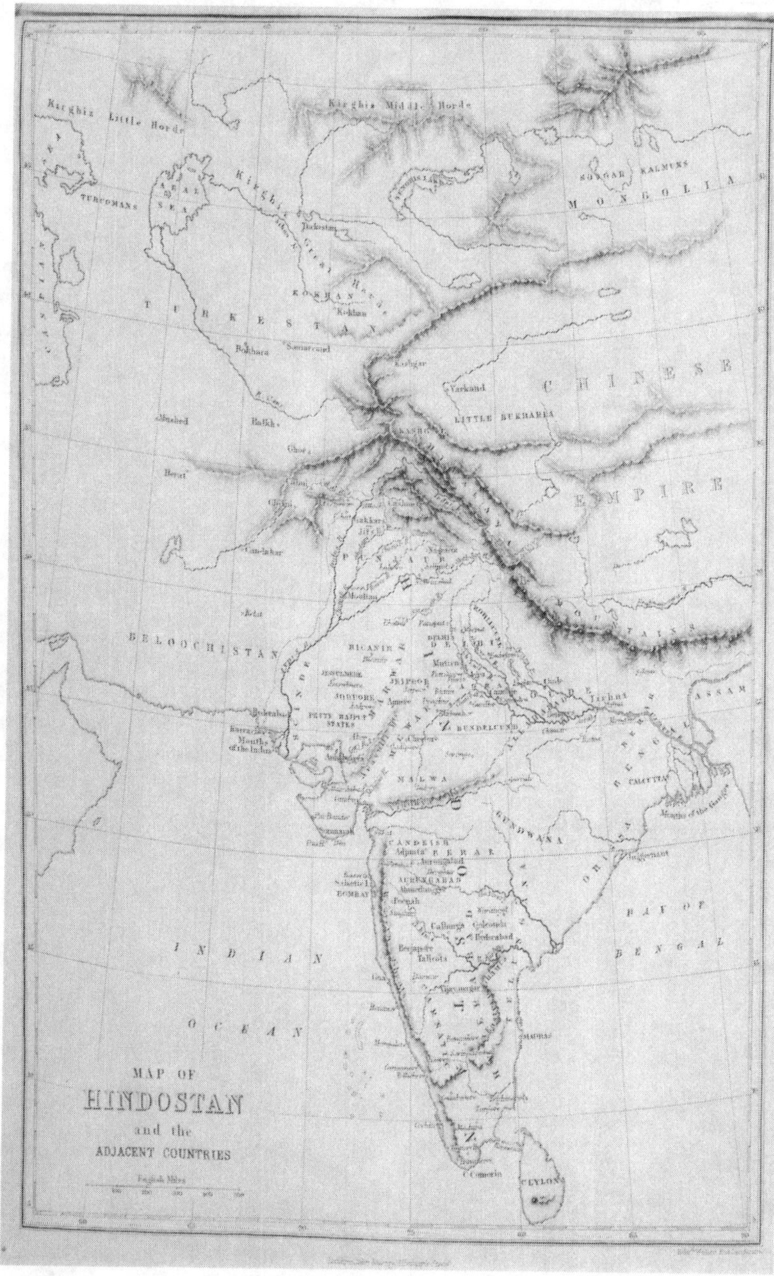
MAP OF
HINDOSTAN
and the
ADJACENT COUNTRIES
English Miles
Kirghiz Little Horde
Kirghiz Middle Horde
ARAL SEA
TURCOMANS
SONGAR KALMUKS
MONGOLIA
TURKESTAN
KOKHAN
Bokhara
Samarcand
Kashgar
Yarkand
LITTLE BUKHARIA
CHINESE
EMPIRE
Balkh
Herat
Candahar
BELOOCHISTAN
BICANIR
JEYPOOR
JODPORE
BUNDELCUND
MALWA
ASSAM
CALCUTTA
Mouths of the Ganges
GUNDWANA
CANDEISH
BERAR
AURUNGABAD
BOMBAY
Poonah
Hyderabad
BAY OF
BENGAL
INDIAN
OCEAN
MADRAS
C. Comorin
CEYLON

ALBEMARLE STREET, LONDON,
January, 1866.

MR. MURRAY'S

GENERAL LIST OF WORKS.

ALBERT (PRINCE). THE SPEECHES AND ADDRESSES of H.R.H. THE PRINCE CONSORT, on Public Occasions; with an Introduction giving some Outlines of his Character. Portrait. 8vo. 10*s*. 6*d*.; or Popular Edition. Portrait. Fcap. 8vo, 1*s*.

ABBOTT'S (REV. J.) Philip Musgrave; or, Memoirs of a Church of England Missionary in the North American Colonies. Post 8vo. 2*s*.

ABERCROMBIE'S (JOHN) Enquiries concerning the Intellectual Powers and the Investigation of Truth. 14*th Edition*. Fcap. 8vo. 6*s*. 6*d*.

——— Philosophy of the Moral Feelings. 13*th Edition*. Fcap. 8vo. 4*s*.

ACLAND'S (REV. CHARLES) Popular Account of the Manners and Customs of India. Post 8vo. 2*s*.

ÆSOP'S FABLES. A New Translation. With Historical Preface. By Rev. THOMAS JAMES. With 100 Woodcuts, by TENNIEL and WOLF. 50*th Thousand*. Post 8vo. 2*s*. 6*d*.

AGRICULTURAL (THE) JOURNAL. Of the Royal Agricultural Society of England. 8vo. *Published half-yearly*.

AIDS TO FAITH: a Series of Theological Essays. By various Writers. Edited by WILLIAM THOMSON, D.D., Lord Archbishop of York. 8vo. 9*s*.

CONTENTS.

Rev. H. L. MANSEL—*Miracles*.
BISHOP OF KILLALOE—*Christian Evidences*.
Rev. DR. MCCAUL—*Prophecy and the Mosaic Record of Creation*.
Rev. CANON COOK — *Ideology and Subscription*.
Rev. GEORGE RAWLINSON—*The Pentateuch*.
ARCHBISHOP OF YORK—*Doctrine of the Atonement*.
BISHOP OF ELY.—*Inspiration*.
BISHOP OF GLOUCESTER AND BRISTOL.—*Scripture and its Interpretation*.

AMBER-WITCH (THE). The most interesting Trial for Witchcraft ever known. Translated from the German by LADY DUFF GORDON. Post 8vo. 2*s*.

ARMY LIST (THE). *Published Monthly by Authority*. 18mo. 1*s*. 6*d*.

ARTHUR'S (LITTLE) History of England. By LADY CALLCOTT. 150*th Thousand*. Woodcuts. Fcap. 8vo. 2*s*. 6*d*.

ATKINSON'S (MRS.) Recollections of Tartar Steppes and their Inhabitants. Illustrations. Post 8vo. 12*s*.

AUNT IDA'S Walks and Talks; a Story Book for Children. By a LADY. Woodcuts. 16mo. 5*s*.

AUSTIN'S (JOHN) LECTURES ON JURISPRUDENCE; or, the Philosophy of Positive Law. 3 Vols. 8vo. 39*s*.

——— (SARAH) Fragments from German Prose Writers. With Biographical Notes. Post 8vo. 10*s*.

B

ADMIRALTY PUBLICATIONS; Issued by direction of the Lords Commissioners of the Admiralty:—

A MANUAL OF SCIENTIFIC ENQUIRY, for the Use of Travellers. Edited by Sir JOHN F. HERSCHEL, and Rev. ROBERT MAIN. *Third Edition.* Woodcuts. Post 8vo. 9*s.*

AIRY'S ASTRONOMICAL OBSERVATIONS MADE AT GREENWICH. 1836 to 1847. Royal 4to. 50*s.* each.

——— ASTRONOMICAL RESULTS. 1848 to 1858. 4to. 8*s.* each.

——— APPENDICES TO THE ASTRONOMICAL OBSERVATIONS.

1836.—I. Bessel's Refraction Tables.
II. Tables for converting Errors of R.A. and N.P.D. into Errors of Longitude and Ecliptic P.D. } 8*s.*

1837.—I. Logarithms of Sines and Cosines to every Ten Seconds of Time.
II. Table for converting Sidereal into Mean Solar Time. } 8*s.*

1842.—Catalogue of 1439 Stars. 8*s.*
1845.—Longitude of Valentia. 8*s.*
1847.—Twelve Years' Catalogue of Stars. 14*s.*
1851.—Maskelyne's Ledger of Stars. 6*s.*
1852.—I. Description of the Transit Circle. 5*s.*
II. Regulations of the Royal Observatory. 2*s.*
1853.—Bessel's Refraction Tables. 3*s.*
1854.—I. Description of the Zenith Tube. 3*s.*
II. Six Years' Catalogue of Stars. 10*s.*
1856.—Description of the Galvanic Apparatus at Greenwich Observatory. 8*s.*
1862.—I. Seven Years' Catalogue of Stars. 10*s.*
II. Plan of the Building and Ground of the Royal Observatory, Greenwich.
III. Longitude of Valentia. } 3*s.*

——— MAGNETICAL AND METEOROLOGICAL OBSERVATIONS. 1840 to 1847. Royal 4to. 50*s.* each.

——— ASTRONOMICAL, MAGNETICAL, AND METEOROLOGICAL OBSERVATIONS, 1848 to 1863. Royal 4to. 50*s.* each.

——— ASTRONOMICAL RESULTS. 1848 to 1863. 4to.

——— MAGNETICAL AND METEOROLOGICAL RESULTS. 1848 to 1863. 4to. 8*s.* each.

——— REDUCTION OF THE OBSERVATIONS OF PLANETS. 1750 to 1830. Royal 4to. 50*s.*

——————— LUNAR OBSERVATIONS. 1750 to 1830. 2 Vols. Royal 4to. 50*s.* each.

——————— 1831 to 1851. 4to. 20*s.*

BERNOULLI'S SEXCENTENARY TABLE. *London,* 1779. 4to.

BESSEL'S AUXILIARY TABLES FOR HIS METHOD OF CLEARING LUNAR DISTANCES. 8vo.

——— FUNDAMENTA ASTRONOMIÆ: *Regiomontii,* 1818. Folio. 60*s.*

BIRD'S METHOD OF CONSTRUCTING MURAL QUADRANTS. *London,* 1768. 4to. 2*s.* 6*d.*

——— METHOD OF DIVIDING ASTRONOMICAL INSTRUMENTS. *London,* 1767. 4to. 2*s.* 6*d.*

COOK, KING, AND BAYLY'S ASTRONOMICAL OBSERVATIONS. *London,* 1782. 4to. 21*s.*

ENCKE'S BERLINER JAHRBUCH, for 1830. *Berlin,* 1828. 8vo. 9*s.*

GROOMBRIDGE'S CATALOGUE OF CIRCUMPOLAR STARS. 4to. 10*s.*

ADMIRALTY PUBLICATIONS—*continued.*

HANSEN'S TABLES DE LA LUNE. 4to. 20*s.*

HARRISON'S PRINCIPLES OF HIS TIME-KEEPER. PLATES 1797. 4to. 5*s.*

HUTTON'S TABLES OF THE PRODUCTS AND POWERS OF NUMBERS. 1781. Folio. 7*s.* 6*d.*

LAX'S TABLES FOR FINDING THE LATITUDE AND LONGITUDE. 1821. 8vo. 10*s.*

LUNAR OBSERVATIONS at GREENWICH. 1783 to 1819. Compared with the Tables, 1821. 4to. 7*s.* 6*d.*

MASKELYNE'S ACCOUNT OF THE GOING OF HARRISON'S WATCH. 1767. 4to. 2*s.* 6*d.*

MAYER'S DISTANCES of the MOON'S CENTRE from the PLANETS. 1822, 3*s.*; 1823, 4*s.* 6*d.* 1824 to 1835, 8vo. 4*s.* each.

——— THEORIA LUNÆ JUXTA SYSTEMA NEWTONIANUM. 4to. 2*s.* 6*d.*

——— TABULÆ MOTUUM SOLIS ET LUNÆ. 1770. 4to. 5*s.*

——— ASTRONOMICAL OBSERVATIONS MADE AT GOTTINGEN, from 1756 to 1761. 1826. Folio. 7*s.* 6*d.*

NAUTICAL ALMANACS, from 1767 to 1869. 8vo. 2*s.* 6*d.* each.

——— SELECTIONS FROM THE ADDITIONS up to 1812. 8vo. 5*s.* 1834-54. 8vo. 5*s.*

——— SUPPLEMENTS, 1828 to 1833, 1837 and 1838. 8vo. 2*s.* each.

——— TABLE requisite to be used with the N.A. 1781. 8vo. 5*s.*

POND'S ASTRONOMICAL OBSERVATIONS. 1811 to 1835. 4to. 21*s.* each.

RAMSDEN'S ENGINE for DIVIDING MATHEMATICAL INSTRUMENTS. 4to. 5*s.*

——— ENGINE for DIVIDING STRAIGHT LINES. 4to. 5*s.*

SABINE'S PENDULUM EXPERIMENTS to DETERMINE THE FIGURE OF THE EARTH. 1825. 4to. 40*s.*

SHEPHERD'S TABLES for CORRECTING LUNAR DISTANCES. 1772. Royal 4to. 21*s.*

——— TABLES, GENERAL, of the MOON'S DISTANCE from the SUN, and 10 STARS. 1787. Folio. 5*s.* 6*d.*

TAYLOR'S SEXAGESIMAL TABLE. 1780. 4to. 15*s.*

——— TABLES OF LOGARITHMS. 4to. 3*l.*

TIARK'S ASTRONOMICAL OBSERVATIONS for the LONGITUDE of MADEIRA. 1822. 4to. 5*s.*

——— CHRONOMETRICAL OBSERVATIONS for DIFFERENCES of LONGITUDE between DOVER, PORTSMOUTH, and FALMOUTH. 1823. 4to. 5*s.*

VENUS and JUPITER: OBSERVATIONS of, compared with the TABLES. *London*, 1822. 4to. 2*s.*

WALES' AND BAYLY'S ASTRONOMICAL OBSERVATIONS. 1777. 4to. 21*s.*

WALES' REDUCTION OF ASTRONOMICAL OBSERVATIONS MADE IN THE SOUTHERN HEMISPHERE. 1764—1771. 1788. 4to. 10*s.* 6*d.*

BAIKIE'S (W. B.) Narrative of an Exploring Voyage up the Rivers Quorra and Tshadda in 1854. Map. 8vo. 16*s.*

BANKES' (THE HON. GEORGE) STORY OF CORFE CASTLE, with documents relating to the Time of the Civil Wars, &c. Woodcuts. Post 8vo. 10*s.* 6*d.*

BARBAULD'S (MRS.) Hymns in Prose for Children. With 112 Original Designs. Small 4to. 5*s.* Or Fine Paper, 7*s.* 6*d.*

BARROW'S (SIR JOHN) Autobiographical Memoir, including Reflections, Observations, and Reminiscences at Home and Abroad. From Early Life to Advanced Age. Portrait. 8vo. 16*s.*

——— Voyages of Discovery and Research within the Arctic Regions, from 1818 to the present time. 8vo. 15*s.*

——— Life, Exploits, and Voyages of Sir Francis Drake. With numerous Original Letters. Post 8vo. 2*s.*

BARRY'S (SIR CHARLES) Life. By his Son, Rev. Alfred Barry, D.D. With Illustrations. 8vo. (*In the Press.*)

BATES' (H. W.) Records of a Naturalist on the River Amazons during eleven years of Adventure and Travel. *Second Edition.* Illustrations. Post 8vo. 12*s.*

BEES AND FLOWERS. Two Essays. By Rev. Thomas James. Reprinted from the "Quarterly Review." Fcap. 8vo. 1*s.* each.

BERTHA'S Journal during a Visit to her Uncle in England. Containing a Variety of Interesting and Instructive Information. *Seventh Edition.* Woodcuts. 12mo.

BIRCH'S (SAMUEL) History of Ancient Pottery and Porcelain: Egyptian, Assyrian, Greek, Roman, and Etruscan. With 200 Illustrations. 2 Vols. Medium 8vo. 42*s.*

BLUNT'S (REV. J. J.) Undesigned Coincidences in the Writings of the Old and New Testament, an Argument of their Veracity: containing the Books of Moses, Historical and Prophetical Scriptures, and the Gospels and Acts. *9th Edition.* Post 8vo. 6*s.*

——— History of the Church in the First Three Centuries. *Third Edition.* Post 8vo. 7*s.* 6*d.*

——— Parish Priest; His Duties, Acquirements and Obligations. *Fourth Edition.* Post 8vo. 7*s.* 6*d.*

——— Lectures on the Right Use of the Early Fathers. *Second Edition.* 8vo. 15*s.*

——— Plain Sermons Preached to a Country Congregation. *Second Edition.* 3 Vols. Post 8vo. 7*s.* 6*d.* each.

——— Essays on various subjects. 8vo. 12*s.*

BISSET'S (ANDREW) History of England during the Interregnum, from the Death of Charles I. to the Battle of Dunbar, 1648–50. Chiefly from the MSS. in the State Paper Office. 8vo. 15*s.*

BERTRAM'S (JAS. G.) Harvest of the Sea: a Contribution to the Natural and Economic History of British Food Fishes. With 50 Illustrations. 21*s.*

BLAKISTON'S (CAPT.) Narrative of the Expedition sent to explore the Upper Waters of the Yang-Tsze. Illustrations. 8vo. 18*s.*

BLOMFIELD'S (BISHOP) Memoir, with Selections from his Correspondence. By his Son. *2nd Edition.* Portrait, post 8vo. 12*s.*

BOOK OF COMMON PRAYER. Illustrated with Coloured Borders, Initial Letters, and Woodcuts. A new edition. 8vo. 18*s.* cloth; 31*s.* 6*d.* calf; 36*s.* morocco.

BORROW'S (GEORGE) Bible in Spain; or the Journeys, Adventures, and Imprisonments of an Englishman in an Attempt to circulate the Scriptures in the Peninsula. 3 Vols. Post 8vo. 27*s.*; or *Popular Edition*, 16mo, 3*s.* 6*d.*

——— Zincali, or the Gipsies of Spain; their Manners, Customs, Religion, and Language. 2 Vols. Post 8vo. 18*s.*; or *Popular Edition*, 16mo, 3*s.* 6*d.*

——— Lavengro; The Scholar—The Gipsy—and the Priest. Portrait. 3 Vols. Post 8vo. 30*s.*

——— Romany Rye; a Sequel to Lavengro. *Second Edition.* 2 Vols. Post 8vo. 21*s.*

——— WILD WALES: its People, Language, and Scenery. *Popular Edition.* Post 8vo., 6*s.*

BOSWELL'S (JAMES) Life of Samuel Johnson, LL.D. Including the Tour to the Hebrides. Edited by Mr. CROKER. Portraits. Royal 8vo. 10*s.*

BRACE'S (C. L.) History of the Races of the Old World. Post 8vo. 9*s.*

BRAY'S (MRS.) Life of Thomas Stothard, R.A. With Personal Reminiscences. Illustrated with Portrait and 60 Woodcuts of his chief works. 4to.

BREWSTER'S (SIR DAVID) Martyrs of Science, or the Lives of Galileo, Tycho Brahe, and Kepler. *Fourth Edition.* Fcap. 8vo. 4*s.* 6*d.*

——— More Worlds than One. The Creed of the Philosopher and the Hope of the Christian. *Eighth Edition.* Post 8vo. 6*s.*

——— Stereoscope: its History, Theory, Construction, and Application to the Arts and to Education. Woodcuts. 12mo. 5*s.* 6*d.*

——— Kaleidoscope: its History, Theory, and Construction, with its application to the Fine and Useful Arts. *Second Edition.* Woodcuts. Post 8vo. 5*s.* 6*d.*

BRINE'S (Capt.) Narrative of the Rise and Progress of the Taeping Rebellion in China. Plans. Post 8vo. 10*s.* 6*d.*

BRITISH ASSOCIATION REPORTS. 8vo. York and Oxford, 1831-32, 13*s.* 6*d.* Cambridge, 1833, 12*s.* Edinburgh, 1834, 15*s.* Dublin, 1835, 13*s.* 6*d.* Bristol, 1836, 12*s.* Liverpool, 1837, 16*s.* 6*d.* Newcastle, 1838, 15*s.* Birmingham, 1839, 13*s.* 6*d.* Glasgow, 1840, 15*s.* Plymouth, 1841, 13*s.* 6*d.* Manchester, 1842, 10*s.* 6*d.* Cork, 1843, 12*s.* York, 1844, 20*s.* Cambridge, 1845, 12*s.* Southampton, 1846, 15*s.* Oxford, 1847, 18*s.* Swansea, 1848, 9*s.* Birmingham, 1849, 10*s.* Edinburgh, 1850, 15*s.* Ipswich, 1851, 16*s.* 6*d.* Belfast, 1852, 15*s.* Hull, 1853, 10*s.* 6*d.* Liverpool, 1854, 18*s.* Glasgow, 1855, 15*s.*; Cheltenham, 1856, 18*s.*; Dublin, 1857, 15*s.*; Leeds, 1858, 20*s.* Aberdeen, 1859, 15*s.* Oxford, 1860, 25*s.* Manchester, 1861, 15*s.* Cambridge, 1862, 20*s.* Newcastle, 1863, 25*s.* Bath, 1864, 25*s.*

BROUGHTON'S (LORD) Journey through Albania and other Provinces of Turkey in Europe and Asia, to Constantinople, 1809—10. *Third Edition.* Illustrations. 2 Vols. 8vo. 30*s.*

——— Visits to Italy. 3*rd Edition.* 2 vols. Post 8vo. 18*s.*

BRITISH CLASSICS. A New Series of Standard English Authors, printed from the most correct text, and edited with notes. 8vo.

Already Published.

I. GOLDSMITH'S WORKS. Edited by PETER CUNNINGHAM, F.S.A. Vignettes. 4 Vols. 30*s*.

II. GIBBON'S DECLINE AND FALL OF THE ROMAN EMPIRE. Edited by WILLIAM SMITH, LL.D. Portrait and Maps. 8 Vols. 60*s*.

III. JOHNSON'S LIVES OF THE ENGLISH POETS. Edited by PETER CUNNINGHAM, F.S.A. 3 Vols. 22*s*. 6*d*.

IV. BYRON'S POETICAL WORKS. Edited, with Notes. 6 vols. 45*s*.

In Preparation.

LIFE AND WORKS OF POPE. Edited by REV. WHITWELL ELWIN.

HUME'S HISTORY OF ENGLAND. Edited, with Notes.

LIFE AND WORKS OF SWIFT. Edited by JOHN FORSTER.

BUBBLES FROM THE BRUNNEN OF NASSAU. By an Old MAN. *7th Edition*, with Illustrations. Post 8vo. 7*s*. 6*d*.

BUNYAN (JOHN) and Oliver Cromwell. Select Biographies. By ROBERT SOUTHEY. Post 8vo. 2*s*.

BUONAPARTE'S (NAPOLEON) Confidential Correspondence with his Brother Joseph, sometime King of Spain. *Second Edition*. 2 vols. 8vo. 26*s*.

BURGON'S (Rev. J. W.) Christian Gentleman; or, Memoir of Patrick Fraser Tytler. *Second Edition*. Post 8vo. 9*s*.

——— Letters from Rome, written to Friends at Home. Illustrations. Post 8vo. 12*s*.

BURN'S (COL.) Dictionary of Naval and Military Technical Terms, English and French, and French and English. *Fourth Edition*. Crown 8vo. 15*s*.

BURR'S (G. D.) Instructions in Practical Surveying, Topographical Plan Drawing, and on sketching ground without Instruments. *Fourth Edition*. Woodcuts. Post 8vo. 6*s*.

BUTTMAN'S LEXILOGUS; a Critical Examination of the Meaning of numerous Greek Words, chiefly in Homer and Hesiod. Translated by Rev. J. R. FISHLAKE. *Fifth Edition*. 8vo. 12*s*.

——— CATALOGUE OF IRREGULAR GREEK VERBS. With all the Tenses extant—their Formation, Meaning, and Usage, accompanied by an Index. Translated, with Notes, by Rev. J. R. FISHLAKE. *Fifth Edition*. Revised by Rev. E. VENABLES. Post 8vo.

BUXTON'S (SIR FOWELL) Memoirs. With Selections from his Correspondence. By his Son. Portrait. 8vo. 15*s*. *Abridged Edition*, Portrait. Fcap. 8vo. 2*s*. 6*d*.

——— (CHARLES, M.P.) IDEAS OF THE DAY ON POLICY. 8vo.

BYRON'S (LORD) Life, Letters, and Journals. By THOMAS MOORE. Plates. 6 Vols. Fcap. 8vo. 18*s.*

——— Life, Letters, and Journals. By THOMAS MOORE. Portraits. Royal 8vo. 9*s.*

——— Poetical Works. Portrait. 6 Vols. 8vo. 45*s.*

——— Poetical Works. Plates. 10 Vols. Fcap. 8vo. 30*s.*

——— Poetical Works. 8 Vols. 24mo. 20*s.*

——— Poetical Works. Plates. Royal 8vo. 9*s.*

——— Poetical Works. Portrait. Crown 8vo. 6*s.*

——— Childe Harold. With 80 Engravings. Small 4to. 21*s.*

——— Childe Harold. With 30 Vignettes. 12mo. 6*s.*

——— Childe Harold. 16mo. 2*s.* 6*d.*

——— Childe Harold. Vignettes. 16mo. 1*s.*

——— Childe Harold. Portrait. 16mo. 6*d.*

——— Tales and Poems. 24mo. 2*s.* 6*d.*

——— Miscellaneous. 2 Vols. 24mo. 5*s.*

——— Dramas and Plays. 2 Vols. 24mo. 5*s.*

——— Don Juan and Beppo. 2 Vols. 24mo. 5*s.*

——— Beauties. Selected from his Poetry and Prose. Portrait, Fcap. 8vo. 3*s.* 6*d.*

CARNARVON'S (LORD) Portugal, Gallicia, and the Basque Provinces. From Notes made during a Journey to those Countries. *Third Edition.* Post 8vo. 3*s.* 6*d.*

——— Recollections of the Druses of Lebanon. With Notes on their Religion. *Third Edition.* Post 8vo. 5*s.* 6*d.*

CAMPBELL'S (LORD) Lives of the Lord Chancellors and Keepers of the Great Seal of England. From the Earliest Times to the Death of Lord Eldon in 1838. *Fourth Edition.* 10 Vols. Crown 8vo. 6*s.* each.

——— Lives of the Chief Justices of England. From the Norman Conquest to the Death of Lord Tenterden. *Second Edition.* 3 Vols. 8vo. 42*s.*

——— Shakspeare's Legal Acquirements Considered. 8vo. 5*s.* 6*d.*

——— Life of Lord Chancellor Bacon. Fcap. 8vo. 2*s.* 6*d.*

——— (GEORGE) Modern India. A Sketch of the System of Civil Government. With some Account of the Natives and Native Institutions. *Second Edition.* 8vo. 16*s.*

——— India as it may be. An Outline of a proposed Government and Policy. 8vo. 12*s.*

——— (THOS.) Short Lives of the British Poets. With an Essay on English Poetry. Post 8vo. 3*s.* 6*d.*

CALLCOTT'S (LADY) Little Arthur's History of England. 150*th Thousand.* With Woodcuts. Fcap. 8vo. 2*s.* 6*d.*

CASTLEREAGH (The) DESPATCHES, from the commencement of the official career of the late Viscount Castlereagh to the close of his life. Edited by the Marquis of Londonderry. 12 Vols. 8vo. 14*s*. each.

CATHCART'S (Sir George) Commentaries on the War in Russia and Germany, 1812-13. Plans. 8vo. 14*s*.

CAVALCASELLE and CROWE'S History of Painting in Italy, from the Second to the Sixteenth Century, from recent researches, as well as from personal inspection of the Works of Art in that Country. With 70 Illustrations. Vols. I. and II. 8vo. 42*s*.

——— **Notices of the Lives and Works of the** Early Flemish Painters. Woodcuts. Post 8vo. 12*s*.

CHARMED ROE (The); or, The Story of the Little Brother and Sister. By Otto Speckter. Plates. 16mo. 5*s*.

CHORLEY'S (H. F.) STUDIES OF THE MUSIC OF MANY NATIONS; including the Substance of a Course of Lectures delivered at the Royal Institution. 8vo. (*In the Press.*)

CHURTON'S (Archdeacon) Gongora. An Historical Essay on the Age of Philip III. and IV. of Spain. With Translations. Portrait. 2 Vols. Small 8vo. 15*s*.

CICERO: HIS LIFE AND TIMES. With his Character viewed as a Statesman, Orator, and Friend. With a Selection from his Correspondence and Orations. By William Forsyth, Q.C. With Illustrations, 2 vols. Post 8vo. 18*s*.

CLAUSEWITZ'S (Carl Von) Campaign of 1812, in Russia. Translated from the German by Lord Ellesmere. Map. 8vo. 10*s*. 6*d*.

CLIVE'S (Lord) Life. By Rev. G. R. Gleig, M.A. Post 8vo. 3*s*. 6*d*.

COLCHESTER (The) PAPERS. The Diary and Correspondence of Charles Abbott, Lord Colchester, Speaker of the House of Commons, 1802-1817. Edited by his Son. Portrait. 3 Vols. 8vo. 42*s*.

COLERIDGE (Samuel Taylor). Specimens of his Table-Talk. *New Edition.* Portrait. Fcap. 8vo. 6*s*.

COLONIAL LIBRARY. [See Home and Colonial Library.]

COOK'S (Rev. Canon) Sermons Preached at Lincoln's Inn Chapel, and on Special Occasions. 8vo. 9*s*.

COOKERY (Modern Domestic). Founded on Principles of Economy and Practical Knowledge, and adapted for Private Families. By a Lady. *New Edition.* Woodcuts. Fcap. 8vo. 5*s*.

CORNWALLIS (The) Papers and Correspondence during the American War,—Administrations in India,—Union with Ireland, and Peace of Amiens. Edited by Charles Ross. *Second Edition.* 3 Vols. 8vo. 63*s*.

COWPER'S (Mary, Countess) Diary while Lady of the Bedchamber to Caroline Princess of Wales, 1714—20. Edited by Hon. Spencer Cowper. *Second Edition.* Portrait. 8vo. 10*s*. 6*d*.

CRABBE'S (Rev. George) Life, Letters, and Journals. By his Son. Portrait. Fcap. 8vo. 3*s*.

——— **Life and Poetical Works. Plates. 8 Vols. Fcap.** 8vo. 24*s*.

——— **Life and Poetical Works. Plates. Royal 8vo. 7*s*.**

CROKER'S (J. W.) Progressive Geography for Children. *Fifth Edition.* 18mo. 1*s.* 6*d.*

——— Stories for Children, Selected from the History of England. *Fifteenth Edition.* Woodcuts. 16mo. 2*s.* 6*d.*

——— Boswell's Life of Johnson. Including the Tour to the Hebrides. Portraits. Royal 8vo. 10*s.*

——— Essays on the Early Period of the French Revolution. 8vo. 15*s.*

——— Historical Essay on the Guillotine. Fcap. 8vo. 1*s.*

CROMWELL (OLIVER) and John Bunyan. By ROBERT SOUTHEY. Post 8vo. 2*s.*

CROWE'S AND CAVALCASELLE'S Notices of the Early Flemish Painters; their Lives and Works. Woodcuts. Post 8vo. 12*s.*

——— History of Painting in Italy, from 2nd to 16th Century. Derived from Historical Researches as well as inspection of the Works of Art in that Country. With 70 Illustrations. Vols. I. and II. 8vo. 42*s.*

CUMMING'S (R. GORDON) Five Years of a Hunter's Life in the Far Interior of South Africa; with Anecdotes of the Chace, and Notices of the Native Tribes. *New Edition.* Woodcuts. Post 8vo. 5*s.*

CUNNINGHAM'S (ALLAN) Poems and Songs. Now first collected and arranged, with Biographical Notice. 24mo. 2*s.* 6*d.*

CURETON (REV. W.) Remains of a very Ancient Recension of the Four Gospels in Syriac, hitherto unknown in Europe. Discovered, Edited, and Translated. 4to. 24*s.*

CURTIUS' (PROFESSOR) Student's Greek Grammar, for the use of Colleges and the Upper Forms. Translated under the Author's revision. Edited by DR. WM. SMITH. Post 8vo. 7*s.* 6*d.*

——— Smaller Greek Grammar for the use of the Middle and Lower Forms, abridged from the above. 12mo. 3*s.* 6*d.*

——— First Greek Course; containing Delectus, Exercise Book, and Vocabularies. 12mo. 3*s.* 6*d.*

CURZON'S (HON. ROBERT) ARMENIA AND ERZEROUM. A Year on the Frontiers of Russia, Turkey, and Persia. *Third Edition.* Woodcuts. Post 8vo. 7*s.* 6*d.*

——— Visits to the Monasteries of the Levant. *Fifth Edition.* Illustrations. Post 8vo. 7*s.* 6*d.*

CUST'S (GENERAL) Annals of the Wars of the 18th & 19th Centuries. 9 Vols. Fcap. 8vo. 5*s.* each.

——— Lives and Characters of the Warriors of the 17th Century who have Commanded Fleets and Armies before the Enemy. 2 Vols. Post 8vo. 16*s.*

DARWIN'S (CHARLES) Journal of Researches into the Natural History of the Countries visited during a Voyage round the World. Post 8vo. 9*s.*

——— Origin of Species by Means of Natural Selection; or, the Preservation of Favoured Races in the Struggle for Life. Post 8vo. 14*s.*

——— Fertilization of Orchids through Insect Agency, and as to the good of Intercrossing. Woodcuts. Post 8vo. 9*s.*

——— Domesticated Animals and Cultivated Plants; or, the Principles of Variation, Inheritance, Re-version, Crossing, Inter breeding, and Selection under Domestication. With Illustrations. Post 8vo. (*In Preparation.*)

DAVIS'S (NATHAN) Visit to the Ruined Cities of Numidia and Carthaginia. Illustrations. 8vo. 16s.

——— (SIR J. F.) Chinese Miscellanies: a Collection of Essays and Notes. Post 8vo. 6s.

DAVY'S (SIR HUMPHRY) Consolations in Travel; or, Last Days of a Philosopher. *Fifth Edition.* Woodcuts. Fcap. 8vo. 6s.

——— Salmonia; or, Days of Fly Fishing. *Fourth Edition.* Woodcuts. Fcap. 8vo. 6s.

DELEPIERRE'S (OCTAVE) History of Flemish Literature. From the Twelfth Century. 8vo. 9s.

DENNIS' (GEORGE) Cities and Cemeteries of Etruria. Plates. 2 Vols. 8vo. 42s.

DERBY'S (EDWARD, EARL OF) Translation of the Iliad of Homer into English Blank Verse. *Fifth Edition, Revised.* 2 Vols. 8vo. 24s.

DIXON'S (W. HEPWORTH) Story of the Life of Lord Bacon. Portrait. Fcap. 8vo. 7s. 6d.

DOG-BREAKING; the Most Expeditious, Certain, and Easy Method, whether great excellence or only mediocrity be required. With a Few Hints for those who Love the Dog and the Gun. By LIEUT.-GEN. HUTCHINSON. *Fourth Edition.* With 40 Woodcuts. Crown 8vo. 15s.

DOMESTIC MODERN COOKERY. Founded on Principles of Economy and Practical Knowledge, and adapted for Private Families. *New Edition.* Woodcuts. Fcap. 8vo. 5s.

DOUGLAS'S (GENERAL SIR HOWARD) Life and Adventures; From Notes, Conversations, and Correspondence. By S. W. FULLOM. Portrait. 8vo. 15s.

——— Theory and Practice of Gunnery. *5th Edition.* Plates. 8vo. 21s.

——— Military Bridges, and the Passage of Rivers in Military Operations. *Third Edition.* Plates. 8vo. 21s.

——— Naval Warfare with Steam. *Second Edition.* 8vo. 8s. 6d.

——— Modern Systems of Fortification, with special reference to the Naval, Littoral, and Internal Defence of England. Plans. 8vo. 12s.

DRAKE'S (SIR FRANCIS) Life, Voyages, and Exploits, by Sea and Land. By JOHN BARROW. *Third Edition.* Post 8vo. 2s.

DRINKWATER'S (JOHN) History of the Siege of Gibraltar, 1779-1783. With a Description and Account of that Garrison from the Earliest Periods. Post 8vo. 2s.

DU CHAILLU'S (PAUL B.) EQUATORIAL AFRICA, with Accounts of the Gorilla, the Nest-building Ape, Chimpanzee, Crocodile, &c. Illustrations. 8vo. 21s.

DUFFERIN'S (LORD) Letters from High Latitudes, being some Account of a Yacht Voyage to Iceland, &c., in 1856. *Fourth Edition.* Woodcuts. Post 8vo.

——— Lispings from Low Latitudes, or the Journal of the Hon. Impulsia Gushington. With 24 Plates. 4to. 21s.

DYER'S (THOMAS H.) History of Modern Europe, from the taking of Constantinople by the Turks to the close of the War in the Crimea. 4 Vols. 8vo. 60*s*.

EASTLAKE'S (SIR CHARLES) Italian Schools of Painting. From the German of KUGLER. Edited, with Notes. *Third Edition*. Illustrated from the Old Masters. 2 Vols. Post 8vo. 30*s*.

EASTWICK'S (E. B.) Handbook for Bombay and Madras, with Directions for Travellers, Officers, &c. Map. 2 Vols. Post 8vo. 24*s*.

EDWARDS' (W. H.) Voyage up the River Amazon, including a Visit to Para. Post 8vo. 2*s*.

ELDON'S (LORD) Public and Private Life, with Selections from his Correspondence and Diaries. By HORACE TWISS. *Third Edition*. Portrait. 2 Vols. Post 8vo. 21*s*.

ELLIS (REV. W.) Visits to Madagascar, including a Journey to the Capital, with notices of Natural History, and Present Civilisation of the People. *Fifth Thousand*. Map and Woodcuts. 8vo. 16*s*.

——— (MRS.) Education of Character, with Hints on Moral Training. Post 8vo. 7*s*. 6*d*.

ELLESMERE'S (LORD) Two Sieges of Vienna by the Turks. Translated from the German. Post 8vo. 2*s*.

——————— Campaign of 1812 in Russia, from the German of General Carl Von Clausewitz. Map. 8vo. 10*s*. 6*d*.

——————— Poems. With Illustrations. Crown 4to.

——————— Essays on History, Biography, Geography, and Engineering. 8vo. 12*s*.

ELPHINSTONE'S (HON. MOUNTSTUART) History of India—the Hindoo and Mahomedan Periods. *Fifth Edition, Revised*. Map. 8vo. 18*s*.

ENGEL'S (CARL) Music of the Most Ancient Nations; particularly of the Assyrians, Egyptians, and Hebrews; with Special Reference to the Discoveries in Western Asia and in Egypt. With 100 Illustrations. 8vo. 16*s*.

ENGLAND (HISTORY OF) from the Peace of Utrecht to the Peace of Versailles, 1713–83. By LORD MAHON (Earl Stanhope). *Library Edition*, 7 Vols. 8vo. 93*s*.; or *Popular Edition*, 7 Vols. Post 8vo. 35*s*.

——————— From the First Invasion by the Romans, down to the Present Year of Queen Victoria's Reign. By MRS. MARKHAM. *New and Cheaper Edition*. Woodcuts. 12mo. 4*s*.

——————— (THE STUDENT'S HUME). From the Invasion of Julius Cæsar to the Revolution of 1688. By DAVID HUME. Corrected and continued to 1858. Edited by WM. SMITH, LL.D. Woodcuts. Post 8vo. 7*s*. 6*d*.

——————— A Smaller History of England for Young Persons. By DR. WM. SMITH. Woodcuts. 18mo. 3*s*. 6*d*.

——————— Little Arthur's History of England. By LADY CALLCOTT. Woodcuts. 18mo. 2*s*. 6*d*.

ENGLISHWOMAN IN AMERICA. Post 8vo. 10*s*. 6*d*.

ESKIMAUX and English Vocabulary, for Travellers in the Arctic Regions. 16mo. 3*s*. 6*d*.

ESSAYS FROM "THE TIMES." Being a Selection from the LITERARY PAPERS which have appeared in that Journal. *Seventh Thousand.* 2 vols. Fcap. 8vo. 8*s.*

ETHNOLOGICAL SOCIETY OF LONDON, TRANSACTIONS. New Series. Vols. I., II., and III. 8vo.

EXETER'S (BISHOP OF) Letters to the late Charles Butler, on the Theological parts of his Book of the Roman Catholic Church; with Remarks on certain Works of Dr. Milner and Dr. Lingard, and on some parts of the Evidence of Dr. Doyle. *Second Edition.* 8vo. 16*s.*

FAMILY RECEIPT-BOOK. A Collection of a Thousand Valuable and Useful Receipts. Fcap. 8vo. 5*s.* 6*d.*

FARRAR'S (REV. A. S.) Critical History of Free Thought in reference to the Christian Religion. Being the Bampton Lectures, 1862. 8vo. 16*s.*

——— (F. W.) Origin of Language, based on Modern Researches. Fcap. 8vo. 5*s.*

FEATHERSTONHAUGH'S (G. W.) Tour through the Slave States of North America, from the River Potomac to Texas and the Frontiers of Mexico. Plates. 2 Vols. 8vo. 26*s.*

FERGUSSON'S (JAMES) Palaces of Nineveh and Persepolis Restored. Woodcuts. 8vo. 16*s.*

——— History of Architecture in all Countries: from the Earliest Times to the Present Day. With 1200 Illustrations. 2 Vols. 8vo. Vol. I. 42*s.*

——— History of the Modern Styles of Architecture: forming the Third and Concluding Volume of the above work. With 312 Illustrations. 8vo. 31*s.* 6*d.*

——— Holy Sepulchre and the Temple at Jerusalem; being the Substance of Two Lectures delivered at the Royal Institution, 1862 and '65. Woodcuts. 8vo. 7*s.* 6*d.*

FISHER'S (REV. GEORGE) Elements of Geometry, for the Use of Schools. *Fifth Edition.* 18mo. 1*s.* 6*d.*

——— First Principles of Algebra, for the Use of Schools. *Fifth Edition.* 18mo. 1*s.* 6*d.*

FLOWER GARDEN (THE). By REV. THOS. JAMES. Fcap. 8vo. 1*s.*

FONNEREAU'S (T. G.) Diary of a Dutiful Son. Fcap. 8vo. 4*s.* 6*d.*

FORBES' (C. S.) Iceland; its Volcanoes, Geysers, and Glaciers. Illustrations. Post 8vo. 14*s.*

FORSTER'S (JOHN) Arrest of the Five Members by Charles the First. A Chapter of English History re-written. Post 8vo. 12*s.*

——— Grand Remonstrance, 1641. With an Essay on English freedom under the Plantagenet and Tudor Sovereigns. *Second Edition.* Post 8vo. 12*s.*

——— Sir John Eliot: a Biography, 1590—1632. With Portraits. 2 Vols. Crown 8vo. 30*s.*

——— Biographies of Oliver Cromwell, Daniel De Foe, Sir Richard Steele, Charles Churchill, Samuel Foote. *Third Edition.* Post 8vo. 12*s.*

FORD'S (RICHARD) Handbook for Spain, Andalusia, Ronda, Valencia, Catalonia, Granada, Gallicia, Arragon, Navarre, &c. *Third Edition.* 2 Vols. Post 8vo. 30s.

——— Gatherings from Spain. Post 8vo. 3s. 6d.

FORSYTH'S (WILLIAM) Life and Times of Cicero. With Selections from his Correspondence and Orations. Illustrations. 2 Vols. Post 8vo. 18s.

FORTUNE'S (ROBERT) Narrative of Two Visits to the Tea Countries of China, 1843-52. *Third Edition.* Woodcuts. 2 Vols. Post 8vo. 18s.

——— Third Visit to China. 1853-6. Woodcuts. 8vo. 16s.

——— Yedo and Peking. With Notices of the Agriculture and Trade of China, during a Fourth Visit to that Country. Illustrations. 8vo. 16s.

FOSS' (Edward) Judges of England. With Sketches of their Lives, and Notices of the Courts at Westminster, from the Conquest to the Present Time. 9 Vols. 8vo. 114s.

FRANCE (HISTORY OF). From the Conquest by the Gauls to Recent Times. By Mrs. MARKHAM. *New and Chaper Edition.* Woodcuts. 12mo. 4s.

——— (THE STUDENT'S HISTORY OF). From the Earliest Times to the Establishment of the Second Empire, 1852. By W. H. PEARSON. Edited by WM. SMITH, LL.D. Woodcuts. Post 8vo. 7s. 6d.

FRENCH (THE) in Algiers; The Soldier of the Foreign Legion—and the Prisoners of Abd-el-Kadir. Translated by Lady DUFF GORDON. Post 8vo. 2s.

GALTON'S (FRANCIS) Art of Travel; or, Hints on the Shifts and Contrivances available in Wild Countries. *Third Edition.* Woodcuts. Post 8vo. 7s. 6d.

GEOGRAPHY, ANCIENT (THE STUDENT'S MANUAL OF). By Rev. W. L. BEVAN. Woodcuts. Post 8vo. 7s. 6d.

——— MODERN (THE STUDENT'S MANUAL). By Rev. W. L. BEVAN. Woodcuts. Post 8vo. *In the Press.*

——— Journal of the Royal Geographical Society of London. 8vo.

GERMANY (HISTORY OF). From the Invasion by Marius, to Recent times. By Mrs. MARKHAM. *New and Cheaper Edition.* Woodcuts. 12mo. 4s.

GIBBON'S (EDWARD) History of the Decline and Fall of the Roman Empire. Edited, with Notes, by DEAN MILMAN and M. GUIZOT. *A New Edition.* Preceded by his Autobiography. And Edited, with Notes, by Dr. WM. SMITH. Maps. 8 Vols. 8vo. 60s.

——— (The Student's Gibbon); Being an Epitome of the above work, incorporating the Researches of Recent Commentators. By Dr. WM. SMITH. Woodcuts. Post 8vo. 7s. 6d.

GIFFARD'S (EDWARD) Deeds of Naval Daring; or, Anecdotes of the British Navy. New Edition. Fcap. 8vo. 3s. 6d.

GOLDSMITH'S (OLIVER) Works. A New Edition. Printed from the last editions revised by the Author. Edited by PETER CUNNINGHAM. Vignettes. 4 Vols. 8vo. 30s.

GLADSTONE'S (RIGHT HON. W. E.) Financial Statements of 1853, 60, 63, and 64; also his Speeches on Tax-Bills, 1861, and on Charities, 1863. *Second Edition.* 8vo. 12*s.*

——— Address on the Place of Ancient Greece in the Providential Order of the World. *Fourth Edition.* 8vo. 2*s.* 6*d.*

——— Wedgwood: an Address delivered at Burslem. Woodcuts. Post 8vo. 2*s.* *A Cheap Edition,* 1*s.*

GLEIG'S (REV. G. R.) Campaigns of the British Army at Washington and New Orleans. Post 8vo. 2*s.*

——— Story of the Battle of Waterloo. Post 8vo. 3*s.* 6*d.*

——— Narrative of Sale's Brigade in Affghanistan. Post 8vo. 2*s.*

——— Life of Robert Lord Clive. Post 8vo. 3*s.* 6*d.*

——— Life and Letters of Sir Thomas Munro. Post 8vo 3*s.* 6*d.*

GONGORA; An Historical Essay on the Times of Philip III. and IV. of Spain. With Illustrations. By ARCHDEACON CHURTON. Portrait. 2 vols. Post 8vo. 15*s.*

GORDON'S (SIR ALEX. DUFF) Sketches of German Life, and Scenes from the War of Liberation. From the German. Post 8vo. 3*s.* 6*d.*

——— (LADY DUFF) Amber-Witch: A Trial for Witchcraft. From the German. Post 8vo. 2*s.*

——— French in Algiers. 1. The Soldier of the Foreign Legion. 2. The Prisoners of Abd-el-Kadir. From the French. Post 8vo. 2*s.*

GOUGER'S (HENRY) Personal Narrative of Two Years' Imprisonment in Burmah. *Second Edition.* Woodcuts. Post 8vo. 12*s.*

GRAMMARS (LATIN and GREEK). See CURTIUS; SMITH; KING EDWARD VITH., &c. &c.

GREECE (THE STUDENT'S HISTORY OF). From the Earliest Times to the Roman Conquest. By WM. SMITH, LL.D. Woodcuts. Post 8vo. 7*s.* 6*d.*

——— (A SMALLER HISTORY OF, FOR YOUNG PERSONS). By DR. WM. SMITH. Woodcuts. 16mo. 3*s.* 6*d.*

GRENVILLE (THE) **PAPERS.** Being the Public and Private Correspondence of George Grenville, including his PRIVATE DIARY. Edited by W. J. SMITH. 4 Vols. 8vo. 16*s.* each.

GREY (EARL) on Parliamentary Government and Reform; with Suggestions for the Improvement of our Representative System, and an Examination of the Reform Bills of 1859—61. *Second Edition.* 8vo. 9*s.*

——— (SIR GEORGE) Polynesian Mythology, and Ancient Traditional History of the New Zealand Race. Woodcuts. Post 8vo. 10*s.* 6*d.*

GRUNER'S (LEWIS) Brick and Terra-Cotta Buildings of Lombardy, Fourteenth and Fifteenth Centuries. From careful Drawings and Restorations. Engraved and printed in Colours. Illustrations. Small folio. *Nearly Ready.*

GUIZOT'S (M.) Meditations on the Essence of Christianity, and on the Religious Questions of the Day. Post 8vo. 9*s.* 6*d.*

GROTE'S (GEORGE) **History of Greece. From the Earliest Times** to the close of the generation contemporary with the death of Alexander the Great. *Fourth Edition.* Maps. 8 vols. 8vo. 112*s.*

——— PLATO, and the other Companions of Socrates. 3 Vols. 8vo. 45*s.*

——— (MRS.) Memoir of Ary Scheffer. Post 8vo. 8*s.* 6*d.*

——— Collected Papers. 8vo. 10*s.* 6*d.*

HALLAM'S (HENRY) **Constitutional History of England, from the** Accession of Henry the Seventh to the Death of George the Second. *Seventh Edition.* 3 Vols. 8vo. 30*s.* Or Popular Edition, 3 Vols., Post 8vo, 18*s.*

——— History of Europe during the Middle Ages. *Tenth Edition.* 3 Vols. 8vo. 30*s.* Or Popular Edition, 3 Vols., Post 8vo, 18*s.*

——— Literary History of Europe, during the 15th, 16th and 17th Centuries. *Fourth Edition.* 3 Vols. 8vo. 36*s.* Or Popular Edition, 4 Vols., Post 8vo., 24*s.*

——— Literary Essays and Characters, Extracted from the above Work. Fcap. 8vo. 2*s.*

——— Historical Works. Containing History of England,—Middle Ages of Europe,—Literary History of Europe. 10 Vols. Post 8vo. 6*s.* each.

——— (ARTHUR) Remains; in Verse and Prose. With Preface, Memoir, and Portrait. Fcap. 8vo. 7*s.* 6*d.*

HAMILTON'S (JAMES) **Wanderings in North Africa.** With Illustrations. Post 8vo. 12*s.*

HART'S ARMY LIST. (*Quarterly and Annually.*) 8vo. 10*s.* 6*d.* and 21*s.* each.

HANNAH'S (REV. DR.) **Bampton Lectures for 1863; the Divine** and Human Elements in Holy Scripture. 8vo. 10*s.* 6*d.*

HAY'S (J. H. DRUMMOND) **Western Barbary, its wild Tribes and** savage Animals. Post 8vo. 2*s.*

HEAD'S (SIR FRANCIS) **Horse and his Rider.** Woodcuts. Post 8vo. 5*s.*

——— Rapid Journeys across the Pampas. Post 8vo. 2*s.*

——— Bubbles from the Brunnen of Nassau. With Illustrations. Post 8vo.

——— Emigrant. Fcap. 8vo. 2*s.* 6*d.*

——— Stokers and Pokers; or, N.-Western Railway. Post 8vo. 2*s.*

——— Fortnight in Ireland. Map. 8vo. 12*s.*

——— (SIR EDMUND) Shall and Will; or, Future Auxiliary Verbs. Fcap. 8vo. 4*s.*

HEBER'S (BISHOP) **Journey through the Upper Provinces of India,** from Calcutta to Bombay, with an Account of a Journey to Madras and the Southern Provinces. *Twelfth Edition.* 2 Vols. Post 8vo. 7*s.*

——— Poetical Works, including Palestine, Europe, The Red Sea, Hymns, &c. *Sixth Edition.* Portrait. Fcap. 8vo. 6*s.*

HERODOTUS. A New English Version. Edited, with Notes and Essays, historical, ethnographical, and geographical, by Rev. G. RAWLINSON, assisted by SIR HENRY RAWLINSON and SIR J. G. WILKINSON. *Second Edition.* Maps and Woodcuts. 4 Vols. 8vo. 48*s.*

HAND-BOOK—TRAVEL-TALK. English, French, German, and Italian. 18mo. 3s. 6d.

———— NORTH GERMANY, HOLLAND, BELGIUM, and the Rhine to Switzerland. Map. Post 8vo. 10s.

———— KNAPSACK GUIDE—BELGIUM AND THE RHINE. Post 8vo. (*In the Press.*)

———— SOUTH GERMANY, Bavaria, Austria, Styria, Salzberg, the Austrian and Bavarian Alps, the Tyrol, Hungary, and the Danube, from Ulm to the Black Sea. Map. Post 8vo. 10s.

———— KNAPSACK GUIDE—THE TYROL. Post 8vo. (*In the Press.*)

———— PAINTING. German, Flemish, and Dutch Schools. Edited by DR. WAAGEN. Woodcuts. 2 Vols. Post 8vo. 24s.

———— LIVES OF THE EARLY FLEMISH PAINTERS, with Notices of their Works. By CROWE and CAVALCASELLE. Illustrations. Post 8vo. 12s.

———— SWITZERLAND, Alps of Savoy, and Piedmont. Maps. Post 8vo. 9s.

———— KNAPSACK GUIDE—SWITZERLAND. Post 8vo. 5s.

———— FRANCE, Normandy, Brittany, the French Alps, the Rivers Loire, Seine, Rhone, and Garonne, Dauphiné, Provence, and the Pyrenees. Maps. Post 8vo. 10s.

———— KNAPSACK GUIDE—FRANCE. Post 8vo. (*In the Press.*)

———— PARIS AND ITS ENVIRONS. Map. Post 8vo. 5s.

———— SPAIN, Andalusia, Ronda, Granada, Valencia, Catalonia, Gallicia, Arragon, and Navarre. Maps. 2 Vols. Post 8vo. 30s.

———— PORTUGAL, LISBON, &c. Map. Post 8vo. 9s.

———— NORTH ITALY, Piedmont, Liguria, Venetia, Lombardy, Parma, Modena, and Romagna. Map. Post 8vo. 12s.

———— CENTRAL ITALY, Lucca, Tuscany, Florence, The Marches, Umbria, and the Patrimony of St. Peter's. Map. Post 8vo. 10s.

———— ROME AND ITS ENVIRONS. Map. Post 8vo. 9s.

———— SOUTH ITALY, Two Sicilies, Naples, Pompeii, Herculaneum, and Vesuvius. Map. Post 8vo. 10s.

———— KNAPSACK GUIDE—ITALY. Post 8vo. 6s.

———— SICILY, Palermo, Messina, Catania, Syracuse, Etna, and the Ruins of the Greek Temples. Map. Post 8vo. 12s.

———— PAINTING. The Italian Schools. From the German of KUGLER. Edited by Sir CHARLES EASTLAKE, R.A. Woodcuts. 2 Vols. Post 8vo. 30s.

———— LIVES OF THE EARLY ITALIAN PAINTERS, AND PROGRESS OF PAINTING IN ITALY, from CIMABUE to BASSANO. By MRS. JAMESON. *A New Edition.* Woodcuts. Post 8vo. *In the Press.*

———— NORWAY. Map. Post 8vo. 5s.

———— DENMARK, SWEDEN, and NORWAY. Maps. Post 8vo. 15s.

HAND-BOOK—GREECE, the Ionian Islands, Albania, Thessaly, and Macedonia. Maps. Post 8vo. 15*s*.

——— TURKEY, Malta, Asia Minor, Constantinople, Armenia, Mesopotamia, &c. Maps. Post 8vo.

——— EGYPT, Thebes, the Nile, Alexandria, Cairo, the Pyramids, Mount Sinai, &c. Map. Post 8vo. 15*s*.

——— SYRIA AND PALESTINE, Peninsula of Sinai, Eidom, and Syrian Desert. Maps. 2 Vols. Post 8vo. 24*s*.

——— BOMBAY AND MADRAS. Map. 2 Vols. Post 8vo. 24*s*.

——— RUSSIA, POLAND, and FINLAND. Maps. Post 8vo. 12*s*.

——— MODERN LONDON. A Complete Guide to all the Sights and Objects of Interest in the Metropolis. Map. 16mo. 3*s*. 6*d*.

——— WESTMINSTER ABBEY. Woodcuts. 16mo. 1*s*.

——— KENT AND SUSSEX, Canterbury, Dover, Ramsgate, Sheerness, Rochester, Chatham, Woolwich, Brighton, Chichester, Worthing, Hastings, Lewes, Arundel, &c. Map. Post 8vo. 10*s*.

——— SURREY AND HANTS, Kingston, Croydon, Reigate, Guildford, Winchester, Southampton, Portsmouth, and Isle of Wight. Maps. Post 8vo. 10*s*.

——— BERKS, BUCKS, AND OXON, Windsor, Eton, Reading, Aylesbury, Uxbridge, Wycombe, Henley, the City and University of Oxford, and the Descent of the Thames to Maidenhead and Windsor. Map. Post 8vo. 7*s*. 6*d*.

——— WILTS, DORSET, AND SOMERSET, Salisbury, Chippenham, Weymouth, Sherborne, Wells, Bath, Bristol, Taunton, &c. Map. Post 8vo. 7*s*. 6*d*.

——— DEVON AND CORNWALL, Exeter, Ilfracombe, Linton, Sidmouth, Dawlish, Teignmouth, Plymouth, Devonport, Torquay, Launceston, Truro, Penzance, Falmouth, &c. Maps. Post 8vo. 10*s*.

——— NORTH AND SOUTH WALES, Bangor, Carnarvon, Beaumaris, Snowdon, Conway, Menai Straits, Carmarthen, Pembroke, Tenby, Swansea, The Wye, &c. Maps. 2 Vols. Post 8vo. 12*s*.

——— SOUTHERN CATHEDRALS OF ENGLAND—Winchester, Salisbury, Exeter, Wells, Chichester, Rochester, Canterbury. With 110 Illustrations. 2 Vols. Crown 8vo. 24*s*.

——— EASTERN CATHEDRALS OF ENGLAND—Oxford, Peterborough, Norwich, Ely, and Lincoln. With 90 Illustrations. Crown 8vo. 18*s*.

——— WESTERN CATHEDRALS OF ENGLAND—Bristol, Gloucester, Hereford, Worcester, and Lichfield. With 50 Illustrations. Crown 8vo. 16*s*.

——— FAMILIAR QUOTATIONS. From English Authors. *Third Edition*. Fcap. 8vo. 5*s*.

HESSEY (REV. DR.). Sunday—Its Origin, History, and Present Obligations. Being the Bampton Lectures for 1860. *Second Edition*. 8vo. 16*s*. Or *Third and Popular Edition*. Post 8vo.

HICKMAN'S (WM.) Treatise on the Law and Practice of Naval Courts-Martial. 8vo. 10*s*. 6*d*.

HOME AND COLONIAL LIBRARY. A Series of Works adapted for all circles and classes of Readers, having been selected for their acknowledged interest and ability of the Authors. Post 8vo. Published at 2s. and 3s. 6d. each, and arranged under two distinctive heads as follows:—

CLASS A.

HISTORY, BIOGRAPHY, AND HISTORIC TALES.

1. SIEGE OF GIBRALTAR. By JOHN DRINKWATER. 2s.
2. THE AMBER-WITCH. By LADY DUFF GORDON. 2s.
3. CROMWELL AND BUNYAN. By ROBERT SOUTHEY. 2s.
4. LIFE OF SIR FRANCIS DRAKE. By JOHN BARROW. 2s.
5. CAMPAIGNS AT WASHINGTON. By REV. G. R. GLEIG. 2s.
6. THE FRENCH IN ALGIERS. By LADY DUFF GORDON. 2s.
7. THE FALL OF THE JESUITS. 2s.
8. LIVONIAN TALES. 2s.
9. LIFE OF CONDE. By LORD MAHON. 3s. 6d.
10. SALE'S BRIGADE. By REV. G. R. GLEIG. 2s.
11. THE SIEGES OF VIENNA. By LORD ELLESMERE. 2s.
12. THE WAYSIDE CROSS. By CAPT. MILMAN. 2s.
13. SKETCHES OF GERMAN LIFE. By SIR A. GORDON. 3s. 6d.
14. THE BATTLE OF WATERLOO. By REV. G. R. GLEIG. 3s. 6d.
15. AUTOBIOGRAPHY OF STEFFENS. 2s.
16. THE BRITISH POETS. By THOMAS CAMPBELL. 3s. 6d.
17. HISTORICAL ESSAYS. By LORD MAHON. 3s. 6d.
18. LIFE OF LORD CLIVE. By REV. G. R. GLEIG. 3s. 6d.
19. NORTH - WESTERN RAILWAY. By SIR F. B. HEAD. 2s.
20. LIFE OF MUNRO. By REV. G. R. GLEIG. 3s. 6d.

CLASS B.

VOYAGES, TRAVELS, AND ADVENTURES.

1. BIBLE IN SPAIN. By GEORGE BORROW. 3s. 6d.
2. GIPSIES OF SPAIN. By GEORGE BORROW. 3s. 6d.

3 & 4. JOURNALS IN INDIA. By BISHOP HEBER. 2 Vols. 7s.

5. TRAVELS IN THE HOLY LAND. By IRBY and MANGLES. 2s.
6. MOROCCO AND THE MOORS. By J. DRUMMOND HAY. 2s.
7. LETTERS FROM THE BALTIC. By a LADY. 2s.
8. NEW SOUTH WALES. By MRS. MEREDITH. 2s.
9. THE WEST INDIES. By M. G. LEWIS. 2s.
10. SKETCHES OF PERSIA. By SIR JOHN MALCOLM. 3s. 6d.
11. MEMOIRS OF FATHER RIPA. 2s.

12. 13. TYPEE AND OMOO. By HERMANN MELVILLE. 2 Vols. 7s.

14. MISSIONARY LIFE IN CANADA. By REV. J. ABBOTT. 2s.
15. LETTERS FROM MADRAS. By a LADY. 2s.
16. HIGHLAND SPORTS. By CHARLES ST. JOHN. 3s. 6d.
17. PAMPAS JOURNEYS. By SIR F. B. HEAD. 2s.
18. GATHERINGS FROM SPAIN. By RICHARD FORD. 3s. 6d.
19. THE RIVER AMAZON. By W. H. EDWARDS. 2s.
20. MANNERS & CUSTOMS OF INDIA. By REV. C. ACLAND. 2s.
21. ADVENTURES IN MEXICO. By G. F. RUXTON. 3s. 6d.
22. PORTUGAL AND GALLICIA. By LORD CARNARVON. 3s. 6d.
23. BUSH LIFE IN AUSTRALIA. By REV. H. W. HAYGARTH. 2s.
24. THE LIBYAN DESERT. By BAYLE ST. JOHN. 2s.
25. SIERRA LEONE. By a LADY. 3s. 6d.

*** Each work may be had separately.

HILLARD'S (G. S.) Six Months in Italy. 2 Vols. Post 8vo. 16s.

HOLLWAY'S (J. G.) Month in Norway. Fcap. 8vo. 2s.

HONEY BEE (The). An Essay. By Rev. Thomas James. Reprinted from the "Quarterly Review." Fcap. 8vo. 1s.

HOOK'S (Dean) Church Dictionary. *Ninth Edition.* 8vo. 16s.

——— (Theodore) Life. By J. G. Lockhart. Reprinted from the "Quarterly Review." Fcap. 8vo. 1s.

HOOKER'S (Dr. J. D.) Himalayan Journals; or, Notes of an Oriental Naturalist in Bengal, the Sikkim and Nepal Himalayas, the Khasia Mountains, &c. *Second Edition.* Woodcuts. 2 Vols. Post 8vo. 18s.

HOPE'S (A. J. Beresford) English Cathedral of the Nineteenth Century. With Illustrations. 8vo. 12s.

HORACE (Works of). Edited by Dean Milman. With 300 Woodcuts. Crown 8vo. 21s.

——— (Life of). By Dean Milman. Woodcuts, and coloured Borders. 8vo. 9s.

HOUGHTON'S (Lord) Poetical Works. Fcap. 8vo. 6s. 6*d.*

HUME'S (The Student's) History of England, from the Invasion of Julius Cæsar to the Revolution of 1688. Corrected and continued to 1858. Edited by Dr. Wm. Smith. Woodcuts. Post 8vo. 7s. 6*d.*

HUTCHINSON (Gen.) on the most expeditious, certain, and easy Method of Dog-Breaking. *Fourth Edition.* Enlarged and revised, with 40 Illustrations. Crown 8vo. 15s.

HUTTON'S (H. E.) Principia Græca; an Introduction to the Study of Greek. Comprehending Grammar, Delectus, and Exercise-book, with Vocabularies. *Third Edition.* 12mo. 3s. 6*d.*

IRBY AND MANGLES' Travels in Egypt, Nubia, Syria, and the Holy Land. Post 8vo. 2s.

JAMES' (Rev. Thomas) Fables of Æsop. A New Translation, with Historical Preface. With 100 Woodcuts by Tenniel and Wolf. *Forty-eighth Thousand.* Post 8vo. 2s. 6*d.*

JAMESON'S (Mrs.) Lives of the Early Italian Painters, from Cimabue to Bassano, and the Progress of Painting in Italy. *New Edition.* With Woodcuts. Post 8vo.

JESSE'S (Edward) Gleanings in Natural History. *Eighth Edition.* Fcp. 8vo. 6s.

JOHNSON'S (Dr. Samuel) Life. By James Boswell. Including the Tour to the Hebrides. Edited by Mr. Croker. Portraits. Royal 8vo. 10s.

——— Lives of the most eminent English Poets. Edited by Peter Cunningham. 3 vols. 8vo. 22s. 6*d.*

JOURNAL OF A NATURALIST. Woodcuts. Post 8vo. 9s. 6*d.*

KEN'S (Bishop) Life. By a Layman, Author of "Life of the Messiah." *Second Edition.* Portrait. 2 Vols. 8vo. 18s.

——— Exposition of the Apostles' Creed. Extracted from his "Practice of Divine Love." Fcap. 1s. 6*d.*

——— Approach to the Holy Altar. Extracted from his "Manual of Prayer" and "Practice of Divine Love." Fcap. 8vo. 1s. 6*d.*

KENNEDY'S (General Sir J. Shaw) Notes on the Battle of Waterloo. With a Memoir of his Life and Services, and a Plan for the Defence of Canada. With Map and Plans. 8vo. 7*s*. 6*d*.

KING'S (Rev. S. W.) Italian Valleys of the Alps; a Tour through all the Romantic and less-frequented "Vals" of Northern Piedmont. Illustrations. Crown 8vo. 18*s*.

——— (Rev. C. W.) Antique Gems; their Origin, Use, and Value, as Interpreters of Ancient History, and as illustrative of Ancient Art. Illustrations. 8vo. 42*s*.

KING EDWARD VIth's Latin Grammar; or, an Introduction to the Latin Tongue, for the Use of Schools. *Seventeenth Edition*. 12mo. 3*s*. 6*d*.

——— First Latin Book; or, the Accidence, Syntax, and Prosody, with an English Translation for the Use of Junior Classes. *Fifth Edition*. 12mo. 2*s*. 6*d*.

KIRK'S (J. Foster) History of Charles the Bold, Duke of Burgundy. Portrait. 2 Vols. 8vo. 30*s*.

KERR'S (Robert) GENTLEMAN'S HOUSE; or, How to Plan English Residences, from the Parsonage to the Palace. With Tables of Accommodation and Cost, and a Series of Selected Views and Plans. *Second Edition*. 8vo. 24*s*.

——— Ancient Lights; a Book for Architects, Surveyors, Lawyers, and Landlords. 8vo. 5*s*. 6*d*.

KING GEORGE THE THIRD'S CORRESPONDENCE WITH LORD NORTH, 1769-82. Edited, with Notes and Introduction, by W. Bodham Donne. 2 vols. 8vo. Published by permission. From the Royal Library at Windsor. (*In the Press*.)

KUGLER'S Italian Schools of Painting. Edited, with Notes, by Sir Charles Eastlake. *Third Edition*. Woodcuts. 2 Vols. Post 8vo. 30*s*.

——— German, Dutch, and Flemish Schools of Painting. Edited, with Notes, by Dr. Waagen. *Second Edition*. Woodcuts. 2 Vols. Post 8vo. 24*s*.

LAYARD'S (A. H.) Nineveh and its Remains. Being a Narrative of Researches and Discoveries amidst the Ruins of Assyria. With an Account of the Chaldean Christians of Kurdistan; the Yezedis, or Devil-worshippers; and an Enquiry into the Manners and Arts of the Ancient Assyrians. *Sixth Edition*. Plates and Woodcuts. 2 Vols. 8vo. 36*s*.

——— Nineveh and Babylon; being the Result of a Second Expedition to Assyria. Plates 8vo. 21*s*. On *Fine Paper*, 2 Vols. 8vo. 30*s*.

——— Popular Account of Nineveh and Babylon. A New Edition. With Woodcuts. Post 8vo. (*In the Press*.)

LESLIE'S (C. R.) Handbook for Young Painters. With Illustrations. Post 8vo. 10*s*. 6*d*.

——— Autobiographical Recollections, with Selections from his Correspondence. Edited by Tom Taylor. Portrait. 2 Vols. Post 8vo. 18*s*.

——— Life of Sir Joshua Reynolds. With an Account of his Works, and a Sketch of his Cotemporaries. By C. R. Leslie and Tom Taylor. Illustrations. 2 Vols. 8vo. 42*s*.

LETTERS FROM THE BALTIC. By a LADY. Post 8vo. 2s.

——— MADRAS. By a LADY. Post 8vo. 2s.

——— SIERRA LEONE. By a LADY. Edited by the HONOURABLE MRS. NORTON. Post 8vo. 3s. 6d.

LEWIS' (SIR G. C.) Essay on the Government of Dependencies. 8vo. 12s.

——— Glossary of Provincial Words used in Herefordshire and some of the adjoining Counties. 12mo. 4s. 6d.

——— (M. G.) Journal of a Residence among the Negroes in the West Indies. Post 8vo. 2s.

LIDDELL'S (DEAN) History of Rome. From the Earliest Times to the Establishment of the Empire. With the History of Literature and Art. 2 Vols. 8vo. 28s.

——— Student's History of Rome, abridged from the above Work. With Woodcuts. Post 8vo. 7s. 6d.

LINDSAY'S (LORD) Lives of the Lindsays; or, a Memoir of the Houses of Crawfurd and Balcarres. With Extracts from Official Papers and Personal Narratives. *Second Edition.* 3 Vols. 8vo. 24s.

——— Report of the Claim of James, Earl of Crawfurd and Balcarres, to the Original Dukedom of Montrose, created in 1488 Folio. 15s.

——— Scepticism; a Retrogressive Movement in Theology and Philosophy. 8vo. 9s.

LISPINGS from LOW LATITUDES; or, the Journal of the Hon. Impulsia Gushington. Edited by LORD DUFFERIN. With 24 Plates, 4to. 21s.

LITTLE ARTHUR'S HISTORY OF ENGLAND. By LADY CALLCOTT. *150th Thousand.* With 20 Woodcuts. Fcap. 8vo. 2s. 6d.

LIVINGSTONE'S (DR.) Popular Account of his Missionary Travels in South Africa. Illustrations. Post 8vo. 6s.

——— Narrative of an Expedition to the Zambezi and its Tributaries; and of the Discovery of Lakes Shirwa and Nyassa. 1858-64. By DAVID and CHARLES LIVINGSTONE. Map and Illustrations. 8vo. 21s.

LIVONIAN TALES. By the Author of "Letters from the Baltic." Post 8vo. 2s.

LOCKHART'S (J. G.) Ancient Spanish Ballads. Historical and Romantic. Translated, with Notes. *New Edition.* Illustrations. 4to. 21s. *Or Popular Edition*, Post 8vo. 2s. 6d.

LONDON'S (BISHOP OF) Dangers and Safeguards of Modern Theology. Containing Suggestions to the Theological Student under present difficulties. *Second Edition.* 8vo. 9s.

LOUDON'S (MRS.) Instructions in Gardening for Ladies. With Directions and Calendar of Operations for Every Month. *Eighth Edition.* Woodcuts. Fcap. 8vo. 5s.

LUCAS' (SAMUEL) Secularia; or, Surveys on the Main Stream of History. 8vo. 12s.

LUCKNOW: a Lady's Diary of the Siege. Fcap. 8vo. 4s. 6d.

LYELL'S (SIR CHARLES) Elements of Geology; or, the Ancient Changes of the Earth and its Inhabitants considered as illustrative of Geology. *Sixth Edition.* Woodcuts. 8vo. 18s.

——— Geological Evidences of the Antiquity of Man. *Third Edition.* Illustrations. 8vo. 14s.

LYTTELTON'S (LORD) Ephemera. Post 8vo. 10*s.* 6*d.*

LYTTON'S (SIR EDWARD BULWER) Poems. *New Edition.* Post 8vo. 10*s.* 6*d.*

MACPHERSON'S (MAJOR S. C.) Memorials of Service in India, while Political Agent at Gwalior during the Mutiny, and formerly employed in the Suppression of Human Sacrifices in Orissa. Edited by his Brother. With Portrait and Illustrations. 8vo. 12*s.*

MAHON'S (LORD) History of England, from the Peace of Utrecht to the Peace of Versailles, 1713—83. *Library Edition.* 7 Vols. 8vo. 93*s.* *Popular Edition,* 7 Vols. Post 8vo. 35*s.*

——— "Forty-Five;" a Narrative of the Rebellion in Scotland. Post 8vo. 3*s.*

——— History of British India from its Origin till the Peace of 1783. Post 8vo. 3*s.* 6*d.*

——— Spain under Charles the Second; 1690 to 1700. *Second Edition.* Post 8vo. 6*s.* 6*d.*

——— Historical and Critical Essays. Post 8vo. 3*s.* 6*d.*

——— Story of Joan of Arc. Fcap. 8vo. 1*s.*

——— Addresses. Fcap. 8vo. 1*s.*

——— Life of William Pitt, with Extracts from his MS. Papers. *Second Edition.* Portraits. 4 Vols. Post 8vo. 42*s.*

——— Miscellanies. *Second Edition.* Post 8vo. 5*s.* 6*d.*

——— Condé, surnamed the Great. Post 8vo. 3*s.* 6*d.*

——— Belisarius. *Second Edition.* Post 8vo. 10*s.* 6*d.*

M'CLINTOCK'S (CAPT. SIR F. L.) Narrative of the Discovery of the Fate of Sir John Franklin and his Companions in the Arctic Seas. *Twelfth Thousand.* Illustrations. 8vo. 16*s.*

M'CULLOCH'S (J. R.) Collected Edition of RICARDO'S Political Works. With Notes and Memoir. *Second Edition.* 8vo. 16*s.*

MACDOUGALL (COL.) On Modern Warfare as Influenced by Modern Artillery. With Plans. Post 8vo. 12*s.*

MAINE (H. SUMNER) On Ancient Law: its Connection with the Early History of Society, and its Relation to Modern Ideas. *Third Edition.* 8vo. 12*s.*

MALCOLM'S (SIR JOHN) Sketches of Persia. Post 8vo. 3*s.* 6*d.*

MANSEL (REV. H. L.) Limits of Religious Thought Examined. Being the Bampton Lectures for 1858. *Fourth Edition.* Post 8vo. 7*s.* 6*d.*

MANSFIELD (SIR WILLIAM) On the Introduction of a Gold Currency into India: a Contribution to the Literature of Political Economy. 8vo. 3*s.* 6*d.*

MANTELL'S (GIDEON A.) Thoughts on Animalcules; or, the Invisible World, as revealed by the Microscope. *Second Edition.* Plates. 16mo. 6*s.*

MANUAL OF SCIENTIFIC ENQUIRY, Prepared for the Use of Officers and Travellers. By various Writers. Edited by Sir J. F. HERSCHEL and Rev. R. MAIN. *Third Edition.* Maps. Post 8vo. 9*s.* (*Published by order of the Lords of the Admiralty.*)

MARKHAM'S (Mrs.) History of England. From the First Invasion by the Romans, down to Recent Times. *New and Cheaper Edition.* Woodcuts. 12mo. 4s.

——— History of France. From the Conquest by the Gauls, to Recent Times. *New and Cheaper Edition.* Woodcuts. 12mo. 4s.

——— History of Germany. From the Invasion by Marius, to Recent Times. *New and Cheaper Edition.* Woodcuts. 12mo. 4s.

——— (Clements, R.) Travels in Peru and India, for the purpose of collecting Cinchona Plants, and introducing Bark into India. Maps and Illustrations. 8vo. 16s.

MARKLAND'S (J. H.) Reverence due to Holy Places. *Third Edition.* Fcap. 8vo. 2s.

MARRYAT'S (Joseph) History of Modern and Mediæval Pottery and Porcelain. With a Description of the Manufacture. *Second Edition.* Plates and Woodcuts. 8vo. 31s. 6d.

——— (Horace) Jutland, the Danish Isles, and Copenhagen. Illustrations. 2 Vols. Post 8vo. 24s.

——— Sweden and Isle of Gothland. Illustrations. 2 Vols. Post 8vo. 28s.

MATTHIÆ'S (Augustus) Greek Grammar for Schools, abridged from the Larger Grammar. By Blomfield. *Ninth Edition.* Revised by Edwards. 12mo. 3s.

MAUREL'S (Jules) Essay on the Character, Actions, and Writings of the Duke of Wellington. *Second Edition.* Fcap. 8vo. 1s. 6d.

MAYNE'S (Capt.) Four Years in British Columbia and Vancouver Island. Its Forests, Rivers, Coasts, and Gold Fields, and Resources for Colonisation. Illustrations. 8vo. 16s.

MELVILLE'S (Hermann) Typee and Omoo; or, Adventures amongst the Marquesas and South Sea Islands. 2 Vols. Post 8vo. 7s.

MILLS' (Rev. John) Three Months' Residence at Nablus, with an Account of the Modern Samaritans. Illustrations. Post 8vo. 10s. 6d.

MILMAN'S (Dean) History of the Jews, from the Earliest Period, brought down to Modern Times. *New Edition.* 3 Vols. 8vo. 36s.

——— Christianity, from the Birth of Christ to the Abolition of Paganism in the Roman Empire. *New Edition.* 3 Vols. 8vo. 36s.

——— Latin Christianity; including that of the Popes to the Pontificate of Nicholas V. *New Edition.* 9 Vols. 8vo. 81s.

——— Character and Conduct of the Apostles considered as an Evidence of Christianity. 8vo. 10s. 6d.

——— Translations from the Agamemnon of Æschylus and Bacchanals of Euripides; with Passages from the Lyric and Later Poets of Greece. With Illustrations, crown 8vo. 12s.

——— Life and Works of Horace. With 300 Woodcuts. 2 Vols. Crown 8vo. 30s.

——— Poetical Works. Plates. 3 Vols. Fcap. 8vo. 18s.

——— Fall of Jerusalem. Fcap. 8vo. 1s.

——— (Capt. E. A.) Wayside Cross. A Tale of the Carlist War. Post 8vo. 2s.

MEREDITH'S (Mrs. Charles) Notes and Sketches of New South Wales. Post 8vo. 2*s.*

MESSIAH (THE): A Narrative of the Life, Travels, Death, Resurrection, and Ascension of our Blessed Lord. By a Layman. Author of the "Life of Bishop Ken." Map. 8vo. 18*s.*

MICHIE'S (Alexander) Siberian Overland Route from Peking to Petersburg, through the Deserts and Steppes of Mongolia, Tartary, &c. Maps and Illustrations. 8vo. 16*s.*

MODERN DOMESTIC COOKERY. Founded on Principles of Economy and Practical Knowledge and adapted for Private Families. *New Edition.* Woodcuts. Fcap. 8vo. 5*s.*

MOORE'S (Thomas) Life and Letters of Lord Byron. Plates. 6 Vols. Fcap. 8vo. 18*s.*

——— Life and Letters of Lord Byron. Portraits. Royal 8vo. 9*s.*

MOTLEY'S (J. L.) History of the United Netherlands: from the Death of William the Silent to the Synod of Dort. Embracing the English-Dutch struggle against Spain; and a detailed Account of the Spanish Armada. Portraits. 2 Vols. 8vo. 30*s.*

MOUHOT'S (Henri) Siam, Cambojia, and Lao; a Narrative of Travels and Discoveries. Illustrations. 2 vols. 8vo. 32*s.*

MOZLEY'S (Rev. J. B.) Treatise on Predestination. 8vo. 14*s.*

——— Primitive Doctrine of Baptismal Regeneration. 8vo. 7*s.* 6*d.*

MUNDY'S (General) Pen and Pencil Sketches in India. *Third Edition.* Plates. Post 8vo. 7*s.* 6*d.*

——— (Admiral) Account of the Italian Revolution, with Notices of Garibaldi, Francis II., and Victor Emmanuel. Post 8vo. 12*s.*

MUNRO'S (General Sir Thomas) Life and Letters. By the Rev. G. R. Gleig. Post 8vo. 3*s.* 6*d.*

MURCHISON'S (Sir Roderick) Russia in Europe and the Ural Mountains. With Coloured Maps, Plates, Sections, &c. 2 Vols. Royal 4to. 5*l.* 5*s.*

——— Siluria; or, a History of the Oldest Rocks containing Organic Remains. *Third Edition.* Map and Plates. 8vo. 42*s.*

MURRAY'S RAILWAY READING. Containing:—

Wellington. By Lord Ellesmere. 6*d.*
Nimrod on the Chase, 1*s.*
Essays from "The Times." 2 Vols. 8*s.*
Music and Dress. 1*s.*
Layard's Account of Nineveh. 5*s.*
Milman's Fall of Jerusalem. 1*s.*
Mahon's "Forty-Five." 3*s.*
Life of Theodore Hook. 1*s.*
Deeds of Naval Daring. 3*s.* 6*d.*
The Honey Bee. 1*s.*
James' Æsop's Fables. 2*s.* 6*d.*
Nimrod on the Turf. 1*s.* 6*d.*
Art of Dining. 1*s.* 6*d.*
Hallam's Literary Essays. 2*s.*
Mahon's Joan of Arc. 1*s.*
Head's Emigrant. 2*s.* 6*d.*
Nimrod on the Road. 1*s.*
Croker on the Guillotine. 1*s.*
Hollway's Norway. 2*s.*
Maurel's Wellington. 1*s.* 6*d.*
Campbell's Life of Bacon. 2*s.* 6*d.*
The Flower Garden. 1*s.*
Lockhart's Spanish Ballads. 2*s.* 6*d.*
Taylor's Notes from Life. 2*s.*
Rejected Addresses. 1*s.*
Penn's Hints on Angling. 1*s.*

MUSIC AND DRESS. By a Lady. Reprinted from the "Quarterly Review." Fcap. 8vo. 1*s.*

NAPIER'S (Sir Chas.) Life; chiefly derived from his Journals and Letters. By Sir W. Napier. *Second Edition.* Portraits. 4 Vols. Post 8vo. 48*s.*

——— (Sir Wm.) Life and Letters. Edited by H. A. Bruce, M.P. Portraits. 2 Vols. Crown 8vo. 28*s.*

——— English Battles and Sieges of the Peninsular War. *Fourth Edition.* Portrait. Post 8vo. 9*s.*

NAUTICAL ALMANACK. Royal 8vo. 2*s.* 6*d.* (*By Authority.*)

NAVY LIST. (*Published Quarterly, by Authority.*) 16mo. 2*s.* 6*d.*

NEW TESTAMENT (THE) Illustrated by a Plain Explanatory Commentary, and authentic Views of Sacred Places, from Sketches and Photographs. Edited by ARCHDEACON CHURTON and REV. BASIL JONES. With 110 Illustrations. 2 Vols. Crown 8vo. 30*s.* cloth; 52*s.* 6*d.* calf; 63*s.* morocco.

NICHOLLS' (SIR GEORGE) History of the English, Irish and Scotch Poor Laws. 4 Vols. 8vo.

——— (Rev. H. G.) Historical Account of the Forest of Dean. Woodcuts, &c. Post 8vo. 10*s.* 6*d.*

NICOLAS' (SIR HARRIS) Historic Peerage of England. Exhibiting the Origin, Descent, and Present State of every Title of Peerage which has existed in this Country since the Conquest. By WILLIAM COURTHOPE. 8vo. 30*s.*

NIMROD On the Chace—The Turf—and The Road. Reprinted from the "Quarterly Review." Woodcuts. Fcap. 8vo. 3*s.* 6*d.*

O'CONNOR'S (R.) Field Sports of France; or, Hunting, Shooting, and Fishing on the Continent. Woodcuts. 12mo. 7*s.* 6*d.*

OXENHAM'S (REV. W.) English Notes for Latin Elegiacs; designed for early Proficients in the Art of Latin Versification, with Prefatory Rules of Composition in Elegiac Metre. *Fourth Edition.* 12mo. 3*s.* 6*d.*

PARIS' (Dr.) Philosophy in Sport made Science in Earnest; or, the First Principles of Natural Philosophy inculcated by aid of the Toys and Sports of Youth. *Ninth Edition.* Woodcuts. Post 8vo. 7*s.* 6*d.*

PEEL'S (SIR ROBERT) Memoirs. Edited by EARL STANHOPE and Right Hon. E. CARDWELL. 2 Vols. Post 8vo. 7*s.* 6*d.* each.

PENN'S (RICHARD) Maxims and Hints for an Angler and Chess-player. *New Edition.* Woodcuts. Fcap. 8vo. 1*s.*

PENROSE'S (F. C.) Principles of Athenian Architecture, and the Optical Refinements exhibited in the Construction of the Ancient Buildings at Athens, from a Survey. With 40 Plates. Folio. 5*l.* 5*s.*

PERCY'S (JOHN, M.D.) Metallurgy of Iron and Steel; or, the Art of Extracting Metals from their Ores and adapting them to various purposes of Manufacture. Illustrations. 8vo. 42*s.*

PHILLIPP (CHARLES SPENCER MARCH) On Jurisprudence. 8vo. 12*s.*

PHILLIPS' (JOHN) Memoirs of William Smith, the Geologist. Portrait. 8vo. 7*s.* 6*d.*

——— Geology of Yorkshire, The Coast, and Limestone District. Plates. 4to. Part I., 20*s.*—Part II., 30*s.*

——— Rivers, Mountains, and Sea Coast of Yorkshire. With Essays on the Climate, Scenery, and Ancient Inhabitants. *Second Edition,* Plates. 8vo. 15*s.*

PHILPOTTS' (BISHOP) Letters to the late Charles Butler, on the Theological parts of his "Book of the Roman Catholic Church;" with Remarks on certain Works of Dr. Milner and Dr. Lingard, and on some parts of the Evidence of Dr. Doyle. *Second Edition.* 8vo. 16*s.*

POPE'S (ALEXANDER) Life and Works. *A New Edition.* Containing nearly 500 unpublished Letters. Edited, with a NEW LIFE, Introductions and Notes, by REV. WHITWELL ELWIN. Portraits. 8vo. (*In the Press.*)

PORTER'S (Rev. J. L.) Five Years in Damascus. With Travels to Palmyra, Lebanon and other Scripture Sites. Map and Woodcuts. 2 Vols. Post 8vo. 21*s*.

——— Handbook for Syria and Palestine: including an Account of the Geography, History, Antiquities, and Inhabitants of these Countries, the Peninsula of Sinai, Edom, and the Syrian Desert. Maps. 2 Vols. Post 8vo. 24*s*.

PRAYER-BOOK (Illustrated), with 1000 Illustrations of Borders, Initials, Vignettes, &c. Edited, with Notes, by Rev. Thos. James. Medium 8vo. 18*s*. cloth; 18*s*. 6*d*. calf; 36*s*. morocco.

PRECEPTS FOR THE CONDUCT OF LIFE. Extracted from the Scriptures. *Second Edition*. Fcap. 8vo. 1*s*.

PUSS IN BOOTS. With 12 Illustrations. By Otto Speckter. 16mo. 1*s*. 6*d*. or Coloured, 2*s*. 6*d*.

QUARTERLY REVIEW (The). 8vo. 6*s*.

RAMBLES in the Syrian Deserts among the Turkomans and Bedaweens. Post 8vo. 10*s*. 6*d*.

RAWLINSON'S (Rev. George) Herodotus. A New English Version. Edited with Notes and Essays. Assisted by Sir Henry Rawlinson and Sir J. G. Wilkinson. *Second Edition*. Maps and Woodcut. 4 Vols. 8vo. 48*s*.

——— Historical Evidences of the truth of the Scripture Records stated anew. *Second Edition*. 8vo. 14*s*.

——— Five Great Monarchies of the Ancient World, Chaldæa, Assyria, Media, Babylonia, and Persia. Illustrations. 4 Vols. 8vo. 16*s*. each.

REJECTED ADDRESSES (The). By James and Horace Smith. Fcap. 8vo. 1*s*.

RENNIE'S (D. F.) British Arms in Peking, 1860; Kagosima, 1862. Post 8vo. 12*s*.

——— Peking and the Pekingese: Being a Narrative of the First Year of the British Embassy in China. Illustrations. 2 Vols. Post 8vo. 24*s*.

——— Story of Bhotan and the Dooar War; including Sketches of a Residence in the Himalayas and Visit to Bhotan in 1865. Map and Woodcut. Post 8vo.

REYNOLDS' (Sir Joshua) Life and Times. Commenced by C. R. Leslie, R.A., continued and concluded by Tom Taylor. Portraits and Illustrations. 2 Vols. 8vo. 42*s*.

——— Descriptive Catalogue of his Works. With Notices of their present owners and localities. By Tom Taylor and Charles W. Franks. With Illustrations. Fcap. 4to. (*In the Press*.)

RICARDO'S (David) Political Works. With a Notice of his Life and Writings. By J. R. M'Culloch. *New Edition*. 8vo. 16*s*.

RIPA'S (Father) Memoirs during Thirteen Years' Residence at the Court of Peking. From the Italian. Post 8vo. 2*s*.

ROBERTSON'S (Canon) History of the Christian Church, from the Apostolic Age to the Concordat of Worms, A.D. 1123. *Second Edition*. 3 Vols. 8vo. 38*s*.

ROBINSON'S (Rev. Dr.) Later Biblical Researches in the Holy Land. Being a Journal of Travels in 1852. Maps. 8vo. 15*s.*

———— Physical Geography of the Holy Land. Post 8vo. 10*s.* 6*d.*

ROME (The Student's History of). From the Earliest Times to the Establishment of the Empire. By Dean Liddell. Woodcuts. Post 8vo. 7*s.* 6*d.*

———— (A Smaller History of, for Young Persons). By Wm. Smith, LL.D. Woodcuts. 16mo. 3*s.* 6*d.*

ROWLAND'S (David) Manual of the English Constitution; Its Rise, Growth, and Present State. Post 8vo. 10*s.* 6*d.*

———— Laws of Nature the Foundation of Morals. Post 8vo. 6*s.*

RUNDELL'S (Mrs.) Domestic Cookery, adapted for Private Families. *New Edition.* Woodcuts. Fcap. 8vo. 5*s.*

RUSSELL'S (J. Rutherfurd) History of the Heroes of Medicine. Portraits. 8vo. 14*s.*

RUXTON'S (George F.) Travels in Mexico; with Adventures among the Wild Tribes and Animals of the Prairies and Rocky Mountains. Post 8vo. 3*s.* 6*d.*

SALE'S (Sir Robert) Brigade in Affghanistan. With an Account of the Defence of Jellalabad. By Rev. G. R. Gleig. Post 8vo. 2*s.*

SANDWITH'S (Humphry) Siege of Kars. Post 8vo. 3*s.* 6*d.*

SCOTT'S (G. Gilbert) Secular and Domestic Architecture, Present and Future. *Second Edition.* 8vo. 9*s.*

———— (Rev. Robert, D.D., Master of Baliol) Sermons, preached before the University of Oxford. Post 8vo. 8*s.* 6*d.*

SCROPE'S (G. P.) Geology and Extinct Volcanoes of Central France. *Second Edition.* Illustrations. Medium 8vo. 30*s.*

SENIOR'S (N. W.) Suggestions on Popular Education. 8vo. 9*s.*

SHAFTESBURY (Lord Chancellor); Memoirs of his Early Life. With his Letters, &c. By W. D. Christie. Vol. I. Portrait. 8vo. 10*s.* 6*d.*

SHAW'S (T. B.) Student's Manual of English Literature. Edited, with Notes and Illustrations, by Dr. Wm. Smith. Post 8vo. 7*s.* 6*d.*

———— Specimens of English Literature. Selected from the Chief English Writers. Edited by Wm. Smith, LL.D. Post 8vo. 7*s.* 6*d.*

SIERRA LEONE; Described in Letters to Friends at Home. By A Lady. Post 8vo. 3*s.* 6*d.*

SIMMONS (Capt. T. F.) on the Constitution and Practice of Courts-Martial; with a Summary of the Law of Evidence as connected therewith, and some Notice of the Criminal Law of England, with reference to the Trial of Civil Offences. *5th Edition.* 8vo. 14*s.*

SOUTH'S (John F.) Household Surgery; or, Hints on Emergencies. *Seventeenth Thousand.* Woodcuts. Fcp. 8vo. 4*s.* 6*d.*

SMILES' (SAMUEL) Lives of British Engineers; from the Earliest Period to the Death of Robert Stephenson; with an account of their Principal Works, and a History of Inland Communication in Britain. Portraits and Illustrations. 3 Vols. 8vo. 63*s*.

——— Lives of Boulton and Watt. Comprising a History of the Invention and Introduction of the Steam Engine. With Portraits and 70 Illustrations. 8vo. 21*s*.

——— Story of George Stephenson's Life, including a Memoir of Robert Stephenson. With Portraits and 70 Woodcuts. Post 8vo. 6*s*.

——— James Brindley and the Early Engineers. With Portrait and 50 Woodcuts. Post 8vo. 6*s*.

——— Self-Help. With Illustrations of Character and Conduct. Post 8vo. 6*s*.

——— Industrial Biography: Iron-Workers and Tool Makers. A companion volume to "Self-Help." Post 8vo. 6*s*.

——— Workmen's Earnings—Savings—and Strikes. Fcap. 8vo. 1*s*. 6*d*.

SOMERVILLE'S (MARY) Physical Geography. *Fifth Edition.* Portrait. Post 8vo. 9*s*.

——— Connexion of the Physical Sciences. *Ninth Edition.* Woodcuts. Post 8vo. 9*s*.

STANLEY'S (DEAN) Sinai and Palestine, in Connexion with their History. Map. 8vo. 16*s*.

——— Bible in the Holy Land. Woodcuts. Fcap. 8vo. 2*s*. 6*d*.

——— St. Paul's Epistles to the Corinthians. 8vo. 18*s*.

——— History of the Eastern Church. Plans. 8vo. 12*s*.

——— Jewish Church. ABRAHAM TO THE CAPTIVITY. 2 Vols. 8vo. 16*s*. each.

——— Historical Memorials of Canterbury. Woodcuts. Post 8vo. 7*s*. 6*d*.

——— Sermons in the East, with Notices of the Places Visited. 8vo. 9*s*.

——— Sermons on Evangelical and Apostolical Teaching. Post 8vo. 7*s*. 6*d*.

——— ADDRESSES AND CHARGES OF BISHOP STANLEY. With Memoir. 8vo. 10*s*. 6*d*.

SOUTHEY'S (ROBERT) Book of the Church. *Seventh Edition.* Post 8vo. 7*s*. 6*d*.

——— Lives of Bunyan and Cromwell. Post 8vo. 2*s*.

SPECKTER'S (OTTO) Puss in Boots. With 12 Woodcuts. Square 12mo. 1*s*. 6*d*. plain, or 2*s*. 6*d*. coloured.

——— Charmed Roe; or, the Story of the Little Brother and Sister. Illustrated. 16mo.

SMITH'S (Dr. Wm.) Dictionary of the Bible; its Antiquities, Biography, Geography, and Natural History. Illustrations. 3 Vols. 8vo. 105*s.*

——— Concise Dictionary of the Bible, condensed from the above Dictionary for Families and Students. Illustrations. Medium, 8vo. 21*s.*

——— Dictionary of Christian Antiquities: from the Times of the Apostles to the Age of Charlemagne. Illustrations. Medium. 8vo. (*In preparation*)

——— Greek and Roman Antiquities. Woodcuts. 8vo. 42*s.*

——— Greek and Roman Biography and Mythology. Woodcuts. 3 Vols. 8vo. 5*l.* 15*s.* 6*d.*

——— Greek and Roman Geography. Woodcuts. 2 Vols. 8vo. 80*s.*

——— Classical and Biblical Atlas. Small folio. (*In preparation.*)

——— Classical Dictionary for the Higher Forms in Schools, compiled from the above works. With 750 Woodcuts. 8vo. 18*s.*

——— Smaller Classical Dictionary, abridged from the above Work. Woodcuts. Crown 8vo. 7*s.* 6*d.*

——— Smaller Dictionary of Greek and Roman Antiquities, compiled from the larger Work. Woodcuts. Crown 8vo. 7*s.* 6*d.*

——— Latin-English Dictionary for the Higher Forms in Schools. Based on the Works of Forcellini and Freund. With Tables of the Roman Calendar, Measures, Weights, and Money. 8vo. 21*s.*

——— Smaller Latin-English Dictionary, abridged from the above Work. 12mo. 7*s.* 6*d.*

——— New English-Latin Dictionary, compiled from original sources. 8vo. and 12mo. (*In the Press.*)

——— Small Classical Mythology for Schools. With Illustrations. 12mo.

——— Latin-English Vocabulary; for Phædrus, Cornelius Nepos, and Cæsar. *2nd Edition.* 12mo. 3*s.* 6*d.*

——— Principia Latina—Part I. A Grammar, Delectus, and Exercise Book, with Vocabularies. *6th Edition.* 12mo. 3*s.* 6*d.*

——— Part II. A Reading-book of Mythology, Geography, Roman Antiquities, and History. With Notes and Dictionary. *3rd Edition.* 12mo. 3*s.* 6*d.*

——— Part III. A Latin Poetry Book. Hexameters and Pentameters; Eclog. Ovidianæ; Latin Prosody, &c. *2nd Edition.* 12mo. 3*s.* 6*d.*

——— Part IV. Latin Prose Composition. Rules of Syntax, with Examples, Explanations of Synonyms, and Exercises on the Syntax. *Second Edition.* 12mo. 3*s.* 6*d.*

——— Student's Greek Grammar for the Higher Forms. By Professor Curtius. Post 8vo. 7*s.* 6*d.*

——— Smaller Greek Grammar, abridged from the above Work. 12mo. 3*s.* 6*d.*

——— Student's Latin Grammar for the Higher Forms. Post 8vo. 7*s.* 6*d.*

——— Smaller Latin Grammar, abridged from the above Work. 12mo. 3*s.* 6*d.*

STANHOPE'S (EARL) Life of William Pitt. With Extracts from his MS. Papers. *Second Edition.* Portraits. 4 Vols. Post 8vo. 42*s.*

——— Miscellanies. *Second Edition.* Post 8vo. 5*s.* 6*d.*

——— Life of Belisarius. Post 8vo. 10*s.* 6*d.*

——— Life of Condé. Post 8vo. 2*s.* 6*d.*

——— History of England, from the Peace of Utrecht to the Peace of Versailles, 1713-83. *Library Edition.* 7 vols. 8vo. 93*s.* *Or Popular Edition.* 7 vols. Post 8vo. 5*s.* each.

——— History of British India, from its origin till the Peace of 1783. Post 8vo. 3*s.* 6*d.*

——— "Forty-Five;" a Narrative of the Rebellion in Scotland. Post 8vo. 3*s.*

——— Spain under Charles the Second. Post 8vo. 6*s.* 6*d.*

——— Historical and Critical Essays. Post 8vo. 3*s.* 6*d.*

STUDENT'S HUME. A History of England from the Invasion of Julius Cæsar to the Revolution of 1688. By DAVID HUME. Corrected and continued to 1858. Woodcuts. Post 8vo. 7*s.* 6*d.* Questions on, 2*s.*

*** A Smaller History of England. 12mo. 3*s.* 6*d.*

——— HISTORY OF FRANCE; from the Earliest Times to the Establishment of the Second Empire, 1852. By W. H. PEARSON, M.A. Woodcuts. Post 8vo. 7*s.* 6*d.*

——— HISTORY OF GREECE; from the Earliest Times to the Roman Conquest. With the History of Literature and Art. By WM. SMITH, LL.D. Woodcuts. Crown 8vo. 7*s.* 6*d.* (Questions. 2*s.*)

*** A SMALLER HISTORY OF GREECE. 12mo. 3*s.* 6*d.*

——— HISTORY OF ROME; from the Earliest Times to the Establishment of the Empire. With the History of Literature and Art. By Dean LIDDELL. Woodcuts. Crown 8vo. 7*s.* 6*d.*

*** A SMALLER HISTORY OF ROME. 12mo. 3*s.* 6*d.*

——— GIBBON; an Epitome of the History of the Decline and Fall of the Roman Empire. By EDWARD GIBBON. Incorporating the Researches of Recent Commentators. Woodcuts. Post 8vo. 7*s.* 6*d.*

——— MANUAL OF ANCIENT GEOGRAPHY. By REV. W. L. BEVAN, M.A. Woodcuts. Post 8vo. 7*s.* 6*d.*

——— MODERN GEOGRAPHY. By Rev. W. L. BEVAN. Woodcuts. Post 8vo. (*In the Press.*)

——— ENGLISH LANGUAGE. By GEORGE P. MARSH. Post 8vo. 7*s.* 6*d.*

——— ENGLISH LITERATURE. By T. B. SHAW, M.A. Post 8vo. 7*s.* 6*d.*

——— SPECIMENS OF ENGLISH LITERATURE. Selected from the Chief Writers. By THOMAS B. SHAW, M.A. Post 8vo. 7*s.* 6*d.*

——— SCRIPTURE HISTORY: the Old and New Testament. Maps and Woodcuts. 2 Vols. Post 8vo. 7*s.* 6*d.* each.

——— BLACKSTONE: a Systematic Abridgment of the Entire Commentaries. By R. MALCOLM KERR, LL.D. Post 8vo. 7*s.* 6*d.*

ST. JOHN'S (CHARLES) Wild Sports and Natural History of the Highlands. Post 8vo. 3*s*. 6*d*.

——— (BAYLE) Adventures in the Libyan Desert and the Oasis of Jupiter Ammon. Woodcuts. Post 8vo. 2*s*.

STEPHENSON (GEORGE and ROBERT). The Story of their Lives. By SAMUEL SMILES. With Portraits and 70 Illustrations. Medium. 8vo. 21*s*. Or Popular Edition, Post 8vo. 6*s*.

STOTHARD'S (THOS.) Life. With Personal Reminiscences. By MRS. BRAY. With Portrait and 60 Woodcuts. 4to. 21*s*.

STREET'S (G. E.) Gothic Architecture in Spain. From Personal Observations during several journeys through that country. Illustrations. Medium 8vo. 50*s*.

——— Brick and Marble Architecture of Italy in the Middle Ages. Plates. 8vo. 21*s*.

SWIFT'S (JONATHAN) Life, Letters, Journals, and Works. By JOHN FORSTER. 8vo. (*In Preparation.*)

SYME'S (PROFESSOR) Principles of Surgery. *5th Edition.* 8vo. 12*s*.

TAIT'S (BISHOP) Dangers and Safeguards of Modern Theology, containing Suggestions to the Theological Student under Present Difficulties. 8vo. 9*s*.

TAYLOR'S (HENRY) Notes from Life, in Six Essays on Money, Humility and Independence, Wisdom, Choice in Marriage, Children, and Life Poetic. Fcap. 8vo. 2*s*.

THOMSON'S (ARCHBISHOP) Sermons, Preached in the Chapel of Lincoln's Inn. 8vo. 10*s*. 6*d*.

THREE-LEAVED MANUAL OF FAMILY PRAYER; arranged so as to save the trouble of turning the Pages backwards and forwards. Royal 8vo. 2*s*.

TREMENHEERE'S (H. S.) The Franchise a Privilege and not a Right, proved by the Political Experience of the Ancients. Fcap. 8vo. 2*s*. 6*d*.

TRISTRAM'S (H. B.) Great Sahara. Wanderings South of the Atlas Mountains. Map and Illustrations. Post 8vo. 15*s*.

TWISS' (HORACE) Public and Private Life of Lord Chancellor Eldon, with Selections from his Correspondence. Portrait. *Third Edition.* 2 Vols. Post 8vo. 21*s*.

TYLOR'S (E. B.) Researches into the Early History of Mankind, and the Development of Civilization. Illustrations. 8vo. 12*s*.

TYNDALL'S (JOHN) Glaciers of the Alps. With an account of Three Years' Observations and Experiments on their General Phenomena. Woodcuts. Post 8vo. 14*s*.

TYTLER'S (PATRICK FRASER) Memoirs. By REV. J. W. BURGON, M.A. 8vo. 9*s*.

VAUGHAN'S (REV. DR.) Sermons preached in Harrow School. 8vo. 10*s*. 6*d*.

VENABLES' (Rev. R. L.) Domestic Scenes in Russia. Post 8vo. 5*s.*

WAAGEN'S (Dr.) Treasures of Art in Great Britain. Being an Account of the Chief Collections of Paintings, Sculpture, Manuscripts, Miniatures, &c. &c., in this Country. Obtained from Personal Inspection during Visits to England. 4 Vols. 8vo.

WALSH'S (Sir John) Practical Results of the Reform Bill of 1832. 8vo. 5*s.* 6*d.*

VAMBERY'S (Arminius) Travels in Central Asia, from Teheran across the Turkoman Desert, on the Eastern Shore of the Caspian to Khiva, Bokhara, and Samarcand in 1863. Map and Illustrations. 8vo. 21*s.*

WELLINGTON'S (The Duke of) Despatches during his various Campaigns. Compiled from Official and other Authentic Documents. By Col. Gurwood, C.B. 8 Vols. 8vo. 21*s.* each.

——— Supplementary Despatches, and other Papers. Edited by his Son. Vols. I. to XII. 8vo. 20*s.* each.

——— Selections from his Despatches and General Orders. By Colonel Gurwood. 8vo. 18*s.*

——— Speeches in Parliament. 2 Vols. 8vo. 42*s.*

WILKINSON'S (Sir J. G.) Popular Account of the Private Life, Manners, and Customs of the Ancient Egyptians. *New Edition.* Revised and Condensed. With 500 Woodcuts. 2 Vols. Post 8vo. 12*s.*

——— Handbook for Egypt.—Thebes, the Nile, Alexandria, Cairo, the Pyramids, Mount Sinai, &c. Map. Post 8vo. 15*s.*

——— (G. B.) Working Man's Handbook to South Australia; with Advice to the Farmer, and Detailed Information for the several Classes of Labourers and Artisans. Map. 18mo. 1*s.* 6*d.*

WILSON'S (Bishop Daniel) Life, with Extracts from his Letters and Journals. By Rev. Josiah Bateman. *Second Edition.* Illustrations. Post 8vo. 9*s.*

——— (Genl. Sir Robert) Secret History of the French Invasion of Russia, and Retreat of the French Army, 1812. *Second Edition.* 8vo. 15*s.*

——— Private Diary of Travels, Personal Services, and Public Events, during Missions and Employments in Spain, Sicily, Turkey, Russia, Poland, Germany, &c. 1812-14. 2 Vols. 8vo. 26*s.*

——— Autobiographical Memoirs. Containing an Account of his Early Life down to the Peace of Tilsit. Portrait. 2 Vols. 8vo. 26*s.*

WORDSWORTH'S (Canon) Journal of a Tour in Athens and Attica. *Third Edition.* Plates. Post 8vo. 8*s.* 6*d.*

——— Pictorial, Descriptive, and Historical Account of Greece, with a History of Greek Art, by G. Scharf, F.S.A. *New Edition.* With 600 Woodcuts. Royal 8vo. 28*s.*